Intelligent Connectivity

Intelligent Connectivity

AI, IoT, and 5G

Abdulrahman Yarali
Coordinator of Cybersecurity Network Management
POC for Center for Academic Excellence Cyber Defense Education
Murray State University, KY, USA

This edition first published 2022
© 2022 John Wiley & Sons Ltd

The right of Abdulrahman Yarali to be identified as the author of this work has been asserted in accordance with law.

Registered Offices
John Wiley & Sons, Inc., 111 River Street, Hoboken, NJ 07030, USA
John Wiley & Sons Ltd, The Atrium, Southern Gate, Chichester, West Sussex, PO19 8SQ, UK

Editorial Office
The Atrium, Southern Gate, Chichester, West Sussex, PO19 8SQ, UK

For details of our global editorial offices, customer services, and more information about Wiley products visit us at www.wiley.com.

Wiley also publishes its books in a variety of electronic formats and by print-on-demand. Some content that appears in standard print versions of this book may not be available in other formats.

Library of Congress Cataloging-in-Publication Data

Names: Yarali, Abdulrahman, author.
Title: Intelligent connectivity : AI, IoT, and 5G / Abdulrahman Yarali.
Description: Hoboken, NJ, USA : Wiley, 2022. | Includes bibliographical
    references and index.
Identifiers: LCCN 2021033024 (print) | LCCN 2021033025 (ebook) | ISBN
    9781119685180 (hardback) | ISBN 9781119685234 (adobe pdf) | ISBN
    9781119685210 (epub)
Subjects: LCSH: Internet of things. | 5G mobile communication systems. |
    Artificial intelligence–Industrial applications.
Classification: LCC TK5105.8857 .Y369 2022 (print) | LCC TK5105.8857
    (ebook) | DDC 004.67/8–dc23
LC record available at https://lccn.loc.gov/2021033024
LC ebook record available at https://lccn.loc.gov/2021033025

Cover Design: Wiley
Cover Image: © metamorworks/Shutterstock

Set in 9.5/12.5pt STIXTwoText by Straive, Pondicherry, India
Printed and bound by CPI Group (UK) Ltd, Croydon, CR0 4YY

C9781119685180 _230921

This book is dedicated to my kids, Fatemeh Zahra and Sadrodin Ali

Contents

Preface

The Oxford English Dictionary defines intelligence as acquiring and applying knowledge and skills. Its three definitions of intelligence demonstrate that humans and devices, buildings, and computers can possess such knowledge and skills. Intelligent connectivity is a concept that foresees the combination of high-speed fifth-generation (5G) networks, Artificial Intelligence (AI), and the Internet of Things (IoT) to accelerate technological development and structural changes paving the roads to enable new disruptive digital services. AI, 5G, and IoT advances are now enhancing each other, making the fifth wave of computing. The convergence of IoT, 5G wireless, and AI technologies are said to be some of the most exciting times for computing and technology and will usher in a new age of intelligent connectivity. Intelligent connectivity is not about a single product or device but a very complicated ecosystem expected to play a major role in bringing industry 4.0. These technologies work in sync with ubiquitous hyper-connectivity, giving the users contextualized and personalized experiences. This phenomenon will significantly impact people, industries, governments, and organizations, transforming our way of life and work. The prospects at hand would be intelligent transport in self-driving cars, intelligent healthcare systems, intelligent public safety and security systems, smart farming, smart city, entertainment, workplace, and many other sectors. Therefore, openness and exchanges across industries are needed.

Various AI applications range from Machine Learning, Deep Learning, Automation, and Autonomy, to Human–Machine Teaming. The implementation of AI through the IoT in different sectors of human life will significantly impact the field of business and job employment. However, AI is a pivotal enabler of intelligent connectivity, currently in its infancy, and human beings are just into the so-called "narrow" or "weak AI" today. Whether to deploy AI in the cloud or at the edge of network connectivity, many real-life applications, and use cases opt for a hybrid cloud-edge approach.

5G networks provide higher data rates than 4G/LTE leveraging directional antennas, millimeter-wave radio frequency, and edge computing solutions. In addition to higher data transfer rates, the 5G provides ultra-low latency, ideally less than 1-ms delay needed for some portable or mobile apps and services, for example, haptic internet, virtual reality, industrial automation, and robotics. The 5G network, unlike 4G/LTE, presents a focused purpose-built technology designed and specifically engineered to facilitate the connected devices and automation system. The prospect positions 5G as a facilitator and catalyst to the next industrial age, referred to as industry 4.0. There is a clear need to forecast beyond smart factories, intelligent goods, and services towards enterprise as a whole and offer new unique benefits of the higher capacity urban wireless application.

IoT refers to a collection of standards for a new generation of "smart" products. These "smart" products, like embedded systems, have computer hardware integrated into them that allows for the gathering, processing, and contextualizing of data from their environment and sharing it across a network. Smart connected products provide more excellent reliability, expanding opportunities, much high utilization of the product, and its capabilities of transcending traditional products. It involves strategic choices of creating and capturing products, newly generated data, and relationship with conventional business partners. It highlights the opportunities of smart products produced through smart products, which are named 'Internet of Things.' IoT devices can be self-adapting, self-configuring, and interoperable. IoT devices use several communication protocols, including ones used by mobile phones. The deployment of 5G can help expand IoT devices deployment while reducing the networks' complexity that utilizes them as the number of devices increases. Together, 5G and IoT technology could allow for faster deployment of networks for virtually every application at the business and consumer levels of industry and commerce. However, when both technologies are combined with AI, intelligent connectivity becomes possible.

All these ever-evolving technologies need to work together to create immersive experiences other than creating several separate devices for consumers. Almost half of the global population (3.8 billion people) are now mobile internet users, forecast to reach 61% (5 billion) by 2025. According to the Global Mobile Suppliers' Association, the Global Mobile Economy will be valued at $4.9 trillion by 2024 as 5G Ramps Up. 4G will continue to grow over the coming years, increasing to 56% of connections by 2025. Mobile operators are expected to spend $1.1 trillion worldwide between 2020 and 2025 in mobile CAPEX, roughly 80% of which will be on 5G networks. Fifty operators had launched 3GPP-compliant 5G commercial services across 27 countries; 328 operators in 109 countries were investing in 5G.

Finally, smartphones play a key role in humans' intellectual connectivity lives. Smartphones are forecast to account for four of every five connections by 2025, up from 65% in 2019. The rise of many digital assistants, such as Amazon Alexa, has not demised smartphones with their basic functions, expected to be improved continuously and comprehensively to continue to strengthen their key role in the 5G and the IoT ecosystem.

The world of AI, 5G data networks, and the rapidly growing IoT devices can be very helpful but may present numerous flaws as they are all new and rapidly developing technologies. It is important to note that the 5G network has better security than the 3G and 4G networks. Still, it has been said that some of the classic vulnerabilities and security flaws from 3G and 4G networks were directly carried over to the developing 5G network, thus presenting additional security flaws right out of the gate. Both AI and the IoT will benefit from the development of 5G networks where businesses can use such devices, which will be tied to the growing 5G network, and can serve several purposes throughout the business market, among other areas.

In this book, the chapters cover the fusion of AI, IoT, 5G, Blockchain technologies, and the cutting-edge applications that cater to customers' personalized needs, very lucrative for businesses who want to reap the many benefits from a line of intelligent products or intelligent services.

We are very pleased that the technology, academic, and industry communities discuss this important and fast-growing industry. We are certain that this book's content will shed some light on this subject. The chapters presented in this book discuss technologies, design, implementation, AI applications, IoT, and 5G. The challenges and issues faced in providing applications and services to meet user experiences ubiquitously and securely are presented.

Acknowledgement

I would like to express my gratitude to all those who provided support and discussions, talked things over, read, wrote, offered comments, allowed me to quote their remarks and assisted in the editing and proofreading. I would like to give special thanks to all my graduate and undergraduate students in CNM302, CNM320, CNM322, CNM323, CNM397, CNM421, and CNM571 classes of our distinction program of Cybersecurity and Network Management at Murray State University, Kentucky. This book would never have found its way to the publisher without these students.

Abdulrahman Yarali

Introduction

Intelligent Connectivity: Fusion of AI, IoT, and 5G

Operations are revolutionized by information technology through smart connected products that help in device miniaturization and by processing power and wireless connectivity. Smart connected products provide greater reliability, expanding opportunities, and much high utilization of the product and its capabilities of transcending traditional products. It involves strategic choices of creating and capturing products, newly generated data, and relationship with conventional business partners.

Intelligent connectivity is essentially the combination of high-speed fifth generation (5G) networks, Artificial Intelligence (AI), and the Internet of Things (IoT). Combining these technologies results in structural changes about how devices communicate by improving both the performance and efficiency to pave the road for Digital Transformations. The analysis and vision in this intelligent connectivity are processed through the digital transformation of the data collected by sensing devices, machines, and the IoT. Intelligent connectivity is much more than just faster and more efficient communications. It opens up a whole world of personalized and ambitious applications very lucrative for businesses who want to reap the many benefits from a line of intelligent products or intelligent services. While there are many areas in which consumers would see substantial benefits from using intelligent connectivity, Entertainment, Workplace Productivity, and Smart Living have been the groups with substantial benefits. Through a fusion of these advanced technologies, it would be possible to create or enhance technologies that can provide a better quality of life, better security and public safety, and significantly greater efficiency to almost any industry, making the fifth wave of computing.

Intelligent connectivity will significantly impact industry, individuals, and society. This phenomenon will significantly impact people, industries, governments, and organizations, transforming our way of life and work, marking the beginning of a new digital era defined by highly contextualized and personalized experiences. Augmented and virtual reality will change the way we watch live sports and music concerts, drones will deliver packages to our homes, and virtual personal assistants will manage our lives for us. New 5G networks, AI, and the upscaling of the IoT will change the world, intelligently connecting everyone and everything to a better future. The fusion of AI, IoT, and 5G will drastically improve the network capacity, responsiveness, and output. It will make it possible for the operators to tailor the connectivity of each application, hence increasing the application of AI, data analytics, and regulating the IoT.

1

Technology Adoption and Emerging Trends

1.1 Introduction

In the last few decades, the world has been changing at a faster rate than before. The immense growth in the global network has left billions of people hyper-connected to each other. Thus, there has been tremendous growth and spread of new ideas and technological innovations (Desjardins 2018). Due to different technological trends, changes in high-tech advances, and demographics, it is expected that the next two decades will experience an exponential and historic transformation (Bayern 2019). The advancement of networking and serverless computing is expected to reshape all the business processes in the next few years. Even though technology has been disrupting different industries, it will reshape gradually in the coming decades since players have been forced to integrate technological advances in their businesses (Arnold and Shadnam 2014). New technologies and scientific breakthroughs have been paraded since they are relentless, and they continue to unfold. Technological advancements are achieved every day, and thus it is expected that they will continue to disrupt people, businesses, and the world at large. Policymakers and different societies need to prepare for technology's future since it is expected that our economy's current status quo will keep changing in the coming years. Ad technology continues to grow so the government should create an environment where citizens will continue to prosper even after different emerging technologies disrupt people's lives and businesses (Bayern 2019). In today's world, we are in the middle of the business revolution, where technology is transforming different business entities. Different businesses will continue to focus on different core technological trends such as mobility, cloud computing, and big data (UN 2018).

In the last few years, there has been a proliferation and convergence of mobile networks, devices, applications, and operating systems. Thus, most businesses around the world are willing to take advantage of and expand their mobile technology (Arnold and Shadnam 2014). As a result, the consumerization of Information Technology (IT) devices and trends in BYOD (Buy Your Own Device) has enabled people to use their devices to work while in motion; this has led to an increase in employee's productivity since they can respond to all the market changes and embrace all the opportunities that might arise. The emergence of mobility as a business tech model has played a significant role in reducing equipment costs and has provided the employees with a sense of employment (Desjardins 2018). They have the freedom to work from any location, and they have an increased level of accessing information. Therefore, employees in different business entities can perform more tasks outside their offices than before. The emergence of big data is expected to change business dynamics in various organizations. In the next two decades, the volume of data available to different enterprises will grow dramatically (Kambala 2018). Big data is expected to change insights about the customers, operational costs, and all the relevant aspects of different business models worldwide. The emergence of cloud computing has enabled businesses to compete at a higher level since the traditional software and systems are no longer required. In the next two decades, cloud computing is expected to grow at a higher level since organizations will focus on business models that they can use to reduce operational costs. In today's world, cloud technology enables organizations to segment and use diverse resources easily and at a lower cost. It has also enabled the implementation of high-performing infrastructures that can be accessed by using mobile devices, and thus they have had widespread adoption.

The future of business technology is expected to get better. In the next two decades, different trends will define business and change all the dynamics of business operations worldwide. Some businesses have already begun integrating their core business process and products with Artificial Intelligence (AI) (Kambala 2018). This indicates that AI will be used to influence and run different business resources in the future. The emergence of cloud computing has fueled the automation of the business process, and thus the outcomes of business processes are expected to change in the next two decades. The connectivity of tomorrow is another key aspect that is expected to transform businesses shortly. The establishment of different technologies such as 5G networks, mesh networks, and edge computing is expected to enhance new products and services whereby they will be completed efficiently and reliably. The presence of intelligent interfaces is expected to transform how people interact with different machines and data while, at the same time, moving beyond marketing will contextualize customer experience and establish closer relationships between customers and the organizations. It is essential to acknowledge that technology is proliferating and more breakthroughs will be realized. The presence of disruptive technologies is a demonstration that there will be a rapid rate of changes. Organizations should identify different approaches to enhance their performance and implement changes due to technological changes. Change is inevitable, and thus organizations should be flexible and be ready for the ever-changing technological advancements (Makela 2012). This research paper will focus on the future of business technology and how adopting different technology trends will define the next two decades. Figure 1.1 is a Gartner Hype Cycle depicting some 30 technology profiles that will significantly change society and business over the next 5–10 years (Panetta 2020).

1.2 Trends in Business Technology

There have been many technological breakthroughs in the last decade, including advanced smartphones, Internet of Things (IoT), AI, self-driving cars, and now 5G and 6G cellular technologies. Development of IoT, 5G, and AI continues to evolve to the point of convergence on

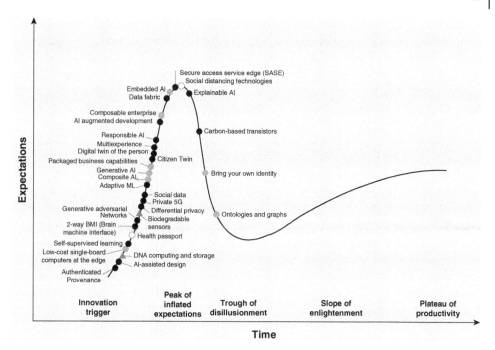

Figure 1.1 Hype cycles for emerging technologies, 2020 (Panetta 2020).

preexisting tech and future technologies as a whole, evolving to the point of everyday life, which encompasses everything from health to industrial systems. The implementation of 5G coming into place allows devices to push data across networks at bigger capacities. However, with devices and systems converging, security implementations need to be in the for-front for IoT, 5G, and AI, which will play a huge role in the future of communications of systems and continue to evolve for a more sophisticated and efficient system throughout the world.

1.2.1 Trends that Could Disrupt the Industry

Various vital trends will disrupt the industry in the future. In this case, some of these trends include AI, where it is expected to benefit businesses and society at large, extended reality, data veracity, frictionless business, and the IoT. The emergence of AI has promised to change the world, and in the last few years, it has positively impacted people's lives. Different businesses are currently capitalizing on the potentials of AI; hence they acknowledge that it will revolutionize many different businesses in the next two decades. AI is more than a tool, and has changed the functionalities of different businesses (Kambala 2018). AI will continue to revolutionize digital marketing and ads based on a business or an organization's core values. The presence of extended reality aimed at ending the distance has transformed the way people work and live. In the next few years, this form of technology is expected to limit people's distance, information, and experiences. As a result, the business will benefit from these changes since employees can work from any location, resulting in higher productivity and turnover (Manyika et al. 2013). In two decades, data veracity will transform how people run data and help businesses deal with different vulnerabilities.

Data veracity is an emerging trend meant to determine if business insights may be corrupted and help the management avoid skewed decisions. It is essential for the organizations to address the issues associated with data bias, inaccurate and manipulated data trends, and ensure they run the organization effectively. Organizations need to redesign themselves as they get ready to embrace frictionless businesses to build to a partner at scale. One of the emerging trends is that businesses are depending on technology-based partnerships as they seek to grow. The associations are meant to expand the partner networks faster than before (Manyika et al. 2013). The establishment of robust digital ecosystems will enhance business relationships between the organizations, which will guarantee a brighter future. IoT is another emerging technology that will continue to revolutionize business in the next two decades (Kambala 2018). It involves the interconnection of different devices over the internet, allowing people to communicate and run various applications. IoT will enable people to control their home heating, lighting, sprinklers, and many other appliances through their mobile devices (Manyika et al. 2013). These solutions have revolutionized business, and it is a trend that is expected to grow tremendously in the next few decades. It is expected that the integration of IoT will affect and disrupt many businesses since it provides unprecedented opportunities through process automation and data-gathering processes.

1.2.2 Adopting New Technologies

The emergence of new technologies has forced businesses, competitors, and other industries to adapt to remain relevant in the market. Over the last few years, organizations have been integrating the upcoming technologies to gain a competitive advantage as they strive to increase their return on investment (Ramey 2012). They are using the latest tech to enhance the attention of the customers towards their products and services. Some have already implemented smart manufacturing, digital marketing, and many other emerging technologies to promote their brand as they strive to increase their market share (Manyika et al. 2013). Before adopting new technologies, businesses are considering several processes and steps to ensure successful integration. The first step is to establish the organization's technology and evaluate how it will change the organization. Based on priorities, the organization will opt for the systems that are accessible, reliable, and affordable. Once it has been established, the organization then considers productive support where difficulties are mitigated during integration (Makela 2012). Employees are trained, and user manuals are provided to have an easier time implementing the new technology. The next step is ensuring there is no impulse to rush since it could result in poor implementation. It means that pilot programs should be introduced where the new technology is tested before implementing the entire organization.

Another essential step is transparency; in this case, clarity aims to reduce the friction that may arise when the new technology is introduced. Employees should be updated on the new developments since they might resist the new technology and derail its implementation (Desjardins 2018). Organizations are building value for their technology, and this is achieved by communicating with the employees and providing all the benefits that are to be achieved after the new technology has been implemented. Once integrated, the organizations have to maintain the momentum; since technological changes are frequently happening, the organizations focus on implementing newer technologies that will enhance their performance and increase their growth (Makela 2012). Maintaining momentum means that the technological changes must be communicated to the employee to oversee the changes and enhance their implementation. Despite their size and reachability, organizations are exploring different means of increasing their productivity, efficiency, and performance. As a result, they must implement newer technologies to accomplish their mission (Manyika et al. 2013). Therefore, introducing new technologies is vital since it will play a critical role in running a successful organization. It is expected that in the next two decades, technology will revolutionize business since they will become fully dependent on technology.

1.2.3 Best Practices and Risks Associated with Emerging Technologies

As technology continues to grow, there are both best practices and risks that are associated with it. In this case, the best practices of the emerging technology involve efficiency whereby, since time does not stand still, there is a need to have things done quickly and accurately. New technologies are constantly changing business dynamics since people can easily interact and exchange ideas and transform their organizations. Another best practice that has been established by the presence of technological advancement is safety. In this case, industries and manufacturing sites are safer, and thus hazards that could affect peoples' health has been minimized (UN 2018). In the healthcare sector, the business has changed tremendously since different technological machinery has enhanced the diagnosis of different diseases and infections. Thus, it is easier to get cured.

Even though human habits have led to pollution and the degradation of the environment, emerging technologies are designed to improve environmental conservation (Veletsianos 2018). As a result, the inventions are eco-friendly. In the next few decades, it is expected that inventors will continue designing technologies that are friendly to the environment as they are geared towards ecological conservation. Emerging technologies have enabled people to express their creative ideas, and they have transformed the world, especially in the business sector (Whitmire 2014). Even though there are numerous advantages associated with emerging technologies, they are posing some risks in various areas. Once an idea has been published on the internet, either positive or negative, it is difficult to remove it and can easily be traced back to the owner. As a result, some individuals can post misleading information that could impact businesses negatively (Ramey 2012). Global networks have enabled people with sinister motives to spearhead negative propaganda towards their competitors, hurting businesses. In the recent past, identity theft has been a significant issue where users cannot protect their virtual image. Therefore, even though the emerging technology has benefitted individuals and organizations, the negative issues need to be addressed so that technology advancements can be achieved successfully.

As organizations strive to adopt the best practices imposed by emerging technologies, they should ensure that they implement strategies that will help them deal with emerging technology risks. In some instances, a small organization may find it challenging to implement some emerging technologies since it could be expensive. In such scenarios, such an organization should seek opportunities to merge or lease the available technology to realize its goals and objectives (Veletsianos 2018). In the future, it is expected that due to emerging technologies, people will lose their jobs. The government should use the ideal strategies to prepare people for such changes since it could disrupt the economy. Since change is inevitable, the next two decades will present challenges to the government. A lot needs to be done to ensure that the population will remain active despite becoming displaced from employment due to technological advancements and implementation in different organizations.

1.2.4   Power of Disruptive Technologies

Even though disruptive technologies continue to emerge and change business worldwide, various products, services, and business models are driven by these changes. The development of mobile apps has revolutionized business (Veletsianos 2018). As technology continues to disrupt business performance and their reliability, businesses can shift their performance by ensuring they have applications where employees can work and enhance their productivity. The presence of mobility has enabled employees to work from any location. These applications can track their performance, identify their weaknesses, and suggest the ideal work methods where they need to change. IoT is a disruptive technology that will continue to disrupt businesses worldwide. It is a technology that presents diverse opportunities where an organization can identify different services that can be run using connectivity powered by IoT devices. Organizations have the opportunity to focus on cloud technology since most of the organization is considering its use since it can be used to help them minimize their costs (UN 2018). Providing cloud services is expected to generate huge revenues since most organizations seek platforms to minimize their operational costs (Whitmire 2014). Another aspect that businesses could tap from disruptive technologies is business models such as digital marketing and online surveys, which can easily help organizations tap into different markets.

The banking industry has been experiencing changes in the technological world. In this case, numerous banking techs have been developed to make their banking processes easier (Ramey 2012). One of the major aspects that banks should diversify is to develop paper-free processes where customers can apply for loans, make payments, and many other services that will save time. This will enhance the banks' performance since customers want to get services in the comfort of their homes. Due to the emergence of disruptive technologies, online shopping has been on the rise. Different stores have been developing applications and cloud services where customers can do online shopping and acquire different products. In this case, there is a need to harmonize their processes, ensure customers get ideal services, and enhance their performance at different operation levels. Even though disruptive technologies may render people jobless, they should acquire the necessary education services that will help them to adapt to change and build innovative products that will help them to keep up with the ever-changing technological aspects. In the future, business dynamics will continue to change, and thus people should be prepared for these changes and ensure they provide reliable services at all levels of the organization (Ramey 2012).

1.2.5   Driving Strategy Around Our Priority

Since technology will keep changing and growing, there is a need to establish strategies based on the organizational priorities that promote technological investments. The organization should have enough capital to focus on specific technological implementations.

They should have money to run all the required processes to realize technological investments and goals. It is essential to identify employees who have the ideal skills to help the organization focus on a specific strategy and implement all the necessary processes. In many instances, lack of skills among the employees may negatively impact the organization's performance, which means that they cannot achieve the vision and mission set forth for achievement (Manyika et al. 2013). The technological achievements should be prioritized to achieve the most important goals within the shortest time possible.

1.2.6 Strategic Partnerships to be Pursued

The presence of digital transformation has prompted key decision-makers in the IT industry to establish partnerships that are meant to develop solutions to various problems in businesses. While looking for solutions for various issues in the business world, alliances among the vendors are essential since it could help them establish the ideal solutions for different problems they encounter (Norton, Littmann, and Prabhu 2019). The majority of businesses seek partnerships from different vendors since they can easily increase enterprise organizations' performance. In the recent past, organizations have been forced to accelerate their digital innovations to integrate their vendor partnerships and effect an ideal transformation. Strategic partnerships enhance customer relations with the organization. Simultaneously, the executives mainly identify the opportunities for growth where they can define various joint ventures and alliances that are meant to propel them to success. In various business entities, leaders assert that 27% of their technology strategies and roadmaps are mainly driven by external events such as competition, changes in the market, and requests from their customers (Norton, Littmann, and Prabhu 2019).

Establishing alliances and partnerships is a key factor since it helps their customers despite competitive situations. Some of the partnerships established in the past include Citrix and Microsoft, and another instance is where Google and Salesforce launched partnerships (Deloitte 2015). These partnerships aim to enable the organizations to provide comprehensive solutions to various business and IT-related challenges to the customers. The main attributes of these strategic partnerships include enhancing customer services and response time, a better understanding of business goals and objectives, support services after selling, the long-term viability of the organizations, enhancing knowledge in the product portfolio, and creating an ideal insight and growing expertise in the technology (Afshar 2019). The presence of alliances and partnerships has been part of human life for many decades. Therefore, it is crucial to establish a strategic partnership in the business world since it could help an organization become innovative and create some of the best solutions.

There has been a tremendous growth of partnerships. They are driven by the benefits of sharing risks and pooling resources, technology convergence, and deconstruction of the industry where knowledge is diffused. Once these partnerships have been established, the partners can acquire new capabilities in their line of business. Thus, it is a win–win situation for both entities. These partnerships should pursue innovativeness; in this case, none of the partners should innovate alone. They should work together as a team and come up with solutions together. The partners involved should understand that none of them has a lock on user preferences since all consumers are moving targets (Deloitte 2015). Partnerships are meant to establish superior knowledge capital and an environment where there is a robust exchange of information to build long-lasting solutions. As partners, organizations should provide a great experience to their customers and not value the exchange. They should also strike the ideal balance between scale and customization in the areas of their operations (Afshar 2019). Another essential strategy is that the involved organizations should treat these partnerships to achieve the intended outcomes.

1.3 AI-Fueled Organizations

AI has experienced tremendous growth due to the numerous advantages it provides to different business entities. In today's world, organizations are implementing AI as they look forward to implementing machine learning capabilities over the existing frameworks of data management (Afshar 2019). Over the next few years, it is expected that the organization will move towards an autonomous intelligence where the majority of the procedures will be digitized and robotized to enhance performance. The majority of the organizations have been harnessing the full potential of AI, and they are exploring the enterprise opportunities presented by this form of technology (Tredinnick 2017). In the next few years, organizations are determined to ensure their move to an AI-fueled environment. Thus, they need to rethink how people and machines interact within a working environment. AI is expected to change businesses, and, in this case, organizations will experience positive growth since the running costs are expected to decrease with time (Tredinnick 2017). Therefore, it is essential for management teams to consider machine learning and other necessary technological tools to enhance the core business processes and operations in different enterprises. Deployment of these specialized tools is expected to improve data-driven decision-making processes since it will offer a new contribution and strategic business models (Norton, Littmann, and Prabhu 2019).

In the coming years, organizations are expected to move towards autonomous intelligence, where various processes in the organization will be digitized and automated. As a result, machines, bots, and their systems will act directly upon the system's intelligence. The evolution of AI has undergone various processes (Indrasen 2017). The first stage was assisted intelligence, where humans comprehended the data and generated their insights. The second stage is augmented intelligence, where machine learning provides an augment based on human decisions. The third and the final stage is autonomous intelligence; it is the most advanced, and this is the level where AI decides and executes autonomously. Through AI, organizations have experienced tremendous growth since the management teams can positively impact the organization. Due to various business sectors' demands, organizations are looking beyond the discrete initiatives to implement AI since it has proven to be one of the essential strategies of enhancing business performance (Indrasen 2017). The majority of the organizations have been scanning their operations and implementing AI since the initiatives involved could benefit the entire organization.

In the next two decades, the number of businesses that will adapt to implement AI will increase significantly since they can use all the cognitive technologies to achieve and implement their strategic goals (Tredinnick 2017). It is essential to note that the role of AI in an organization is to develop vital cognitive tools and strategies that are meant to promote their performance. The use of AI has led to the deployment of various system models such as cloud-native, a platform that will become one of the biggest operating systems, a packet-adjunct model, and the open-algorithm model, developed to meet specific needs in different business platforms (Harris 2011). In many organizations, it is essential to realize data management, which has led to a growth in AI-fueled organizations. Therefore, it is ideal for establishing an environment that will promote dynamic data governance, storage, and architecture. AI will offer an environment where data is processed, analyzed, and acted upon at a high rate and speed. Even though organizations may consider deploying AI tools, there is a need for organizational and cultural changes. This means that employees should gather more skills to analyze, model, and develop skills to enhance their interaction with this emerging technology in the business world. People speculate that in the next two decades, AI will replace the human workforce. However, it is expected that augmented intelligence will boost instead of replacing human skills (EDICOM 2018). In this case, critical and emotional intelligence and value judgments among the people is expected to grow.

In the last few years, the buzz over AI has been on the rise since penetrating C-suites of various organizations in the world. As a result, there has been a growth in AI investment, and businesses are adopting this technology to enhance their performance (Afshar 2019). It is expected that AI success in different organizations will be numerous and diverse since it helps them perform better. Even though not every organization has implemented AI, the external investments in technology have been tripling since 2013 (Deloitte 2015). Some organizations are using AI in parts of their organization. Still, in two decades, it is expected that the majority of the companies will adopt the technology to be fully utilized in the entire organization. The five AI technology categories include robotics, computer vision, language, machine learning, and virtual agents (Harris 2011). Different organizations have implemented these categories of technologies in their departments based on their needs and the necessity of usage. Therefore, AI will experience tremendous growth in two decades since businesses are expected to tap into this technology to achieve their goals and maximize their income (Tredinnick 2017).

1.4 Connectivity of Tomorrow

The number of network-connected devices is rising every day, and thus the implication of both wired and wireless technologies is critical in providing the future of the digital economy. The increase of new connectivity has prompted the business to adopt the newest technologies to run their operations (Prysmian 2017). Growth in fiber cables means that organizations will continue to invest in various infrastructures to deal with their connectivity needs, even in future decades. Both private and governmental organizations are investing heavily in technology since the current trends are meant to make organizations better in terms of digital infrastructures (Conan 2018). The recent trends and changes in technology mean that business is based on fiber-connected backbone networks since service providers are working towards achieving future-proof networks. In the next two decades, organizations will have the best services for running their business entities. In the future, demand for quality and excellent network services will increase, and thus organizations will focus on reliable and fault-proof networks (Tempels 2016). The connectivity of tomorrow is expected to become even better since service providers are innovative and are determined to design and develop solutions that will meet customer's needs.

In the last few years, global communications were achieved through satellite systems where connectivity was slow, expensive, and with limited bandwidth. Due to the demand for more capacity and faster networks, both terrestrial and undersea fiber cables were developed, making communication quicker and easier (Prysmian 2017). Even though microwave networks are still in use, manufacturers have modified them, and currently they can do higher capacities over longer distances. They can now meet customer's needs, which has enhanced communication in different sectors. The presence of 3G, 4G, and 5G networks means that businesses can adopt mobility where employees can work from any location as long they meet all the organization's requirements (Conan 2018). It is expected that in the next two decades, better networks and technologies will be developed and will enhance the performance of different business entities. It is essential to acknowledge that advanced technologies in networking are the current boost of business' future in the digital world. It is meant to offer connectivity that is destined to drive new services and products to transform all the necessary operating models.

Based on tomorrow's connectivity, digital transformation in businesses is achieved through data and networking technologies that are cognitive, with the adoption of IoT, blockchains, and advanced analytics to fuel and implement connectivity progress. Figure 1.2 depicts the importance of AI, IoT, and 5G integration to accelerating technological development.

The connectivity of tomorrow will be enhanced by the presence of emerging technological innovativeness such as 5G, deployment satellites orbiting at lower distances, meshed networks, an edge in computing, and the presence of ultra-modern and broadband solutions (Tempels 2016). The connectivity of tomorrow will enhance network function virtualization and will help organizations manage and evolve their connectivity options. As tomorrow's connectivity continues to take shape, various advanced building blocks of connectivity must be considered. The first building block is 5G; in this case, the fifth

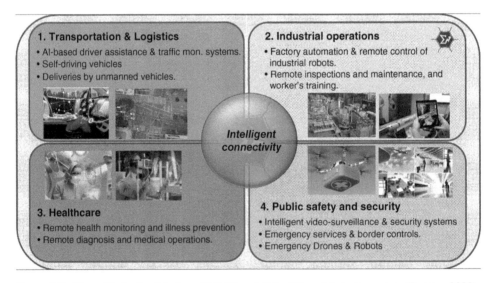

Figure 1.2 The critical role of fusion of IoT, 5G, and AI in different industry sectors (Durmus 2020).

generation of cellular technology is expected to change and redefine the new wireless interfaces for smartphones. It provides faster speeds, low latencies, and the ability to connect many smart devices in the network. This means that different protocols coexist and meet the user requirements seamlessly (Tredinnick 2017). It is a unifying and pervasive technology that brings together different networking capabilities needed to change information flow and density at a specific scale (Tempels 2016). Low earth orbit satellites are also expected to redefine the connectivity of tomorrow.

These clustered satellites can provide high-performance connectivity to earth instead of traditional geostationary satellites (Millicom 2017). They are expected to play a critical role in different businesses since they can provide infrastructure tools to organizations in remote areas such as mining and transportation. The establishment of network function virtualization is also expected to redefine tomorrow's connectivity in the business sector. In this case, the Network Virtualization Function (NVF) replaces various networking functions such as routing, switching, encryptions, and deployment of firewalls (Norton, Littmann, and Prabhu 2019). It is eliminating various options in networking, such as load balancing and virtualization of software. It is a technology that depends on the deployment of commodity services, which are scaled either horizontally or vertically depending on the current demand. It is expected that this technology will change all the dynamics in tomorrow's connectivity, especially in the business world. As technology continues to grow, tomorrow's connectivity is expected to change various dynamics in the next two decades, especially in the business environment. There is a growing demand where the end device should expedite real-time computation and ensure low latency. There is also a need to ensure that all the connected devices can monitor and manage various organizations' different resources and services. Therefore, as technology continues to grow, it is expected that it will affect many businesses in the next two decades and manage their operations.

1.4.1 Intelligent Interfaces

In the current technological advancements, the intelligent interface enables communication between two or more entities. The system's intelligence aspect means that the interface can predict what the user wants to do; thus, the system can predict the actions of the mind (Yasar 2019). Due to their technological advances, intelligent interfaces can be helpful while undertaking specific tasks. The intelligence factor enables the system to use the information gathered appropriately. In today's world, individuals have embraced technology, and they interact with it through various intelligent services, and the trend is expected to get better in the future. The presence of intelligent services has enabled people to move from traditional keyboards to touchscreens, while others use voice commands and other upcoming technologies. Therefore, businesses are expected to experience extreme growth from technology advancements since user interfaces will enable people to undertake various procedures more simply. A change in the engagement patterns provides a seamless and natural interaction method (Arxiv 2019).

In the next two decades, the business tech will experience advancements in innovative voice capabilities, which will allow communication with multifunctional systems in natural and active conversations. Since intelligent interfaces are integrated with systems based on AI, they can reply to various non-verbal commands (Yasar 2019). The current interfaces can combine some of the latest human-centered design techniques with some leading telecommunication technologies. Some of these technologies include computer vision, conversational voices, and auditory analytics, and some also consider the use of virtual reality. It is expected that these interfaces will become too complex and inflexible, while some people argue that some of the interfaces may not change when people's needs change (Arxiv 2019). In some instances, the interfaces do not work with each other. In the business world, an interface is intelligent if it can adapt to different users' needs and learn different concepts and techniques. An interface is also intelligent if it can anticipate the user's needs and initiate and provide different user suggestions (Hazard and Singh 2016). It is also intelligent if it can explain various actions that it may undertake.

Business-related intelligent interfaces have a specific architecture that determines their functionalities. They have a particular rule that governs their performance; they have frame descriptions and contain discrimination networks; they also contain sub-Sumption hierarchies and an inference engine. Other essential entities of the architecture include associative memory, matching, and the presence of autonomous agents. Intelligent interfaces are built with a perspective of human–computer interaction; the interfaces aimed at promoting businesses are designed so that they are clearer and have increased efficiency. Information is presented effectively and they offer better support while undertaking various tasks and goals (Hazard and Singh 2016). In the next two decades, intelligent interfaces will undergo a considerable transformation, making business technology better and easier. The presence of these interfaces is to offer services to the buyer and then provide the buyer with another buying opportunity. It is designed to benefit them in various areas, such as tracking the customer's habits while offline, providing new products and solution sets, and creating real-time context-aware and automated feedback loops based on the customer's feedback (Yasar 2019). The technology aims to make business interaction better and increase the revenues of the organizations.

Therefore, it is expected that more designs will be implemented, which will transform businesses around the globe. The system is meant to enhance efficiency, bandwidth capabilities, and cloud-edge computing to ensure the services are rendered at an optimum rate (Arxiv 2019). Intelligent interfaces are meant to enhance the functionality of the system and make the user's experience better. The future of technology is still open, and it is expected that complex systems will be developed and will transform the entire business industry. Organizations need to choose the ideal intelligent systems that will suit their objectives and goals. Even though there might be challenges during their implementation, there is a need to equip employees with skills to adapt to changes and support their implementation. In the next two decades, failure to adapt to change will cost many organizations because they will not be able to analyze and implement changes in the business sector (Hazard and Singh 2016).

1.5 Moving Beyond Marketing

Business tech has experienced exceptional growth and it is expected that the same trends will continue in the next decades. It is essential to note that organizations are creating value out of their social business. Therefore, the adoption of social value is an indication that organizations are experiencing business maturity. The world of marketing is becoming personalized and contextualized. This is attributed to teamwork between IT and marketing teams, where they work together and establish tools geared towards emerging technologies. These teams' goal is to guarantee that the organization's marketing strategies are transformed, and the organization can face competition and penetrate their market (Kraus, Harms, and Fink 2010). Moving beyond marketing means that technology has enabled organizations to treat every individual fairly since they understand their preferences and behaviors (Kane, Palmer, and Phillips 2014). As a result, it is possible to create strategic engagements and identify the best methods that they can use to deliver their services.

Technologies used in marketing have been undergoing a renaissance. Thus, the future is intensive on channel-focused solutions such as mobile platforms, management of content tools, and social platforms enhancement. The trends in moving beyond marketing are focused on adopting a new generation of marketing strategies and systems meant to deliver an unprecedented level of intimacy to the customers and deliver the ideal goals with precision. It is a process that requires the gathering of data, strategic decision-making, and enabling organizations to create dynamic, individualized, and personalized experiences for the customers (Kraus, Harms, and Fink 2010). This aims to deepen the customer's emotional connections and drive business growth due to loyalty from the customers. The future of marketing is to ensure that customer expectations are met. Thus, the organizations need to ensure that the needs, wants, and previous interactions with the customers are satisfied and understood. Moving beyond marketing means that organizations must seek long-standing relationships between them and their service providers in conjunction with the advertisement agencies (Kraus, Harms, and Fink 2010). It is essential to ensure that data management and customer management are done to meet customer's needs and expectations.

In the future, organizations need to integrate more data and technology in their formal practices since it will help them deploy the ideal consumer experience. In today's digital world, customers are in the driver's seat and determine their financial performance. Since there are endless options and channels in the market, organizations must remain competitive to create a differential experience while delivering their services. Even though moving beyond marketing is one of the best ideas in the ever-changing technological features, it is essential to consider some of the process risks (Kraus, Harms, and Fink 2010). In this case, some of the threats include fraud and cyber threats presented by scenarios where credentials are stolen, limitations while securing data from various touchpoints, and regulations implemented to control the market force (Kane, Palmer, and Phillips 2014). Even though these challenges may impact the movement beyond marketing, organizations should seek turnaround strategies to overcome the problems to enhance their performance in the market.

Another aspect that promises to impact the movement beyond marketing is that a business is considered social. It is professed as a significant factor in today's world, and it is expected to transform marketing in the future (Kane, Palmer, and Phillips 2014). Statistics indicate that social business will continue to transform various industries since technology has experienced exponential growth where people are seeking services online. Therefore, marketing strategies will continue to change so that organizations can reach as many people as possible. Millions of people are connected to the internet, and thus social business will continue to grow as more people become connected to the internet. As a result, marketing strategies will also change since the traditional marketing modes will soon become outdated. Technology will continue to transform marketing strategies, and, in the future, organizations must develop innovative strategies that will enable them to tap more customers (Kane, Palmer, and Phillips 2014). The presence of social business maturity in an organization is meant to help them achieve their goals. Organizations need to have visionary leaders who will implement innovative ideas to help the organization move beyond marketing.

1.6 Cloud Computing

Cloud computing technology enables businesses to manage their data resources online. In recent years, the term has been evolving and can depict scenarios where storage and computing needs are done by third parties (Carr 2017). It is a term used to refer to the internet operating in the cloud; it provides a scenario where data can be stored and made accessible through an internet connection. It is a process where businesses can access their information virtually, and creates a flexible and global mode of accessing data at any time from any location. Globally, most businesses have explored and have chosen the cloud as the favorite mode of storage (Samuels 2018). In recent years, the cloud has been used for database backups, software development, and some are using it for end-to-end modern computing. Based on current innovations, the future of cloud computing will be based on hybrid cloud options where security benefits will be explored. There is flexibility since virtualized servers are used for scalability and rapid response. Organizations will continue to investigate the hybrid cloud due to the presence of advanced security levels. It is possible to secure sensitive data using high-level security servers (Chorafas 2012). It is also expected that the multicloud model will continue to develop where different enterprises will run various applications over different and separate clouds.

The presence of multiple clouds is aimed at protecting business entities from unexpected outages, and is a key security feature that prevents denial of service attacks. There is an issue; it is possible to lock out a vendor without affecting the delivery of services. In business technology, cloud computing presents potential opportunities and capabilities since it opens a new world of jobs, services, applications, and different platforms (Samuels 2018). In the next decades, thousands of possibilities will emerge and push cloud computing technology to the maximum. It is a technology that will enable vendors and different providers to board and develop new ways of selling their products to the cloud users through technology. Therefore, it is a technology that has been opening new platforms for various designers and developers (Chorafas 2012). Organizations can conduct different businesses at affordable rates and in a professional manner. The future of cloud computing is bright because it is a powerful and expansive technology aimed at providing extreme benefits to users. It offers reliability, security, and boasts superb performance where both the users and service providers have incredible options for the services rendered (Carr 2017). The drivers of cloud technology include improving speed during service delivery, greater flexibility by reacting to the changing conditions of the market, and enabling continuity of business in various entities.

The future of cloud computing is bright because the industry is moving towards greatness and openness. Therefore, in the next two decades, it is expected that cloud computing technology will provide an environment whereby the traditional hardware will be separated from the software (Chorafas 2012). Another futuristic aspect of cloud computing is that a low-power processor will necessitate a decline in cloud service prices from different service providers. Since digital services are prone to security breaches, it is expected that data security mechanisms will become more superior. It begins with physical data security at the data centers where data will be encrypted, and only the end-user can access it (Carr 2017). It is a technology that will enhance technological breakthroughs for various organizations since they are determined to explore different services that will regulate tomorrow's technological advancements (IEEE 2013). Cloud computing has numerous advantages; they include reducing costs, scalability, business continuity, efficiency in terms of collaboration, and flexible working practices. Business entities are looking for technologies that will help them minimize their costs in the current world. Cloud computing is one of the infrastructural technologies that various organizations could use to minimize their costs and enhance their products and services (Samuels 2018).

1.7 Cybersecurity, Privacy, and Risk Management

Even as business technology's future continues to get brighter, there is a need to reconsider cybersecurity, privacy, and risk management issues. As technology continues to advance, the risks become more, and thus security becomes a significant aspect that needs to be addressed (Cleary and Felici 2014). In the last few years, new laws have been developed to regulate how service providers collect, use, retain, disclose, and dispose of user information. The number of cyber-attacks and data breaches has been rising rapidly; the organization needs to take the necessary precautions to protect their data. The future of business technology is expected to experience data privacy and regulatory space (Herbane 2010). In 2018, the EU regulatory space started to make sweeping changes regarding privacy and data security policies. All the organizations were meant to implement the laws that govern how they manage and share user data. Cybersecurity, privacy, and risk management are essential in any organization; the stakes are more significant than ever since the risks will continue to grow. They will continue to face risks associated with privacy and security practices. Thus, organizations need to implement ideal policies to enhance security and protect user data (Maras 2015).

Cybersecurity involves protecting and recovering networks, network devices, and various programs from any form of cyber-attack. In the current IT world, cyber-attacks are common, and if networks are not well protected, the attacks could result in the destruction of sensitive data and money extortion. Privacy aims to secure user information and protect it from getting into the wrong hands. Personal information is confidential, and thus it is one of the distinct components of information security. Therefore, it is essential to enhance privacy to ensure user data is protected and cannot be accessed by unauthorized users. Risk management involves the identification, analysis, and assessment of various risks in cyberspace. It involves studying and analyzing the information technology infrastructures and identifying all the possible vulnerabilities that negatively impact different systems

(Maras 2015). Once the assessment has been done, the ideal risk management should be carried out where program priorities are identified and various processes are initiated to monitor, control, and minimize the risks. Under cybersecurity, privacy and risk management, internal and external threats are established to identify risk management's ideal framework. It is essential to define the communication lines involving all the stakeholders to highlight the consequences of the risks. In this manner, the risk status can be analyzed, helping to formulate a solution. It is a process that needs prioritization to reduce the chances of risk occurrence while at the same time establishing processes that will enhance risk review processes.

In the next two decades, it is expected that more regulations will be developed as organizations will continue to adopt technological advancements to enhance their performance. As more organizations implement digital technology, the risks associated with it will continue to rise. Therefore, the management team's mandate is to enhance privacy, implement the ideal cybersecurity techniques, and establish a risk management process that will help them deal with cyberspace threats (Rademaker 2016). Some of the risks that may expose an organization to hackers or intruders include limited configuration security, lack of patch management, lack of a proper encryption process, and code security weaknesses. These weaknesses expose systems and could harm the organization's data. Therefore, it is essential to implement cybersecurity techniques, privacy, and a risk management process that will ensure the organization is protected at any given time (Rademaker 2016). Some of the ideal mechanisms that could strengthen cybersecurity include enhancing network security, operating system (OS) and database security, front end security, authorizations for users, communication security, and the presence of emergency concepts, where backup and disaster recovery processes are defined. The explosion in internet penetration is a significant boost to organizations worldwide. Cybersecurity is a major concern that needs to be addressed since the same organizations are exposed to major threats (Cleary and Felici 2014). Business technology's future is bright, but organizations need to consider the ideal practices that will keep them protected from cyber threats, risks, and privacy issues.

1.8 Conclusion

In conclusion, the future of business tech will continue to experience exponential growth as more organizations will continue to implement the latest technological advancements to run various functions and processes. In the next two decades, different technology trends are expected to disrupt the industry, while competitors are expected to implement the latest technological models to increase their market share (Desjardins 2018). AI is expected to dominate the market since most of the world's organizations consider the use of AI to reduce their operating costs. In two decades, the number of AI-fueled organizations will increase significantly as these organizations seek to enhance their performance and provide high-quality products and services (Tredinnick 2017). Another aspect that is expected to redefine the connectivity of tomorrow is the rising number of connected devices. The number of network-connected devices is multiplying, leading to a positive impact on wireless and wired technology ecosystems. Therefore, tomorrow's connectivity will enhance different services where the organization will choose the ideal mode of services to meet customer needs. As business tech continues to grow, the number of products, services, and business models is expected to rise. Innovations within organizations are expected to rise to meet customers' ever-increasing demands (Herbane 2010). Organizations can drive the technology strategy through their investments to ensure that they meet their customers' demands and requirements.

Despite the rise in technological advancements, organizations need to consider strategic partnerships or acquisitions to increase their market share. Partnerships and acquisitions are meant to provide organizations with a competitive edge, and it is a strategy that could help them gain more customers and provide more services and products. In the next two decades, more acquisitions and partnerships will be done as organizations will be seeking to enhance their modes of operation (Maras 2015). Growth in cloud computing has helped companies minimize their costs since the solution is better than traditional modes of operation. The presence of cloud computing has also promoted intelligent interfaces that promise a better future for the business. Cybersecurity, privacy, and risks management is a major issue that needs to be addressed by organizations. Despite the rising growth in technology, data security is a major aspect that should be addressed. There is a need to enhance cybersecurity protocol, implement privacy models, and implement the ideal risk management processes used during threats. Therefore, the future of business tech is bright, but organizations should be ready to experience disruptions and changes as they embrace the ever-changing trends in the industry.

References

Afshar, V. (2019). Top digital transformation tech investment priorities for 2019: cloud, cybersecurity, and AI | ZDNet. https://www.zdnet.com/article/top-digital-transformation-tech-investment-priorities-for-2019-cloud-cybersecurity-and-ai/ (accessed 22 June 2021).

Arnold, B. and Shadnam, M. (2014). Innovation goals in software development for business applications. *Evolving Trends In Engineering And Technology* 1: 53–62. https://doi.org/10.18052/www.scipress.com/etet.1.53.

Arxiv (2019). Intelligent user interfaces. https://arxiv.org/ftp/arxiv/papers/1702/1702.05250.pdf (accessed 22 June 2021).

Bayern, M. (2019). The future of business tech: six trends that will define the next two decades. https://www.techrepublic.com/article/the-future-of-business-tech-6-trends-that-will-define-the-next-two-decades/ (accessed 22 June 2021).

Carr, N. (2017). What is the future of cloud computing? Five exciting predictions. https://medium.com/predict/what-is-the-future-of-cloud-computing-5-exciting-predictions-f96a047c0de8 (accessed 22 June 2021).

Chorafas, D. (2012). *Cloud Computing Strategy*. Washington, DC: Chief Information Officer, Department of Defense.

Cleary, F. and Felici, M. (2014). *Cyber Security and Privacy*. Cham: Springer International Publishing.

Conan, Y. (2018). New mobile places, the challenge of connectivity for tomorrow's hyperplaces – Call for case studies: Modu Magazine. https://www.modumag.com/activity/

new-mobile-places-the-challenge-of-connectivity-for-tomorrows-hyperplaces-call-for-case-studies/ (accessed 22 June 2021).

Deloitte (2015). *Technology Investments: A Strategic Priority, and Digital, Analytics and Big Data the Key Bets for 2015* [Ebook] 2e. https://www2.deloitte.com/au/en/pages/media-releases/articles/deloitte-cio-report-240315.html (accessed 22 June 2021).

Desjardins, J. (2018). The eight major forces shaping the future of the global economy. https://www.visualcapitalist.com/the-8-major-forces-shaping-the-future-of-the-global-economy/ (accessed 22 June 2021).

Durmus, M. (2020). The Fusion of 5G, IoT, and AI.

EDICOM (2018). Investment in technology and digital transformation – Spanish business priorities in 2018. https://www.edicomgroup.com/en_US/news/11086-investment-in-technology-and-digital-transformation-spanish-business-priorities-in-2018.html (accessed 22 June 2021).

Harris, M. (2011). *Artificial Intelligence*. New York: Marshall Cavendish Benchmark.

Hazard, C. and Singh, M. (2016). Privacy risks in intelligent user interfaces. *IEEE Internet Computing 20* (6): 57–61. https://doi.org/10.1109/mic.2016.116.

Herbane, B. (2010). Risk management on the internet. *Risk Management 7* (1): 71–72. https://doi.org/10.1057/palgrave.rm.8240206.

IEEE (2013). IEEE cloud computing. *IEEE Transactions On Cloud Computing 1* (2): 230–230. https://doi.org/10.1109/tcc.2013.24.

Indrasen, P. (2017). Why business intelligence needs Artificial Intelligence (AI) and advanced natural language generation (NLG). *Journal Of Environmental Science, Computer Science and Engineering and Technology 6* (4) https://doi.org/10.24214/jecet.b.6.4.266274.

Kambala, C. (2018). What the Internet of Things means for businesses – DZone IoT. https://dzone.com/articles/what-the-internet-of-things-means-for-businesses (accessed 22 June 2021).

Kane, G., Palmer, D., and Phillips, A. (2014). Moving beyond marketing: Generating social business value across the enterprise. https://www2.deloitte.com/insights/us/en/topics/emerging-technologies/social-business-study-mit-smr.html (accessed 22 June 2021).

Kraus, S., Harms, R., and Fink, M. (2010). Entrepreneurial marketing: Moving beyond marketing in new ventures. *International Journal of Entrepreneurship and Innovation Management 11* (1) https://doi.org/10.1504/IJEIM.2010.029766.

Makela, L. (2012). Top three technology trends with the biggest impact on companies. https://www.digitalistmag.com/innovation/2012/09/26/top-three-technology-trends-with-the-biggest-impact-on-companies-017435 (accessed 22 June 2021).

Manyika, J., Chui, M., Bughin, J.et al. (2013). Disruptive technologies: advances that will transform life, business, and the global economy. https://www.mckinsey.com/~/media/McKinsey/Business%20Functions/McKinsey%20Digital/Our%20Insights/Disruptive%20technologies/MGI_Disruptive_technologies_Executive_summary_May2013.ashx (accessed 22 June 2021).

Maras, M. (2015). Internet of Things: Security and privacy implications. *International Data Privacy Law 5* (2): 99–104. https://doi.org/10.1093/idpl/ipv004.

Millicom (2017). *Digital Connectivity for Tomorrow's World* [Ebook] 2e. Millicom. https://www.millicom.com/media/3246/millicom_annual_report_2017.pdf(accessed 22 June 2021).

Norton, K., Littmann, D., and Prabhu, A. (2019). Connectivity of tomorrow: The spectrum and potential of advanced networking. https://www2.deloitte.com/insights/us/en/focus/tech-trends/2019/future-of-connectivity-advanced-networking.html (accessed 22 June 2021).

Panetta, K. (2020). Five trends drive the Gartner hype cycle for emerging technologies, 2020. https://www.gartner.com/smarterwithgartner/5-trends-drive-the-gartner-hype-cycle-for-emerging-technologies-2020/ (accessed 22 June 2021).

Prysmian (2017). Debating the connectivity of tomorrow – Stories – Stories | Prysmian Group. https://www.prysmiangroup.com/en/stories/debating-the-connectivity-of-tomorrow (accessed 22 June 2021).

Rademaker, M. (2016). Assessing cyber security 2015. *Information & Security: An International Journal 34*: 93–104. https://doi.org/10.11610/isij.3407.

Ramey, K. (2012). Use of technology in business – To gain competitive advantage – Use of technology. https://www.useoftechnology.com/technology-business-competitive-advantage/ (accessed 22 June 2021).

Samuels, M. (2018). Computing the future: What is next for the cloud industry? https://www.raconteur.net/technology/future-cloud-computing (accessed 22 June 2021).

Tempels, M. (2016). *Connectivity Today and Tomorrow* [Ebook] 1e. Telenet Business.

Tredinnick, L. (2017). Artificial Intelligence and professional roles. *Business Information Review 34* (1): 37–41. https://doi.org/10.1177/0266382117692621.

UN (2018). Strategy on new technologies. https://www.un.org/en/newtechnologies/images/pdf/SGs-Strategy-on-New-Technologies.pdf (accessed 22 June 2021).

Veletsianos, G. (2018). The defining characteristics of emerging technologies and emerging practices. https://www.veletsianos.com/2016/06/13/defining-characteristics-of-emerging-technologies-and-emerging-practices/ (accessed 22 June 2021).

Whitmire, B. (2014). Increase your competitive advantage using technology. http://www.pinnacleofindiana.com/blog/blog/2014/01/21/increase-your-competitive-advantage-using-technology/ (accessed 22 June 2021).

Yasar, B. (2019). Intelligent interfaces: Reimagining the way humans, machines, and data interact. https://www2.deloitte.com/content/dam/Deloitte/uk/Documents/technology/deloitte-uk-tech-trends-2019-chapter5-intelligent-interfaces.pdf (accessed 22 June 2021).

2

Telecommunication Transformation and Intelligent Connectivity

2.1 Introduction

The telecommunication industry is one of many that have gone through important modifications. Several organizations retained their on-premise telecommunication platforms. However, there has been an incessant adoption of cloud-hosted telephony resolves (Ismail 2019). Worldwide telecommunications indicate that the industry is susceptible to modifications in technology cycles, client requirements, and competition's actions. These various modifications are experienced in many forms. Today in society, technology has such an important role in people and their everyday lives. The advancement of technology has always been a changing feat, and the changing of technology is crucial to maintain more advanced lives. Technology is used for personal use; it is now making its way into everyday life. It is also gaining hold of the industrial manufacturing and health care sectors of society. When we think of technology, a lot of people think of computers and cell phones. These are great things to think of, but now there are a few new advancements that are drawing in consumers and businesses worldwide. These are Internet of Things (IoT) devices and fifth generation (5G) networks that can support these IoT devices. These are two new concepts to the technology world. Today, however, it seems they are more than just a concept. These technologies are already being used and utilized for personal use and the industrial manufacturing and health care sectors.

There have been many advantages in technology in the last decade breakthroughs. Smartphones, the IoTs, and the introduction to Artificial Intelligence (AI) and its usage within different aspects of our lives have paved the digital era's road to pervasive connectivity. With such great technological changes and their adaptation in different aspects of life, enhancement and increased productivity have been the result. However, humanity did not stop there as we aimed for higher ground with technology, which resulted in more intelligent connectivity. This included the fusion of different technologies, which fostered a path towards much more advanced outcomes. To explore and realize the full potential of the IoT future to capture massive data from the pervasive connectivity of devices, will require investment and coexistence of new technologies. Fourth generation (4G) technology has been around for almost a decade since it was first introduced commercially in December 2009 (Telia Company 2019). With greater advancements, significant outcomes and

Intelligent Connectivity: AI, IoT, and 5G, First Edition. Abdulrahman Yarali.
© 2022 John Wiley & Sons Ltd. Published 2022 by John Wiley & Sons Ltd.

improvements are being made. This includes the fusion of 5G, IoT, and AI. It focuses on fostering a future that is much more intelligent and will result in a better life where everyone is connected in a much more advanced and intelligent way. AI, ML (Machine Learning), Blockchain, and IoT are the top technologies currently used by businesses to increase efficiency, productivity, and increase their competitiveness in this fast-paced digital era transformation. Figure 2.1 shows companies' investment details on the implementation of these new technologies (Vinugayathri n.d.).

It has been found that IoT now has almost 25 billion devices being connected, with a prediction of 80 billion connected devices by 2025. AI has led to the computer IQ level of 10 000+ to enhance performance and efficiency, and 5G interoperable, flexible, high-speed, reliable, high capacity with almost zero delay network connection will reach 1.2 billion by 2025 worldwide (Sterlite Tech 2019).

These technologies will form the basis for what is being colloquially defined as Intelligent Connectivity. Through these technologies, it will become possible to transition to a digitally driven, sustainable world. Figure 2.2 depicts the detail of AI, IoT, and 5G Intelligent Connectivity (Sterlite Tech 2019).

The future of technology relies on Intelligent Connectivity. High-speed 5G and sixth generation (6G) networks with IoT technology and AI make up Intelligent Connectivity. A fact that is gradually becoming a reality as IoT technology is improved upon, 5G becomes the new communication standard for mobile devices and AI becomes increasingly commonplace in businesses. The applications for business, agriculture, education, transportation, and public safety is already showing promise as a concept. As it becomes commonplace, it could lead to a revolution that is as big – if not bigger – than the concept of personal computers.

At its most basic, AI refers to machines that can compute to extend their functionalities to such an extent that they can "learn," displaying the presence of "intelligence" among such artificial constructs (Katsaros and Dianati 2017). This fundamental difference is significant to consider as it should contrast with human intelligence at large. Current AI literature shows the importance of creating "intelligent agents" as a practical manifestation of the technology wherein the specific machines could perceive everything is happening in the environment and successfully capitalizing upon it to reach

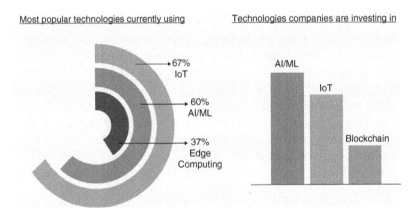

Figure 2.1   Investment and usage of the most popular technologies.

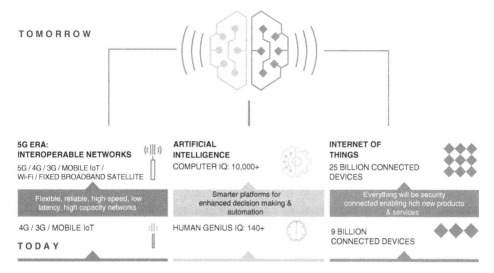

Figure 2.2 The fusion of 5G, AI, and IoT (GSMA International 2018).

their own goals. Moreover, a higher consideration is that, apart from learning, the machines should become able to "mimic" human cognition in the most accurate way imaginable.

However, it is essential to highlight what these programs may learn in general because "mimicking" human cognition is extremely hard to process many different things associated with the different subject-based ideas since they have not been explored yet. That specifically brings in necessities that could essentially address the most prescient challenges standing in front of all humankind (Siau and Wang 2018). One of the most important among them is communication, which has become unimaginably fast over time. However, by all indications the 5G network technology straightforwardly points towards the fact that creating these networks could present remarkably prescient challenges (Pagé and Dricot 2016). This fact is most evident by the routines that prominently manage and direct pathways among the immense complexities of what makes a complete and comprehensive network at large. However, the motivation behind such a high=performing network requirement is also an issue that needs addressing.

In terms of 5G networks, it is notable that the primary motivation for the development and advancement is mainly the strain of technologies, such as the IoT. This correctly points towards the mode of innovation of giving everyday commonplace objects and mechanical devices communication and processing capabilities. In almost all of these cases, human intervention needs these object operations and their functionalities. That means these objects or "things" would have to execute their functions with no or minimum possible human intervention (Siau and Wang 2018). Thus, IoT development could lead to a drastic increase in computing devices or specific nodes across the network at large. It is entirely plausible that the current versions would not support billions of such devices, which would also increase dramatically with every passing moment (Yazıcı, Kozat, and Sunay 2014). This issue explicitly highlights the need to implement 5G networks in terms of expectations and objectives. However, what these specific standards imply is altogether different. First of all, it is essential to focus on the present perspectives about AI, alongside all of their critical factors and commonalities.

2.1.1 Learning Algorithm and Its Connections to AI

It is apparent that the case of "learning" is most definitely an essential way of directing what needs to be an intrinsic guiding factor across all forms and manifestations of AI technology. The learning algorithm is mostly used in a sub-domain of techniques known as machine learning. The technology innovation happens to operate apropos to neural networks, at which point the sophisticated manifestations of execution are significantly reflective of important aspects of a notable issue (Andrieu et al. 2003). Many different learning algorithms are continually being developed with a definite outlook on autonomy and decision-making. Some notable examples of basic learning algorithms include logic regression, linear regression, decision trees, random forests, etc. It is essential to note that all of these program commonalities involve extrapolation from data obtained through testing and training, so that projections or build models can be manifested automatically (West 2016).

Moreover, these are notable tools that help pull data points together from a confusing and significantly large repository of variable qualities of data. The potential that these learning algorithms hold is quite apparent. They serve as essentially theoretical guides that provide effective solutions all across the board. However, it is also vital to address what their actual application looks like.

2.1.2 Machine Learning as a Precursor to AI

The learning algorithms discussed in the section above constitute the overall topic or subject of machine learning. This involves the study and innovation of both the algorithms and statistical frameworks where essential and critical tasks can be ensured without a specific pattern, depending upon how inference and adaptation should work. Essentially speaking, machine learning operations are viewed as being a "subset" of AI in which the algorithms implemented could effectively create a separate mathematical model through the full realization of the available data, but without the presence of a specific embedded task that has been constantly defined (Andrieu et al. 2003). At present, machine learning is being used. There is a definitive closeness detected for the technology in computational statistics, which can be immensely beneficial to everyone involved. There are many forms of learning made possible by this strain of technologies. However, AI is tied with that specific active learning event, which works based on choosing the exact variables to work upon selectively at the beginning itself (Arel, Rose, and Karnowski 2010). As a result of this, there is a significant decrease in costs accrued in terms of time and output. Therefore, machine learning holds a prominent position, which could be why fully-fledged AI technologies could be developed in many ways. It is essential to "proverbially" go down to a far deeper extent than what one can imagine (West 2016). This is the overall effect of what machine learning could achieve concerning the technology of AI, and reflects far greater possibilities, all of which would be rendered quite possible even if the need for knowledge goes deeper than what one might imagine.

2.1.3 Deep Learning and Realization of AI

Deep Learning constitutes a part of the broader family of machine learning based upon the notion of artificial neural networks (ANNs). However, that is specifically a limited viewpoint of the technology at large. This has also been known for the inclusion of propositional formulae organized by multiple generative models, such as the specific nodes present in the deep belief model (deep neural networks) and deep Boltzmann machines (Chen and Zhao 2014). Across deep learning, the most apparent form of realization is the passage of data through multiple layers, wherein the data in question becomes more abstract and composite by the fold. ANNs formulate an essential aspect of this form of technology as it aims to be inspired by the biological neural networks in living beings. Particularly, these systems, when implemented, can improve themselves instead of doing some specific tasks at hand. However, one must also consider the deep neural network option, as it is an ANN but with multiple inputs and output layers. The network moves based on calculating the probability of multiple outputs and presents the seemingly most appropriate options in light of a given problem (Katsaros and Dianati 2017). Through their implementation with computer vision, speech recognition, network filtering, social media filtering, etc., deep learning has achieved a completely different domain, which has moved close to the manifestation of actual AI in terms of the improvement factor.

2.1.4 Consideration of the Next Generation Wireless Technology

Communication is always at the forefront of all conversations about human innovation and realization. One of the most consequential developments to happen all across this specific domain involves that of wireless communication. In that specific definition, telephone services are provisioned to remote phone devices, allowing free movement instead of just being fixed at a single location as it had been in the past. These devices specifically receive and can send radio signals with cellular base stations fixed in proximity and utilize high-performing antennas (Hassabis et al. 2017). These are then connected to cable communication networks and switching systems that perform the translation of the all-important data, which is being transmitted as audio signals. The 5G constitutes next-generation cellular system technology, where the Third Generation Partnership Project (3GPP) defines it as the 5G New Radio (5G NR) to indicate the developments and innovations across cellular technology as well as other systems (Al-Falahy and Alani 2017). This transition and evolvement follow that of past generations of second generation (2G), third generation (3G), and fourth generation (4G) networks, respectively, in the past. The 5G NR will carry forward all the wireless communication expectations of the past while also including essential functions that contribute to the enhancements of private networks, which may have a wide field of applications across domains like the IoT and critical industrial sector communications at large.

The prospective plans have not actualized in reality. Instead, there are many speculations apparent across the board. Of note is the implementation of millimeter waves, which have shorter ranges but are tremendously faster than the microwave standard. However, the considerations for accessibility and communicative qualities have been put into question, and it remains to be seen how the research and development can overcome it (Simsek et al. 2016). However, it is also essential to note other technological enhancements. For example, this is specifically apparent from the prospect of Multiple-Input Multiple-Output (MIMO) (Chen and Zhao 2014), which should provide the necessary quality of transmission through the cell system antennas connected to a specific device. This configuration and arrangement will ensure that the device receives various data streams in question through parallel transmissions.

At present, three specific implementation plans have been reserved that form the prospective aim of the entire field of 5G technology at large. The first one is Enhanced Mobile Broadband (eMBB), which will act as the successor of the highest standard of internet services at the moment, the Fourth Generation Long-Term Evolution (4G LTE) Broadband services (Chen and Zhao 2014). These should have a better capacity, faster connections, and a higher quality of throughput, which will intrinsically allow for a higher degree of communications than at any time before. The Ultra-Reliable Low-Latency Communications (uRLLC) refers to enhancing the network variables that could promote robust and uninterrupted communications under any given setting. On the other hand, Massive Machine Type Communications (mMTC) would allow for a greater inclusion of low-cost, low-power devices across a network with a significant focus upon high scalability and better battery performance (French and Shim 2016). According to the International Telecommunications Union's (ITU) IMT 2020 standard, the connectivity speed benchmark has been kept only slightly higher than that which 4G LTE provided.

2.1.5 Potential of AI and 5G Network Technology Together

The 5G networks must present a chaotic and confusing structure in its innate formation that has not yet been anticipated by those present in the telecommunication industry. If there is no proper mode of assurance, the sheer growth that should occur horizontally across the board could result in extremely critical scenarios (Sánchez, Sánchez-Picot, and De Rivera 2015). Moreover, the entire scenario is quite inimitably challenging, to say the least (Al-Falahy and Alani 2017). Therefore, the AI routines applicable in the form of machine and deep learning, alongside the potential algorithms, could nevertheless prove to be extremely beneficial and could lead to the necessary innovations required across both technologies.

It is essential to consider that the MIMO possibilities are achievable, especially considering the case of what deep learning brings to the table. With the help of such a technology, it is entirely plausible that cell site distribution and leveraging associated processes will become completely possible (Katsaros and Dianati 2017). In addition to this, site maintenance and repair operations could also be managed better, especially when considering that the 5G Network case is spread quite widely. Many learning algorithms could be implemented to satisfactorily deal with the multidimensional data in 5G that will often coalesce, transform, or shift from one specific type to another (Akyildiz, Wang, and Lin 2015). Essentially speaking, the chaotic nature of 5G would be best brought under control by the effective use across its systems.

Conversely, the AI routines bring forth the recognition of a large quantity of data for them to operate in a desirable way. This is especially related to the entire case of self-improvement, which has also been noted as an essential potential of deep learning ANN systems (Siau and Wang 2018). The 5G technology would supposedly put all concerns to rest by processing data without any possibility of delays or other limitations. Experts predict that this will ensure that the current projected increase in connectivity speed of 15–20% would almost double if AI is specifically brought and implemented through this approach (Chen and Zhao 2014). Moreover, it must not be denied what it would mean for the future of both these technologies. There should be a potential for creating even more capable and powerful systems if definite results are derived from such an arrangement.

However, there are also risk considerations. It must not be forgotten that the large amounts of data that need to be produced for the AI to work properly will require a great availability of sources (Palattella et al. 2016). Therefore, it can be assumed that there could be a critically threatening scenario for all those involved in the industry when there could be a great and constant demand for more data (Duan and Wang 2015). In the past, many software companies illegally sold the private data of users to many unscrupulous entities who remain active throughout the internet. Thus, cybersecurity is an issue that must be considered to a critical extent.

2.2 Cybersecurity Concerns in the 5G World

By the time 5G networks and systems arrive in full force, there will be a great deal of consideration with regards to numerous security aspects. The criticality of addressing cybersecurity concerns has been growing over the years, as the impact of such instances eventually became quite widespread. Moreover, there is little awareness of all the risks evident at present, and the likeliness of cyberattacks affecting individuals greatly increases (French and Shim 2016). The 5G technology holds immense potential for realizing many IoT devices and making sure that their processes are as effective as possible (Akyildiz, Wang, and Lin 2015). This will inevitably lead to an explosion in the number of IoT devices connected to the internet, directly or indirectly. Moreover, there would be a significant increase in interconnectivity across the board. This specifically means that a single attack can cause maximum harm in terms of coverage, which is possible since these devices will be connected to multiple sub-networks to provide agility and flexibility in operations.

Additionally, security concerning dissemination will also become a definite challenge. When considering IoT technologies, it is necessary to highlight a bit of revelation about the exact nature of the change. IoT is everyday "things" that people usually use in their daily lives. However, they are then optimized to function with the inserted capabilities of doing the functions they were meant to do, and more (Al-Falahy and Alani 2017). Turning ordinary objects into specific IoT devices is challenging across every instance. It is also no wonder that these concerns that are being raised will extend to the provisioning of actual security allocations for these particular and different devices (Li, Da Xu, and Zhao 2018). Security solutions also follow monitoring protocols in real-time and are often limited by the network's bandwidth capability (Arel, Rose, and Karnowski 2010). However, there is a constant look-out for user performance upon the specified bandwidth through these specifications. The advent of 5G may make all these legacy strains of security solutions completely obsolete.

Moreover, another cybersecurity concern that realistically exists relates to the specific issues that reflect on the situation from another perspective altogether. In terms of realizing IoT, it is quite apparent that people would depend upon technology even more than the situation now. Therefore, the higher area of attack could find very subtle and non-noticeable ways in which to significantly disrupt users' daily lives in a critical and very damaging fashion (Siau and Wang 2018). As a consequence, it becomes clear that the entire scenario reflects a situation that needs to address security across multiple dimensions at large.

IoT devices are the ultimate manifestations of what automation is supposed to be. However, this is not specifically focused upon 5G networks squarely, as it will also require the same treatment. The rise in security allocations that are automated across widespread systems has been quite prescient for some time. However, because of the existing challenges in the proper form of integration that many architectures and interfaces have encountered (Arel, Rose, and Karnowski 2010), the requirements state that security must synchronize with the data at every possible level, irrespective of the physical property or software. This fact is more problematic, especially when the software divide has become extremely complex. This is all in addition to the prescient need in case AI becomes an indelible part of 5G technology at large (Yazıcı, Kozat, and Sunay 2014). It will inimitably mean that there should be a significant increase in the stakes since the convergence of both will raise the requirement of data required for the AI systems to work correctly (Hassabis et al. 2017). All of this places a great deal of risk for the entire prospect of 5G technology and the networks.

2.2.1 5G's Potential in Making Security a Priority

A notable case to highlight is that there is still time for 5G to be released to the world. Although some technology instances have started to appear across some countries, they are not fully realized, and nor do they provide full-fledged coverage in these places. One may assume that this specific technological advancement is still in its testing phase. However, what needs to be discussed is all about addressing concerns that must emanate from its highest stage, which involves setting goals and all the necessary policies to realize this specific aim at large (Akyildiz, Wang, and Lin 2015). Therefore, the International Telecommunication Union must update the goals that it has already set for realizing 5G technology to its fullest extent. This should result in the full realization of 5G technology for the public to be postponed for quite some time. That would also compel everyone associated with the predicament to work towards the goal in a way that is most critically and effectively imaginable (Ghahramani 2015). Moreover, the necessities that predict the success of the 5G technology will depend upon how well it can shift the technology landscape. It has happened repeatedly that a significant development in the communication aspects led to the total transformation of everything that was at hand about the technological aspects (Arel, Rose, and Karnowski 2010). It is also essential to highlight the fact that factors pervading throughout the field need to tackle the very complex problem. Additionally, the innovation should also look towards upgrading the security solutions with the help of what the AI routines encounter at large. Although this is a significantly challenging scenario, there is no doubt that there are numerous focal points available for addressing the need for capitalization.

2.2.2 Key Features

The entire field of the 5G network is significantly affected due to a wide variety of factors. However, it is extremely important to address the necessary features that pervade all across the board. These are the most important points of focus that will have a significant consequence across the circumstances that possess the innate potential to create the necessary changes as and when they are required.

2.2.2.1 Peak Data Rate

The peak data rate's essential position is essential since it showcases the exact improvements and advancements that have taken place across a single technology domain. However, the peak data rate essentially indicates the fastest rate at which any particular device can transfer data at any given time (Abdelwahab et al. 2016). According to the International Telecommunication Union (ITU), this value should be somewhere in the 10–20 GB per second for any given network in terms of the allowance to be deemed complete as a 5G network.

2.2.2.2 Mobile Data Volume

The allowances brought forth will allow for more devices to work almost unabatedly across the board. However, it also ensures a maximum possible realization that the average usage efficiency would also increase (Duan and Wang 2015). This will inimitably point towards the definitive and consequential increase in the total volume of data that is transferred, handled, or used globally at any given space of time. Under the presumption that 5G will start arriving by the end of 2021, experts predict that it should carry approximately 32% of the global data traffic (Abdelwahab et al. 2016). By that time, the overall volumes of data consumption will be around 131 Exabyte (billion GB) at the end of each month.

2.2.2.3 Mobility

It is almost a confirmatory factor that mobility should improve by leaps and bounds due to much mobile data traffic and mobile data connections (Dong et al. 2017). This would inimitably also result in the betterment spectrum and energy efficiency all across the board. It would be possible for users who are moving faster than even $500\,\mathrm{km\,h^{-1}}$ to get nothing but unabated and unproblematic network performance.

2.2.2.4 Connected Devices

It has already been showcased that the main impact of 5G technology and networks will be on the field of IoT at large. Therefore, the assumption is that everything in association with the number of devices should experience unmitigated growth in terms of the number to the greatest extent (O'Leary 2013). The very definition of counting devices should essentially change since the advancements that will take place will turn almost every household object into a self-functioning IoT device (Arel, Rose, and Karnowski 2010). The bare minimum of this figure should mean about a million devices within every square kilometer, which means that the 5G network could easily support many devices within that specific area.

2.2.2.5 Energy Efficiency

One of the essential factors that require addressing and action is the matter of energy. The very nature of existence dictates that there will be consumption at every moment. At present, this has put concern into many factors that question the very fabric of sustainability. Since the entire case of the usage in the network will drastically increase the apparent volume of use, it is quite natural that there is a need for less consumption of energy by way of making the connections more efficient upon the devices and their energy sources (Andrieu et al. 2003). Thus, it becomes imperative that the energy consumption in 5G network-connected devices should be almost 10% lower than what had been required in 4G network-connected devices.

2.2.2.6 Service Deployment

Instead of 5G network availability, the service deployments need to happen in phases, mainly because the entire scenario involves significant changes across the previous 4G allocation infrastructure and allocation. This will inimitably mean that the entire case at hand is reflective of a significant amount of investment as well (Abdelwahab et al. 2016). For large multinational businesses, to have their services translate to 5G in terms of deploying them will inimitably mean that there could be spending upwards of 100 million USD in general.

2.2.2.7 Reliability

The ITU seemingly has not been able to converge upon a specific reliability criterion that is both accurate and pervasive. Despite this, some advancement has been made, especially by such as URLLC, which states that it must have a minimum of 10^{-5} (0.001%) of 20 long byte packets. These are then measured if they are being delivered within 1 ms (Arel, Rose, and Karnowski 2010). Moreover, the overall case can be seen through a general mode of measurement, with bit error rates (BER). This essentially calculates the accuracy and efficiency that exist concerning data packet loss under any possible condition. Moreover, the case with 5G Networks, when considered with the layered MIMO framework, indicates channel diversity and contributing gain across the link budget, either for uplinks or downlinks.

2.2.2.8 Latency

Within a network, latency indicates the time required to get it to the destination across a certain network's follow-through. In 5G specifically, the latency is referred to as "air latency," and the target for achievement is supposed to be 1–4 ms (Abdelwahab et al. 2016). Despite this, the tests have revealed that 5G routines showcase a latency in the range of 8–12 ms at large.

2.3 Positive Effects of Addressing Cybersecurity Challenges in 5G

One of the essential factors that have become apparent over time is that connectivity on the network is perhaps the most important factor. Not only do they reflect how well a specific technology performs, but they also address the possibility of horizontal usage and pervasiveness at large. Not only are these the factors that affect the entire case of technological innovation and advancement of what will happen, but also how effective they actually will be must be considered in full detail (Al-Falahy and Alani 2017). Experts note that 5G connectivity's goal should reflect upon the widespread impact that 4G had over time (Hassabis et al. 2017); inasmuch as what will lead to the ubiquity of IoT and many other revolutionary technologies across the board. This will inimitably bring forth the question of cybersecurity, as has already been delineated beforehand.

However, the potential for creating change has become evident through the basic condition that the 5G network connectivity is still in its infancy. There must be some requirements that would require a proper form of addressing this (Chen and Zhao 2014). A prominent factor among these is setting up policy benchmarks that significantly reflect everything essential about the requirements that would not just pervade through the 5G networks but also the technologies that will operate upon it (O'Leary 2013). This might indicate an increase in the goals set by numerous organizations and individuals, but cybersecurity concerns on the network are most likely to affect more people in more critical ways.

The prevailing thought is that to address the cybersecurity issues, there is a need for AI routines implementation. Particularly, the machine learning aspects should play a very important role in such a significant need for detecting security threats across the different aspects of the 5G network (Jiang et al. 2017). The network will have multiple layers of both inputs and outputs and implement necessary perspectives that will speak about the continual monitoring of the different nodes that pervade all across the network at large (Dong et al. 2017). Moreover, proper machine learning should be able to "learn" about these threats, even when they might not be evident under any condition, which will inimitably identify these attacks in real-time. Additionally, it should also indicate whether the overall conditions that pervade across the entire field should be updated (Hansen et al. 2015). This is an essential aspect of ensuring proper cybersecurity because the remedial measures become developed and implemented spontaneously and responsively.

One cannot deny the sheer advantage of having such an approach in the first place. However, some considerations need to be made. For one, Mobile Operators should be the initial purveyors of AI routines because they are responsible for managing all issues and factors that may arise within a network (Jiang et al. 2017). Another major concern is the scenario of whether the developments that the routines develop by themselves will be possible when considering the exponential increase of coverage, complexities, and domains that 5G technology will bring forth (Dong et al. 2017). This indicates that there needs to be significant effort put in to develop the operators' AI capabilities (Pagé and Dricot 2016). This will inimitably mean that the AI technologies will also undergo a critical increase in their capabilities and experience full flexibilities and versatilities in terms of the volume and type of problems they might face at large.

2.4 Intelligent Connectivity Use-Cases

As the terminology indicates, AI will integrate and make the overall 5G network of the world "intelligent" in terms of the network's standard expectations. This has a wide range of definitions, and the difference in their operations is normal because there exist so many implementation scenarios in the first place (Hansen et al. 2015). These are all the necessary use-cases wherein the 5G network will play a very consequential role in promoting feasibility and enhancement in daily operations. Therefore, these are an essential discussion that must be kept in mind because of all the opportunities and challenges they bring and compel the board's technologies to move forward.

2.4.1 Transportation and Logistics

Advanced Driver Assistance Systems (ADAS) have existed for some time. They are mainly utilized to highlight the necessary technological developments and implementation so that there is a definite increase in car and road safety, respectively. These systems are developed to automate, adapt, and actuate certain aspects of the vehicle so that every possible instance of accidents or any other misfortune is avoided (Dong et al. 2017). ADAS exists in many different versions, but 5G network connectivity and AI routines indicate interesting scenarios. Among the many options that have been presented, it might include enhancing the cabin area and focus on driving factors better than ever before (Mellit et al. 2009). The AI-enhanced cameras will respond to any inconsistencies in the situation, such as intoxication, drowsiness, distraction, fatigue, etc.

2.4.2 AI-based Driver Assistance and Monitoring

In addition to this, AI involvement will also inherently involve specifying and managing necessary tasks if something happens. There are already many different enhancements in ADAS that identify different strategies to bring about an avoidance in case accidents do happen. However, with the help of AI routines as well as IoT implementation, there would be computer vision and sensor fusion that will ensure adherence to safety precautions that inimitably help in the reduction of a great deal of damage at large (Duan and Wang 2015). Moreover, this will also involve real-time passenger and driving movement tracking, which greatly enhances the user experience within the vehicle itself. Gesture recognition and the interaction through normative language are all essential features that lay the necessary groundwork for more intervention-based technologies at large (Lemley, Bazrafkan, and Corcoran 2017). The electronic enhancements of "under the hood" circuity will also undergo significant enhancement when considered under the perspective of IoT in 5G developments (French and Shim 2016). All of this makes it possible that the entire field of operating the car requires minimal human input, while also ensuring that essential and required contingencies are deployed if something is wrong with the vehicle itself.

2.4.3 Self-Driving Vehicles

However, the most consequential aspect of AI implementation in modern vehicles is self-driving technology. It has been something that the entire automotive industry has been working towards for a very long time, and the effects delineate the exact circumstances (Hansen et al. 2015). One of the most obvious challenges is that people want AI to drive their vehicles, but they also want to be driven in the same way. This goes beyond what one would expect to be following safety rules and might consider the speed and the responsive behavior when other vehicles are on the road (Ge, Li, and Li 2017). This means that there needs to be a significant contribution to decision-making capabilities within the AI routines in addition to sensory and cognitive functions. Moreover, self-driving vehicles can also be looked upon as IoT devices themselves, or a series of the same working towards a highly complex human goal. It should also specifically involve consideration for communications. Under these circumstances, there should be a focus on vehicle-to-vehicle (V2V) or vehicle-to-communication (V2X) aspects (Dong et al. 2017). However, the specific processes that lead the vehicle to drive itself are pursued in many different ways.

2.4.4 Deliveries with Unmanned Vehicles

The consideration for cases of transportation would not be complete without the implementation of technologies across logistics. Specifically, with the rise of online shopping and many other smart warehouse operations, logistics, as an entire subject unto itself, has become quite a consequential topic to address (Martini et al. 2015). However, the supply chain would become fully automated by the inclusion, which has already garnered attention from many of the biggest retailers (French and Shim 2016). This involves selecting the best delivery pathway that sophisticated algorithms need to handle, which can be executed by the AI routines within the delivery vehicles themselves. Moreover, the fast and efficient processing of all the necessary data involved also indicates better service provision under any circumstance (Ge, Li, and Li 2017). However, many other nuanced challenges are apparent in handling deliveries with unmanned vehicles, which should constitute an inherent part of innovating and implementing new IoT inventions.

2.5 Industrial and Manufacturing Operations

There has been a significant initiative to automate many different aspects of industrial operations, particularly concerning manufacturing. Remote control mostly refers to the wireless connectivity of controlling operations that require minimal movement interventions (Lemley, Bazrafkan, and Corcoran 2017). The subject of control is industrial robots – mechanical devices that perform human operations previously made possible by human beings. The results are quite obvious in how they allow for faster and more efficient execution, down to the most elemental and commonplace tasks. This inimitably replaces human labor, making manufacturing operations more economical and indicating safer throughput operations.

2.5.1 Factory Automation and Remote Control of Industrial Robots

The implementation with 5G in conjunction with IoT technologies and AI routines will inimitably spell a significant change in the entire prospect of directing and managing industrial robots at large. First of all, it is essential to consider that these robots can become "smart" and become part of the IoT infrastructure when fitted together with sensors working based on highly sophisticated AI software routines. This will allow them to work based on achieving better output as they have been directed (Duan and Wang 2015). However, 5G connectivity is required to ensure that these industrial robots can perform different batches in terms of instantaneous communications. This brings forth the projection of "cloud robotics" and indicates all the necessary developments and facilitation needed to produce4 the advent of such an advanced communication network technology at large.

2.5.2 Remote Inspections and Maintenance, and Worker's Training

The entire case of intelligent connectivity focuses on the realization of manufacturing in other senses than normal. Specifically, it becomes true when one considers the auxiliary operations like inspection, maintenance, and repairs in a remote approach. When one considers the entire case of making several possible operations at once, it is evident that a great amount of time and cost is accrued by any organization (Duan and Wang 2015). Moreover, considering actual cases, many of these areas remain inaccessible under purely human intervention. However, that is most definitely not the case with the remotely controlled IoT technology devices that will inherently provide the necessary operations at any given time or condition. These two factors might specifically convey some hazardous instances, especially when considering the case of human intervention. This can be seen when one considers the specific auxiliary functions that might happen across nuclear plants (Feng et al. 2018). Moreover, these specific operations can also inimitably aid in the necessary training of workers at large. When considering this specific responsibility, in most cases, the content and the strategy required often do not cover the plant's conditions under question (Mellit et al. 2009). However, when translated across very real data and solutions, it can become quite essential to the entire field of operations and can essentially change the fortune of any organization that engages in them.

2.6 Healthcare

The combination of 5G networks, AI, and IoT, respectively, also referred to as Intelligent Connectivity, has the potential of maximizing healthcare facilities to the greatest extent imaginable. It shall effectively facilitate better preventive care while bringing the costs to an affordable rate at large (Feng et al. 2018). This is made possible because healthcare providers can make better use of the resources. Moreover, the remote allowances that have possibly made this possible have quite a few factors involved.

2.6.1 Remote Health Monitoring and Illness Prevention

In particular, among them is the case of remote availability of health monitoring and illness prevention services. This is most notably by the sheer strength and the possibilities brought about by 5G interconnectivity (Kovac and Leskova 2012), as well as support across a wide and varied number of individuals, especially when considering the development and use, which facilitates sophisticated monitoring of different aspects of the body.

However, such innovations and devices would need to disseminate to a commonplace extent. The data are put through AI routines that operate specifically to provide health-based recommendations and solutions. Additionally, these can detect the threat of future health issues as well (Feng et al. 2018). This situation should bring forth a better under-standing and overview that healthcare providers need to have for their patients at any given time (Kovac and Leskova 2012). Moreover, the specific facilities containing medical sup-plies and equipment could then be optimized in terms of their use and strategic resource management.

2.6.2 Remote Diagnosis and Medical Operation

Intelligent connectivity also specifically points towards achieving a desirable state of remote diagnosis and medical operation. At present, both these services under health-care auspices are specifically handled within significant limitations, which do not have significant amounts of management issues at large (Ghahramani 2015). However, through the specific realization of high speed, low latency, and ultra-high reliability, it is entirely plausible that doctors will now be able to provide full examinations from remote locations in fully-fledged audio/video feedback (Feng et al. 2018). The facilitation of diagnosis is also made possible through the above recommendation, which realizes the entire prospect at hand.

2.7 Public Safety and Security

One of the most prominent public safety applications and security is realized through the potential that agencies and governments have in making public or private spaces safer. Surveillance capabilities and security and emergency systems can all create maximum effects by way of facilitating all that is required by increasing and enhancing capabilities and versatility in operations (Ghahramani 2015). However, when these systems become "intelligent" under the connectivity allowances facilitated by 5G network capabilities, sce-narios are bound to change. These specific qualities have been discussed, for both vertical and horizontal enhancements of IoT-based technologies (Ge, Li, and Li 2017). This means that there would be both horizontal and vertical improvement in security alarms, cameras, and sensors, which will also increase in number.

2.7.1 Intelligent Video-Surveillance and Security Systems

In addition to all of this, the specific AI routines and applications, when implemented, will allow for specialized operations and processes to become automated. This becomes evident from the fact that there is automation in terms of analyzing individual move-ments, actions, activities, body language, and everything that might be programmed to enhance the capabilities of detecting the occurrence of a crime or other forms of illegal actions under the law (Ge, Li, and Li 2017). Through the machine learning capabilities, which will undergo development and advancement over time, it is entirely plausible that there will be predictive instances when the entire case of future crimes and offenses could be both predicted, anticipated, and acted upon (Ghahramani 2015). These are all possibilities existing for intelligent connectivity in terms of future video-surveillance and security systems.

2.7.2 Emergency Services and Border Controls

Moreover, one should consider that the significant increase and advancement of the technology sector in terms of video surveillance and security systems should inimitably result in disseminating these technologies across the board (Mahmood et al. 2018). Wherever they might be used, it can be assumed that emergency services could then be provisioned under the very best circumstances imaginable. Both fixed and mounted vehicles will inimitably allow for better response times and efficiency of emergency services. There can also be the possibility of implementing robot devices in environments that are not safe for human interventions by any stretch of the imagination. In any case, these can significantly decrease the damage caused by many different calamities or other instances that put a significant section of the society at risk.

2.7.3 Other Sectors

The potential of intelligent connectivity is not specifically limited across these scenarios. There are many areas and points of concern that might benefit for a critical extent if one considers the sheer advantages that the convergence of 5G networks, AI, and, IoT might bring to the table.

2.7.3.1 Virtual Personal Assistance

A notable case in question is that of the Virtual Personal Assistant, which highlights all aspects of one's activities at the lowest individual level. This indicates a significant amount of consideration for evaluating the factors involved in what personalized services the individual might want at any instance, or at any given time for that matter (Dong et al. 2017). These challenges have been tackled in very different ways by the assistants' actual developers, and they have also addressed them in different ways. One of the major ideas is that a virtual assistant must become compatible with any device in proximity, which would allow any individual to control things that surround them. Therefore, the virtual assistants will need to be integrated with the most advanced capabilities in processing and actuating actions as and when the expectations should arise (Militano et al. 2015). However, the entire breadth of the necessary operations inherently reflects the requirements of very high requirements from communication capabilities, resulting in the adoption of 5G network connectivity. It is therefore quite apparent that virtual personal assistants will greatly undergo improvement over time, especially with intelligent connectivity.

2.7.3.2 3D Hologram Displays

There is also the case with a 3D holographic display, which requires a significant amount of data to operate properly. This is specifically prescient about the most advanced display services that have become standard for software technology consumers at large. Under the present and standard 4G LTE network technology, however, this becomes a problem because the hologram display must be streamed in real-time (Dong et al. 2017). With 5G network implementation, the factors of having increased value in speed and very low latency will inimitably mean that all of this is managed in the best way imaginable. However, there are still many other questions that relate to developing this notable form of technology. The most obvious among these is the specific "output display," where such holograms would be projected (Katsaros and Dianati 2017). Under the current beta testing phase, this is made possible with the facilitation of 3D screens, which require some additional circuitry. Alternative options try exploring "virtual reality" technologies at large to bring forth the sense of this result in a completely roundabout fashion. However, most experts agree upon the fact that this entire projection still has significant room for development, as well as advancements at large.

2.8 Conclusion

It is quite an apparent fact that the entire cast of Intelligent Connectivity speaks greatly about the next-generation communication capabilities to the greatest extent imaginable. However, one would be remiss if there was no mention whatsoever in terms of the advancements in processing and decision making it will bring forth. The point about computing technologies has long been about facilitating services that reflect minimum possible human intervention while also ensuring that there is enough personalized presentation, alongside a properly realized mode of complete cybersecurity at large. This is where AI will find its most consequential applications. There is also no doubt that the entire case of implementing AI brings forth a very high-level requirement of a machine or deep learning, respectively. Looking at the AI as a self-learning entity, it has become clear that addressing all of these factors represents challenges that are very hard to address and relate to. Moreover, the significant amounts of data required to be put into the entire field bring forth the overlying cybersecurity threat scenario reaching its definitive peak. This is the clear dilemma that sectors engaging in 5G connectivity, AI, and IoT must engage to the greatest extent imaginable.

References

Abdelwahab, S., Hamdaoui, B., Guizani, M., and Znati, T. (2016). Network function virtualization in 5G. *IEEE Communications Magazine 54* (4): 84–91.

Akyildiz, I.F., Wang, P., and Lin, S.C. (2015). SoftAir: A software-defined networking architecture for 5G wireless systems. *Computer Networks 85*: 1–18.

Al-Falahy, N. and Alani, O.Y. (2017). Technologies for 5G networks: Challenges and opportunities. *IT Professional 19* (1): 12–20.

Andrieu, C., De Freitas, N., Doucet, A., and Jordan, M.I. (2003). An introduction to MCMC for machine learning. *Machine Learning 50* (1-2): 5–43.

Arel, I., Rose, D.C., and Karnowski, T.P. (2010). Deep machine learning – A new frontier in Artificial Intelligence research. *IEEE Computational Intelligence Magazine 5* (4): 13–18.

Chen, S. and Zhao, J. (2014). The requirements, challenges, and technologies for 5G of terrestrial mobile telecommunication. *IEEE Communications Magazine 52* (5): 36–43.

Dong, P., Zheng, T., Yu, S. et al. (2017). Enhancing vehicular communication using 5G-enabled smart, collaborative networking. *IEEE Wireless Communications 24* (6): 72–79.

Duan, X. and Wang, X. (2015). Authentication handover and privacy protection in 5G Hetnets using software-defined networking. *IEEE Communications Magazine 53* (4): 28–35.

Feng, W., Wang, J., Chen, Y. et al. (2018). UAV-aided MIMO communications for 5G Internet of Things. *IEEE Internet of Things Journal 6* (2): 1731–1740.

French, A.M. and Shim, J.P. (2016). The digital revolution: Internet of Things, 5G, and beyond. *Communications of the Association for Information Systems 38* (1): 40.

Ge, X., Li, Z., and Li, S. (2017). 5G software-defined vehicular networks. *IEEE Communications Magazine 55* (7): 87–93.

Ghahramani, Z. (2015). Probabilistic Machine Learning and Artificial Intelligence. *Nature 521* (7553): 452–459.

GSMA International (2018). New GSMA Report Highlights How 5G, Artificial Intelligence and IoT will Transform the Americas. https://www.gsma.com/newsroom/press-release/new-gsma-report-highlights-how-5g-artificial-intelligence-and-iot-will-transform-the-americas/ (accessed 23 April 2020).

Hansen, J., Lucani, D.E., Krigslund, J. et al. (2015). Network coded software-defined networking: Enabling 5G transmission and storage networks. *IEEE Communications Magazine 53* (9): 100–107.

Hassabis, D., Kumaran, D., Summerfield, C., and Botvinick, M. (2017). Neuroscience-inspired Artificial Intelligence. *Neuron 95* (2): 245–258.

Ismail, N. (2019, January 15). Digital transformation in the telecom industry: what's driving it? Information Age: https://www.information-age.com/digital-transformation-in-the-telecom-industry-123478152/ (accessed 22 June 2020).

Jiang, F., Jiang, Y., Zhi, H. et al. (2017). Artificial Intelligence in healthcare: Past, present, and future. *Stroke and vascular neurology 2* (4): 230–243.

Katsaros, K. and Dianati, M. (e.) (2017). A conceptual 5G vehicular networking architecture. In: *5G Mobile Communications*, 595–623. Cham: Springer.

Kovac, M. and Leskova, A. (2012). Innovative applications of car connectivity network – Way to the intelligent vehicle. *Journal of Systems Integration 3* (4): 51–60.

Lemley, J., Bazrafkan, S., and Corcoran, P. (2017). Deep learning for consumer devices and services: Pushing the limits for Machine Learning, Artificial Intelligence, and Computer Vision. *IEEE Consumer Electronics Magazine 6* (2): 48–56.

Li, S., Da Xu, L., and Zhao, S. (2018). 5G Internet of Things: A survey. *Journal of Industrial Information Integration 10*: 1–9.

Mahmood, K., Khan, M.A., Shah, A.M. et al. (2018). Intelligent on-demand connectivity restoration for wireless sensor networks. *Wireless Communications and Mobile Computing 2018*, 1–10.

Martini, B., Paganelli, F., Cappanera, P. et al. (2015, April). Latency-aware composition of virtual functions in 5G. In: *Proceedings of the 2015 1st IEEE Conference on Network Softwarization (NetSoft)*, 1–6. IEEE.

Mellit, A., Kalogirou, S.A., Hontoria, L., and Shaari, S. (2009). Artificial Intelligence techniques for sizing photovoltaic systems: A review. *Renewable and Sustainable Energy Reviews 13* (2): 406–419.

Militano, L., Araniti, G., Condoluci, M. et al. (2015). Device-to-device communications for 5G Internet of Things. *EAI Endorsed Trans Internet Things 1* (1): 1–15.

O'Leary, D.E. (2013). Artificial Intelligence and big data. *IEEE Intelligent Systems 28* (2): 96–99.

Pagé, J. and Dricot, J.M. (2016). Software-defined networking for low-latency 5G core network. In: *2016 International Conference on Military Communications and Information Systems (ICMCIS)*, 1–7. IEEE.

Palattella, M.R., Dohler, M., Grieco, A. et al. (2016). Internet of Things in the 5G era: Enablers, architecture, and business models. *IEEE Journal on Selected Areas in Communications 34* (3): 510–527.

Sánchez, B.B., Sánchez-Picot, Á., and De Rivera, D.S. (2015). Using 5G technologies in the Internet of Things, handovers, problems, and challenges. In: *2015 9th International Conference on Innovative Mobile and Internet Services in Ubiquitous Computing*, 364–369. IEEE.

Siau, K. and Wang, W. (2018). Building trust in artificial intelligence, machine learning, and robotics. *Cutter Business Technology Journal 31* (2): 47–53.

Simsek, M., Aijaz, A., Dohler, M. et al. (2016). 5G-enabled tactile internet. *IEEE Journal on Selected Areas in Communications 34* (3): 460–473.

Sterlite Tech (2019). Don't just change, transform with intelligent connectivity. https://www.stl.tech/mwc19/pdf/01_Intelligent_Connectivity_Whitepaper_16_01_19_web.pdf (accessed 22 June 2020).

Telia Company (2019). Happy anniversary 4G and welcome 5G. News article, 2019. https://www.teliacompany.com/en/news/news-articles/2019/4g-birthday/ (accessed 22 June 2020).

Vinugayathri (n.d.). AI and IoT blended – what it is and why it matters?. https://www.clariontech.com/blog/ai-and-iot-blended-what-it-is-and-why-it-matters (accessed 22 June 2020).

West, D.M. (2016). How 5G technology enables the health Internet of Things. *Brookings Center for Technology Innovation 3*: 1–20.

Yazıcı, V., Kozat, U.C., and Sunay, M.O. (2014). A new control plane for 5G network architecture with a case study on a unified handoff, mobility, and routing management. *IEEE Communications Magazine 52* (11): 76–85.

3

The Internet of Things (IoT): Potentials and the Future Trends

3.1 Introduction

The integration of standards and technologies and the ability to connect massive smaller devices, objects, and sensors, inexpensively and easily, have created a world that is hyper-connected with bridging the virtual and physical things to generate, process, exchange, and consume data for the Internet of Things (IoT). The IoT is a union of standards, technologies, and connections of devices in the real world that communicate in the online realm. This type of technology is useful in data generation, processing, exchanging, and decision-making. IoT is widely considered to be one of the largest revolutions in the Information age. IoT has several issues related to addressing regulation, security and privacy, and standardization. Once these issues have been resolved, the development and growth of complex IoT applications will take place. This chapter discusses the future of intelligent devices and pervasive connectivity, data sharing, and the creation of partnerships overcoming interoperability issues, security and regulations, technology, and applications while experiencing waves of new technology advancement.

The IoTs is the concept that involves the interconnection of electronic devices or any object that has an "ON" and "OFF" state to a network allowing those devices to establish communication with one another and with the network infrastructure. Figure 3.1 depicts how IoT enables a smarter integration of digital devices and humans by capacities to collect, process, and transmit data to the physical sphere in a smart networked environment.

In an ever-evolving world that sees daily changes in the development of technology, medicine, and economics, IoT allows the practical experience of implementations and applications offered by the devices we use every day. The IoT provides many new and interesting concepts that change the overall complexion of the devices and services that we use; devices can take on new forms and enhance user experience. IoT can also provide ways for the end devices to communicate and provide feedback, such as their surroundings and functionality. Devices such as kitchen appliances, lights, thermostats, computers, cell phones, and medical equipment are being upgraded to be connected to networks. Providing a better user experience increases ease of access and convenience. In order to unlock the true potential of IoT, many questions need to be addressed.

Some important questions include:

Intelligent Connectivity: AI, IoT, and 5G, First Edition. Abdulrahman Yarali.
© 2022 John Wiley & Sons Ltd. Published 2022 by John Wiley & Sons Ltd.

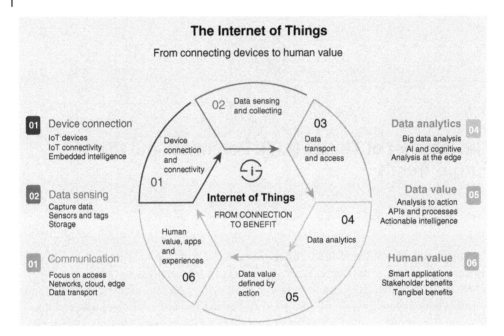

Figure 3.1 IoT network from connectivity to human value (i-SCOOP).

- How far are we from a connected and intelligent future, and how do we get there?
- Why choose IoT? Building your IoT business model: Identifying commercial opportunities and their justification.
- Joining Forces: To what extent does the true value from IoT lie in sharing data and creating partnerships?
- Overcoming Interoperability Challenges: Are we any closer to creating a one size fits all IoT framework?
- Regulation and Security: Will this hinder or enable IoT innovation?
- Lessons on how to successfully innovate while keeping security and privacy at the forefront.
- What's coming next? AI, Drones, Robotics, AR/VR . . . discussing this in detail (technology, applications, etc.).

3.2 Achieving the Future of IoT

IoT is a concept that involves interconnection with devices around the user and devices all over the world. When a user connects to the IoT, the user is communicating with the Internet Service Provider, another user or service, but is actively engaged in an online environment with data communication, real-time information, and active user involvement. The IoT has been an evolving process for many years and continues to develop new and interesting "things" each day. Lately, the question has been how far are we from being in a truly connected and intelligent future and how did we get there? The first part has been a hot topic type question for a few years now, and stems from the idea of what is considered "connected and intelligent." Many new devices now have smart or intelligent integration, completely transforming the identity of all devices that we buy today. For over a decade, we have been privy to these changes via the devices that we buy. Users now are more integrated and connected than ever before. A user in one country can almost effortlessly communicate with a user in another country. The aspects of time are almost made trivial due to the ability to transfer data, the e-mail message, and stream different life forms and recorded content. Is the ability to communicate with someone with little to no effort considered being "connected"? Alternatively, is a device like a smartwatch or a tablet being able to update information about your surroundings as if the weather and the ability to respond to voice commands truly make it "intelligent"?

An intelligent minded device is usually identified with AI, or Artificial Intelligence. AI is intelligence displayed by machines that allow them to understand and adapt to their surroundings. In an article written by Guia Marie Del Prado, she states that "It seems as though not a week passes without yet another AI system overcoming an unprecedented hurdle or outperforming humans." AI is the primary indicator of how well a machine can adapt to its surroundings. A human may consider a trivial task like remembering a date or setting up a schedule. However, an AI system evolves by achieving those simple tasks and producing more results with analytical tools and their form of thought. Therefore, AI is what would be that baseline of what is considered "intelligence" for a device. If we define intelligence by the definition of AI, then new devices all have some form of AI and are actively pursuing ways to improve upon those designs to become more intelligent. The second part of the first question, "how long," can best be described by analytical data gathered from the past decade. According to Business Insider data analytics, they show that the number of smart devices has gone up exponentially over the past few years (Prado 2015).

The issue is not something that can be pinned down to an exact time or date, but be a consistent change in the landscape of IT and the devices and services that people use every day. As time goes on, users can witness advancements to the devices and services used until, eventually, almost every aspect of human life has some form of connection to the online world. The daily human routines will be tied to the online realm and coexist with other users who use the same devices and services. Having almost any form of their lives available online will choose how much of their life exists online and the best way to manage that.

3.3 Commercial Opportunities for IoT

Many businesses face the IoT network infrastructure changes and opportunities that IoT would bring for their company and increase revenue. Most companies have some form of an online presence. Companies can now easily get free or cheap advertisement space and offer user questions, comments, and concerns. The marketing opportunities that the online world can offer to companies can help them to reach a broad market. This can be more productive for the company than other means like newspaper ads or word of mouth; online environments offer these two forms of communication and many more through services like social media and website ads. Online marketing is not the only benefit companies can gain while using online services. Companies can accept the benefit from users' analytical data to gauge things like deals or changes to their goods or services. Analytical tools offered by online/IoT services can easily be a huge game-changer for some companies on a customer base's fringes, possibly having productivity issues or wanting to reinvent or reinvigorate a product service.

The IoT offers the means to increase productivity and innovation to completely reshape and transform a product or service into something almost impossible to achieve. The IoT also makes it possible to improve the quality and overall productivity of businesses. According to Business Insider, these companies have caught multiple investors' attention due to their ability to integrate their services with the IoT. Companies like Honeywell (a company specializing in the industrial IoT and Hitachi, who are helping other companies incorporate IoT systems) are getting a lot of attention to take advantage of the IoT resources (Meola 2016).

The IoT allows businesses to take advantage of a very expansive resource that other businesses did not have the luxury of having before creating the Internet. The IoT not only allows users to input comments and complaints about businesses or services, but it also allows businesses to take these comments and complaints and enhance their products or services to transform and fix flaws that would otherwise be inconvenient to the user. The IoT's benefit goes far beyond checking a comment or informing a user that there is a deal available. Businesses are starting to take advantage of it.

3.4 The Industrial Internet of Things

The Industrial Internet of Things (IIoT) is an upcoming and developing concept in the internet world. The latest technological change is set to create limitless opportunities and risks to businesses and society. Six main enabling technologies are spinning around IIOT to utilize all its functionality and potentials. The fusion of these technologies (see Figure 3.2) creates a platform of IIOT (Benardos and Vosniakos 2017).

The IIoT is the use of smart sensors and actuators to enhance manufacturing and industrial processes. Also known as the industrial Internet or Industry 4.0, IIoT leverages the power of smart machines and real-time analytics to take advantage of the data that dumb machines have produced in industrial settings for years. The driving philosophy behind IIoT is that smart machines are better than humans at capturing and analyzing data in real-time. In addition, they are also better at communicating important information that can be used to drive business decisions faster and more accurately.

Connected sensors and actuators enable companies to pick up on inefficiencies and problems sooner and save time and money in addition to supporting Business Intelligence (BI) efforts. In manufacturing, IIoT holds great potential for quality control, sustainable and green practices, supply chain traceability, and overall supply chain efficiency. In an industrial setting, IIoT is key to processes such as predictive maintenance (PdM), enhanced field service, energy management, and asset tracking.

The IoT revolution can enhance manufacturing, energy, agriculture, transportation, and other industrial departments that directly affect countries' economies. The IIoT is perceived to be able to control the physical world. However, since it is in its early stages of development,

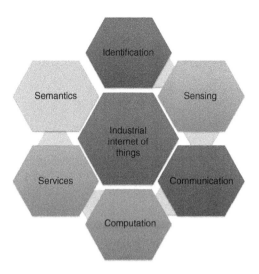

Figure 3.2 IIOT categories of enabling technologies (Benardos 2017).

various questions have been raised regarding its impact on the current industries, value chains, business frameworks, and workforces, and action to ensure its success in the future.

The main business opportunities of IIoT, as per the convention, include greatly enhanced operational efficiency through PdM and remote management. Secondly, there would be an outcome economy through various software and hardware innovations and improved visibility into products and services. Thirdly, there will be emerging interconnected ecosystems. Fourthly, close collaboration with people and machines will lead to high productivity and engage many workforces. Conversely, a majority of businesses are more likely to shift from product to outcome-based services. Governments and businesses will have to deal effectively with risks such as security, privacy, and interoperability to realize the concept's full potential.

The various recommendations for seizing the opportunities for IIoT include establishing global security commons, re-orientation of the overall business strategy, and re-evaluation and updating data protection and liability policies to enhance data flow. It was discovered that, in the future, the four phases of IIoT would include operational efficiency (phase 1) and new products and services (phase 2), which are of the near term. The long term includes outcome economy (phase 3) and an autonomous pull economy. In conclusion, the IIoT will be transformative as it will change competition because of its various potentials.

3.4.1 How IIoT Works

IIoT is a network of intelligent devices connected to form systems that monitor, collect, exchange, and analyze data. Each industrial IoT ecosystem consists of:

- Intelligent assets that can sense, communicate, and store information about themselves;
- Public and private data communications infrastructure;
- Analytics and applications that generate business information from raw data; and
- People.

Edge devices and intelligent assets transmit information directly to the data communications infrastructure. It is converted into actionable information on how a certain piece of machinery is operating, for instance. This information can then be used for PdM, as well as to optimize business processes.

3.4.2 Benefits of IIoT

One of the top touted benefits the IIoT affords businesses is PdM. This involves organizations using real-time data generated from IIoT systems to predict defects in machinery before they occur, enabling companies to take action to address those issues before a part fails or a machine goes down.

Another common benefit is improved field service. IIoT technologies help field service technicians identify potential customer equipment issues before they become major issues, enabling techs to fix the problems before inconvenient customers.

Asset tracking is another IIoT perk. Suppliers, manufacturers, and customers can use asset management systems to track the location, status, and condition of products throughout the supply chain. The system will send instant alerts to stakeholders if the goods are damaged or at risk of being damaged, giving them the chance to take immediate or preventive action to remedy the situation.

IIoT also permits enhanced customer satisfaction. When products are connected to the IoT, the manufacturer can capture and analyze data about how customers use their products, enabling manufacturers and product designers to tailor future IoT devices and build more customer-centric product roadmaps.

IIoT also improves facility management. As manufacturing equipment is susceptible to wear and tear and certain conditions within a factory, sensors can monitor vibrations, temperature, and other factors that might lead to operating conditions that are less than optimal.

3.4.3 IIoT versus IoT

Although the IoT and the IIoT have many technologies in common, including cloud platforms, sensors, connectivity, machine-to-machine communications, and data analytics, they are used for different purposes.

IoT applications connect devices across multiple verticals, including agriculture, healthcare, enterprise, consumer, utilities, government, and cities. IoT devices include smart appliances, fitness bands, and other applications that generally do not create emergencies if something goes amiss.

IIoT applications, on the other hand, connect machines and devices in such industries as oil and gas, utilities, and manufacturing. System failures and downtime in IIoT deployments can result in high-risk situations or even life-threatening situations. IIoT applications are also more concerned with improving efficiency and improving health or safety, versus the user-centric nature of IoT applications.

3.4.4 IIoT Applications and Examples

In a real-world IIoT deployment of smart robotics, ASEA Brown Boveri (ABB), a power and robotics firm, uses connected sensors to monitor the maintenance needs of its robots to prompt repairs before parts break.

Likewise, commercial jetliner maker Airbus has launched what it calls "factory of the future," a digital manufacturing initiative to streamline operations and boost production. Airbus has integrated sensors into machines and tools on the shop floor and outfitted employees with wearable tech, e.g. industrial smart glasses, to cut down on errors and enhance workplace safety.

Another robotics manufacturer, Fanuc, uses sensors within its robotics, along with cloud-based data analytics, to predict the imminent failure of components in its robots. Doing so enables the plant manager to schedule maintenance at convenient times, reducing costs and averting potential downtime.

Magna Steyr, an Austrian automotive manufacturer, is taking advantage of IIoT to track its assets, including tools and vehicle parts, and automatically order more stock when necessary. The company is also testing "smart packaging" enhanced with Bluetooth to track components in its warehouses.

3.4.5 Vendors in IIoT

There are several vendors with IIoT platforms, including:

- Ability by ABB, a power and robotics company;
- IoT System by Cisco, a networking company;
- Field by Fanuc, a supplier of industrial automation equipment;
- Predix by GE Digital, an energy management company;
- Connected Performance Services by Honeywell, a software-industrial company;
- Connyun by Kuka, a manufacturer of industrial robots (created in partnership with Infosys, an IT consulting firm);
- Wonderware by Schneider Electric, an energy management company; and
- MindSphere by Siemens, an industrial manufacturing company.

3.4.6 The Future of IIoT

Bain & company predicted industrial IoT applications would generate more than $300 billion by 2020, double that of the consumer IoT segment ($150 billion).

Similarly, International Data Corporation (IDC) Research reported that the top three industries investing in IIoT in 2018 are manufacturing with $189 billion focusing on asset management; transportation ($85 billion) with a focus on freight monitoring and fleet management, and utilities ($73 billion) with a focus on smart grids. At the same time, consumer IoT spending will reach $62 billion.

More optimistically, Accenture expects IIoT to add $14.2 trillion to the economy in the same period, growing at a 7.3% compound annual growth rate (CAGR) through 2020.

PdM is servicing equipment when it is estimated that service is required within a certain tolerance. PdM is used in railroads, industrial equipment, manufacturing plants, and oil and gas processing.

Maintaining machinery and electronics is most cost-effective if done when it is needed. To that end, PdM systems are designed to ensure that servicing does not happen too soon, wasting money on unnecessary work, or too late, after wear and time have caused undue deterioration. PdM systems can also help plan an inventory for replacement parts and provide input on systems that need a design upgrade because of unacceptable performance.

PdM is enabled by the advances in sensor and communication technologies that are part of the ongoing trends of automation and the IoT, and particularly the Industrial IoT. Those advances enable continuous monitoring and data analytics for mechanical and electrical conditions, operational efficiency, and other performance indicators.

PdM works through sensors, often tied together with PdM software on a wireless sensor and actuator network (WSAN). The software takes into account time, mileage or usage, and the measured, sometimes minute changes from sensors that indicate a need for service before reduced performance or degradation of the equipment occurs. These measurements are often performed on machines while they are running to reduce the impact on production.

Many measurements are taken to estimate the need for service, including:

- Oil and oil contaminant analysis.
- Sound and ultrasound analysis.
- Vibration analysis.
- Infrared analysis.

3.5 Future Impact of IoT in Our Industry

- In 10 years, The IoT will make up two-thirds of the gross domestic product (GDP) globally. That has major impacts on how things will operate at that time. With the rapid replacement of people for computers, there will be a lot more need for people in the IT field and less in the physical manufacturing fields. This means that there will be a great need for more educated workers and potentially no place for uneducated workers whose line/manufacturing jobs have been replaced by robots.
- There are still many unknowns with the IoT, just like the internet when it first started to gain popularity. Like most things that rapidly enter the mainstream, there are always fantastic improvements, but there are always unknowns and issues with the rapid pace that it comes.
- An annual meeting started in 2014 called the Industrial Internet Initiative that focused on IoT and helped start a framework and help educate through workshops, surveys, interviews, etc. There are still struggles for organizations to understand the long-term impacts of IoT and the threat of being left behind. Many evident benefits can come from this advancement.
- Operations will improve through speed and precision and the replacement of people with efficient machines.
- Interconnection of all devices creates mass ease of access and functionality.
- Potential for even greater and more efficient software to be developed to increase nearly every field involved rapidly.
- There will be a large demand for higher-skilled workers and potentially allow current workers to be educated to fill these new roles, creating better jobs than their previous ones.
- Some risks come with the IoT.
- The main risk is security and data privacy. There are always gaps that tend to form with such a rapidly growing field, whether its lack of standards due to development speed or simply overlooked when connecting so many devices and services; now more than ever

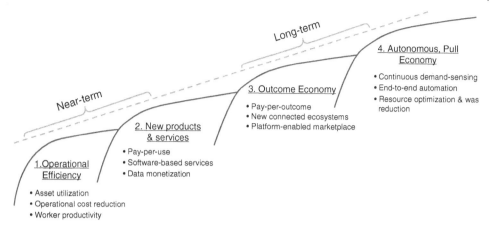

Figure 3.3 The adoption and impact path of the industrial Internet (World Economic Forum 2015).

data security is vital. Our entire lives are online, and without proper precautions, a person or entire company can be found to be breached after it is too late to stop it.

- There is also the risk of fads. That there could be no long-term sustainability for this new phenomenon, and there is a risk of investment vs. not.

There are four phases of the Industrial Internet Evolution. There is a near term representing immediate opportunities (phases 1 and 2) and long term (phases 3 and 4) representing structural changes (World Economic Forum n.d.); see Figure 3.3.

- Near Term
  - Operational Efficiently. This includes things like asset utilization, operational cost reductions, worker productivity.
  - New Products and Services. This includes things like pay-per-use, more software-based services, data monetization increases.
- Long Term
  - Outcome Economy. This includes platform-based market places, connected ecosystems, and pay-per-outcome.
  - Autonomous Pull Economy. This includes resource optimization, waste reduction, end-to-end automation, continuous demand sensing.

3.6 Data Sharing in the IoT Environment

The primary benefit of the IoT is the ability for users to connect and access information through different methods. For this to be possible, users must integrate themselves into this system as much as the devices do; user input and data gathered for analytical tools help continue developing many different devices and services online. Sharing data is a hot topic because users can sometimes feel blindsided by how much information they supply to online resources and are confused when they get ads attributed to what they search or comment about. While this is a gray area in the discussion, the concept of tailoring searches to recently discussed things or items is a very interesting advancement. The overall idea is that the IoT can become an expansive environment and will be dictated by how much people or users want to help push the development.

User input is important for IoT advancement, but the core infrastructure and policy changes must come from the states and nations that the users reside in. Lawmakers and legislators work with and sometimes against the advancement of IoT in different ways. The changes that IoT faces could have global implications. Policies made in one country can have a ripple effect and cause that legislation to be enacted in other countries or cause a restriction of systems due to laws put in place by that country. The real problem is how far these laws and regulations can affect the users from being truly connected online.

While regulations will be discussed later in the paper, the idea of forming partnerships within communities and among different countries allow for endless possibilities. A group of organizations can create a cause it can actively advocate for others. That group of users can advertise, collect, and even rally those other users and actively pursue change through these online environments. The idea of partnerships allows for the usage of resources to manage and consolidate resources. The IoT offers a unique ability that we have not had before. The IoT not only helps for social partnerships, but it can also help on an educational scale. Recently, the Massachusetts Institute of Technology (MIT) has offered new training programs for professionals. According to a Computerworld article, "The courses are targeted at professionals who are trying to think about the future of their companies." The IoT could help startup businesses, with users who work from across the world and use online resources to meet, exchange ideas, and create (Thibodeau 2016). These tools are at the users' disposal and can be utilized in different ways; the direction that IoT goes can be dictated by many different ways and could ultimately be transformed from what is known today to something completely different tomorrow.

3.7 IoT Devices for Environment Operation

Many people and organizations utilize IoT devices to extend efficiency and benefit. In contrast, IoT devices offer incredible comfort; having huge numbers of them in a little space increments complexity in device plan, test, execution, and security. Testing these devices is one of the greatest challenges today's plan engineers and device producers confront. IoT victory requests that they address the 5 C challenges over the whole IoT device life cycle network – coherence, compliance, coexistence, connectivity, and cyber-security.

The IoT is rapidly growing into already detached businesses with applications such as farther machinery, remote surgery, and vitality dissemination in keen networks. Numerous remote advances back these applications. Advances incorporate near-field communication (NFC) for portable installments, geosynchronous satellites for unattended farther climate stations, Bluetooth® (BT), remote Local Area Network (LAN), ZigBee, and point-to-point radio cellular. The network presents modern challenges to originators, particularly for mission basic applications, where profoundly complex frameworks and thick device arrangements must work dependably and without "fall flat." The remote advancing guidelines moreover include complexity to devise improvement and testing.

Whether we are talking around wearable devices that send data to your computer or network-connected movement finders in a domestic alarm system, expanded battery life tops the prerequisites list for unused IoT devices. Shoppers regularly anticipate long battery life for their applications and devices. For illustration, keen agricultural and mechanical sensors must work for long periods regularly more than ten years a long time between charges. Untrustworthy and brief battery life causes a disturbance, instead of making lives simpler, as planned. For those who actualize IoT techniques at the center of their trade, wasteful control utilization becomes problematic.

Remote devices bring comfort to clients. Be that as it may, as utilization of the common remote measures develops, clog causes remote communication disappointment, an issue that is discontinuous and difficult to follow. To address the blockage, benchmarks bodies and administrative offices have issued proposals and controls to guarantee compelling and proficient utilization of the radio range. Administrative bodies incorporate the US Government Communications Commission and the European Commission, which administers the European Union administration. Other administrative bodies incorporate the Korea Communications Commission and Advancement, Science, and Financial Advancement Canada. It is basic for IoT gadget producers to achieve precompliance and compliance testing through the item life cycle from plan to test approval, fabricating, and sending. This makes difference manufacturers achieve first-to-market breakthroughs and remain competitive within the market.

When multiple protocols/devices are in operation near each other, the frequencies can overlap or cause interference, which results in a degradation of the network. Some frequencies are licensed and therefore have more stringent requirements regarding devices that are on nearby frequencies, which helps eliminate some interference, but it does not prevent it. Wireless devices and systems are vulnerable to disturbance, particularly within the shared license-free mechanical, logical, and medical groups at 2.4 and 5 GHz. Since most IoT devices and sensors depend on a dynamic remote association to transmit information, obstructions can be inconvenient to the coming about data. Remote associations might drop discontinuously. Information may get to be undermined and incoherent. Coexistence is a wireless device's capacity to function within other devices' nearness using divergent working conventions. It is basic for steady, dependable communication within the IoT world. The way to guarantee dependable remote organized execution and success within the remote IoT world, particularly in healthcare situations, is to test for radio coexistence legitimately.

Cybersecurity may be a concern for people as well as huge organizations. With the exponential development of family things and a broad array of wireless sensors come frightfulness stories around hacked savvy family things, stresses around character robbery, and ever-increasing concerns, almost information breaches. The cyber-security issue comes to numerous levels, from gadgets to communications, cloud, applications, and clients. Either cybercriminals or negligent users may be the cause. Endeavors ought to discover arrangements that cater to each level to counter cyber-security issues. Cybercriminals utilize advanced methods to pick up a vulnerable IoT device for their attack. Any connected device might act as a portal to important frameworks. It is important to realize what might happen if a programmer picked up national control dissemination or a defense framework through an IoT device.

One of the most important steps in developing an IoT network is which networking protocol you plan to use. Most IoT customers demand reliable connectivity that works even in the most crowded wireless environments without interfering with other ongoing wireless communications. Luckily, there are many wireless protocols available for IoT organized into two groups: short-range and long-range standards.

The coexistence concept will help ensure stability and reliability for IoT devices as they become more commonplace. In this case, it means being able to exist alongside other wireless devices in a network, be it at home or an office. Without coexistence in mind, wireless devices may not be able to detect each other; or worse yet, they may conflict with each other, causing them to malfunction and behave in unexpected ways. The purpose of this coexistence is to determine their ability to maintain functional wireless performance (FWP) in the presence of interference. Four main steps help to ensure IoT devices can work within their environment as intended, starting with protocol selection (Keysight Technology 2019).

3.7.1 Step One: Pick Your Protocol

When choosing an operating medium for your IoT network, careful consideration needs to be given to understanding the differences between protocols, along with their pros and cons. One of the first main considerations to determine is whether you need short or long-range coverage. Just as the name implies, if you do not need coverage to extend long ranges, you should choose a shorter-range protocol, just as a precautionary measure, to lessen the accessibility of your network to non-authorized devices. The short-range technologies include Bluetooth Low Energy (BLE), NFC, ZigBee, Z-Wave, and Wi-Sun. The long-range technologies include Narrowband (NB)-IoT, Cat-M1, LoRa, and SigFox. Each of these technologies features various benefits but may also have some notable drawbacks, depending on the scenario and environment. ZigBee is based on the IEEE 802.15.4 PHY and MAC standard and offers a great deal of functionality. Coexistence and mitigation of interference mean that ZigBee supports usage in tree, star, and mesh networks. The various specifications of ZigBee are as follows: Frequency – 800, 900, 2400 MHz; Bandwidth – 2 MHz; Data Rate – 40 to 250 kbps; Modulation – Binary Frequency Shift Keying (BPSK), Offset Quadrature Phase-Shift Keying (OQPSK); Range – 10 m; Network – Wireless Personal Area Network (WPAN); Applications – Home automation, smart grid; and remote control. Thread is based on the IEEE 802.15.4 PHY and MAC standard and is similar to ZigBee, but instead uses IPv6 over low-power Wireless Personal Area Network (6LoWPAN). Additionally, it uses an encrypted mesh network to securely and reliably connect devices and minimizes interference by using a listen-before-send technique before every data transmission. The specifications of Thread are as follows: Frequency – 800, 900, 2400 MHz; Bandwidth – 2 MHz; Data Rate – 40 to 250 kbps; Modulation – BFSK, Frequency Shift Keying (FSK), OQPSK; Range – 10 m; Network – WPAN; Applications – Mesh network for home and support 6LoWPAN. BLE was created as a low-power, low-data throughput networking option to allow an IoT device to have up to 10 years of operation without recharging. The BLE specifications are as follows: Frequency – 2.4 GHz; Bandwidth – 1 MHz; Data Rate – 1 Mbps; Modulation – GFSK; Range – 50 m; Network – WPAN; Applications – Automotive, healthcare, security, and home entertainment. Z-Wave has the following specifications: Frequency – 868.42 MHz, 908.42 MHz;

Bandwidth – 200 kHz; Data Rate – 9.6 to 100 kbps; Modulation – BFSK, GFSK; Range – 100 m; Network – WPAN; Applications – Remote controls, smoke alarms, and security sensors. Owned by Denmark Zensys, Wi-Sun has the following specifications: Frequency – 800, 900, 2400 MHz; Bandwidth – 200 kHz to 1.2 MHz; Data Rate – 50 kbps to 1 Mbps; Modulation – FSK, Orthogonal Frequency Division Multiplexing (OFDM), OQPSK; Range – 1000 m; Network – WNAN; Applications – FAN and HAN Smart Utility. Wi-Fi has the following specifications: Frequency – Sub GHz; Bandwidth – 1 to 16 MHz; Data Rate – 150 kbps to 78 Mbps; Modulation – OFDM; Range – 1000 m; Network – WLAN; Applications – Target for IoT, wearable devices or extended range. NFC has the following specifications: Frequency – 13.56 MHz; Bandwidth – 1 MHz; Data Rate 848 kbps; Modulation – FSK, Amplitude Shift Keying (ASK); Range – 20 cm; Network – P2P; Applications – Contactless payment, easy other connection (Wi-Fi, BT) identity and access. Long Term Evolution (LTE)-M (Cat-M1) has the following specifications: Frequency – LTE bands; Bandwidth – 1.4 MHz; Data Rate – 200 kbps to 1 Mbps; Modulation – OFDM; Range – 1000 m; Network – WAN; Applications – Lower speed and power versions of LTE in a 3rd Generation Partnership Project (3GPP); Release 12/13. Cat-M1 is expected to be used on machine-to-machine (M2M) applications for industrial IoT. NB-IoT has the following specifications: Frequency – Global Systems for Mobile (GSM)/LTE band; Bandwidth – 180 kHz; Data Rate – up to 250 kbps; Modulation – BPSK, QPSK, opt 16QAM; Range – 10s of km; Network – WAN; Applications – Critical infrastructure and agriculture. LoRa has the following specifications: Frequency – Sub GHz; Bandwidth – 125 kHz; Data Rate – 0.3 to 50 kbps; Modulation – GFSK, CSS; Range – 32 km; Network – WAN; Applications – Critical infrastructure and agriculture. SigFox has the following specifications: Frequency – Sub GHz; Bandwidth – 600 Hz; Data Rate – Up to 500 kbps; Modulation – BPSK, GFSK; Range – 10's of km; Network – WAN; Applications – Critical infrastructure and agriculture. Each of these standards offers various pros and cons when deciding which to use for an IoT network. It is important to keep those in mind when determining the best standard to use in any given situation. Table 3.1 summarizes the differences between important specifications discussed above.

Table 3.1 IoT protocols and specification.

Protocol	Frequencies	Bandwidth	Data rate	Range	Common applications
ZigBee	800, 900, 2400 MHz	2 MHz	40–250 kbps	10 m	Home automation, smart grids, remote control
Thread	800, 900, 2400 MHz	2 MHz	40–250 kbps	10 m	Mesh networks and support for 6LoWPAN
Bluetooth low energy	2.4 GHz	1 MHz	1 Mbps	50 m	Automotive, healthcare, security, and home entertainment
Z-wave	868.42 and 908.42 MHz	200 kHz	9.6–100 kbps	100 m	Remote controls, smoke alarms, security sensors

(Continued)

Table 3.1 (Continued)

Protocol	Frequencies	Bandwidth	Data rate	Range	Common applications
Wi-Sun	800, 900, 2400 MHz	200 kHz–1.2 MHz	50 kbps–1 Mbps	1000 m	Smart utilities, smart grids, and smart metering
Wi-Fi	Sub GHz	1–16 MHz	150 kbps–78 Mbps	1000 m	IoT networks, wearable devices, extended ranges
NFC	13.56 MHz	1 MHz	848 kbps	20 cm	Contactless payments, other identification connections
LTE-M	LTE bands	1.4 MHz	200 kbps–1 Mbps	1000 m	Mainly M2M for industrial IoT
NB-IoT	GSM/LTE bands	180 kHz	250 kbps max	10s of km	Infrastructure and agricultural
LoRa	Sub GHz	125 kHz	0.3–50 kbps	32 km	Infrastructure and agricultural
SigFox	Sub GHz	600 Hz	500 kbps max	10's of km	Infrastructure and agricultural

3.7.2 Step Two: Understand Coexistence

The second step in the development of an IoT network is understanding coexistence. Most customers want the IoT devices they use to work seamlessly together, even if they operate using different standards. Coexistence is defined as the ability for wireless devices or equipment to operate in other devices or equipment that use dissimilar operating protocols. This is important because when two devices operate on close or the same frequency while also being near each other, both devices are usually affected. In most cases, four key factors drive the concern for coexistence. These factors include:

- Increased use of wireless technology for critical equipment connectivity; intensive use of unlicensed or shared spectrum;
- Higher deployment rates of sensitive equipment, including medical devices (intravenous infusion pumps, pacemakers), and emergency detection devices (such as those found in a connected vehicle); and massive deployments of sensors for smart cities, industrial applications, and beyond.

The article of Keysight Technology (2019) gives an example of coexistence by describing a smart hearing aid scenario attempting to communicate with a smartphone while inside a hospital. The key thing to keep in mind with this scenario is that there are numerous other types of devices and wireless communications standards in use due to being inside a hospital. Some of these devices and standards include wireless LAN access points, nurse call stations, Bluetooth devices at the nursing stations, microwave ovens in the pantry, and medical devices such as IV infusion pumps and cardiac monitors reporting patient status that sound alarms based on real-time data. Additionally, patients, family members, and staff will often have a couple of smart devices like smart-phones or smartwatches on them. Many of the devices mentioned above make use of cellular, LTE, Bluetooth, or Wi-F, sometimes depending on the type of device. Whether they be for hospital or personal use, all of the devices will often create at least a small amount of interference or some other hindrance on the performance of the hearing aid's ability to communicate with the smartphone in the scenario. A good practice to ensure coexistence is testing. Coexistence tests evaluate a device's ability to maintain FWP in various wireless environments, even when those environments are device heavy. Testing is important because it is often difficult to take the numerous variables that affect wire-less communications when attempting to calculate environmental factors or make a said environment model. As a side note, Electromagnetic Interference (EMI) and Electromagnetic Compatibility (EMC) testing are not considered as a test of coexistence. Instead, coexistence testing requires equipment under test (EUT) to initiate communi-cations with other companion devices. A signal generator is usually set up to generate an unintended interference signal to cause interference for the device being tested. A signal analyzer is then used to monitor the intended signal between the EUT and its companion device and the unintended signal causing interference. The Key Performance Indicator (KPI) metric is used to monitor performance degradation in the EUT's operation.

3.7.3 Step Three: Pick Your Technique

While there are many possible protocols for an IoT network, it is important to keep in mind that many protocols cannot share channels cooperatively. A prime example of this fact is that Bluetooth devices use a frequency-hopping spread spectrum (FHSS). They cannot detect any 802.11 transmission that uses OFDM or a direct sequence spread spectrum (DSSS) modulation while on the same radio frequencies. In order to overcome these chal-lenges, three techniques were developed to improve the coexistence of IoT networks and devices. These three techniques are as follows: physical separation, frequency separation, and time separation. While each of these techniques overcomes some issues concerning coexistence, they have their challenges as well. The first technique is physical separation.

Physical separation reduces interference by reducing the amount of competition on a shared spectrum and reduces the signal strength to make the signals more localized. The challenge associated with physical separation is that it does not work well in wireless areas that are very dense. This is a rather large challenge since, in most cases, every IoT environ-ment is extremely dense, which is where interference is most abundant. The second tech-nique is frequency separation. This technique can be used to improve the performance of mixed wireless networks by allowing each individual network to operate on different fre-quencies. This ensures that each network's traffic does not interfere with the other net-work's traffic even if those two networks are placed near each other. This technique is often more effective than physical separation but does have a challenge of its own. Many of the different standards used for IoT networks operate within the same frequency band. For example, Bluetooth, Zigbee, and 802.11 channels all operate on the 2.4-GHz ISM band. Additionally, with a shared spectrum, you cannot decide which channels your neighbors use at any given time.

The third technique is time separation. This technique ensures that data transmissions are sent and received at different times to minimize collisions and interference. This technique is easily employed because most networks are designed to transmit data 100% of the time and instead transmit data only in short time slots. This technique's challenge is that most radio standards are not designed to detect other network transmissions or cooperatively share channels. This means that the higher the volume of data, the more time is spent transmitting and sending acknowledgments. In some cases, this will lead to a device becoming deaf to other protocols attempting to transmit a critical data transfer. Additionally, transmissions may collide, which in turn leads to errors or data needing to be retransmitted.

3.7.4 Step Four: Create Your Test Plan

The final step in the selection of an IoT standard to use is creating a test plan. In order to make the creation of a test plan easier to understand, it has been broken down into the following five steps: Characterize the Expected Radio Frequency (RF) Environment, Choose Your Test Signals, Define FWP, Choose a Physical Format, and Perform the Coexistence Test. The first step, known as characterizing the expected RF environment, is very crucial. In this step, field measurements must be performed to construct a model of all signals, signal strength, and spectrums that those signals use in the given environment. In most cases, a Real-Time Spectrum Analyzer (RTSA) is used to continually sample the spectrum with a high-speed analog-to-digital converter (ADC). It is important to keep in mind that the traditional swept spectrum analyzer is often ineffective for gathering field measurements due to the fact that digital devices communicate in very short bursts that will pass before a sweep can be completed. The second step is to choose which test signals to use. The possible signals that can be chosen are the ones discovered in a step by the RTSA. It is important to keep in mind that often three different tiers of test signals must be selected. This is necessary because it is important to have varying numbers of signals in each test tier to see how added traffic will affect the test signals. The third step is to define FWP. The metric used to determine the success or failure of a device under test (DUT) is known as FWP. FWP is important because it defines what types of functions will be possible in the environment. The fourth step is choosing a physical format. There are four ways in which the coexistence test equipment can be configured. The first configuration is a conducted/wired test, which combines both intended and unintended signals and then connects them to whatever is acting in place of an antenna. Some notable attributes of this configuration are that the antenna's effects are excluded from testing. It is possible to account for Multiple-Input Multiple-Output (MIMO) and beamforming, but is potentially challenging, and it is the most repeatable but least realistic test method. The second configuration is the multiple chamber/hybrid test. In this configuration, signals are generated by actual equipment and antennas, and therefore shows the effects of an antenna. Additionally, the EUT and companion device are placed in separate chambers to control, which signals that the EUT is fully exposed. The third configuration is a Radiated-Anechoic Chamber (RAC) test, which is conducted using a semi- or fully anechoic chamber. This is done to ensure that the environment does not affect the repeatability of test results. Antenna effects are also accounted for in this configuration, but the environment may not resemble the actual deployment environment.

The fourth configuration is the Radiated Open Environment (ROE) test. In this configuration, there is no shielded room. Additionally, this test can be used on any device regardless of whether they are in a line-of-sight or non-line-of-sight setup. The drawback is that ambient signals in the environment can affect test results and therefore render results unrepeatable. The fifth and final step in coexistence testing is performing the test itself. A best-practice approach is to stress test the devices integrated wireless module and perform early testing on devices according to the wireless coexistence and interference tests specified by the appropriate standard and, additionally, testing APs, infrastructure, wireless range, coexistence, and roaming to determine coexistence problems.

3.8 Interoperability Issues of IoT

IoT offers many advancements to older devices and allows new devices and services to enter the market. While actively engaging and growing, IoT runs into whether or not devices and services can work together under a specific set of rules, regulations, or interoperability. Some examples of inoperability could include devices of different operating systems (OS), devices with different manufacturers, and devices made at different times. These factors play a role in one way or another on how a device operates. A device is useless if it cannot operate by itself. For any changes in a device, even something as simple as removing a component, there is a risk of device failure.

The main concern is with devices that have different operating systems. These devices can have the hardest time trying to communicate with one another due to issues embedded deep into their programming. These are the hardest obstacles to face because they are designed to function with this operating system and are not usually compatible with other operating systems. A solution would be to integrate multiple operating systems into the device to ensure inoperability with other client devices, but that would cause some issues regarding the choice of the OS or the processing/hardware power required to run two concurrent operating systems. While implausible, a universal operating system could be created to solve this issue, but it would ultimately destroy competition between companies and could cause more unforeseen problems in the future. The discussion is a hard one and will probably be the most important factor in defining evolution of the devices within the IoT.

Another concern is with devices made by different manufacturers. A device, possibly one that shares the same purpose as another device, could have issues operating with that device if both were required to transfer data or communicate with one another; this concern also follows programs, probably with more occurrences. The reasoning behind this is competition; a manufacturer wants their product or service to be the best and wants to have a loyal customer. Competition is good for the market, and is good for the development of the IoT. Still, it could also hurt the eventual product of the IoT due to inoperability through stubbornness. A device that wants to update or change its configuration or what connections it has could affect many other devices that had previously communicated with it. These topics are also a big factor in developing a unified IoT environment if it is even possible to assume it can do so.

In regards to inoperability, the last factor refers to newer devices and how they communicate with legacy devices. Devices that use legacy software programs that are being used by businesses and end-users presently can run into issues with the new products. The biggest concern is whether the users will want to replace these devices with newer ones or not. Many factors can dictate this, mostly including money or ease of use. The monetary price of these devices or services is the main conductor of whether a company or user upgraded now, waits until next year, or holds off until the device is at its end of life.

These concerns are very real and affect all forms of business and user interactions with IoT. The biggest challenge will be to determine how new devices will communicate with older devices and how often older devices will need to be replaced with newer ones to function properly within the IoT environment. While some users and businesses are on the cutting edge of technology and upgrade constantly, some users and businesses face the struggle of either not having enough money to purchase these new products or lack knowledge of the effects these devices can bring to their environment.

3.9 IoT-Cloud – Application

Cloud computing is the practice of using a network of remote servers hosted on the Internet to store, manage, and process data, rather than a local server or a personal computer. Here you are housing your data on an internet-based platform instead of local devices. Some of the advantages of cloud computing are:

- Pay as You Go, pricing model
- Scalability when needed
- Economy of Scale
- Immediate security accreditation
- Multiple data centers easily
- Horizontal scaling

When it comes to cloud computing and IoT, the manufacturing and industrial sectors can progress a lot by implementing them. The industrial revolution can be defined as the process of change from an agrarian and handicraft economy to one dominated by industry and machine manufacturing or a rapid major change in an economy. What ties all these definitions together is change. There are four phases of the industrial revolution now:

Phase 1: Mechanization, waterpower, steam power
Phase 2: Mass production, assembly line, electricity
Phase 3: Computer and automation
Phase 4: Cyber-physical systems

We are currently in the fourth phase. With IoT and Cloud, further advancements can be made in the fourth revolution.

Some key trends driving industrial IoT applications are data convergence from different sites to improve production, easier extraction of factory data, and cloud technology emergence. The emergence of cloud technology makes sure that no piece of data is wasted.

Cloud platforms ingest massive amounts of data and store it cost-effectively. Cloud platforms provide machine learning abilities. When developing IoT for industrial use cases, uses the following checklist:

- Efficiency
- Predicting and avoiding
- Inventory
- Quality
- Asset tracking
- Supply chain

Publish–Subscribe is a messaging pattern where senders of messages, called publishers, do not program the messages to be sent directly to specific receivers, called subscribers. Instead, published messages are categorized into classes without knowledge of which subscribers, if any, there may be. The Publish–Subscribe model allows messages to be broadcast to different parts of a system asynchronously. Here IoT devices are the publishers and send messages to the gateway and a topic; then subscribers get the resources they need. Some benefits of pub/sub are that it makes sure that once the data is published, it stores it till the subscriber sends an acknowledgment back; it is a global service – you do not have to worry when you have sites in different geolocations; and it allows you to separate your upstream deployment from your downstream deployment.

Real-time processing is a big factor in using IoT and Cloud in the industrial sector. Google's Data flow allows you to receive and process streams of data in real-time. You can then use Big Query to process up to a billion rows of data, and it provides a result in seconds. After all these, you can then apply Cloud Machine learning, which is used to provide new insights on how to use data. Some examples of industries using IoT–Cloud are the manufacturing industry, the transportation and shipping industry, asset tracking, energy, etc.

Auto Scaling is another big factor in cloud computing. Here you do not need to buy new equipment when you have more traffic, and you will not be sitting on equipment when traffic is slow. Auto Scaling adds more servers depending on the amount of load coming in, and it also decreases when the traffic slows down.

One of the videos points out that Microsoft leverages customers' existing installed applications and makes cloud migration a breeze. In other words, Microsoft uses tools and platforms that millions of developers already rely on.

In conclusion, IoT-Cloud is the combination to move manufacturing, productivity, and efficiency forward.

3.10 Regulation and Security Issues of IoT

A big concern that the IoT network will face is the regulations imposed on the users by their respective countries. The regulations or laws could affect everything regarding internet infrastructure to the cost of service, and in the recent case of net neutrality could restrict access to certain websites or services online that could benefit the advancement of the IoT. However, these regulations can provide a stable environment that would allow the IoT network to grow and develop within countries that can expand worldwide. Security is also a big factor. When devices are online, and nothing is physical but virtual, users risk losing access to assets. There are many different security practices and forms of encryption as well; the main question is what one works the best and provides the most stable connection most safely.

Regulations are one of the biggest obstacles that the IoT will face with regards to becoming more connected as time goes on. Businesses and users in all parts of the world have to follow the rules and regulations set upon them by laws in their country; trying to bring everyone under a unified set of rules regarding IoT could prove very difficult due to the existing laws. Another concern is that of potential upcoming regulations that could restrict users' access to sites due to their internet service providers (ISPs). Net neutrality has been a highly discussed and debated topic lately. The resolution would change the overall landscape of the IoT if it was repealed. Repealing net neutrality will cause ISPs to dictate what users can and cannot access. Some countries endorse net neutrality, and they may be the best hope in keeping net neutrality alive for the IoT (Smithsonian n.d.). According to an article by *The Guardian*, India's communications regulator endorsed net neutrality stating, "The Internet today is a great platform for innovation, startups, banking, and government applications such as health, telemedicine, education, and agriculture" (Safi 2017). Other countries feel the same way, and they are the best chance we have as users to keep the Internet neutral, which will ultimately benefit the growth of the IoT. Overall, this is just one of the stepping-stones the IoT needs to cross over to continue to grow and develop.

Additionally, the device-to-device interactions should be made inaccessible unless the devices have been paired through elaborate mechanisms. Implementation and maintenance of security is an important factor to consider when progressing with ideas for the IoT. A security method obviously needs to be secure and not detract from users' connections and maintain a sense of transparency to allow for ultimate usability. The decision for a one size fits all security method will probably be one of the toughest decisions that should be made. The security method would also need to be rolled out to legacy devices via patches, causing operability and compatibility issues with other programs and services.

Both security and regulations are important in achieving an IoT connected world. These two factors provide some of the most important factors to ensure the IoT will continue to grow and be adopted by more and more individuals and organizations. Regulations can allow countries to invest in building or improving the infrastructure for IoT properly. Security is important because it allows people to feel safe while browsing online or conducting a currency exchange. It is pivotal to the success of the IoT to provide for the privacy of all users.

3.11 Achieving IoT Innovations While Tackling Security and Regulation Issues

IoT is in its early stages of development. While we have seen many new and different developments, IoT at its core is still developing an identity. For IoT to continue to grow and develop, some things need to be undertaken to allow the IoT to flourish as it connects and enhances our lives. Although there is currently no consensus on how to implement security in IoT on the connected devices and nodes, security for IoT interaction is essential in maintaining impenetrability and enhancement. It should be made in the computation models to ensure that there are authentication levels before allowing users into the closed systems. Security and privacy are very big factors in the regulation and the appeal of the IoT; conveniences like the ease of users accessing data or making purchases are important in making the IoT more central in everyday life. Suppose privacy and security are not the most important factors when dictating how IoT develops. In that case, there will be a drop off in usability due to fears of losing assets or personal data. There are a few ways that users and businesses can help IoT reduce or even prevent privacy and security issues going forward.

Businesses are one of the IoT's primary users and can offer new and unique services that the IoT can utilize to make that business more efficient and profitable. A concern for these businesses is how much data they would need to give to get their metrics. Another concern is their customer data and personal business data; how much of that data is needed and will it be secure enough to protect if something is lost or compromised? Utilizing IoT technologies, businesses can provide data on revenue, sales, and other measurable items, allocating them into analytical tools that the business can use to increase productivity. The business may want to hand the entire data over and may consider whether it is worth investing in the IoT or the analytical tools offered. The IoT needs to offer secure services to businesses in data protection and data recovery if anything is stolen or lost. The IoT can also offer better encryption tools that these companies can utilize to provide a more stable connection for their users.

Users who access webpages, buy things online, or comment on social media are concerned about their privacy and security. As the climate has changed over the past few years concerning the ease of use of services online, users are constantly making purchases and utilizing the newest device or feature to connect with other users who are doing the same. However, users require more effort on their part to remain safe while on the internet. A user could easily fall into a trap like a malicious advertisement or a phishing attempt that could compromise all their data. The users can follow safe browsing guidelines and know what kind of information they give out online. The IoT can also provide users with a safe environment to browse in, and there are services available now that protect users, like good web browsers and antivirus systems. For users and the IoT to work together, they must be willing to adhere to some safe browsing policies and take advantage of antivirus software designed to protect users at the same time as they browse the web or when they download programs. Users can also provide data to these programs and services, so they can be better updated and be provided with the best experience possible. There are user concerns regarding whether these programs or services using user data are really for the user's betterment. Still, in most cases, these programs and services are trying to use this data for the best possible experience for the user, and it ultimately helps the program grow and be more productive.

Users and businesses will always want to try new things or have an easier time doing the things they have already been doing. The IoT presents a unique opportunity for users and businesses to provide data at the cost of a little security and privacy to increase productivity, convenience, or functionality. The important thing to consider on both sides is how much data will be needed and how much data should be given up. The IoT cannot ask for too much data, or it risks not being the same, and the users need to provide more than just a little data to help the products and services perform better. If the two sides can come together, the IoT will have many opportunities to develop and extend user input to develop better products and services for the future. To improve IoT security, we need to (Gerber 2017; DHS 2016) incorporate and implement security at the beginning of the IoT network from the ground up:

- A strong authentication and access control
- Predict and preempt
- Regular update and vulnerability management
- Strategy to detect anomaly by creating a log file of network performance
- Ensure to use secure apps for web, mobile, or any other types of devices, perhaps with authentication for both users and apps
- Transport encryption is recommended for secure transmission
- Build on transparency across devices

3.12   Future of IoT

It has been predicted that the IoT market will see 50 billion connected devices by 2022, creating tremendous opportunities for all parties, from designers to application developers, device makers, data centers, and hardware makers. There are numerous possibilities and challenges associated with the emerging technology of the IoT that are yet to be explored. Like the robust authorization models available in mobile telephony, the IoT will have to deploy systems that enhance confidentiality, tiered authentication processes, and efficient algorithms that deter intrusion. As previously discussed, some of the challenges are (Gartner 2017):

- Security: new security concerns in this digital era and pervasive and automated networking
- Enterprise: security issues that can compromise safety risks
- Consumer Privacy: illusion of privacy and potential of consumer data breaches
- Data: personal data and big data generation, processing, and storage
- Storage Management: zeta data storage requires a cost-effective method
- Server Technologies: types of new servers and more research funding and investment

Overall, the IoT is a great idea being developed and worked on by many different people. It is amazing to see the innovations that come out almost every day. The IoT has the potential to change human lives in many different and unique ways.

The IoT offers a unique opportunity for businesses, non-commercial users, investors, and many others to help progress the IoT and themselves into a more connected world. For the IoT to continue its development and growth, it will need help from users and businesses with the products and services that it offers. It has many products and services to offer, including drones, smart devices, AI, augmented reality, and virtual reality. These products and services will be only a few of the many more that will come about in the future that will ultimately continue to shape the way humans live and interact with each other. The IoT will probably face issues with regulations and laws that could possibly restrict or remove access to some sites or services (i.e. Net Neutrality); these are important issues that must be addressed by the users themselves to help properly maintain and regulate the IoT.

With or without security, IoT will continue to advance whether we are ready or not. To be fair, such developments are exciting and greatly useful to consumers and businesses. The possibilities are only being brushed upon at the moment. IoT is in its infancy, and we need to be reminded of this as we progress with the adaptation and implementation of these advanced devices. The internet itself has and will continue to experience exponential growth. The hunger for data continues to climb as storage prices fall and wireless technologies dominate. It will be interesting to see how this continues as we progress into the digital age.

Another offshoot of this could show up in drones. Military or civilian, hacked drones could cause havoc if left unattended. The flexibility of drones could allow for numerous possibilities for attack, espionage, and directed malice. Connecting drones in mesh networks could prove to be even worse. Some are extremely small, nearly undetectable if used well.

Of course, that depends on the product. When new developments come through, companies may have a real incentive to increase security in their own products. A great example is in cars. When a white hat hacker showed how easy it was to control a Jeep Grand Cherokee's various functions without driver consent, Fiat-Chrysler began to reconsider the setup of their vehicle infotainment systems seriously. And that is just the beginning. With self-driving cars around the corner, this will need to be seriously addressed. If hackers can gain full control of a car, devastating targeted murders or even terrorist attacks could turn vehicles against others.

Therefore, it is important for companies to realize the importance of IoT security and ultimately do something about it. While it may not affect them directly, the collective must address this issue since it will hurt their industry as a whole. What goes around, comes around. Some potential methods could include government regulation or agreed-upon industry standards. Outside of these options, there does not appear to be much that can be done, as there is little financial incentive to increase IoT security at the moment.

What does all of this mean for the future of IoT? Well, not much! The allure of connected devices is simply too strong for companies to slow down. For many, it is double-dipping – consumers get what they want and companies can also reap the rewards of collecting valuable data either for themselves or to sell for others. It is a relatively cost-free way of netting pure profit or cutting R&D costs. The added integration is valuable to many consumers as well, especially with everyone having smartphones in our society.

IoT devices are some of the most insecure, ready-to-abuse pieces of technology on the planet and they are growing in number. The past few years have seen hackers easily utilize thousands of IoT devices in botnet attacks on powerful corporations. Last year, a huge disruption in Level 3 telecommunications was caused via distributed malware and botnets. Conversely, hackers have also used IoT devices as an attack vector into previously well-guarded organizations. For instance, many devices are placed at the edge of networks, outside of any device management policies or firewalls. These devices have extremely rudimentary software. They willingly connect to just about anything, accept almost any form of data, and use no passwords or lockouts. Since they are sold in batches to consumers, they are clones of each other – crack one and you have cracked them all. Also, what consumer will bother updating the firmware on their smart refrigerator, implying that the manufacturer would even provide such a thing? Good idea or not, I do not think I would bother or even know how to check! Outside of a more targeted attack, using such devices in botnets does not affect the consumer themselves, so this is not even an issue for them to begin with.

3.13 Conclusion

These devices and services, and many more that will be developed in the future, are the IoT's lifeblood. These are what keep the users wanting to buy products and what keeps the businesses and investors wanting to spend money to increase development and production. The IoT needs these products to be successful because they offer things to all types of users. The public would appreciate advancements to Augmented Reality because it would allow them to place objects for things like home renovations or for laying out a building project. Drones offer the capabilities to provide aerial delivery services that could prove more efficient than a typical delivery truck or mailing procedures. Virtual reality will keep users engaged and interested in new games or environments in the future. AI will continue to develop and will become smarter and provide new ways to be used by users that enhance almost every aspect of their day-to-day life.

The last service that will be discussed is virtual reality. Virtual reality is composed of projected environments that allow users to generate realistic sensations with the help of physical environments or props. Virtual reality and augmented reality are different. Augmented reality only adds to your current reality view, while virtual reality replaces your reality with a created one. Virtual reality has become more popular with the addition of gaming consoles that provide the user with games that create virtual worlds. The end-users can use real-life objects to interact in that virtual reality. The idea of virtual reality is to allow users to experience different settings that would be impossible otherwise; users can experience previous events in time, movies, games, and other situations that can only be dreamed of. Virtual reality has the highest selling potential of all the others previously discussed because it allows users to experience things that were once thought to be impossible, and it offers the highest chance at continued development from many different businesses that work in the IoT due to limitless possibilities.

Augmented reality, another technology utilizing IoT, has been gaining popularity with users by having integration with devices they use every day, like phones and gaming equipment. Augmented reality is an indirect view of a physical, real-world environment. Augmented reality is in its early infancy stages and will continue to be developed and expanded upon. We will see new and very interesting ways to view our world. Augmented reality provides us with an idea of what life can be if we can change what we see and how we, as users, perceive the world around us. There are four different types of augmented reality (Alkhamisi and Monowar 2013), marker-based, marker-less, projection-based, and superimposition-based augmented reality. The first two, marker-based and marker-less, are the most widely used. According to the website, it explains that marker-less is "As one of the most widely implemented applications of augmented reality, marker-less (also called location-based, position-based, or Global Positioning Systems, GPS) augmented reality, uses a GPS, digital compass, velocity meter, or accelerometer which is embedded in the device to provide data based on your location." Marker-less augmented reality uses your location and finds information regarding stores and services around you to offer you a quick view of your surroundings. These two types of augmented reality can display data like restaurants or provide information or changes to your view by scanning things like QR codes. The website defines the last two, projection-based and superimposition, as more of a visual transformation, allowing objects to come into your view or be added to what you are looking at. "Superimposition based augmented reality either partially or fully replaces the original view of an object with a newly augmented view of that same object." These two types of augmented reality can use light to reflect off surfaces allowing you to touch or move an object or give you an object and allow you to place it almost anywhere. Augmented reality is one of the newer services offered via the IoT and will continue to develop as new devices emerge that allow users to see these augmented views.

Another device that was born in the IoT is that of AI or artificial intelligence. AI are internal components of a device that allow it to comprehend requests, learn from experience, and predict patterns. AI has been evolving for many years and has been most recently displayed with devices such as the Google Home and the Amazon Echo. AI has been developed and modified to be almost able to predict what users will want to search for or how they will spend their day. The goal of AI is to tailor itself to the user's wish and respond to requests or conduct searches as almost second nature. AI devices can also include things like smart devices, which can include anything from a watch to a tablet to a refrigerator. Smart lights can turn off with a voice command or a sound command or dim and brighten at will. A smart refrigerator can adjust the temperature depending on how many items are in the fridge, and a smart thermostat can change the temperature according to settings or via voice commands. AI systems are the primary communication method used by devices in the IoT network and are crucial in developing the IoT's overall productivity.

Drones were among the first real "new devices" that were introduced as an extension of the IoT network. Drones are small, mobile aerial devices that can do everything from transporting items, doing surveillance work, and even filming films and commercials. These devices are a combination of many different factors within the IoT. The drone's design varies from company to company, and most drones have built-in GPS capabilities, allowing them to be located and given coordinates to reach specific destinations. Drones are a prime example of a born device within the IoT and consistently developed into popular use like with Amazon delivery. Drones possess the capabilities to do so much more and constantly evolve with new attachments and enhancements made possible by the development of the IoT.

The IoT gives us the rare opportunity to experience the creation of devices that were once beyond our comprehension. We can now see a world with drones, advanced AI robotics systems, virtual reality, and augmented reality. All of these devices and applications will improve the popularity of the IoT and provide the means to improve upon the overall complexion and infrastructure of the IoT in the future. The implementation of these devices and services, along with others, will spark a consistent trend of developing the IoT system. These devices are only a small sample of what the IoT can provide. There will be many more if the IoT is allowed continued development by businesses, users, and inventors.

References

Alkhamisi, A.O. and Monowar, M.M. (2013). Rise of augmented reality: current and future application areas. https://www.researchgate.net/publication/276494825_Rise_of_Augmented_Reality_Current_and_Future_Application_Areas (accessed 22 June 2021).

Benardos, P.G. and Vosniakos, G.-C. (2017). *Internet of Things and Industrial Applications for Precision Machining*, vol. 261, 440–447. Switzerland: Trans. Tech. Publications Internet-of-Things-and-industrial-applications-for-precision-machining.pdf (researchgate.net).

Prado Guia Del (2015). 18 Artificial Intelligence researchers reveal the profound changes coming to our lives, Business Insider. http://www.businessinsider.com/researchers-predictions-future-artificial-intelligence-2015-10 (accessed 22 June 2021).

DHS, U.S. (2016). *Strategic principles for securing The Internet of Things* , Version 1. Department of Homeland Security.

Gartner (2017). The death of IoT security as you know it. https://www.gartner.com/doc/reprint s?id=1-4KQ5GVY&ct=171117&st=sb (accessed 22 June 2021).

Gerber, A.M. (2017). Top 10 security challenges. Retrieved from: https://developer.ibm.com/dwblog/2017/iot-security-challenges/?lnk=hm.

Keysight Technology (2019). How to ensure IoT devices work in their intended environment: Locate and identify interference. https://www.keysight.com/us/en/assets/7018-06402/ebooks/5992-3467.pdf (accessed 22 June 2021).

Meola, A. (2016). These are the Top IoT Companies to Watch Stocks and Invest in, Business Insider. http://www.businessinsider.com/top-internet-of-things-companies-to-watch-invest-2016-8 (accessed 22 June 2021).

Safi, M. (2017). India's communications regulator endorses net neutrality. *The Guardian*https://www.theguardian.com/technology/2017/nov/29/india-communications-regulator-endorses-net-neutrality-telecom-internet (accessed 22 June 2021).

Smithsonian (n.d.) How other countries deal with NMet neutrality. https://www.smithsonianmag.com/innovation/how-other-countries-deal-net-neutrality-180967558/ (accessed 22 June 2021).

Thibodeau, P. (2016). MIT offers internet of things training for professinals. COMPUTERWORLD from IDG. https://www.computerworld.com/article/3024912/internet-of-things/mit-offers-internet-of-things-training-for-professionals.html.

World Economic Forum (2015). The four phases of industrial internet evolution. WEFUSA_IndustrialInternet_Report2015.pdf (weforum.org) (accessed 22 June 2021).

4

The Wild Wonders of 5G Wireless Technology

4.1 Introduction

The telecommunications sector consists of the companies that enable communication globally; there can be multiple sources to achieve this, ranging from cell phones, internet services, airwaves or cables, to other wired and wireless devices. Telecom companies have created the basic infrastructure that has ensured data in words, voice, audio, or video to be transferred anywhere in the world. Furthermore, the telecommunications industry consists of the following sub-sectors (Lioudis 2018):

- Wireless communications
- Communications equipment
- Processing systems and products
- Long-distance carriers
- Domestic telecom services
- Foreign telecom services

    Diversified communication service
    Advancements in this sector have dramatically changed people's lives across the world, which has posed new challenges and opened new horizons to the industry players. Industry, in general, has the following trends, which in future will surely give the industry a different look:

- First, we will witness the first commercial launch of 5G (fifth generation) in 2018; the advent of 5G, which offers more speed, greater efficiency, and less latency, will be a major push for connected things in the future, which will change the picture of this industry.
- Another emerging category would be autonomous vehicles, which heavily rely on the telecom sector. While autonomous cars have been in the gossip and media for several years, they are gaining popularity and are expected to be warmly welcomed by the masses.
- Apart from the above, it is expected that there would be fewer regulations across the globe, and telecom companies would be exposed to global markets with more freedom and competition.

Intelligent Connectivity: AI, IoT, and 5G, First Edition. Abdulrahman Yarali.
© 2022 John Wiley & Sons Ltd. Published 2022 by John Wiley & Sons Ltd.

- Security and privacy have become key areas of concern from the customer's viewpoint, so advancement in this aspect would be of critical importance because it greatly impacts the demand of services and industry.
- Cross-industry partnerships would be seen on a large scale. It has been the trend for some time now; banking and selling would be more reliant on the telecom industry. Promoting these operations would be fully performed by telecom industry players.

The wireless mobile industry is one of the largest and fastest-growing industries, and is at the beginning of its revolution. Wireless technology has seen exponential growth in the past decade. It continues to evolve to new generations with various advanced features for flexibility and reliability, providing the platform needed to launch scalable, safe, self-organized self-healing, and reliable end-to-end pervasive connectivity solutions that will give many benefits to society.

Wireless communications have brought dramatic changes in the international communication sector, improving informational infrastructure that uses radio waves in place of wires to transmit information. Wireless technology is already playing an essential part in billions of people's lives worldwide. For as long as one can remember, radios and televisions have been entertainment sources informing millions of people, with the information being passed through satellites and with connections to different countries of the world, giving people a chance to converse and share information and do business.

Wireless technologies have a cost advantage as it ensures cheaper connectivity. It is providing access to voice and data networks, even in remote, underserved areas. With this technology, it is possible to connect businesses in different ways, ranging from a desktop computer to a smartphone and tablet. Wireless technologies give an excellent opportunity for economic development, ensuring that services are delivered to developing nations, and can play critical roles, considering how fast they facilitate access to better knowledge and acquisition of information (Badia and Zorzi 2005). For example, WiFi facilitates access to low-income individuals and countries and uses the network to empower its people.

The journey of wireless communication only began to develop about 51 years ago. For technological purposes, 50 years is a short amount of time, and to understand where the wireless network is today is an unimaginable advancement in a short amount of time considering the skyrocketing number of subscriptions. Over this span of 51 years, Wireless Networks underwent various developments: Wireless Personal Area Networks (WPAN), Wireless Local Area Network (WLAN), Ad Hoc Network (Adhoc), or Mesh Networks, Wireless Metropolitan Area Network (WMAN), Wireless Wide Area Network (WWAN), Cellular Networks that span from first-generation (1G) to 5G, and Space Networks.

Broadband telecommunication has seen massive and continuous development in the recent decade. Telecommunication has continuously evolved due to increased public demand for a better and more efficient broadband experience (Norp, Kips, and Loon 2015). The evolution of each generation of wireless technology has been a decade trend to cope with the end-users' demands. Figure 4.1 shows the evolution path of wireless systems.

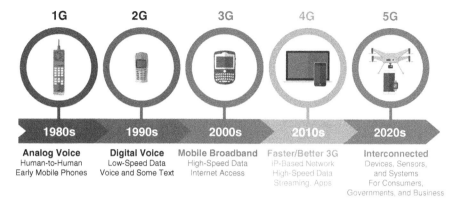

Figure 4.1 Wireless networks evolution (Senate RPC 2019).

4.1.1 First Generation (1G)

1G was the first wireless telephone technology introduced in late 1970. This analog telecommunications standard only offered voice call services to subscribers. 1G was the only reliable network since the early 1970s with a very limited capacity before (2G) was first introduced in the early 1990s.

4.1.2 Second Generation (2G)

1G continued to operate until it was replaced by 2G later in the 1990s. 2G was much enhanced as its signals are digitalized. This new network had various benefits over its predecessors (Garg and Rappaport 2011). The 2G spectrum was significantly more efficient in that it allowed better spectrum utilization and penetrations offering data service. It enabled service providers to offer Short Message Service (SMS) for mobile phones. Technologies such as Global Systems for Mobile (GSM) and CDMA (Coe Division Multiple Access) also offered data roaming services.

4.1.3 Third Generation (3G)

3G was a huge milestone in transmitting the bulk of data and speed of transmission compared to 2G. 3G was introduced in the late 1990s with a wider data bandwidth and faster internet connectivity (Buddhikot et al. 2003). It is applicable to a wireless voice telephone, internet access, wireless internet service, video calls, and mobile television technologies. However, the 3G network infrastructure was not rolled out as it was marketed, and we can say that it was a failure and was interrupted by 4G.

3G or the Universal Mobile Telecommunication Service (UMTS) was an upgrade from GSM via GPRS (General Packet Radio Services) or EDGE (Enhanced Data for GSM Evolution). The standardization work for 3G UMTS was carried out by the Third Generation Partnership Project (3GPP). It had a data rate specification of 144 kbps for rural, 384 kbps for urban outdoor, 2048 kbps for indoor, and a low range outdoor.

4.1.4 Advanced Third Generation (3.5G)

3.5G is a cellular telephone grouping and data technology designed to provide more efficient performance than the 3G network, as an interim advancement towards realizing full 4G capabilities. This platform provided faster and better uplink/download packet access and includes:

- Evolved HSPA (High-Speed Packet Access)
- Long-Term Evolution – Advanced (LTE-A)

4.1.5 Fourth Generation (4G)

4G stands for Fourth Generation Wireless Connection. The network infrastructure is mainly used for the mobile cellular network connection and was implemented to succeed in the proceeding generation networks connection. The network infrastructure was invented in the year 2010 through vigorous research activities and technical implementations, by a body known as International Telecommunications Union–Radio communications (ITU-R). The platform was designed specially for internet access, with speeds of up to 100 Mbps.

4G networks have multiple specifications that have made them accessible for many service providers and network users. Firstly, the network infrastructure can adopt various network frequency component carriers from MHz to GHz, where most of the frequencies are entirely dependent on the geographical locations. Secondly, 4G network connections have a wide bandwidth with data rates varying from 1 Mbps to 2 Gbps. According to the standards laid out by the ITU-R organization, the network bandwidths are supposed to differ with regard to the facilities and equipment used in the connections. For example, for high-speed connections, the rate should vary from 100 Mbps to higher (Thompson et al. 2014, pp. 62–64), including cars and trains, and 1 Gbps transmission rate for low mobility connections, such as pedestrians and stationary devices. Such policies were implemented through the International Mobile Communication Advanced (IMT-Advanced) specifications. 4G networks are applicable and in different network infrastructures such as the WAN (Wide Area Network), WLAN, WMAN, etc. Moreover, the 4G networks have unified IP addresses and seamless broadband integrations. The 4G cellular network is supposed to provide an environment for dynamic data access, HD (high definition) video streaming, and global roaming regarding service delivery. Such services were rarely prevalent in previous mobile network technologies.

In the 4G technology, a combination of standards IEEE 802.11 and IEEE 802.16 for radio technologies ratified by IEEE are used (Khan et al. 2009). These radio technologies meet the ITU-Rs of the 4G requirements (Huang et al. 2012) set in 2008 to have at least a peak speed of 100 Mbps. The IEEE 802.11 VHT (Very High Throughput) has a speed of 1 Gbps for a low user velocity. The goals of 4G implementation are to meet the following objectives:

- To be a completely IP-based integrated system.
- To provide communication indoor and outdoor with speeds of between $100\,MB\,s^{-1}$ and 1 Gbps.
- The 4G also combines the use of WiFi and WiMAX (Worldwide Interoperable Microwave Access) technologies.
- Fourth Generation Long-Term Evolution (4G-LTE).

4G LTE is mobile technology, standardized by the 3GPP, and meets the 4G requirements defined by the International Telecommunications Union (ITU). This technology consists of a wide range of advancements and new features and contents compared to earlier versions of Long-Term Evolution (LTE) and 3G. Commonly referred to as 4G, LTE delivered both the speed and power in mobile devices and smartphones. The 4G LTE works best in the metropolitan area, making it difficult for users in other areas to access it. To overcome this challenge, the mobile services with 4G LTE technology uses combined network types, 3G and 4G LTE (Huang et al. 2012), to meet the following requirements:

- Highly advanced bandwidth and data transfer speeds of up to $1\,GB\,s^{-1}$
- Faster response times as a result of shorter round-trip delay
- Enhanced quality of service control mechanisms
- Lowers mobile implantation cost due to simplified and simple architecture
- Uses Orthogonal Frequency Division Multiplexing (OFDM) for downlink
- Uses Single Carrier Frequency Division Multiple Access (SC-FDMA) for uplink
- Uses Multi-input Multi-output (MIMO) for enhanced throughput
- Reduced power consumption
- Higher Radio Frequency (RF) power amplifier efficiency (less battery power used by handsets)
- Increased ARPU (Annual Revenue Per Unit)

4.1.6 Fifth Generation (5G)

Experts have invested valuable resources to develop next generation wireless technologies and networks. The new 5G network is unique in its own way and uses many new and path-breaking technologies. The new network is expected to increase the range and capacity of communications.

The topic of safety and security has been debated by many researchers and experts, in light of the global focus against terrorism. Businesses are also infringing upon the personal lives of consumers using mobile applications. They are targeting consumers using mobile analytics through their purchase cycles (Blackshaw 2006).

The 5G concept will be ahead of just networking and will be built for various systems that need higher speeds. It will not be limited to the broadband network alone. This path breaking technology will change the way telecommunications is understood and implemented. However, 5G is still on the horizon and many new policies and implications for providers have to be analyzed and considered before it is launched.

5G is set to succeed in the 4G networks and is considered to be the future path of pervasive networks and internet connections. 5G connectivity is considered to have a bandwidth of higher speed than the 4G networks (Gopal and Kuppusamy 2015, pp. 67–72). For example, they are supposed to accommodate a speed that is not less than 1 Gbps. Secondly, different from the frequency bands evident in the 4G connections, 5G spectrums are supposed to hold between 3 and 300 GHz. Moreover, network infrastructure applicable to the 5G cellular networks is almost similar to that of the 4G connections, but with advanced technologies based on the OFDM scheme and integration of some small technologies to enhance the capacity quality and data rates. Furthermore, service delivery is also identical to that of the 4G, but that connectivity will be based on a higher speed connection with higher capacity and a shorter coverage range. The 5G platform, which has not yet been fully developed, represents the next major milestone in mobile network standards boasting features such as (Yarali, Fateh, and Razmi 2016):

- Simultaneous seamless connections for massive cloud deployments.
- Improved signal efficiency.
- Significantly lower latency as compared to 4G.
- Enhanced spectral reliability and efficiency.
- Will help browse, download, and upload data files from any place to anywhere.
- Network energy usage will be reduced, which will, in turn, increase the battery life of the device.
- Will increase the users' density over the unit area many times, which will help users to apply a high bandwidth for a longer period.
- Will also help the Internet of Things (IoT), machine-to-machine communication, and device-to-device communication and will increase object-oriented works and data management.
- Through the deployment of 5G technology, the users will develop frameworks to utilize a machine-to-machine system of communication.
- The roll-out of this architecture will highly increase, improve, and meet business and consumer demands.

5G boasts the following characteristics that are important for high performance:

- Improved reliability and security. Reliability and security are major factors, especially for public safety. With the proliferation of the IoT, the use of 5G in various applications such as plane communication systems provides seamless and uninterrupted coverage for long hours. Automated cars are also a viable use case.
- Traffic prioritization. Critical networks are designed based on the worst use case to achieve the best results. The coverage of network capacities is based on a situation where a huge number of the said network subscribers are in a small area where the network peak is simultaneous. Priority must allow certain users in a similar network a faster response and immediate feedback, for instance, in emergency cases.
- IoT. This is a major driver of 5G, whose major aim is to facilitate automation and seamless communication amongst various devices through the exchange of information. Integrating this technology into manufacturing, environment, and public safety shifts first responder activity to being more proactive rather than reactive. Usually, public safety moves towards the prevention of crime rather than seeking to recover from them.
- Radio Interoperability Performance. 5G is an enhancement of the existing 4G radio interface. In addition to a new radio interface developed with high-frequency millimeter wavelengths, this technology provides capabilities that manage various single physical cases with a different priority network environment.

4.2 5G Architecture

The 5G network has been the most waited for network ever and is expected to offer a very high rate of data transmission (Trivisonno et al. 2015). Figure 4.2a and b show a comparison of Key Performance Indicators (KPIs) of 3G, 4G, and 5G. The target 5G network capabilities often exceed 4G by a large margin.

The international telecommunication union divides this network into three subcategories, which include enhanced mobile broadband (eMBB), also known as the handset, massive machine type communication (mMTC), also known as sensors, and ultra-reliable low-latency communication (uRLLC). 5G will focus mainly on the eMBB and high use of fixed wireless. For 5G to perform, it has to meet all the ITU requirements satisfying IMT-2020, which stipulates a downlink speed of 20 GB (Wamura 2015). 5G uses spectrum with LTE frequency ranging from 600 MHz to 6 GHz with MIMO for capacity and quality purposes. In the millimeter-wave range, it has a frequency range of 24–86 GHz. The 5G system is supposed to have many more capabilities than the other network services, mainly by providing massive connectivity of many devices in a unit area (per square mile km^{-1}), such as an application in the Industrial Internet of Things (IIoT). Qualcomm's projective report (Qualcomm 2019) recommends that 5G will produce up to $3.5 trillion in income in 2035 and uphold upwards of 22 million positions. With availability at the core of this new degree of recurrence, 5G will not just give a genuinely necessary lift to IoT advancement but will additionally present new and worthwhile open doors for private companies. Figure 4.3 shows different uses of 5G network scenarios.

4.2.1 Realizing New 5G Possibilities with the Intelligent Edge

This involves connections between an organization's system, framework, and stored information. 3G was the first cellular innovation to open up the conceivable outcomes of what data could do. Ten years later, the launch of 4G greatly improved consumer experience, giving a lot quicker download speeds and many bespoke applications. It likewise observed new kinds of services take off. In any case, moving from 4G to 5G vows to be more transformational for businesses than past innovative leaps, offering something other than more prominent speed. It is a genuine game-changer, revolutionizing how businesses operate. Organizations should begin taking a gander at the technology to perceive how they could utilize it to gain the upper hand. Businesses that 5G will probably have a significant impact on include:

- Healthcare. 5G's low latency implies that robotic surgeons can carry out remote tasks. 5G permits patient data to be transferred progressively, broken down by Artificial Intelligence (AI) for abnormalities before referral to a clinician.
- Manufacturing. Rolling out 5G is key to the fourth industrial revolution.
- Automotive. Autonomous vehicles will depend on 5G's ultra-low latency for constant communication with other vehicles to avoid accidents; continuous 5G monitoring will identify whether a driver has an ailment and assume control of the vehicle. If necessary, 5G sensors can be utilized by authorities to advance traffic flow within a smart city.

(a)

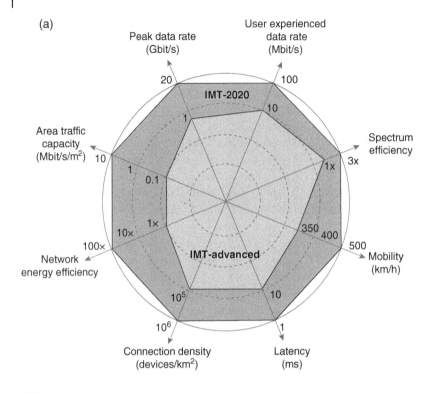

(b)

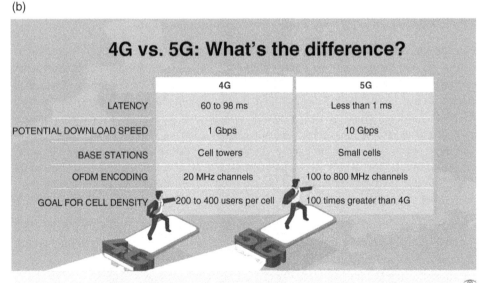

Figure 4.2 (a) KPI comparison of 4G and 5G (International Telecommunication Union 2015). (b) KPI for 3G, 4G, and 5G (Sandra Gittlen 2020).

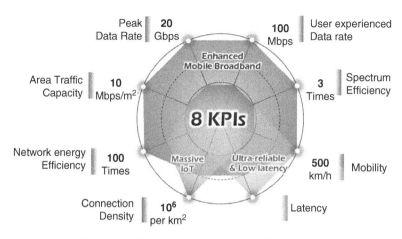

Figure 4.3 KPI for three 5G use cases of eMBB, mMTC, and uRLLC (Lee, 2016).

- Retail. Retailers are progressively mixing physical and virtual experiences by utilizing an Augmented Reality (AR) app. A 5G-enabled Virtual Reality (VR) headset could empower customers to stroll around a virtual showroom or test-drive a vehicle.
- Entertainment. The ultra-low latency of 5G implies that game designers can offload processing to the cloud, so clients do not require powerful consoles; rather, they can enjoy responsive first-person shooters and real-time strategy games. Thanks to 5G's high capacity, thousands of devices can be connected for socially driven AR/VR games.

With the wide adoption of 5G, there would be tremendous progress in real-time communication (Desai 2019), such as:

- Autonomous Vehicles
- Cloud and Virtual Reality Gaming
- Immersive Entertainment
- Instant Movie Streaming
- IoT
- Remote Healthcare
- Smart Cities
- Smart Factories
- Smart Grid
- Smart Homes

In the years to come, 5G technology is set to improve enterprise connections, power the emerging AI innovations, and utilize IoT sensors. Accordingly, there is a need to find out how to put resources into it to change how businesses interact with customers, coordinate new technologies, and break down big data. 5G is the most recent generation of cellular wireless network technology, outperforming the current 4G LTE network connection. It is set to change different business activities from consumer interaction to the storage and analysis of information. This can be achieved by including new antennas on to already set up cell towers, utility poles, and smart buildings. These physical changes construct quicker connections permitting organizations to convey remedies and services at a competitive rate and empower increasingly proficient big data analysis, among other advantages. Numerous pioneers in remote correspondence estimate that by 2023 there will be expanded IoT connections, astounding news for IoT gadget-reliant businesses, service or product providers, or those hoping to incorporate IoT into their present setups.

Ericsson's recent report suggested that 50% of US customers will access 5G in as few as five years (Combs 2021). ABI's Research study demonstrated that 5G technology would almost certainly diminish production times of developing technologies more than 4G connections; subsequently, it is seen by numerous industry specialists as a key component in the mass adoption of XR (Extended Reality) software innovation. 5G tech will increase connection speed, website traffic, and dependability, all of which assist with the boundless integration of innovations to come, stated a report by Qualcomm (2017). Organizational adoption of 5G tech is essential for any Tech business anticipating executing or consolidating consumer services and solutions involving emerging advancements like AR and VR tech.

Quicker internet speeds, expanded traffic, and consistent tech integration are only a couple of the business benefits; here are some more advantages that may cause organizations to consider putting resources into and prioritizing 5G tech. The quantity of IoT gadgets is anticipated to rise with the presentation of 5G speeds. Subsequently, IoT-centered organizations can expect significant effects on their gadgets by upgrading infrastructure diagnoses systems and information insights, fortifying an organization's infrastructure, and bringing down vulnerability of these gadgets. With 5G connections, your business can offer customers an increasingly consistent experience as many uses and new services of emerging innovations by organizations and customers will require an adaptable network ready to furnish a better user experience. With 5G tech, organizations will have the option to make different virtual networks with only one physical system to support companies in giving end-to-end virtual systems incorporating networking and computing and storage functions.

By 2025, the quantity of connected gadgets globally is expected to surpass 74 billion (Claveria 2019). More than hundreds of new gadgets are consistently connecting to the internet whose processing of AI tasks happens in the cloud. As the number keeps swelling, there is a need to reexamine how insight is scaled. In this way, processing must be pushed nearer to the gadget to aid in the expansion of these savvy gadgets. 5G gives the framework for scaling both connectivity and intelligence in this period of hyper-connectivity. With such understanding, the transformative capability of IoT requires a move away from the centralized cloud and toward another model of distributed functions with on-gadget insight.

Gadgets like smartphones, savvy speakers, and responsive sensors that monitor a patient's wellbeing are, as of now, smart, with changing models of on-gadget processing and information sharing by means of the internet and cloud-based resources. Some wide-area IoT gadgets are connected by 4G LTE; however, 5G connectivity will give their future development framework. Today, on-gadget AI can handle local decisions for extended abilities while connected to the cloud. Inherently, concentrated clouds are often a long way from gadgets, meaning higher latency, particularly when the system is congested. In our current age, where everything is connected, on-gadget processing assumes a fundamental role. Nonetheless, devices have inherent impediments, such as power, thermal, and form factors. To conquer them, another upgraded system architecture rises, bringing information processing capabilities closer to gadgets, the smart wireless edge, where on-device processing is augmented by edge cloud computing and is connected by ultra-fast, low-latency 5G.

4.3 5G Applications

Through 5G tech, multiaccess edge computing will help with decongesting an organization's swarmed networks while supporting several gadgets without a moment's delay. This cloud-based network architecture can likewise expand the site's overall performance. Besides taking care of enormous information stacks and conveying results in real-time, it likewise secures client data through local computing versus a centralized network that is in present use (Hatten n.d.). 5G offers something beyond speed. Expanded capacity and ultra-low latency make it perfect for focused, real-time services that could transform businesses. Advances in technology are changing how businesses operate and the services they offer (Price 2019). Figure 4.4 shows various 5G real-time services and applications.

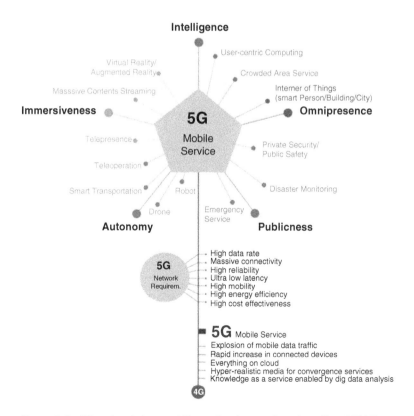

Figure 4.4 5G and real-time mobile applications and services (Desai 2019).

4.3.1   5G and Video Surveillance

Video CCTV (Closed-Circuit TV) has been around since the coax age; cameras were usually connected to a central recording station for later viewings. One could record everything, regardless of whether there was an event or not. Back then, finding the film you needed could have been tedious and time-consuming. The technology has since evolved to cameras using IP interfaces to work in the same way, view from a remote location, and make recordings stored digitally for later access and purged after days. IP cameras had an upgrade as devices can detect motion and record sections before and after a trigger. Also, the integration of PoE (Power over Ethernet) has eliminated the need for power outlets to be available. However, these solutions created many false positives and wasted resources for an event. It should also be mentioned that data wires are involved in both of these technologies because wireless cameras in this age could not come even close to the work 5G would do for CCTV and surveillance. Wireless cameras today and networks require a massive bandwidth to provide the support to keep up with motion detection and transmission of high-definition videos to a recording server.

Nokia predicted that by 2050, 70% of the world's 5G network endpoints would be cameras. 5G can handle all requests and transmissions associated with these camera systems in real-time through the 4K/8K definition's low-latency feeds. Camera quality is half the battle to provide an effective CCTV system to protect infrastructure, towns, and citizens. These 5G enabled cameras can also provide smart analytics that use AI to detect anomalies among crowds and scenery. This equipment can sit at the edge of the network, potentially even offloading some of the bandwidth that would come directly to the system's core to process the outrageous amount of data collected from these cameras. The cameras will not only keep citizens safe in densely populated areas, as the analytics can even look into traffic flow management for other citizens to use as a caution for long delays from accidents or rush hour traffic.

CCTV can be deemed "invasive" by citizens who feel their rights are taken away when cameras are always recording and the data is collected without consent. However, Nokia considers the analytics of the CCTV wireless cameras are smart enough to look for anomalies and mask other people in the frame in real-time, so it only produces the anomaly action and discards the other different pieces of footage. This process is all done without human intervention, and the decisions are made purely by the analytical applications. No longer does someone have to sift through hours of footage to get what they need to see. Heightened security also makes crime less prevalent as acts are easily captured for playback and more likely to obtain footage than the footage that has no aspect of criminal evidence to use against a person.

One of the most promising aspects of using wireless cameras in 5G is placing cameras anywhere they can be mounted. Users can save money by putting cameras in locations that were blinds spots for other systems or hard to reach with data cables and power. Wireless 5G is also an excellent technology for low-power devices and can use just batteries that last years and require little maintenance.

Another exciting feature used in a 5G wireless is network slicing, which can be used with several services aside from wireless camera systems. Network-slicing concepts mirror network segmentation, or VLANs (Virtual Local Area Networks) as they are called, as a way to divide the network for specific uses most suitable for applications. Network slicing, according to the SDxCentral (2018) staff team in 2018, would share the network by a spectrum of 5G, and only those applications that reside on those spectrums can communicate. The art of segmentation further enhances 5G wireless abilities by not making the airspace a giant broadcast network for these devices to spit everything out and overwhelm base stations or core equipment.

4.3.2 5G and Fixed Wireless Access (FWA)

POTS (Plain Old Telephone Service) is a dedicated residential wired connection using a modem system to convert the signals from analog to digital, or vice versa, or using fiber to the home (FTTH) solutions that can provide high-speed data access. Some individuals resort to using hotspots on their mobile devices through a mobile carrier instead of using a cooperation utility. Over the past few years, we have seen increases in the speeds and reliability between these technologies, ranging from 10 MB a second to gigabit Ethernet. Wired data connections are even preferred to some customers as wireless has limitations on long-distance carriers and poor adaptation to high interference environments.

Metaswitch (n.d.) claims 5G can elevate some of these issues by providing an always-on wireless broadband connection called Fixed Wireless Access (FWA). FWA is not a new concept, but its presence in a 5G environment enhances its ability because of the resilient, durable principles 5G offers to users. A precursor to FWA is the WiMAX standard 802.16, which promotes using wireless as a last-mile technology instead of cable or a Digital Single Lens (DSL). WiMAX was thought to replace cable or DSL broadband technologies by providing digital VoIP, IPTV, and data convergence for residential users.

The difference between the WiMAX and FWA technologies resides in what infrastructure each uses to complete the job. Metaswitch (n.d.) explains how WiMAX was mainly a failure because it is proprietary and required a whole new infrastructure to be built for this technology, not to mention the fact that it was costly. FWA employs standardized 3GPP architectures and standard mobile components to deliver its service to residential and even enterprise customers. Standardizing FWA can help other wireless vendors to get behind producing equipment that can integrate smoothly and certainly implement in the areas with existing wired broadband technologies. FWA would have an opportunity in emerging countries where fixed broadband is not currently implemented. FWA promotes connecting even those with the farthest reach to provide a new reality to improve their culture. Country governments have funds set up to implement this technology where needed.

Metaswitch (n.d.) also mentions that FWA is such a vast spectrum that the different levels of service can provide a perfect type of frequency to implement. For example, using lower bands or the wireless spectrum range can provide better distances than much smaller frequencies where coverage is short, but throughput can be comparable to fiber optics. Figure 4.5 shows frequencies between 3 and 27 GHz, which is the ideal frequency for using FWA.

Frequency	FWA?	Coverage	Throughput
700 Mhz	N	Excellent	Poor
3.4–3.8 Ghz	Y	Good	Good
24.25–27.5 Ghz	Y	Poor	Excellent

Figure 4.5 High-level characteristics of proposed 5G frequency bands (metaswitch).

A frequency of 700 MHz is not considered to be right for FWA because even though coverage can reach that far, there is not enough throughput to support the converged technologies and maintain a bandwidth that 5G devices need for services. The narrow beams of 5G can support a much denser population of users and devices with very little interference.

The downside to having the high throughput speeds to perform tasks needed for users is that the signal does not go through building materials very well, similar to how 5 GHz wireless works well inside a room with an access point (AP). However, beyond that, the throughput will decrease as you move away from the AP. By placing the receiving antennas in an outdoor environment, we can resolve low throughput data. The signal can then be transmitted to a router or switch for access.

Metaswitch (n.d.) also mentions how the Customer Premise Equipment (CPE) is not space or power constrained, allowing the FWA antennas to support Multi-Input Multi-Output, better known as MIMO. MIMO can be used with beam-forming techniques to provide a line-of-sight communication with another device rather than use the antenna in an omnidirectional setting that spreads the signal through the air to the other receiver. Line-of-sight provides a higher throughput between devices as the transmitted signal is more concentrated than being dispersed into the air for anyone to grab.

Another positive to using MIMO for the FWA antennas are using different frequencies on the uplink and downlink antennas. These different frequencies can act like separate simultaneous connections so users can have limited contention on their network's access side. The throughput of the device will also increase as bandwidth is segmented between frequencies and will not cause devices to use intensive services to miss a beat.

Metaswitch (n.d.) comments on 5G FWA deployment using a non-standalone architecture that works along with existing 4G eNodeB architecture to reduce deployment risks when first implementing FWA. Backward compatibility is crucial for an application like this, where customers may not invest at first with the newer technology until the legacy becomes too troublesome to maintain. Companies can iron out their issues with first runners rather than everyone giving this option first-hand.

The prerequisites of deploying this technology will rely on the 5G User Plane Function with Multi-access Edge Computer cloud environments to successfully use FWA, which needs the right cloud core infrastructure for creating a service-based architecture and simplified network design.

The 5G network will likewise be essentially more intricate than past generations, which were planned mainly for users' voice and information administrations. Table 4.1 gives a detailed comparison of the last five generations of wireless systems.

The 5G network will uphold three diverse significant capacities of:

- Upgraded portable broadband, which will empower quicker download speeds for users.
- Super solid low-latency for communication, intended for self-drive vehicles and different applications requiring no holes in correspondence.
- Gigantic machine-to-machine interchanges, or the IoT, in which billions of devices continually convey among themselves.

Table 4.1 Mobile generation technology evolution and comparison (Desai 2019).

Features	1G	2G	3G	4G	5G
Data speed and latency	2.0 kbps	14.4–64 kbps 629 ms	2 Mbps 212 ms	200 Mbps to 1 Gbps for low mobility 60–98 ms	1 Gbps and higher <1 ms
Standards	AMPS	TDMA, CDMA, GSM, GPRS, EDGE, 1xRTT	WCDMA, CDMA-2000	Single unified standard	Single unified standard
Technology	Analog	Digital	Broad bandwidth CDMA, IP technology	Unified IP and seamless combination of broadband, LAN/ WAN/ PAN and WLAN	Unified IP and seamless combination of broadband, LAN/WAN/ PAN /WLAN and www
Service	Mobile telephony (voice)	Digital Voice, Short Messaging, Higher capacity packetized	Integrated high-quality audio, video, and data	Dynamic information access, wearable devices	Dynamic information access, wearable devices with AI capabilities
Multiplexing	FDMA	TDMA, CDMA	CDMA	CDMA, OFDM	OFDM, BDMA
Switching	Circuit	Circuit for access network and air interface; Packet for core network and data	Packet except for circuit for air interface	All packet	All packet
Core network	PSTN	PSTN	Packet network	Internet	Internet

4.4 5G Network Architecture

Earlier generations of mobile innovation included devices associated with the network in a center point-and-talk engineering; in 5G, billions of IoT devices will interface with each other in a web-like climate.

One key capability of 5G is network slicing. With network slicing, administrators can part a single physical network into numerous virtual networks. These virtual networks would then be able to be customized to various types of administrations or client segments. This implies that a business can have its own private 5G network customized to its particular business needs. Also, parties will have the option to get new items and administrations all the more rapidly from administrators. Without much of a stretch, these items and administrations can be adjusted as the request changes and develops. Network slicing likewise has online protection advantages and cybersecurity benefits. Suppose that when a cyber-attack happens to one virtual network, the attack will not have the possibility of spreading to another virtual system – the entirety of this method provides more administration and a superior client experience for businesses.

With 5G connections, gadgets will acquire massive quantities of new information, helping organizations to comprehend their infrastructural needs and customer patterns better and improve and secure their systems.

Pundits in the telecommunications industry have considered 5G wireless as a new technology that will make users more connected than ever before. The architecture of networks adapts for every device connected to a centralized piece of equipment to devices using each other to pass and receive information between base stations. 5G has the purpose of expanding the amount of data traversing the networks by adding widgets to the system that generally would not be connected. 5G is also looking to save the energy of these devices in order to have a free experience for years or months on battery-powered devices for remote and rural areas where wires are not feasible and power is not readily available. It also promotes utility automation of products and services such as smart grids, water supply companies, and manufacturing. 5G technology allows for a more efficient way to manage data and give users a way to integrate with their machines. One of the 5G's most considerable principles is a low-latency instantaneous technology, promoting a 20–100 times faster connection than current LTE technologies.

4.5 Security and Issues of 5G

Wireless networks are more vulnerable to more security risks than wired ones. In addition, there are many challenges in wireless networks due to the presence of what is known as node mobility and continual changes in its network topology. There is also a situation that is called intermittent connectivity, which may be caused by periodic or mobility node sleep, which brings more challenges. Due to battery operation, weak transceivers, and small storage or memory, node resource constraints make direct adoption of existing security solutions difficult or even impossible. Some of the significant factors that lead to security problems are the channels in place, mobility, and Man-in-Middle, whereby not all wireless networks are mobile, have scarce resources, limited accessibility, etc.

The big ugly to 5G is the ever-growing need for security and resilient standards to ensure that 5G can handle user volume, data, services, and reliability to support the millions of devices and machines that need access to this network. 5G and users need a balance between the number of user devices and their interaction on a 5G network. 5G is designed to be a 99.999% available network, and if it were to go down, the number of users affected, even in a local geographic area, would be detrimental. We think of 5G as a step for many industries to have real-time access to information over the internet coming from several devices.

However, there are some limitations to the security of the 5G technology. It becomes hugely political concerning who will manufacture the equipment, where the standards come from, who is in charge of deploying the technology, and other variables. These factors are essential for security purposes because it deals with keeping out malicious users. However, security involves ensuring that the system can do its functions to keep up with the constant demand. The Chinese company Huawei is known to the US as a shady entity whose manufacturing process is not reliable and cyber actors can hack equipment. The government in China enforces a policy that requires the company to aid in intelligence if requested. China has significant development with 5G as its government-funded programs look to enhance the technology. This advantage to China is that all other nations will be left in the dark to their knowledge compared to other countries. Standards in China may also not be readily available for those in other nations looking to develop their 5G networks, causing China to monopolize 5G equipment and development. The Chinese have let their standards be proprietary instead of open source, rendering the interoperability of other companies' equipment virtually impossible. No matter how you look at it, components of 5G will be made in China, causing risks for the user data in the networks. To combat this, the US is looking to limit those individuals within their development areas to ensure everyone involved has the same knowledge about how 5G security should work. Even the US is looking to make 5G spectrum licenses available only to vendors who can operate best practices to mitigate against these attacks.

As we can see in millimeter-wave communications, there are significant challenges, such as what is known about an integrated circuit and system design. In this technical problem, challenges arise due to high carrier frequency and small wavelengths in the design of the circuit component and antenna design and specifications in the higher frequency of the millimeter-wave band, which causes a nonlinear distortion of power amplifiers. Apart from phase noise, signal imbalance is also a challenging problem. Some of the researchers work on the integrated circuit of a millimeter wave in the higher frequency band. This includes an on-chip and in-package antenna, radio frequency power amplifier, low noise amplifier, voltage control oscillator mixers, and analog-to-digital converters. The proposed aperture antenna element has excellent gain and bandwidth (Rappaport et al. 2014, p. 111). Some of the designs were brought in to curb the problems related to integrated circuits and design, which brings a more suitable way of reducing the millimeter-wave challenges.

Also, millimeter-wave communications have another major challenge, known as the range and directional communication. In this challenge, we can see from the Friis transmission law that the free space that does not have a direct path loses its way as the frequency space square increases. In this case, the smaller the coverage, the more the strength is of the antenna. The antenna strength does not guarantee an increase in the more extensive coverage. Another problem faced by millimeter-wave communications is shadowing; this is the difference in the electromagnetic signal's power, which causes challenges that affect wireless propagation. Shadowing may not be the same in different areas. Millimeter waves are affected by shadowing (Huang and Wang 2011, p. 67).

Multiuser coordination is also a challenge to millimeter waves. The current millimeter-wave transmission used is for point to point for local or even a personal area network. Due to high spatial reuse and spectral efficiency, cellular networks will need more transmission on several interfering links. A new mechanism may arise and ease coordination of transmission in millimeter networks. Rapid channel fluctuation and connectivity also pose another challenge in millimeter-wave communication; channel coherence is linear to the carrier frequency in a given mobile connectivity time. This means that fluctuations and connectivity will be minimal in the millimeter range.

Processing power consumption is another problem to millimeter-wave communications and poses a challenge in signal transmission. The process of leveraging the gain of a multi-antenna wide bandwidth is the power consumption from conversion that is from the analog to digital system. This situation makes many antennas with a wide bandwidth, contradicting low power and low-cost devices.

4.6   IoT Devices in 5G Wireless

IoT and 5G are two technologies that work together for better and more efficient utilization. IoT provides 5G with the ability to show off its impressive performance by handling millions of devices at one time to process data streams efficiently at extremely high data rates. IoT devices are far and few between, and their technology is all about transferring data. IoT needs a resilient network in place for devices to send their information between one another. In an IoT network, many signaling sensors collect the data and send it off to another device that can record the information or perform a task based on the collected data, known as Machine to Machine or M2M. M2M connectivity does not allow humans to intervene with the devices and to run their course depending on their tasks.

IoT developments have been characterized by six attributes: Anyone, Anywhere, Anytime, Any path, and Any service. The IoT is developing globally, and whole ecosystems are now built upon innervation elements known as the 6Cs stated below:

1) Collect data generated from the connections of devices and information.
2) Connect heterogeneous devices and information.
3) Cache involving stored information in the distributed IoT computing environment.
4) Compute with advanced processing and computation of data and information.
5) Cognize information analytics, insights, extractions, real-time AI processing.
6) Create new interactions, services, experiences, business models, and solutions.

The IoT changes physical objects in the surrounding environment into ecosystems of data, enhancing people's lives as it impacts the future internet landscape, with implications for security and protection while lessening the digital divide. The increased reliance on AI and the IoT on the connectivity network and the seriousness of security challenges build their vulnerabilities in parallel. The internet's continuous and future achievements are connected to how it will react to these dangers as a driver for financial and social developments. Consolidating AI with the IoT guarantees new opportunities, running from new services and forward leaps in science to the growth of human insight and its assembly with the physical and digital world. The up-and-coming age of IoT-combining technologies will require increased human-focused safeguards and organized moral contemplations in their design and deployment. The IoT is overcoming any issues between the virtual, digital, and physical worlds by uniting people, processes, information, and things while producing information through IoT applications and stages. It accomplishes this while tending to security, privacy, and trust issues in an era where the use of emerging technology is expected to increase. IoT is therefore driving computerized change. As a worldwide idea, it requires a typical elevated level definition since it is a worldview including multidisciplinary exercises and has various implications at various degrees of deliberation through the information and knowledge value chain (Vermesan et al. 2018).

IoT unites the essential attributes of Next-Generation Internet (NGI) technology, mobile systems, and ubiquitous connectivity utilizing industrial control systems, sensing, actuating, and control capabilities for actualizing applications in modern vertical domains and across different vertical domains. Interoperability, stage coordination, and normalization are fundamental for digitizing industry applications. IoT gadgets and frameworks that expand on improved detecting, thinking capacities, and computational force at the edge are, as of now, turning into a characteristic piece of an incorporated NGI as opposed to basic augmentations of the internet. Accordingly, the IoT is promising in a hyper associated world. The primary advantage of IoT frameworks is the system impact when various frameworks are incorporated, meeting people's high expectations before it can make genuine cross-space administrations with consistent developments of gadgets and information with an absence of stable usage and assortment of accessible gadgets undermining it. A standard solution for IoT interoperability could bring about a few executions whose viability should be checked and affirmed. The combination of a hyper network, IoT, AI, DLTs (Distributed Ledger Technologies), and edge nodes requires the NGI to address these difficulties. Suggesting the recognizable proof of the correct plans of action and the best possible administration structure, supporting information development across frameworks and distinguishing obligation in the event of any issues is essential, just as comprehension is also needed of how to conquer the present specialized discontinuity in the IoT. With multi-get-to-edge registering and omnipresent hyper availability abilities, the IoT networks and associations are presently ready to process massive data, to be utilized for shrewd purposes by cutting edge AI calculations. The cognitive transformation of IoT applications also allows the use of optimized solutions for individual applications and the integration of immersive technologies (Vermesan et al. 2018).

According to some statistics, the market for IoT applications for agriculture will grow to 75 million device installations by 2020, meaning 20% growth annually (Aleksandrova 2018). The most noticeable effect of IoT on agriculture is the vast amounts of data collected by IoT devices. This data includes data types such as weather conditions, soil quality, draining plant beds, warning farmers of potential risks taken from weather forecasts, animals, or other external entities, and even the growth of crops or livestock (Aleksandrova 2018). With this data, farmers can make much more informed decisions about managing their crops or livestock. In the past, many farmers relied solely on instinct or made their bets on either a farmers' almanac or old superstitions. The collected data is stored in large databases. Notably, these databases are often cloud-based. Cloud-based databases offer cloud storage, meaning on-site storage and analysis are not required. One of the methods used to analyze the massive amounts of data created by IoT devices is association rules (Muangprathub et al. 2019).

Association rules are perfect for efficiently analyzing large amounts of data. IoT's main effect in agriculture is that it increases both efficiency and performance by allowing for more accurate and precise control of the many processes that make up agriculture.

The effects of IoT usage in agriculture have led to some quite notable benefits in the field. Many of these IoT benefits in agriculture give farmers the ability to track and manage their crops or livestock in ways that, before the utilization of IoT, were almost impossible. Analysis of the data mentioned above allows trends to be defined. These trends can be used to compare future data with previous trends to detect anomalies. The detection of defects is important because it gives farmers a warning system of sorts, which provides them with a chance to adjust conditions to help prevent disasters from occurring. Another key benefit of IoT usage is that with accurate and real-time data at their fingertips, farmers can now control internal processes with a much higher degree of accuracy and efficiency. Consequently, farmers have a higher level of production efficiency and much lower costs of the production process. A lower price of production, in turn, allows for a higher quality product to be produced for consumers that is still affordable (Kuprenko 2019).

Several critical components are almost always present in any type of IoT application on a more technical note. The first component is the IoT devices themselves. These devices can range from small wireless sensors that conduct no data analysis to drones capable of collecting, storing, and even processing the collected data locally. The main thing to keep in mind is that no matter what type of IoT device is being used, it will always have some kind of sensor capable of measuring some sort of variable. These sensors are often capable of collecting crop health assessment, irrigation, crop monitoring, crop spraying, planting, and soil and field analysis. The next key component is how IoT devices communicate with themselves and other end-user devices. Applicable wireless standards in the case of agriculture include Bluetooth, BLE (Bluetooth Low Energy), ZigBee, and cellular technologies. Cellular technologies are likely to be the best choice due to the often-wide areas in which IoT devices will be spread to monitor an entire farm. The third component is the database itself, and whether it is a physical database or one in the cloud, which is an essential factor. If it is a physical database, the owner must possess the equipment and knowledge to run a server of their own.

In contrast, a cloud-based database leaves hardware provisioning and knowledge to the service provider. The final component is arguably the most crucial, as IoT without it would almost make the managing of IoT data either impossible or at the least extremely difficult.

The combination of IoT-enabled devices and sensors with 5G and machine learning through AI creates a collaborative and interconnected world that aligns itself around outcomes and innovation (Schmelzer 2019). Using IoT fused with 5G and AI opens many doors, some of which are quite ground-breaking.

The utilization of AI results in analyzing data to be done autonomously, which means that the vast amounts of data collected by IoT devices can be analyzed accurately and efficiently without the need for a human analyzer. Machine learning refers to AI's ability to provide a system to learn and improve from previous experiences automatically without being explicitly programmed (Internet Society 2017). This process translates to the fact that these machines can virtually learn to think and make decisions based solely on collected and stored data. This means that an IoT system for agriculture that utilizes AI can detect a trend of lowering water levels in the soil and then decide to water the field if the water level stays too low or falls below a certain threshold. All of this can be done without human interaction or from a completely remote location.

Where there is no access to wired links is not possible for wireless 5G to come into these scenarios. Think of third world countries or underserved rural areas where telecom companies are not available. 5G can still manage communication in these regions and can do it at high data rates, which is a huge accomplishment for people in these areas who have probably never used a cell phone or experienced high-speed broadband technology. The use of the 5G and IoT mix can help the farmers in remote areas to produce higher yields by letting the technology tend to the plants instead of humans. With the integration of AI technology, the system could build a baseline to the perfect levels of condition needed for the crop's success, taking all the guesswork out of farming.

Another place IoT and 5G work in harmony are in the emergency and medical fields. Many medical devices are digital, such as organ monitors and level monitors; however, some can only transmit data by plugging it up to a local database. If they can transmit wirelessly, the rate is probably not fast enough and has delayed content. This does not mention the alarms, which are only on the device and are not sent to the specialist. With 5G, these devices can instantly upload data to a cloud infrastructure for the specialist to look at in real-time as it is happening to assess whether the patient's condition is getting better or worse. IoT devices with AI integration and 5G make this device extremely reliable. It can also notify someone in the moments before a medical episode occurs so the patient can be brought in under supervised care and not have a fatality or catastrophic event.

Emergency services and first responders can also use 5G for communication between other responders in real-time to quickly and efficiently assess a situation before the worst happens. The massive bandwidth capacity of 5G can push many vitals to a doctor who can be prepped and ready to go before the patient arrives. Global Positioning Systems (GPS) tracking is also said to be an improvement of the 5G networks. This improvement is a more precise GPS location and can help dispatchers find a property that is not obvious because of the area on the road or in a busy neighborhood. The responsiveness and reliability of 5G can save lives because of the amount of time lost with legacy networks.

According to the KPMG (2019) organization, 5G has a considerable front in the manufacturing industry as the cost to implement it is lower than fiber optics and matches the same speeds of up to 10 Gbps. IoT and 5G enable enterprises to connect all parts of their processes to promote efficiency and reliability by providing data to analysts to respond quickly to breakdowns or changes in customer demands, predicting and deciding possible scenarios to maximize profit gain and satisfaction for consumers. The massive amount of data collected in real-time can be a huge time saver for corporations trying to get the leading edge on their products. In addition, these IoT devices can send data with 5G during the manufacturing process to determine quality control of products to minimize loss of materials and funds. If it is caught early enough in the process, someone can be notified and make the machine's necessary changes to keep processing.

KPMG also states how 5G can offer spectrums to be reserved by corporations to use, so their data does not interfere with other devices that may be on the same channel. I could see this being great for an autonomous car business entity, whose devices need to communicate with other base stations or drivers on the road to collect data about traffic patterns for warning the driver or to take over when an accident is about to happen. Segregation of data in this context is a security practice that can improve the overall efficiency of moving large amounts of data and ensure unauthorized stations or devices are not snooping in to manipulate data or collect sensitive data to be exploited. The downside to this is choice in proprietary content and devices available only on that channel. This gives an unfair advantage to that corporation as equipment cannot mix and mingle in the mesh architecture when nodes try to use different communication channels. It should also be mentioned that vendors who control these spectrums may not adhere to some of the best practices put out, conflicting with the data's security and safety moving across this spectrum. If an accident were to occur as a result of terrible network design and poor practice in the case of autonomous cars, a lawsuit could cost that company a lot of money. Even the IoT industry is not as standardized because of its inability to keep up with the always changing principles, so vendors are on their own to design promising products to deliver to consumers.

4.7 Big Data Analytics in 5G

The intermingling of 5G, IoT, and Advanced Data Analytics will upset the Information and Communications Technology (ICT) environment making ready for new plans of action, innovation development, and horde open doors for applications of overall industry verticals that depend on Telecom and IT administrations. 5G vows to empower insightful system and application administrations with networks to remote sensors, gigantic measures of IoT information, and low idleness information transmissions. Big Data analytics will play a significant role in the evolution of 5G standards, enabling intelligence across networks, applications, and businesses (Somisetty 2018).

Not at all like 4G LTE, 5G speaks to a reason constructed innovation, structured and designed to encourage associated gadgets such as computerization frameworks. It will be a facilitator and a quickening agent of the following modern insurgency from multiple points of view, promising to convey high information rates with ultra-low inertness for applications. Data Analytics is at the sweet-spot, taking full advantage of 5G network characteristics such as high bandwidth, low latency, and mobile edge computing (MEC). 5G's ability to support massive connectivity across diverse devices, backed by distributed compute architectures, creates the ability to translate the big data-at-rest and the data-in-motion into real-time insights with actionable intelligence. Data Analytics will play a dual role in the context of 5G. On one side, it will keep supporting different business applications or use-cases over 5G systems, yet on the opposite side, it will assume a basic job in the turnout of 5G and system tasks. Application Intelligence is another area where the 5G application use-case spectrum is very broad, including wearables, smart homes, smart cities, autonomous cars, and industrial automation. IoT and Industry 4.0 are going to be the biggest drivers for 5G applications. Hence, the Context-Aware Engine will become an integral part of 5G to make networks aware of the underlying context and are cognitive enough to provide smart experiences for an individual subscriber on the network with better flow management decisions. In the network intelligence connectivity, 5G networks are inherently complex with multiple layers of virtual functions, virtual and physical RAN assets, spectrum usage, and distributed computing nodes, based on Software-Defined Network/Network Function Virtualization (SDN/NFV) concepts (Hodges 2015). Network analytics will become critical to building a flexible 5G network where roll-out and operational complexity are simplified. It helps network planning and optimization in deciding where to scale specific network functions. Application services will be based on machine learning algorithms that analyze network utilization and traffic data patterns more closely. Thus, Operations and Business Support Systems will have analytics integrated and embedded into their toolset.

Big Data Analytics is inalienably synergistic with other 5G innovation patterns, for example, SDN/NFV and MEC. The key patterns and business drivers that will shape the guide of information examination in 5G are MEC and mobile cloud sensing. Big data and 5G Network make Intelligent and Smart World Mission-critical applications such as public safety and healthcare domain and would need analytics in real-time. Thanks to slicing-based traffic prioritization, MEC-based local analytics, or the latency improvements promised by the new 5G air interface, 5G lays a foundation for supporting mission-critical edge analytics and tactile internet applications. 5G makes it possible and not just to trigger actuators to trigger response actions within a fraction of seconds. All data seamlessly travels from the cloud to many endpoints and vice-versa (Wang et al. 2015). For IoT over 5G, the mass amount of information being created by the IoT has the power to revolutionize everything from manufacturing to healthcare to the layout and functioning of smart cities, allowing them to work more efficiently and profitably than ever before (Ismail 2017). For Information Monetization, Telco's 4G/LTE have just been utilizing information to improve administration quality and client experience. Be that as it may, with the numerous prospects of 5G to arrange administrations joined with IoT and AI, they will investigate new plans of adaptation, such as canny endeavor application administrations. Predictive maintenance is the leading use-case of Industry 4.0, helping in predicting failures before they occur by leveraging AI, anticipated to have an increasing role in ICT, and rapidly becoming integrated into many aspects of communication, applications, and content commerce (Scully 2017). Psychological Analytics in 5G will transform itself into a machine or deep learning and develop to the unique situation degree. It will predict what will occur straightaway, recommends the following best activity or step, gains from the past standards of conduct for taking the ideal choice, and for completely self-ruling applications will robotize the following activity. Investigation created experiences can progressively drive the dynamics. With the speed of 5G, more data will be gathered and prepared, quicker than at any time in recent memory, prompting intellectual insight applications. Technical challenges and a path to 5G include High-Speed Data-In-Motion, Advanced Cloud Infrastructure Support, Support for Application and Network Intelligence, End-to-End Security, and Real-Time Actionable Insights. In a simple network with limited capabilities, data analytics is of marginal importance: the network can only carry so much data, and there is not that much network data to collect or act on. 5G networks look to be anything but limited or simple, making analytics key to delivering on the 5G promise and making full use of 5G resources.

5G is vulnerable to the volume of data to infiltrate these networks. Billions of devices are on networks today, and it is only the beginning. 5G networks have to be strong enough to assess the risks that involve outages and denial of service. Systems will no longer service just those for voice and data, but will also be a massive undertaking of machine-to-machine communications.

The world of IoT has begun to change the way data is processed between devices. No longer will network architecture be thought of as hub and spoke, but more like a mesh network. Every device will be connected. These benefits as devices can have redundancy paths if one point is not functional, and tools push a larger bandwidth because of the distance between them. However, the downside to having a mesh network could include rogue devices being placed within a network and sitting silently collecting data or redirecting data collected to a central location that sifts through this looking for personal information. We will see the volume of data on 5G networks between the IoT devices, autonomous machines, user data, and devices we do not already know exponentially. This vast amount of data and metadata associated with these devices have to be encrypted end-to-end to ensure data is not vulnerable to the outside. The hard part about having all this data and encrypting it is the current architecture looking for malicious activity traversing these networks. The enormous amount of data coming into a network will be challenging to determine the malicious activity hackers are trying to push through the firewalls of your system. The capacity is going to flood anything networks already have in place. Solutions will need to be reworked and hardware will have to be upgraded to service the users and data on these networks. The use of AI will need to integrate into the systems to learn behaviors of the kinds of packets traveling between networks.

4.8 AI Empowers a Wide Scope of Use Cases

The AI baseline can become very predictive and it is easy to see anomalies coming across the network wire. How the architecture has to be reworked in the 5G space is somewhat daunting. 5G networks run on a RAN, or Radio Access Network, where devices connect to a base station, and the data is transmitted to a core network for routing to another system and the destination. 5G technologies identify the edge network where user devices are versus the core network that houses routing and switch equipment, which is difficult from a security standpoint. However, in the Mesh network, devices nearby may use each other as a leg to send information to the base stations because of their proximity and large bandwidth requirements. These devices can easily act as a man-in-the-middle attack, take the information, send it to another destination, or modify the packet's contents before it is sent off. Even in the core network base stations, we can see backdoors implemented for unauthorized access into these systems to be used in a middle-in-the-man attack. While being in a mesh configuration environment seems to be an excellent option to offload some of the load from base stations, it could be a hazardous feature. Devices could be infected or under attack for a malicious purpose, obtaining a cyber-data actor to use their gain.

While the preparation of data-intensive deep learning models happens in the cloud, inference, the act of responding to new situations using the predictive power of a trained AI model, should occur near the user to make decisions and continuously take action. Decentralizing the cloud for a more distributed framework, utilizing both edge cloud and on-gadget processing similarly conveys lower latency so that gadgets can be progressively responsive. 5G was imagined to be the uniting connectivity fabric that can connect everything and everyone, and it is intended to help and grow the IoT ecosystem. Thus, with the headways in on-gadget AI, edge cloud computing, and 5G, the wireless edge will bring new and improved experiences and a wide scope of use cases.

The intelligent wireless edge will turn into the foundation for driving cutting edge user experiences. The consistent mix of on-gadget AI, edge cloud computing, and 5G networking empower new nodes and services. It also changes existing ones for both individual and expert use with its more extensive bandwidth and low latency to enhance mobile experiences better than ever (Qualcomm 2019). With the savvy wireless edge, we can increase the ability of on-gadget AI with the edge cloud for new advantages, from greater photography to progressively instinctive augmented reality experiences, numerous more current use cases empowered, and far better 5G upgraded smartphone experiences (Carter 2019). With AI-empowered cameras, new 5G cell phones can offer usefulness equivalent to that of the best in class DSLR (Digital Single Lens Reflex) cameras. AI improved features with the blend of on-gadget intelligence, cloud computing, and 5G connectivity to transform voice technology can make a genuine individual partner that can be progressively responsive, proactive, and mindful. The present cloud-driven virtual assistants offer limited privacy and few options for personalization.

4.9 Conclusion

The 5G network will be characterized by its increased power, strength, efficiency, and speed, promising features that will take the mobile industry to the next level. With the 5G network's presence, the mobile industry will be considered the main key to the IoT. This name is given to the act whereby every activity will be tied to the internet and mobile network. The mobile industry will lead to billions of sensors, door locks, smartwatches, and health monitors. Additionally, the mobile industry will be characterized by increased scalability, flow, and latency to meet all of its overarching demands. A consideration of these factors gives a clear look at the opportunity and efficiency presented to the mobile industry by developing the 5G network in the year 2020 and beyond. From a look at the recent occurrence after the deployment of the 3G and 4G networks, it is clear that by the year 2021 the 5G network will present them with new realities, increased speed, gratification, efficiency, and a lightning-fast response. The following are some of the expected characteristics of 5G networks (Yarali, Fateh, and Razmi 2016):

- Ultra-high capacity and Massive MIMO
- Multi-hop transmission and New spectrum
- Wide area coverage and Full duplex
- Ultra-dense networks and NFV

The 5G wireless will advance the current typical experience when using networking infrastructure for professional and leisure activities. The expansion of IoT devices produces the quality analytics necessary to improve data's overall processing and can be integrated with 5G and AI to give predictive answers in a real-time format for users and analysts. The use of CCTV over the 5G network can enhance how surveillance is captured. Events are tracked and protected by citizens' privacy while providing safe spaces for a decline in criminal activity. 5G also helps to improve the home front for an alternative to wired broadband with speeds to match fiber optics and the provision of backward compatibility for development to promise minimal cost for excellent service. Countries have specific security needs and face unique threats. Tracking these threats will require integrating the new 5G protocol within an existing framework. This may present many challenges to developing countries.

Integration of 5G to the existing networks will depend on many national imperatives. Financial power, national security policy, the status of the legacy narrowband solutions, and commitment from private mobile operators, who own the spectrum and operate the services, will remain critical.

References

Aleksandrova, M. (2018) *IoT in Agriculture: Five Technology Uses for Smart Farming and Challenges to Consider*. DZone IoT Zone: Available: https://dzone.com/articles/iot-in-agriculture-five-technology-uses-for-smart

Badia, L. and Zorzi, M. (2005). A technical and microeconomic analysis of wireless LANs. In: *IEEE Wireless Communications and Networking Conference*, vol. 2005. https://doi.org/10.1109/wcnc.2005.1424758.

Blackshaw, P. (2006). The consumer-controlled surveillance culture. *Clicz*, Accessed 12 June 2018: www.clickz.com/the-consumer-controlled-surveillance-culture/69332/.

Buddhikot, M., Chandranmenon, G., Han, S. et al. (2003). Integration of 802.11 and third-generation wireless data networks. In: *INFOCOM 2003. Twenty-Second Annual Joint Conference of the IEEE Computer and Communications*, IEEE \Societies, vol. 1, 503–512. IEEE.

Carter, J. (2019, January 14). 10 Ways 5G will change daily life. Retrieved from TechRadar: https://www.techradar.com/news/10-ways-5g-will-change-daily-life.

Claveria, K. (2019, April 13). 13 stunning stats on the Internet of Things. Retrieved from VisionCritical: https://www.visioncritical.com/blog/internet-of-things-stats.

Combs, V. (2021). 5G Prediction: 53% of the world's population will have coverage by 2025. Retrieved from: 5G Prediction: 53% of the world's population will have coverage by 2025 – TechRepublic.

Desai, R. (2019). 5G, December 1, 2019. Retrieved from: https://drrajivdesaimd.com/2019/12/01/5g/.

Garg, V.K. and Rappaport, T.S. (2011). *Wireless Network Evolution: 2G to 3G*. Prentice-Hall PTR.

Gittlen, S. (2020) Enterprise 5G: Guide to planning, architecture, and benefits.Retrieved from: https://searchnetworking.techtarget.com/ Enterprise-5G-Guide-to-planning-architecture-and-benefits.

Gopall, B.G. and Kuppusamy, P.G. (2015). A comparative study on 4G and 5G technology for wireless applications. *IOSR Journal of Electronics and Communication Engineering (IOSR-JECE)* 10 (6), ver. III: 67–72. ISSN: 2278-2834 and 2278-8735.

Hatten, M. (n.d.). What is 5G Tech, and how will it impact your business? Retrieved from MONDO: https://www.mondo.com/blog-5g-tech/.

Hodges, J. (2015, June 9). The role of big data & advanced analytics in SDN/NFV. Retrieved from ACCEDIAN: https://accedian.com/wp-content/uploads/2015/06/BTE15_The-Role-of-Big-Data-and-Advanced-Analytics-in-SDN-NFV.pdf.

Huang, K. and Wang, Z. (2011). *Millimeter-Wave Communication Systems*. Hoboken, NJ: Wiley.

Huang, J., Qian, F., Gerber, A. et al. (2012). A close examination of performance and power characteristics of 4G LTE networks. In: *Proceedings of the 10th International Conference on Mobile Systems, Applications, and Services*, 225–238. ACM.

Internet Society (2017). Artificial Intelligence and Machine Learning: Policy paper. Retrieved from: https://www.internetsociety.org/resources/doc/2017/ artificial-intelligence-and-machine-learning-policy-paper/.

International Telecommunication Union (2015). Recommendation itu-r m.2083-0 (09/2015), IMT Vision – Framework and overall objectives of the future development of IMT for 2020 and beyond. Retrieved from https://www.itu.int/dms_pubrec/itu-r/rec/m/r-rec-m. 2083-0-201509- i!!pdf-e.pdf.

Ismail, N. (2017, January 19). How big data and analytics are fuelling the IoT revolution. Retrieved from Information Age: https://www.information-age.com/ big-data-analytics-fuelling-iot-revolution-123464081/.

Khan, A.H., Qadeer, M.A., Ansari, J.A., and Waheed, S. (2009). 4G as a next-generation wireless network. In International Conference on. In: *Future Computer and Communication, 2009, ICFCC 2009*, 334–338. IEEE.

KPMG (2019). Converging 5G and IoT. (2019, June 11). Retrieved May 1, 2020, from: https://home.kpmg/xx/en/home/campaigns/2019/06/converging-5g-and-iot.html.

Kuprenko, V. (2019). IoT in agriculture: Why it is a future of connected farming world. Retrieved from: https://theiotmagazine.com/iot-in-agriculture-why-it-is-a-future-of-connected-farming-world-70b64936627c?gi=b3fc8b0243c6.

LEE (2016). Paving the way for 5G, ETRI. Retrieved from https://5g-ppp.eu/wpcontent/uploads/2016/11/06_10-Nov_Session-3_Lee-JunHwan.pdf.

Lioudis, N. (2018). *Investopedia, LLC*. 13 June 2018. blog.

Metaswitch (n.d.). What is 5G Fixed Wireless Access (FWA)? Retrieved May 1, 2020, from: www.metaswitch.com/knowledge-center/reference/what-is-5g-fixed-wireless-access-fwa.

Muangprathub, J., Boonnam, N., Kajornkasirat, S. et al. (2019). IoT and agriculture data analysis for smart farm. *Computers and Electronics in Agriculture* 156: 467–474. Retrieved from: https://www.sciencedirect.com/science/article/abs/pii/S0168169918308913.

Norp, A., Kips, A., and Van Loon, J.M. (2015). US Patent No. 9, 178, 822. Washington, DC: US Patent and Trademark Office.

Price, C. (2019, November 29). What does 5G mean for your business? Retrieved from Telegraph: https://www.telegraph.co.uk/business/5g-in-sport/what-does-5g-mean-for-businesses/.

Qualcomm (2017, August 16). We are making on-device AI ubiquitous. Retrieved from OnQ Blog: https://www.qualcomm.com/news/onq/2017/08/16/we-are-making-device-ai-ubiquitous?cmpid=oofyus181544.

Qualcomm (2019). *Realizing New 5G Possibilities with the Iintelligent Wireless Edge*. Fierce Wireless fierce-wireless-ebrief-realizing-new-5g-possibilities-with-the-intelligent-wireless-edge.pdf (qualcomm.com).

Rappaport, T.S. Jr., Heath, R.W., Daniels, R.C., and Murdock, J.N. (2014). *Millimeter-Wave Wireless Communications*. Upper Saddle River, NJ: Prentice-Hall.

Schmelzer, R. (2019, October 1). *Making the Internet of Things (IoT) More Intelligent with AI*. Forbes. Retrieved from: https://www.forbes.com/sites/cognitiveworld/2019/10/01/making-the-internet-of-things-iot-more-intelligent-with-ai/#3c0930defd9b.

Scully, P. (2017, March 21). Market Report. Retrieved from IoT Analytics: https://iot-analytics.com/report-us11-billion-predictive-maintenance-market-by-2022/.

SDXCentral, 2018. What is 5G network slicing? (2018, January 2). Retrieved May 1, 2020, from: https://www.sdxcentral.com/5g/definitions/5g-network-slicing/.

Senate, R.P.C. (2019). The importance of 5G. Retrieved from: https://www.rpc.senate.gov/policy-papers/the-importance-of-5g.

Somisetty, M. (2018). Big data analytics in 5G. Retrieved from IEEE: https://futurenetworks.ieee.org/images/files/pdf/applications/Data-Analytics-in-5G-Applications030518.pdf.

Thompson, J., Ge, X., Wu, H. et al. (2014). 5G wireless communication systems: Prospects and challenges [Guest Editorial]. *IEEE Communications Magazine* 52.2: 62–64.

Trivisonno, R., Guerzoni, R., Vaishnavi, I., and Soldani, D. (2015). SDN-based 5G mobile networks: Architecture, functions, procedures, and backward compatibility. *Transactions on Emerging Telecommunications Technologies* 26 (1): 82–92.

Vermesan, O., Eisenhauer, M., Serrano, M. et al. (2018). *The Next Generation Internet of Things – Hyperconnectivity and Embedded Intelligence at the Edge*, 19–102. River Publishers.

Wamura, M. (2015). NGMN view on 5G architecture. In: *81st IEEE Vehicular Technology Conference (VTC Spring)*, 1–5.

Wang, X., Han, G., Du, X. et al. (2015). Mobile cloud computing in 5G: Emerging trends, issues, and challenges. *IEEE Network* 29 (2): 4–5.

Yarali, A., Fateh, M., and Razmi, N. (2016). 5G Mobile Communication Systems: Innovation, convergence and ubiquitous connectivity. *The Twelfth ICNS International Conference on Networking and Services*, 2016.

5

Artificial Intelligence Technology

5.1 Introduction

Artificial Intelligence (AI) started in 1956 when John McCarthy used this term for the first time when he started a research group that included scientists and researchers from different disciplines such as complexity theory, neuron nets, and language simulation. There was a workshop on AI that was called the Dartmouth Summer Research Project on Artificial Intelligence. This was the first time when researchers tried to develop the "thinking machines" concept. McCarthy picked the artificial intelligence name for neutrality. This was to abstain from highlighting the ways adopted for the field of "thinking machines," which included complex information processing, cybernetics, and automata. The main theme of this conference was "The study to proceed based on the conjecture that every aspect of learning or any other feature of intelligence can in principle be so precisely described that a machine can be made to stimulate it." (Marr 2018). The modern dictionary defines AI as a sub-field of computer science that machines can learn from human intelligence; machines are like humans, not becoming humans. The definition given by the English Oxford Living Dictionary about AI is, "The theory and development of computer systems able to perform tasks normally requiring human intelligence, such as visual perception, speech recognition, decision-making, and translation between languages." Britannica defines AI as "The ability of a digital computer or computer-controlled robot to perform tasks commonly associated with intelligent beings." (SAS 2019)

To understand what AI stands for today, it is important to know the term and know the foundation. AI can be termed as a science of training systems in order to emulate human work with the help of automation and learning. The main aim is to let the machine learn and apply the logic and also the reason to develop an understanding with the help of data. In simple words, the machines learn from the data it gets with the help of identification patterns and the relationships within the data itself. The machine can ingest a large amount of data, information, extracting the main features, determine the way of analyzing, and write code to execute the analysis and production of intelligent output. This is all done by an automated process; once this becomes operational, this process will occur along with minimal intervention from the human counterparts.

Intelligent Connectivity: AI, IoT, and 5G, First Edition. Abdulrahman Yarali.
© 2022 John Wiley & Sons Ltd. Published 2022 by John Wiley & Sons Ltd.

- Building Blocks and Main Elements
- AI is based on the following technologies:
- Forecasting
- Optimization
- Natural language processing (NLP)
- Computer vision
- Deep learning
- Machine learning

AI makes use of technology to accomplish tasks that, in the past, might have been only done using human intelligence. The AI sector has managed to bring admirable transformation all over the world to corporations as they make a race to comprehend and incorporate this emerging technology into their daily operations. AI technology is, at the moment, predominant in several areas of everyday living. At present, the progress of AI is astounding. There is a need to be aware of three primary AI concepts of deep learning, machine learning, and neural networks. At this time, the universal race being witnessed to progress, financially support, and acquire AI technology and start-ups is gaining momentum. AI is being used in healthcare, finance manufacturing, transport, education, and energy. Based on a recent report, it is apparent that no city is equipped to deal with AI head-on. All cities need to make considerable enhancements to make preparations for the effects of state-of-the-art tech.

To put it plainly, AI is the capability of a computer program or otherwise a machine to go about thinking just like human beings. AI makes use of technology to accomplish tasks that, in the past, might have been only done using human intelligence (McCarthy 1988). This concept can range from learning to solving problems. AI is bound to mold humanity's future more than any other technology that has been seen before. Due to this fact, several people hold the misguided notion that AI was crafted to take human beings' place and assume any tasks that are carried out by humans in their day-to-day routine at home and work as well.

On the other hand, AI is being progressed to enhance human life and increase the skills and abilities of every human task. Humanity is sitting on an era where human beings and machines will partner even with more cohesion. Several nations have made publications and official announcements on national AI strategies that maximize the potential of technology in becoming global leaders. The AI industry has been top headlines in recent times, all for good reasons. The AI sector has managed to bring admirable transformation all over the world to corporations as they make a race to comprehend and incorporate this emerging technology into their daily operations. AI has been present with humanity for a relatively long time and is not a new concept. However, what has changed in the past few years is the power of computing, the applicability of AI to jobs, and cloud-based service selections. The influence of AI on marketing is ever progressing. There are predictions that it might amount to close to $40 billion by 2025. A good number of companies are aware of AI. However, some sectors are not sure and are unaware of the immense benefits and how they can go about adopting AI to enhance marketing. Progress in AI translates to product developers creating innovative and cutting-edge products and services that up to recent times would not have been feasible in the standard marketing budget. These fresh and innovative products and services gaining entry into the market make the adoption of AI have a decreased risk with much attention paid to making available practical and immediate effective results. Several past efforts ended up in costly and custom-progressed marketing technology projects that left behind scars.

AI can mimic the human brain. This makes it exceptional amid other technologies because it can learn and find solutions to problems that would, under normal circumstances, need human intelligence instead. Comprehensively, AI includes natural language and processing, pattern identification, visual perception, and decision making. All these processes working in tandem give AI vast potential in some industries and many economic sectors. These processes can take care of constant challenges to development, like the deficiency of infrastructure or underdeveloped healthcare and financial sectors, leaving several people lacking in service. Even though AI might have revolutionary potential, it has existed for many decades, at least in its most rudimentary form. First-generation AI capable computers engaged in chess games and found solutions to puzzles and carried out other comparatively forthright roles.

Nevertheless, the complexity level of AI has revolutionized intensely in the past 10 years or so. AI technology is, at the moment, predominant in some areas of daily living. For instance, Google Maps uses AI to get conversant with traffic patterns and develop effective routes enthusiastically. Smartphones make use of AI to identify faces and verbal commands. AI makes it possible to effectively spam filters in email programs. Smart assistants like Alexa are also made possible through AI. These are minimal examples of familiar technology that control the capabilities that AI has. AI applications can be traced in virtually every sector at the moment, from finance and healthcare to marketing. As expected, the progress and implementation of AI do not come without its fair share of controversy. The debate concerning the risks and the benefits of this exceptional and revolutionary technology tends to go towards extremes. Many observers predict that AI could bring destruction to job opportunities and, in the long run, pose a threat to human beings (Frey and Michael 2017). Some suggestions point towards a probable positive effect of AI on GDP growth, but virtually all emphasize developed economies. Overall, the combined effect is projected to hinge on several factors, including technological development, open-source data, and skills. Some nations have the probability of gaining more than others. The effect on jobs is mainly undefined as it is reliant on the specific economic industry and the skill component of the labor force.

5.2 Core Concepts of Artificial Intelligence

The elements of AI (optimization, forecasting, computer vision, machine learning, deep learning, and natural process learning) can be used all together or independently to make an AI capability. Defining a capability in AI is the main operational task that a machine is required to perform, and needs to consider the main aim to be achieved. In AI, the capabilities can be continuously learned and adjusted as per the changing conditions in the data. Figure 5.1 depicts the top 10 use cases for AI revenue-generating applications. Following are the AI capabilities in a business context:

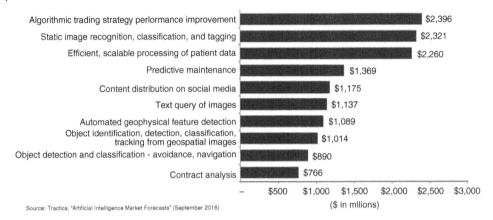

Figure 5.1 AI revenue, top 10 use cases, world markets – 2025 (TM Capital 2017).

- Prediction. This involves getting long and short-term variability in the data to forecast energy consumption.
- Image recognition. Determining if the nodes on a CT scan are benign or malignant.
- Classification. Evaluating the track images of animals and classifying them as per their species to support wildlife conservation efforts.
- Pattern recognition. Understanding customer trends may include buying behavior and identifying anomalies in spending to prevent fraudulent behavior.
- Speech to text. Transcribing call center agents' voice messages into the text to detect sentiment and other evaluations.
- Natural language generation. Summarizing and analyzing large document collection.
- Cognitive search. Personalizing recommendations by matching the search results and buying patterns of the customers who have bought similar items.
- Natural language interaction. Generating reports on sales and making future predictions with the help of software (SAS 2019).

At the moment, the progress of AI is astounding. Attempts made to develop AI ideas in the past 20 years have ended up in some remarkable innovations (Turing 1948). Autonomous vehicles, big data, and medical research are amazing applications resulting from AI development. It is necessary to understand three primary concepts: deep learning, machine learning, and neural networks to gain complete comprehension of some of the inner concepts of AI like NLP, data mining, and driving software. Even though some people may be under the impression that AI and machine learning are interchangeable terms, AI is, in most cases, regarded as a broader term, with machine learning being a subset of the former. All three AI concepts, machine learning, neural networks, and deep learning, can make it possible for hardware and software robots to think and act in a dynamic manner outside the code's restrictions. Getting a comprehension of these basics can result in more complex AI topics, including superintelligence and AI, artificial general intelligence, and ethics in AI. Machine learning algorithms develop a mathematical model grounded on sample data referred to as training data to arrive at predictions or decisions minus being overtly programmed to carry out the task (Samuel 1959). Machine learning algorithms are put to use in various applications like computer vision and email filtering. It is hard or infeasible to come up with a conventional algorithm for effectively carrying out a task.

5.3 Machine Learning and Applications

Machine learning is the scientific study of algorithms and statistical representations that computer systems use to carry out a particular job minus the use of clear guidelines, and in its place being reliant on inference and patterns (Mohri, Rostamizadeh, and Talwalkar 2012). The average person has likely been in contact with AI in their daily activities. For instance, take Gmail; there is no doubt that there are benefits from the automatic filtering feature. If one owns a smartphone, there are chances that they benefit from Siri, Bixby, and Cortana in filling out their calendars. If one owns a new generation vehicle, they have probably experienced benefits from a driver-aid feature during driving. As helpful as these software products might be, they cannot learn all on their own. They cannot think outside their written code. Machine learning is a subset of AI that gives machines the capability to learn a job minus a preexisting code. In the plainest of terms, machines are granted many trial examples for a specific job. In the course of these trials, machines learn and adapt their approaches to attain these set goals. For instance, an image-recognition machine could be given close to a million pictures for analysis (Mohri, Rostamizadeh, and Talwalkar 2012). Following infinite variations, the machine needs to identify faces, patterns, and shapes, amongst other things. AI is a blend of technologies, with machine learning being one of the most dominant methods used for hyper-personalized marketing. AI machine learning uses conventions to reconsider the model, re-examine the data, and perhaps make a decision without interference from a human being. This feature is the turning point where everything changes on all possible customer-product demands and is faster than something a human can do.

5.4 Deep Learning

The big question is how to get a machine to learn more than just one particular job. It is also a question of what happens when there is a need for it to have the ability to take what has been learned from photograph analysis and make use of the same knowledge to evaluate various data sets. This needs computer specialists to develop general-purpose learning algorithms that aid machines in learning additional tasks (Schmidhuber 2015). An excellent example of deep learning in practice is AlphaGo Project pioneered by Google. It is written in Lua C++ and Python code (Jordan and Mitchell 2015). The AlphaGo AI could counter professional Go players. Something that had been assumed to be unattainable provided the game had such complexity and dependence on fixated practice and the human instinct to master.

5.5 Neural Networks Follow a Natural Model

In most cases, deep learning is made feasible using artificial neural networks that mimic neurons and brain cells (Hinton et al. 2012). Artificial neural networks were motivated by things that can be found in everyday biology. The neural net models use math and computer science guidelines to imitate the procedures that go through the human brain, thus making more room for general learning. An artificial neural network makes attempts to mimic the procedures of densely interlinked brain cells. However, instead of being constructed from biology, these neurons and nodes are constructed from codes. Neural networks comprise three layers: a hidden layer, an input layer, and an output layer (Hinton et al. 2012). At times these layers comprise millions of nodes. Data is filled into the input layer. Inputs are accorded with a specific weight and interlinked nodes enlarge the link's weight in the course of their travel. If the data unit makes it to a specific threshold, it can pass on to the following layer. To obtain information from experience, machines compare outputs from a neural network and then proceed to change connections, thresholds, and weights based on the variances among them.

5.6 Classifications of Artificial Intelligence

AI can be grouped into three various types of system:

- Analytical. Analytical AI has just featured in line with cognitive intelligence, thereby creating a cognitive setup of the world by using learning grounded on previous experiences to give information on coming judgments.
- Human-inspired. Human motivated AI possesses elements from cognitive as well as emotional intelligence. It gives a comprehension of human emotion and cognitive factors and gives them consideration in making important decisions.
- Humanized AI. Humanized AI gives an insight into all kinds of capabilities like emotional, cognitive, and social intelligence. It can be self-conscious as well as being self-aware in its interactions.

5.7 Trends in Artificial Intelligence

The worldwide race that is currently being witnessed to progress, financially support, and acquire AI technology and startups is gaining momentum. Commercial uses of AI are increasing in progressed and developing economies. AI has the potential to turn up the growth of GDP in progressed markets and those that are emerging. In the energy sector, AI has the potential to enhance the transmission of power. In the healthcare industry, diagnosis and drug discovery ought to immensely gain help from AI. In the education sector, AI has the potential to enhance the learning setting as well as its outcomes. It can improve the preparation for youth at the time of transition to the workspace. In the manufacturing industry, AI can aid in designing improved products in the aspects of quality, costs, functionality, and enhancing analytical maintenance. AI can aid in the extension of financial services and credit services to the people who need them. The prospective effect of AI on logistics and transport moves a long way past automation and road security, thereby extending the whole logistics sequence. However, taking China and India from the equation, emerging markets have managed to get only a small share of international investment in this progressed technology (Kaplan and Haenlein 2019). Figure 5.2 depicts the leading AI sector investment.

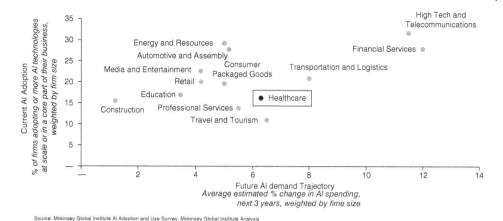

Source: Mckinsey Global Institute AI Adoption and Use Survey: Mckinsey Global Institute Analysis

Figure 5.2 Sectors leading to AI adoption technology (TM Capital 2017).

5.7.1 Artificial Intelligence in Energy

The potential of AI in the energy sector, in most cases, influences the tech's capability to evaluate increasingly comprehensive systems in real-time and enhance them in a manner not feasible with otherwise conservative information technology. The timing is specifically casual with the energy grid in a prevalent change to recurrent renewable generation from endless base load systems. This is a modification that significantly augments system complications. As a case in point, AI can be put to use in the enhancement of distributed energy resources such as rooftop solar photovoltaic cells and batteries to equate the capacity and load. Electricity meter information can be disaggregated using heuristics machine learning. As a result, the creation of intuitions for extra energy savings can be realized. In addition to that, sales from renewable energy and deployment can be hastened using AI. It can also deliver augmented energy effectiveness at the grid level by bringing down standby stashes of thermal baseload creation through the permission of the grid to keep track of renewables and load more keenly. In turn, this capability brings down the use of coal, gas, and oil and, in so doing, reduces greenhouse gases. Correspondingly, using its increased degree of flexibility, AI can augment the creation of renewables by lifting the ceiling on the number of renewables housed. At the building phase, AI can increase effectiveness through machine learning to make predictions on building heating and cooling loads on the grounds of weekday, weather, and the time of day. AI can also sanction clients using improved disaggregation of electricity meter information, making room for resource conservation using behavior change.

5.7.2 Artificial Intelligence in Healthcare

There happen to be several uses for AI technology in the healthcare industry. This technology is undergoing development at a swift pace and is already being put to use in numerous applications ranging from helping in arriving at a diagnosis to enhancing operational healthcare workflow effectiveness. A good number of these application objectives is to carry out the activities assumed by human beings but at an improved pace with increased accuracy and more reliability, making them prospectively beneficial in resource-limited settings with constrained access to medical professionals and additional health professionals. Top uses of AI in the healthcare sector include (Kuperman, Reichley, and Bailey 2006):

- AI improved medical diagnostics and imaging that is constructed to enhance the reliability and speed of evaluation and has the potential to be specifically beneficial in settings where there is a deficiency of radiologists or trained doctors.
- AI triage pugs in telehealth settings and accordingly a preconsulting triage. It goes further by flagging prospective diagnosis to save time for the physicians.
- Patient information and risk evaluations. AI gives promise to machine learning and data analytics on patient information such as electronic health data, making it possible for predictive diagnosis and, in the long run, enhancing the results.
- Discovery of drugs. Deep learning methods that make use of convolutional neural networks happen to be very useful in making predictions on which molecular constructions might end up yielding efficient drugs (Schmidhuber 2015). Applications are currently being designed by development departments, in-house research, and independent startups keen on vertical systems. These entities are keen to enhance the rate of drug discovery. AI likewise offers support for personalized medicine or otherwise, targeting medicines founded on personal genetics and additional genomic evaluation.
- Pharmaceutical supply chain. Making use of AI to process real-time information and come up with predictive endorsements is supposed to drive data-motivated supply chains, thereby enhancing effectiveness and cost management.

The healthcare AI market in the US exceeded $320 million a few years ago, and is predicted to rise to more than a 38% compound annual growth rate (CAGR) by 2024, and is estimated to grow by more than a 38% CAGR through 2028. The global healthcare AI market is expected to grow at a 39.4% CAGR to over $10 billion by 2028 (see Figure 5.3) (Global Market Insight 2017).

5.7.3 Artificial Intelligence in Education

AI tech can, by dramatic means, improve the ways through which students learn outside and within the confines of their classrooms. This service is in addition to the expansion of relevance, access, and effectiveness of education. Machine learning can customize learning content by providing faculty and teachers with actionable instruction from students'

Source: Markets and Markets: Global Market Insights, Inc.

Figure 5.3 Global healthcare AI market growth through 2024 (TM capital 2017).

performance to comprehend better and take care of their needs. AI can also enhance online tutoring, aid teachers in the automation of routine tasks like grading and fill gaps in the curricula, and give students a fast response to aid in improved comprehension of ideas at their pace and with an improved individualization level. The use of AI in education can enhance learning settings as well as learning results. It can also save faculty members and teachers time and make room for them to direct their attention to learners with special requirements and make curricula also relevant to industry and employers' wants.

AI in education also can democratize education through the provision of standard teaching in non-traditional learning settings. AI can also grant parents a more significant role in their children's education using new implements and platforms. It can decentralize education to reduce the sizes of classes, campuses, and schools. All these listed applications might be useful to academia and create on-the-job training programs with improved efficiency. AI applications can better organize the youth to transition to the working setting using specialized work readiness programs. It also aids adults in remaining competitive using customized up/reskilling programs. Specialists make predictions of immense potential for AI in evaluations, language learning, intelligent tutoring, the expansion of global classrooms, and matchmaking between the demands for and supply of talents.

5.7.4 Artificial Intelligence in Manufacturing

Manufacturing makes available several prospects for AI technologies with inventions comprising software and hardware alike. The top uses include:

- Intelligent Computer-Aided Design (CAD) systems can be interfaced with process imitation implements to look for the ultimate means to manufacture a specific product. A case in point is deciding between the traditional molding and three-dimensional (3D) printing for plastic parts. As has already been witnessed with CAD systems, where the cost has dropped down to 1% of what it used to be two decades ago, such implements could quickly grow to be affordable and thereby widespread, even in sprouting markets.
- Yield improvements result from the root cause evaluation of malfunctioning products and enhanced manufacturing procedures in real-time to increase output. AI can aid in instances when the customary statistical review has already been completely developed, and where benefits and costs validate it. Several AI applications are currently being developed by startups keen on development in the industry and in-house any time that benefits and costs evaluation can give them validation. Getting access to large sets of information and data analysts, who also happen to be technical specialists in the particular application under scrutiny, is essential in the successful deployment of AI in the manufacturing process and product engineering areas.
- This is inclusive of AI in CAD systems to develop improved products in the context of cost, function, and quality. This sector is by far the most promising for the manufacturing industry because of CAD software resolution scalability. A generative design that uses large databases can yield an optimized product in its functionality, manufacturability, and cost.
- Product management. AI improved prognostic maintenance by enhancing asset productivity by using data to prepare for chance machine breakdowns, especially when

customary statistical evaluation implements have been completely set up and benefits and costs validate tallying AI to them. Into the bargain, context-aware and collaborative robots can identify their settings, thereby making it possible for them to change their actions based on what is required of them. Functions can also be modified in real-time.

5.7.5 Artificial Intelligence in Financial Services

Artificial Intelligence is in the offing to have a game-determining effect in the financial services sector in six prominent sections (Marwala and Hurw`itz 2017):

- Timely discovery and prevention of cybersecurity threats. Generative Adversarial Networks can develop fabricated and actual data sets and learn through time, augmenting identification and confirmation accuracy.
- Attaining intuitions that can precisely make predictions on client tendencies. A perfect example is the use of AI to look into a prospective borrower's past tendency and make precise predictions on their worth in terms of credit. Among the many applications under this is the IBM Watson.
- Giving support to financial entities through the fulfillment of KYC/AML guidelines given that AI can recall, learn, and stay in line with all applicable regulations. This has the potential to considerably bring down operating costs in an increasingly comprehensive regulatory existence.
- Chatbots with many similarities to humans, like the most popular application, Siri, can intelligently engage with clients, respond to asked questions, and bring downloads for customer service departments. An example of such a chatbot provider is NextIt.
- Visual identification and validation can identify clients and documents, thereby offering a streamline to procedures like account generation and insurance and loan initiation. As a case in point, Irisguard provides support for the identification of clients.
- AI technology and data analytics offer support to client access to mortgage financing, especially for those that happen to be in informal employment and applicants with faulty documentation. Aavas, which is a specialized housing finance corporation located in India, banks on data analytics and AI, and implements and evaluates the credit worth and inclination of households with undocumented and documented proceeds to reimburse loans acquired.

5.7.6 Artificial Intelligence in Transport

Self-operative vehicles tend to dominate talk of AI when it comes to transportation. However, the impacts of AI in the transport and logistics industry go way beyond this and even roads. A whole spectrum of transportation is supposed to go without drivers and crews, including ships, railways, and several delivery vehicles, all of which can be viable in the short to medium term. AI tech has immense prospects to take care of challenges in transport, especially in conjunction with safety, predictability, reliability, effectiveness, and environmental matters like pollution. AI is the ability to give inventions in the management of traffic for resolutions to more effectively aid in law enforcement, avert accidents, fatalities, crashes, and route cars. Routes can be enhanced to reduce traffic and upsurge reliability, while ideal transit networks for communities can be constructed with improved traffic signals and additional transport infrastructure (Prakken 2017). Routes for delivery trucks and motorcycles within the city can be modified for much swifter delivery times while commute times can be lowered for individuals.

These resolutions affect pollution as route improvement brings down the use of fuel and emission of different transport types, including cars, ships, and trucks, to name a few. The impacts of AI in logistics and transport stretch further than automation and road security management to cover the whole logistics chain straight from the origin to the eventual destination of goods and cargo. AI can make faster delivery timelines available to shippers and augmented dependability at decreased costs to send products by sea from factories to land disbursement points. AI can also increase precision in making predictions concerning arrival times for container ships and identify trends and dangers in shipping ports and lanes. Machine learning can aid in analyzing historical shipping information by considering factors like slow or busy shipping lines and weather patterns, which can, in turn, pinpoint duplications, inefficiencies, and errors. AI can also help to provide digital leasing marketplaces for the wholesale maritime sector, just like VesselBolt is currently doing. AI tech is likewise being used to imitate human perception and cognitive skills like reading, seeing, hearing, and the interpretation of sensory information. This has profits for user interfaces on ships, including speech recognition programs responsible for the direct control of equipment.

5.8   Challenges of Artificial Intelligence

AI is one of the fastest-growing and invested in technologies right now. The idea of AI is to take extremely lager amounts of data and make intuitive and fast decisions that will lead to greater efficiency and productivity. AI is heavily invested in by the US, China, and India, with most investments being in technology. IBM, Microsoft, Amazon, Google, and Facebook are the top companies investing in this technology. Taylor-made computer ships are now being created quickly and cheaply, which will help support AI applications. AI will push companies into learning algorithms for their business efficiency and service growth. However, the rapid development of AI is changing multiple industries and redesigning the rules of strategy. Big data is a good example of how people analyze an abundance of data by using AI to promote their companies to be more effective than those of their associates. The utilization of AI will gradually be a global trend, such as companies with investment funds, VC firms, or other corporate investors. Figure 5.4 depicts the essential landscape of enterprise AI companies (Yao 2020).

AI also does not have a perfect track record, as it still is just a machine, and machines can still make mistakes. Fully autonomous vehicles come to mind when I hear that. The amount of algorithms and programming that goes into a system like that is daunting. Sometimes a bug can be small and cause little problems or large and cause big issues. This risk will be something companies will have to deal with and mitigate to the best of their abilities. AI's assessment is not based on the models themselves but on organizations' ability to use them. Even though the use of AI strategies has monetary potential, concerns such as data security, protection, and potential tilting issues need to be addressed.

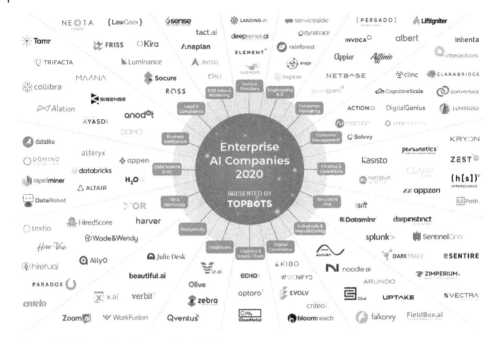

Figure 5.4 Enterprise AI companies, 2020.

5.8.1 Data

Data linked matters are most likely the ones that a good number of corporations are supposed to experience. It is a mutual fact that the constructed system is as good as the information fed into it. Companies need to consider several things before they decide to implement AI into their businesses. With data being the principal element of AI resolutions, a series of challenges can emerge.

5.8.1.1 Data Quantity and Quality

The quality of any system is reliant on the kind of data that is put into it. AI systems need enormous training datasets. AI learns from accessible information in a manner that is likened to humans. However, to pinpoint patterns, AI needs more data than human beings. It sounds sensible once you think about it, given that human beings get better at tasks given to them with more experience in performing them. The difference is that AI can evaluate data at a high speed that is unattainable for human beings. This makes learning using AI faster. The more improved the data given, the more enhanced the results will be provided.

5.8.1.2 Data Labeling

Some years back, much of the data being used was textual or structured. With the Internet of Things coming into play, a considerable part of this data comprised videos and images. There is nothing at fault with this situation, and it might look like there is no difficulty present. However, the problem is that a number of the systems making use of machine learning or otherwise deep learning have to be trained under supervision, so they need data that has labeling. The fact that humanity is responsible for generating massive quantities of data does not help matters either. It has reached a point where there is a scarcity of people needed to label data generated by the second. Databases exist that have made labeled data available, including ImageNet. ImageNet is a database that has well over 14 million images. All of these databases are annotated on a manual basis by ImageNet contributors. Even though more precise data could be accessible somewhere else in several instances, several computer vision experts use ImageNet because their image data always comes with labeling.

5.8.1.3 Clarity

As they are numerous "black box" models, an inevitable conclusion is arrived at like a prediction but lacks an explanation. If the finding given by the system overlaps with information that is already in hand and is thought to be right, there is a chance that one might not question it. However, the challenge comes when the conclusion given disagrees with available information. There is then a need to ascertain just how the conclusion was arrived at. In most instances, the decision on its own is never satisfactory. For example, it is hard for doctors to trust one suggestion when the matter concerns a patient's health. Strategies like Local Interpretable Model-Agnostic Explanations have the objective of augmenting the transparency given by models. In this case, in the instance where AI decides that a specific patient is suffering from the flu, then it will follow through and indicate the parts of data that resulted in this decision, like headaches, sneezing, but without the patient's demographics like weight and age. By being accorded the reason that motivates a decision, it is easier to evaluate just how much a model can be trusted.

5.8.1.4 Case-Specific Learning

The intelligence used by human beings guides them to use the experience gained from one field in a different one. This is referred to as the transfer of learning. Human beings can transfer learning from one setting to another with a similar context. AI keeps on having challenges in transferring its experiences from one series of occurrences to the next. There happen to be no surprises; it is evident that AI is specialized and supposed to implement a particular task. It is constructed to provide an answer to just one question. In fact, why would we even expect it to give answers to a different question in addition to that? On the other side of things, the experience needed by AI in completing a certain task can be valuable to another related to it. It is feasible to use this experience in place of having to come up with a whole new model from the ground up. Transfer learning is a method that makes all this feasible. The AI model undergoes training to implement a specific job and then goes ahead to apply the same learning to a similar but different event. This translates to having a developed model for task A being used as a starting point for a model used in completing task B.

5.8.1.5 Bias

Bias is a matter that causes worry for most people. Accounts of AI systems undergoing prejudice against women or based on race find themselves in the headlines from time to time. The real question is founded on how this happens because there is no way that AI on its own can harbor evil intentions. Making such an assumption would likewise translate to

AI being conscious and having the ability to arrive at self-motivated decisions. In reality, AI arrives at these decisions using accessible data. AI does not hold any opinions. However, it learns from the views held by others. It is at this point that bias takes place.

Bias can happen because of a series of reasons beginning with the means to gather data. Suppose the data is gathered using a survey method published in a magazine. It is important to note that the data is a reproduction of those who read the magazine and could be restricted to a social category. In such an instance, it is not right to say that the dataset available represents the whole population. There is another way to develop bias – the way that data is probed. A selection of people using a system could have preferred features and fail to use the rest of the available features. In such an instance, AI cannot learn about the functions that are not being put to use with the same frequency. Another aspect that has to be regarded when it comes to bias is that data comes from human beings. People tend to tell lies. People are responsible for the spread of stereotypes, which is exactly what took place in Amazon. During recruitment, the AI recruiter turned out to have a bias on the grounds of gender. Because technical departments in Amazon were male-dominated, the system learned that male applicants would be favorable and ended up penalizing any resumés that were inclusive of the term "women."

5.8.1.6 Model Accuracy

AI has its errors. Human judgment finds its way into algorithms and, at times, leads to discriminatory results. As noted earlier, there are several reasons that datasets can end up being biased (Buckley and Mozur 2019). Challenges like this can make AI generate outcomes and predictions that are deficient in precision and accuracy. Bad reasoning can also be counted as an additional cause of mistakes by AI. With AI systems being advanced, it can be progressively challenging to comprehend the network's procedures. If an AI system makes a mistake, it becomes hard to pinpoint the precise place that something went amiss.

Imagine a situation where the decision concerns a self-operated car making an unexpected turn or avoiding to hit a pedestrian. In response to such challenges, experts had to come up with developments like Whitebox Testing. Whitebox Testing was developed for deep learning systems. This development is responsible for testing the neural network using a large number of inputs and pinpoints, at which point the reactions are faulty and need to be mended. The big question is whether the mistakes that are made by AI are harmful. It has become certain that this is not always the case. This is all reliant on how the system is put to use. If AI is used for driving vehicles, cybersecurity, and military use, then there is a lot more to lose. If the system settles on a man's choice as opposed to that of a woman with the same capacity in skills, then it becomes an ethical matter. However, in some instances, the mistakes made are very silly.

5.8.1.7 People

Deficiency in the comprehension of AI with non-technical personnel is an issue. The implementation of AI needs the management to have an inner comprehension of contemporary AI tech. This ought to be inclusive of their restrictions and prospects. Regrettably, the AI world is full of a series of misconceptions regarding AI. This ranges from ordinary matters like the necessity to hire an in-house data expert to sci-fi caprices concerning smart robots' eventuality, bringing an end to humanity (Ford and Colvin 2015). This deficiency in

AI proficiency and knowledge slows down the adoption of AI in some sectors. An additional everyday mistake resulting from this lack of understanding is working with impossible objectives in mind. The most fundamental way of bringing a solution to this problem is, to begin with, education. At first thought, this solution could be a little discouraging, but education does not directly translate to becoming a data expert. However, it is vital to take a critical look around the industry and take note of the significant players and identify the use cases they have deployed. Learning about the prevailing prospects of AI is essential, whether through personal effort or using insight from an AI expert. When a little bit of knowledge is gained, it will be easier to manage prospects because it will be evident what AI can and cannot make available for respective businesses.

5.8.1.8 Deficiency of Field Experts

To come up with an efficient AI solution and platform, there is a need for available business perspective comprehension and technical proficiency. Inopportunely, in most cases, it is one or the other. In most cases, business managers and CEOs lack the technical skill needed to pull off AI adoption. On the other hand, most data experts are not interested in how the models will work in everyday life. The number of AI specialists who know how to apply the tech developed in a specific business challenge is minimal. In addition to that, there are also very few data scientists as a whole. Companies aside from Apple, Google, Facebook, Amazon, and Microsoft are going through hurdles to attract prominent skills. Even in cases where they are making an effort to come up with an in-house team, they are never sure that their manpower is qualified and equipped to deal with the job description. It is hard to know if top-quality solutions are being made available if there is no adequate technical know-how. Medium and small businesses may be deficient in the concept of AI adoption for reasons of restricted budgetary allocations. Despite this, outsourcing a data team has grown to become a viable option in the present.

5.8.1.9 Business

Suppose a company or business culture does not make room for AI requirements, together with challenges in pinpointing business use cases. In that case, they are part of the most significant hurdles to implementing AI. Identifying AI business cases requires managers to have intrinsic comprehension of AI tech with their prospects and restrictions. The deficiency in AR proficiency could act as an impediment to AI adoption in several corporations. At this point, another challenge arises. Some companies take on the AI prospect with just a little bit too much optimism with a clear approach. The implementation of AI needs a strategic method, putting in place objectives, pinpointing Key Performance Indicators (KPIs), and keeping track of the Return on Investment. If this is not done, it may be hard to evaluate the results reeled in by AI and compare the assumptions to assess the success or otherwise of the investment.

5.8.1.10 Challenges in Evaluating Vendors

Like employing data experts, in the deficiency of technical proficiency, it is easy to be fooled. AI in businesses is a relatively emerging field. It is specifically susceptible to numerous corporations making exaggerations on their experience when in fact they may have inadequate knowledge of how to use AI to solve actual business challenges. A perfect idea in such a case is to use Clutch's websites to pinpoint leaders in the development of AI. It is also a good idea to look at what corporations are considered to have in their portfolio. An additional strategy would be to start with a simple initial step in the right direction, which can be in the form of a workshop with the vendor that is considered the most promising. In this way, it will be possible to ascertain whether the vendor understands the business's strategies, has the needed skills, and takes care of the company's needs.

5.8.1.11 Challenges with Integration

Incorporating AI into a prevailing system is a procedure that is more complex than just adding a plugin into a browser. The elements and interfaces that are to be used in addressing business requirements have to be put in place. A section of the guidelines is hard-coded. There is also a need to consider the needs of infrastructure, labeling, data storage, and feeding information into the system (Lieto, Lebiere, and Oltramari 2018). After that, there is model training and making tests on the efficiency of the AI developed, thereby coming up with a feedback loop to continually enhance models founded on people's data sampling and actions to bring down the quantity of data in storage-run models more swiftly. At the same time, there is a need to keep on giving precise outcomes. The question arises on how one is supposed to know if this model is working and if the whole process is a feasible approach. It is important to join efforts with the vendors to ensure that everyone has a lucid comprehension of the procedure. It will likewise need the vendor to have a wider skill span and not just be restricted to the construction of models. With AI implementation being done using a strategic approach and performed in a step-by-step manner, the danger of failure is managed. After the successful incorporation of AI into the system, there will still be a need to offer training to people to enable them to learn how to use the model and interpret the results obtained. The vendor ought to advise on how to go about daily use of the model and make suggestions on how to make developments on AI if it is possible to do so.

5.8.1.12 Legal Matters

Various things have to be put under consideration before going on to implement AI into a business. At times, the legal system becomes difficult to maintain technology development and matters arise at this point. What happens in the case where AI results in damage? If someone gets hurt or something gets damaged due to AI, then who is supposed to be accountable in such a situation? Is it the company that developed the AI application or is it the company that ordered it? At the moment, there happens to be a lack of guidance on what has to be done in such instances (McCauley 2007). An additional matter is the issue of the General Data Protection Regulation (GDPR). With GDPR, data has grown to be a commodity that needs to be handled with a lot of care, although there could be a challenge in gathering data. There is the question of what type of data can be gathered, as well as finding the best way to handle big data in a GDPR-compliant manner. There is also the matter of sensitive data that might not look so sensitive at first glance. Even though this might have legal implications, it is still a challenge that can harm a business; for example, any data whose leakage poses a threat to the business's status or its stature ought to be regarded as sensitive. For example, take the instance of when the data related to personnel training and courses finds its way out of the system. This situation, at first, might not seem threatening. However, when there is some type of ordinary position, like training on bullying at the workplace, the information could be the subject of misinterpretation. It can result in damage to the operations of the company.

5.9 Funding Trends in Artificial Intelligence

With the ever-increasing need for the use of AI in the commercial sector, the race to get AI tech and start-ups is steadily going up. From agriculture to retail, significant companies in almost every sector are making efforts to incorporate machine learning into their products. Most probably, as a consequence, machine learning can be found at the head of AI tech investments (Mou 2019). Machine learning instead of learning with regards to logic and rule takes place using experience and surveillance. Instead of having a programmer in charge of writing commands to resolve a problem, the program then comes up with a personal algorithm grounded on example information and output that is desired.

Most importantly, the machine is in charge of programming itself. Looking back to January of 2019, a sprouting technology research organization called Venture Scanner evaluated well over 2000 AI start-ups and grouped them into 13 functional groups that cumulatively managed to raise $48 billion in funding from 2011. Start-ups coming up with machine learning applications account for half of this monetary support. These corporations make use of computer algorithms to enhance a section of their operations routinely. These companies include Drive.ai, CustomerMatrix, Cylance, and Ayasdi. A lot of additional AI classifications have pioneered and put out massive prospectives for development and progress. Maybe as a result of this speedy development in the AI sector, there is, at the moment, a small shortage of AI proficiency in several workforces.

In turn, this is putting a gas pedal to the race to get hold of early-stage AI corporations with a favorable tech and workforce. Significant acquisitions include the purchase made by Amazon of Sqrrl, an AI cybersecurity startup, and the acquisition of Zenedge, a cybersecurity company, by Oracle. Even though tech giants keep searching for AI skills and technology, retail, customary insurance, and healthcare officials are eying the same prize. Some of the most significant deals ever made in AI history include acquiring New York-based Flatiron Health for $1.9 billion by Roche Holdings in 2018 and the acquisition of the auto tech startup Argo AI for over $1 billion by Ford Motor in 2017. Google has come out the winner with the acquisition of AI startups with 14 acquisitions under its belt. The progress of VC monetary support has abided by the same path since 2012. Looking back at 2017 alone, AI garnered a total of $12 billion from VC corporations. This happens to be twice the amount recorded in 2016. Since 2013, a total of 42% of the AI corporations that were acquired happened to have had VC support.

5.9.1 Artificial Readiness

The big question is whether any city in the world has fully anticipated the challenges that will come together with AI. No town is equipped to deal with AI head-on because of a recent report. Despite this, together with numerous other AI prospects, dangers from its capability to substitute human personnel or otherwise from the tech's unethical employment have likewise grown to be more evident. According to the Global Cities Artificial Intelligence Disruption Index published by Oliver Wyman Forum, 105 essential cities are making preparations for the AI era. The report was written on the grounds of interviews with partners like academics and government officials. The report is meant to evaluate the readiness considering comprehensive parameters, the direction that the city is taking, a city's comprehension of AI, linked risks, its equivalent plans, and its capability to implement the objectives and asset base that have been set to rely on. In each of the four listed classifications, London, Singapore, Shenzhen, and Stockholm come first. However, not even one of these cities features in the top 20 in four categories, and none of them shows in the top 10 using more than two of the listed classifications. This translates to no city being anywhere near ready for the challenges that are yet to come. All cities need to make considerable enhancements to make preparations for the effects of the state-of-the-art tech. Evaluating AI readiness is not anything close to exact science at the prevailing time using some of the efforts in past years that have been made. At the moment, it seems like a number of the qualities that could count as making a city prepared to counter AI are in the offing are likened to those that place them high on ratings of suitable places to implement business ideas. There are three types of AI readiness.

5.9.2 Foundational Readiness

A prerequisite for AI is suitable interfaces and infrastructure. Expertise and skills could be inadequate, which is why the following ought to be taken into account:

- Cloud resources as a base for AI, specifically in areas like NLP and image.
- Infrastructure platform to comprehend whether prevailing data center facilities will be appropriate for AI workloads.
- Software packages.
- Data sources have to be accessible and available.

5.9.3 Operational Readiness

Appropriate governance and management methods are important to ensure the sustainability of AI solutions. Therefore, a review of the following is suggested:

- Cybersecurity. Possible security dangers come from the exploitation of input data into AI, interfering with the models.
- Agile delivery.
- Skills and expertise. The lack of it is a recurrent trial for establishments in the initial steps of AI.
- Governance, compliance, and risk. The association between AI and governance is multi-layered and intricate. With the expansion of its use, AI consequentially brings extra complications.
- Operational management.

5.9.4 Transformational Readiness

This could be the most critical area of readiness in AI. It is characterized by whether a company can effectively maximize its worth by using AI. AI is supposed to have either of the following effects: make automatic a section of the business process, meaning the business needs to have the ability to embrace the consequential modifications, or offer backup for enhanced decision making in the line of management. There are various ways through which the business can have the ability to embrace these changes:

- Business acceptance. The AI solution ought to be adapted to business requirements right through the everyday activities of front-line employees and the people affected.
- Business prospects. The chances of success for AI solutions are also reliant on how it unveils new prospects for growth of the business.
- Strategic leadership. It is undoubtedly essential to have the right mindset to motivate the delivery of AI solutions and models straight from the top of the business.
- Lucidity of the business case. The business case ought to be inclusive of a lucid and casted benchmark of what necessitates success.

AI is heavily based on specialized processors that support the central processing unit (CPU). The more improved and efficient CPUs might not boost the training speed of the AI model. During inferencing, the AI model requires more hardware to operate complex mathematical tasks for speeding up processes such as face detection and expression recognition. In the upcoming years, there are many chip manufacturers such as NVIDIA, Intel, ARM, and AMD that will ship special chips that would increase the processing time of AI applications. These chips are going to optimize the special cases that are related to computer vision and speech recognition. There are many chances that the healthcare and automobile industry will be relying on such applications. Hyper-scale infrastructure companies like Google and Amazon will be investing more in AI chips programs and applications such as the Application Specific Integrated Circuit (ASIC) (Tekoäly 2018).

5.10 Conclusion

AI is a software development focused on creating intelligent machines and projects. Artificial intelligence has the motivation to imitate human intelligence and perform tasks like humans. In practice, this implies the ability of a machine or program to think and learn. Typically, the term AI implies a machine or program for imitating human intelligence. Computer-aided intelligence has become an integral part of the technology business. AI experienced three phases in the historical context of AI in the 1950s: the supposed period of neural systems from 1980 to 2000, the age of machine learning, and the current deep learning era. A neural system is a type of programmed learning consisting of interconnected substances (such as neurons) that process the data as it responds to external information sources and transmits data between each element. The method requires several steps to detect associations and determine the meaning of indistinct data. Machine learning automates the development of exposure models. It uses different strategies, such as, for example, neural systems, research tasks, measurements, and materials science to discover data that is excluded from the data without appearing clearly in the view or reaching what is to be achieved. Deeper learning is more like machine learning but in a deeper dimension. The goal of deep learning is to use an algorithm to create a fearful system that can deal with the given problems. It is used in particular to solve problems in which arrangements with conventional techniques require exceptionally complex patterns. For example, through deep learning, speech, images, and content are distinguished or monitored.

An algorithm is a well-ordered strategy to tackle problems. It is constantly used for the management of data, estimates, and other numerical and Personal Computer (PC) activities. It is an accurate determination of the guidelines to perform a task or solve a problem. Algorithms can perform multiple tasks effectively and immediately if the correct data is included in the framework.

References

Buckley, C. and Mozur, P. (2019). *How China Uses High-Tech Surveillance to Subdue Minorities.* New York: The New York Times.

Ford, M. and Colvin, G. (2015). *Will Robots Create more Jobs than They Destroy?* New York: The Guardian.

Frey, C.B. and Michael, A.O. (2017). The future of employment: How susceptible are jobs to computerization? *Technological Forecasting and Social Change* 114: 254–280.

Global Market Insights (2017). Healthcare AI Market Size, Competitive Market Share & Forecast, 2024. https://www.globenewswire.com/news-release/2017/05/11/982356/0/en/Healthcare-Artificial-Intelligence-Market-worth-over-10bn-by-2024-Global-Market-Insights-Inc.html (accessed 22 June 2021).

Hinton, G., Deng, L., Yu, D. et al. (2012). neural networks for acoustic modeling in speech recognition – The shared views of four research groups. *IEEE Signal Processing Magazine* 29 (6): 82–97.

Jordan, M. and Mitchell, T. (2015). Machine learning: Trends, perspectives, and prospects. *Science*: 255–260.

Kaplan, A. and Haenlein, M. (2019). Siri, Siri, in my hand: Who's the fairest in the land? On the interpretations, illustrations, and implications of Artificial Intelligence. *Business Horizons* 62: 15–25.

Kuperman, G., Reichley, R., and Bailey, T. (2006). Using commercial knowledge bases for clinical decision support: Opportunities, hurdles, and recommendations. *Journal of the American Medical Informatics Association* 13 (4): 369–371.

Lieto, A., Lebiere, C., and Oltramari, A. (2018). The knowledge level in cognitive architectures: Current limitations and possible developments. *Cognitive Systems Research*: 39–55.

Marr, B. (2018, February 14). The key definitions of Artificial Intelligence (AI) that explain its importance. https://www.forbes.com/sites/bernardmarr/2018/02/14/the-key-definitions-of-artificial-intelligence-ai-that-explain-its-importance/#bf566164f5d8 (accessed 22 June 2021).

Marwala, T. and Hurwitz, E. (2017). *Artificial Intelligence and Economic Theory: Skynet in the Market.* London: Springer.

McCarthy, J. (1988). Review of the question of Artificial Intelligence. *Annals of the History of Computing*: 224–229.

McCauley, L. (2007). AI armageddon and the three laws of robotics. *Ethics and Information Technology*: 9, 153–9, 164.

Mohri, M., Rostamizadeh, A., and Talwalkar, A. (2012). *Foundations of Machine Learning*. London: The MIT Press.

Mou, X. (2019). *Artificial Intelligence: Investment Trends and Selected Industry Uses*. New York: EM Compass.

Prakken, H. (2017). On the problem of making autonomous vehicles conform to traffic law. *Artificial Intelligence and Law*: 341–363.

Samuel, A. (1959). Some studies in machine learning using the game of checkers. *IBM Journal of Research and Development*: 210–229.

SAS (2019). Artificial Intelligence – What it is and why it matters. https://www.sas.com/en_us/insights/analytics/what-is-artificial-intelligence.html (accessed 22 June 2021).

Schmidhuber, J. (2015). Deep learning. *Scholarpedia*: 32832.

Tekoäly (2018). Tekoälyn historia. http://xn--tekoly-eua.info/tekoaly_historia/ (accessed April 6, 2018).

TM capital (2017). The next generation of medicine: Artificial Intelligence and Machine Learning. https://www.tmcapital.com/wp-content/uploads/2017/11/TMCC20AI20Spotlight20-202017.10.2420vF.PDF (accessed 22 June 2021).

Turing, A. (1948). Machine Intelligence. In: *The Essential Turing: The Ideas that Gave Birth to the Computer Age* (ed. B.J. Copeland), 412. London: Oxford University Press.

Yao, M. (2020). The essential landscape of enterprise AI companies. https://www.topbots.com/enterprise-ai-companies-2020/ (accessed 22 June 2021).

6

AI, 5G, and IoT: Driving Forces Towards the Industry Technology Trends

6.1   Introduction

The world of Artificial Intelligence (AI), fifth-generation data networks (5G), and the rapidly growing Internet of Things (IoT) devices can be beneficial to us, but also present numerous flaws as they are all new and rapidly developing technologies. It is important to note that the 5G network has better security than the third generation (3G) and forth generation (4G) networks. Still, it has been said that some of the classic vulnerabilities and security flaws from 3G and 4G networks were directly carried over to the developing 5G network, thus presenting additional security flaws right out of the gate. Both AI and the IoT will benefit from the development of 5G networks where businesses can use such devices, which will be tied to the growing 5G network, and can serve several purposes throughout the business market, among other areas.

When it comes to consumer-based electronic devices, they are certainly on the rise. As technology improves, these devices will consume more bandwidth and data than ever before. The increase in data and bandwidth consumption from newly emerging technologies could include the ability to interpret human speech on-the-fly and identify various patterns throughout data or documents from a mobile device. This data can even adjust business efficiency, increasing overall profits with endless possibilities for automation in manufacturing. This is where the development of 5G data networks come into play. 5G networks will have the bandwidth needs for current and future data-hungry devices in a growing technological world.

AI technology is growing from ordinary scientists' simple tools to as far as the use within the professional development community for higher intelligence use. These various organizations can use AI technology to fill the current gap in the data science area, a big game-changer for data science! This also always gives end-consumers the ability to take their business and personal data wherever they go. This is a big deal when making end-consumers happy while retaining their privacy with their online data.

When it comes to data processing, with the help of 5G, AI, and the IoT, modern technology demands that data management and processing capabilities should have the data possessors brought to the data itself rather than sending the collected data processing elsewhere. This may also include the data processing and distributed data stores included within the data management process in order to guarantee that support is offered where

Intelligent Connectivity: AI, IoT, and 5G, First Edition. Abdulrahman Yarali.
© 2022 John Wiley & Sons Ltd. Published 2022 by John Wiley & Sons Ltd.

the received critical data is being stored. 5G network technology will be revolutionary to end-consumers, businesses, and data processing centers worldwide.

6.2 Fifth Generation of Network Technology

The new 5G data networks will likely introduce many new network-connected devices along with it, and many of those devices will probably have capabilities and new functions we cannot imagine. The technology is so unique that it is still in rapid development, even though some larger cities will have 5G access when this document is published. 5G networks introduce a world of technological ease and sophistication, which was not possible in the past. Multiple virtual networks can be both supported and created, which can assist various markets and corporations.

Mobile IoT can benefit from 5G because they will support more connections with increased speeds and much lower latency. This could increase overall profits or even maximize business or corporate revenue, all from a little Mobile IoT device!

5G networks will also enable drones to make quick and secure deliveries straight to customers' homes. The 5G network will help coordinate large fleets to fly safely and avoid hitting buildings and other drones en route (GSMA 2018). This would be made possible with an AI-based on-board computer that collects data via in-flight sensors, will always monitor the drone's surrounding environment, and be able to adjust to almost any situation while in flight.

The development of 5G is quite revolutionary, with high capacity, network slicing, low latency, and incredibly fast speeds (Mo 2019). With the increase in data speeds with 5G, there is a lot of "wiggle room" for bandwidth control. Since 5G has the ability for network slicing, it can control the IoT uses that have various bandwidth needs for large or small amounts of data that need to be rapidly sent over the internet.

6.3 Internet of Things (IoT)

As the IoT technology grows and develops over time, it will likely mold into a global network with securely managed devices that will be slowly integrated into our day-to-day lives. This advancement will improve the overall quality of public life as we know it. Businesses will also have access to the luxuries of 5G networks. The 5G network will become an excellent opportunity for the growth of the IoT, which will have massive bandwidth, better coverage, and overall faster speeds compared to the previous cellular networks. Figure 6.1 depicts the vast reality of IoT descriptions and definitions. As illustrated in the schematic diagram, the top right section shows sensing and data collecting IoT smart objects with an IP address. The upper left section shows the connectivity of everything via a handheld device such as a smartphone – the internet of people. The lower part of the picture shows IoT non-IP connectivity – industry IoT (i-Scoop, n.d.).

5G also has capabilities to arm and disarm security alarms, sensors, and IP cameras, with real-time, high-quality videos for enhanced remote surveillance, which could help reduce the chances of theft or crime in general. The combination of AI with the massive capacity and endless possibilities that comes with 5G networks would significantly improve sensor-based systems, decreasing overall energy consumption.

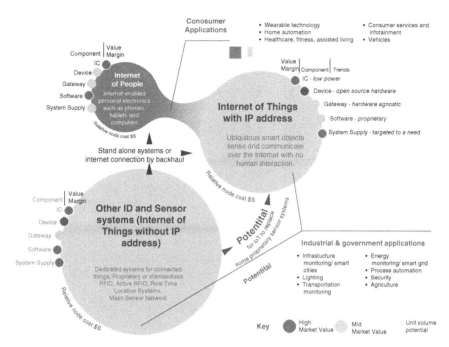

Figure 6.1 IoT map illustration and definition (i-Scoop).

It has been said that 5G, as we know it, was initially built primarily for the IoT devices and their intended uses, not just for the average consumer with a cell phone. IoT can be viewed as a "three-layer cake" in layman's terms (Mo 2019):

1) The very bottom layer where the IoT devices such as the GE engine, Google Nest, or Amazon Echo are.
2) The center layer where a communication "pipe" or network such as 5G provides internet connectivity between the devices themselves and the cloud servers.
3) Finally, the top layer where the IoT software applications are powered by AI, their algorithms, and Business Intelligence.

When it comes to IoT devices, there is no specific company or agency in charge of the IoT. Businesses and corporations will often find IoT devices and their software applications beneficial when used within a manufacturing or production environment. It should be known that the IoT devices are not an entirely separate entity from the internet itself but more of an extension or branch of the internet as we know it, which is continuing to grow daily. It has been estimated that the concept of the IoT is likely to be a widespread game-changer to the global economic system. However, it is still far too early to be certain as the IoT devices and their technology are still under rapid development.

Experts predict that IoT devices and their computing software will be revolutionary to the Information Technology fields, especially due to their small size and computing efficiency for the price (Mo 2019). When pairing IoT devices with the new 5G network, a whole new computing world in information technology (IT) will be developed for small, energy-efficient computing uses. The IoT technology even allows vehicles of all types and models to be equipped with technologies for a safer commute using an intelligent mass transportation system everywhere, all with the combined use of 5G networking technology (Fischer 2015).

The IoT devices and their corresponding technologies will make cities appear as "computers in the open air," where general public foot-traffic will have the ability to interact with the city's IoT technology systems in real-time out on the street. With the growing demand for technology, there will always be constant access to any kind of information one could ever want. Thanks to the IoT technology, these services have advanced to a whole new level with interactive technology right on the street corner. Some IoT technology experts have predicted that with the massive growth and expansion of the IoT technology, we will soon be living in an entirely "hyper-connected" society, where there will be seamless integration of everything. Perhaps this move will cause the internet to vanish and become a wholly separate phenomenon (Fischer 2015).

While they are in no way responsible for the IoT technology or the devices themselves, the United States Department of Defense has been a huge leader in the underlying development of the IoT devices and technology (Fischer 2015). Numerous other companies have assisted in the research and development of the IoT devices, but the United States Department of Defense is the largest contributor by far. The National Science Foundation has also participated in other contributing activities associated with various IoT technologies and software development.

The IoT devices are being deployed and developed daily for new uses in various industries, especially in the manufacturing sector. Some networking experts argue that the current network framework used for spectrum allocation may not benefit the IoT devices as well as it could be. For now, there are not any universally recognized technical standards for the IoT devices or their corresponding software uses, but that may change as the IoT technology grows and develops over time.

Cybersecurity for the IoT may be complicated by several things, such as the complexity and pervasiveness of networks and the increasing demand for industrial automation for cost-cutting measures, which may severely affect network security and network and device authentication. Cybersecurity legislation has addressed multiple issues concerning IoT applications, such as notification of data breaches and information sharing, but nothing has been "set in stone" for now.

- Spectrum Access Radio is a type of frequency spectrum that is considered a critical link in all kinds of IoT device communication systems. Affordable and reliable access to it is a significant requirement to accommodate the billions of new IoT devices expected to be deployed and go online, just within the next decade alone.
- According to Congressional Research, there are no official bills that have been introduced in the last two congressional meetings that directly relate to the IoT devices and their peripheral devices (Fischer 2015). Numerous bills have been introduced to Congress that refer directly to general concepts of the IoT technology, such as smart-connected vehicles, smart cities, cyber-physical systems, and the public smart-city grid. The IoT world is still under rapid development today but is expected to take off rapidly with the development of 5G networking technology to back it up.

6.4 Industrial Internet of Things

When it comes to the industrial sector of the IoT, many of these devices require extremely low latency for maximum operation efficiency, depending on their intended application. This is where 5G network technology comes into place. Low latency 5G networks are achieved initially through architecture where 5G networks only have 1 ms latency, compared to the standard Fourth Generation Long-Term Evolution (4G LTE) network with about 20–30 ms latency (Mo 2019). The 5G network is revolutionary when it comes to the Industrial Internet of Things (IIoT).

5G with the IIoT is a merger of the internet, intelligence, and electronic devices, all of which will be routed through the developing 5G network. It could help reduce the chances of theft or any other crime in general with devices that operate on the 5G network and support more connections with increased speeds and much lower latency. AI will have the ability to better grow and function efficiently with 5G technology that can make any process more efficient and improve our overall quality of life. The evolution and widespread use of 5G and AI technology is heavily anticipated, which is suspected to be revolutionary as the technology ages and is eventually perfected and implemented globally.

With the IIoT, businesses could be remotely operated and/or managed from the other end of the world at any time, if needed! With the intelligent connectivity of the IIoT, a business firm can interact with customers from any part of the world at any given time, leading to an increase in sales and an overall rise in the profit margin with reduced costs throughout the business.

- The data collected from IIoT devices can help businesses understand customers better and even bring in changes in various areas of the company to suit future consumer needs. This level of personalized customer experience is the only thing that will differentiate a specific brand from the rest of the industry, with an increase in financial income and profits and a positive impact on a company with higher conversion rates and an overall increase in customer loyalty. This approach is key to a striving company in today's evolving and monopolizing market.
- Digitization with IIoT devices can bring in that uniqueness to a business and offer unique opportunities to corporations to re-position their company in the market while creating advanced service offers for current and future customers. This move can make a business stand out from the rest of the market by using the IIoT devices efficiently.
- As businesses and corporations are rearranging themselves in the digitalization sector and making the shift towards intelligent connectivity with the smart IIoT devices, this is also a good time to be re-positioned in today's market by understanding customers' trends and demands. It is essential to understand consumer needs with 5G network technology, consumer IoT devices, and personalized and innovative services for the average person. This is key to a striving and successful company and consumer in today's growing and revolutionizing market, using the IIoT devices and 5G network technology.

6.5 IoT in the Automotive Industry

It has been predicted that technological advancements and changes will have significantly increased in the automotive industry alone in the next decade. In the automotive industry, end-consumer demands must be met in full for a modern-day tech-filled experience when researching, purchasing, and driving a new automobile. Today's technological advancements, combined with the development of the IoT technology, put the automotive industry under a lot of pressure for a rapid transition to modern technology in a vehicle. That is why inventions such as the IoT devices and AI make such a huge impression on today's automobile industry. The primary focus for auto manufacturers will be on smart-connected automobiles using the IoT technology. All this combined suggests new and revolutionizing trends applied within the automobile industry yearly.

- The consumer's overall automotive experience is being customized to their needs with modern technology trends. Unfortunately, these trends also pose numerous security risks and vulnerabilities. These technological advancements in the automobile industry are being implemented much sooner than expected. The automobile industry today has already been permanently changed, for good. We already have basic smart connected automobile technology and fully electric cars paving the path for more advancements soon!
- Of course, these modern automobile trends are still under rapid development today. Nevertheless, these developments and trends will likely forever change the basic automotive industry's manufacturing processes and how we use and operate these smart-connected automobiles as drivers. Unfortunately, the automotive manufacturing industry has recently decided to move away from national and regional manufacturing/production of certain cars for a broader connection and approach to the overall automotive manufacturing technology supply chain.

The trucking industry already utilizes many modern technological advancements with the IoT and smart-connected sensors to allow drivers and their employers to view and monitor the truck's information in real-time to ensure fuel efficiency and driver and truck safety.

Additionally, Lyft and Uber's services have started a new trend from owning personal vehicles for a service-based "private" transportation versus taking the local public transit bus. Partnerships are also rapidly growing with these ride-sharing companies. Online rumors say Volkswagen is currently developing its ride-sharing application, as well, although, if true, the development could fall through or become another top competitor in that market. This trend is just the start of the ever-growing ride-sharing path!

As we know, the automotive industry has made a considerable shift from a product-centered to a data-driven industry combined with the fusion of AI, IoT technology, and Big Data in this industry. New technology for predictive maintenance is based on unique sensors combined with the IoT technology that records and logs data on the automobile's current performance in real-time. The data is then sent to the "cloud," where any potential malfunctions of a vehicle's hardware, software, and physical components are evaluated.

After this recorded information is reviewed and processed automatically, the driver will then be notified of any necessary mechanical or software services to have completed in order to avoid any incidents or potential permanent damage to the automobile internally or electronically. This eliminates any guesswork when it comes to vehicle maintenance or repair, including anything else mechanically! Drivers can immediately be notified of any potentially serious on-board issues.

The system software can also predict any issues before they happen, thanks to AI technology. This is also likely to reduce the vast number of recalls that occur every year for newer vehicles. This system is likely to become so advanced that it will track something as simple as tire wear with carefully placed wheel-well sensors combined with AI and IoT technology. With over-the-air technology in automobiles, dealers and automobile companies can track common issues with their automobiles in real-time, a serious game-changer with safety in the automobile industry and manufacturing processes.

Another possibility with the combination of AI and the IoT technology is remote wireless service from anywhere at any given time. A digital interface in automobiles allows continuous over-the-air updates to automobile software. This eliminates the current necessity of having to go to the dealership with your car to have the computer software fixed and reprogrammed, assuming they even do it at all! This remote technology also allows for software fixes that could increase fuel efficiency or save battery life in all-electric automobiles.

Tesla's automotive manufacturing company already has this remote technology feature in their automobiles with "over-the-air" updates. Their incorporated automobile technology gives their vehicles the ability to connect to the consumer's home wireless network, where Tesla automobiles can receive software updates just as soon as the updates are released. Their cars receive regular updates that add new features and enhance existing ones over wireless networks (Tesla 2019).

It is no secret that the automobile industry is now the largest data-driven industry globally, next to data information security and protection. Today's world wants the ability to take modern technology wherever we go. Almost all new vehicles come with a wireless internet connection function; this means premium security is also needed and automobile manufacturers understand that.

Data security and overall protection are critical, so data security is always a top priority for technological advancements, especially in the automobile industry. Mass, rapid, widespread changes in the automobile industry still present considerable challenges during the initial development phase. In addition, the overall improvements and end-consumer benefits of these modern technological advancements significantly outweigh any of the challenges that come with them.

As most of us already know, basic, reliable automobiles that only get us from point A to point B are not the only top priority for automotive manufacturers. It also includes mass amounts of technology mixed in. These modern changes and technological improvements impact product development significantly. Although it is still the automobile industry's task to design and manufacture contemporary, reliable vehicles, the new mixture of old manufacturing techniques and new smart technologies requires placing modern-day automotive engineers under tremendous amounts of pressure. As the automotive industry makes a significant change towards modern technological product development in the manufacturing process, the pressure will only increase for it to be completed faster, more efficiently, with a shrinking budget, while produced in mass quantities with fewer resources available. This new trend is only getting started for the automotive side of the IoT.

6.6   IoT in Agriculture

As discussed so far, the IoT has drastically revolutionized and changed how we live and how we operate in areas such as the general manufacturing industry, smart-connected vehicles, and smart-connected cities. Taking all the IoT technology and specifically applying it to the agricultural sector as a whole is where we will all see an enormous impact, even as supermarket produce consumers.

The agricultural industry can use wireless sensors combined with the IoT devices that use specialized communication techniques to process and analyze gathered field information to improve the agricultural industry. Specialized sensors are available for specific agriculture applications, such as soil preparation, crop status, irrigation, and insect and pest detection, which can help the farmers throughout the crop growth stages, from sowing until harvesting, packing, and transportation. The use of unmanned aerial vehicles for crop surveillance and basic field monitoring for optimizing maximum crop yield can drastically change crop production for the agricultural industry.

"The global population is set to touch 9.6 billion by 2050" (Anonymous 2018). With the global population expected to grow to such numbers, the agricultural industry must team up with the IoT technology to accommodate such a rapidly growing and demanding population. With the fusion of IoT devices, commercial and independent farmers will both be able to take advantage of modern technology to cut costs and reduce overall waste and help save the environment from potentially aggressive and unfair farming practices.

As farmers adopt IoT devices with their farming techniques, the overall crop yield will significantly increase. The adoption also includes using wireless field sensors to monitor crops for their health or merely recording yearly local weather patterns to more accurately predict planting a specific type of crop to increase maximum quality and quantity upon each harvest. These sensors can include the ability to detect soil preparation, crop status, irrigation, insect/pest detection, light, humidity, temperature, soil moisture, etc. (Anonymous 2018). The use of wireless IoT sensors alone can help increase crop yield, resulting in increased profits while saving the process's environment.

Although we must face it, this is the real world we are talking about. Integrating this modern IoT technology with decades-old traditional farming techniques and practices is not always going to be easy, or sometimes even possible at times. Farmers do need to be willing to accept change for modern technology to operate at its best for maximum results. The IoT and the world of agriculture can be a great duo together if used correctly. Some older generation farmers may fear new technology such as this, which is very understandable. In general, the IoT devices or technology can be overwhelming to older generation farmers used to basic traditional farming practices with minimal to no advanced modern technologies in the mix. The willingness to accept a modern change is a huge benefit to everyone, even the environment!

IoT devices and their attached wireless sensors can offer unique communication techniques that can be coordinated together for a farmer's specific application, such as soil quality, crop health, or even livestock and their health for the cattle farmers. These various IoT devices and their sensors can be programmed to collect any kind of data necessary to enhance the agricultural experience, which results in better control over internal processes and variables with reduced production risks in the end. IoT devices equipped with AI technology operating on 5G network technology can easily predict the outcome of crop health, yield, and overall growth progress before the crop is even close to harvest. The same can be done with livestock farmers, such as cattle farmers. Specialized wireless sensors can use AI technology to monitor, predict, and log future livestock health and overall wellness outcomes. These sensors can also monitor any new or developing diseases livestock are subject to in the outdoors. This technology can find and track these diseases in the beginning stages before livestock shows any visible signs of illness, often too late for a cure. This advanced technology allows farmers to take immediate action much sooner than before, potentially lifesaving for livestock, preventing livestock farmers' additional financial losses, and thus increasing yearly profits over time.

One of the most popular wireless IoT sensors is the Weather Monitoring Station (Aleksandrova 2018). These stations can collect and monitor local ambient air temperature, humidity, and moisture levels over a specified period. AI technology combined with the IoT devices can then use this recorded information to predict the highest yielding crop type for that year that should be sown for maximum farmer's profits and minimum resource waste upon harvest. This smart connectivity through 5G wireless will provide precision farming.

Another popular IoT device technology used in agriculture is Greenhouse Automation (Aleksandrova 2018). The weather station sensors previously mentioned can be attached to irrigation equipment and/or lighting systems via wireless or Local Area Network (LAN) network technology and be controlled and operated to match specific pre-defined system parameters to maintain or improve crop health. There is a benchmark or normal data comparison with crop health conditions, whether it be soil moisture or specific lighting conditions necessary for a specific crop to grow or improve health. Specialized IoT sensors can be strategically placed throughout crop fields to collect live data. Artificial intelligence, paired with the IoT devices, is fully automated to operate in the most efficient manner possible.

Cattle and livestock monitoring sensors are wearable devices directly attached to livestock to monitor their health and log performance over time (Aleksandrova 2018). These sensors can monitor livestock body temperature, activity, health, and each cow's nutrition intake with down-to-the-minute live data. This data collection can be paired with the IoT technology to help farmers know what feed is best for a breed of livestock or know which ones are healthiest for breeding or slaughter. The use of the IoT technology in the agricultural sector has eliminated the traditional "guessing game" factor that can often be financially fatal, resulting in livestock farmers' financial losses.

One of a crop farmer's largest enemies is the inevitable insects! Thanks to modern technology, the IoT devices and their wireless sensors can monitor insects and unwanted pests. When this IoT technology is directly connected to pesticide equipment, the AI software can automatically deploy pesticide spray for crops if weather conditions are appropriate. Other sensors used for pest detection can include low-power sensors and cameras, high-power thermal sensors, fluorescence image sensors, acoustic sensors, and gas sensors (Biz Intellia 2019). These sensors can detect pests down to the smallest known species that cause crop diseases that are not even visible to the human eye!

Another advantage is the combination of AI and IoT technology, which can help crop farmers throughout crop growth stages by using a series of wireless field sensors paired with cloud computing technology. This integration will predict precisely when to plant a specific crop, based on gathered historical data from exterior on-site weather monitoring stations and their sensors. The AI technology can then use field sensors to mathematically predict when it is best to harvest the crop for maximum crop yield with minimum waste of local resources such as fuel used during the harvest and transport process.

The agricultural IoT devices can also compute how best to pack crop yield and transport it with maximum efficiency based on collected current and historical data combined with local wireless sensors. The AI technology can access local weather condition sensors mapped with current local fuel prices to identify the best day to transport the harvested crop to the local crop purchase center for maximum profit.

One of the most significant advancements using AI and the IoT technology in agriculture is the development and use of unmanned aerial vehicles (also known as drones) for crop surveillance and crop yield optimization mapping. Agricultural drones are becoming very popular in modern-day commercialized agriculture. These drones are used for precision farming with an aerial assessment of field crop health and surveillance, where standard IoT field sensors simply cannot operate. Aerial drones can map current field layouts better and analyze the soil conditions from above. The drone's altitude and image optimization quality can be selected based on the user's input.

Drones can also map objects and areas such as excess tree canopy coverage, shading crops from maximum sunlight, preventing healthy crop growth, excess field water ponding, and drainage. These issues can also cause crop growth and health issues, which can also initiate crop diseases and crop fungus. Aerial drones can be equipped with heat-mapping technology to scan crop fields from above and assess crop growth statistics where improvements can be made in the future (Aleksandrova 2018). The possibilities are nearly endless with agriculture-oriented aerial drones.

Like agricultural aerial drones, unmanned full-size aerial vehicles can be used in agriculture for various large-scale tasks. One of the most common uses is to spray field crops from above. Using an unmanned aerial vehicle allows farmers to spray pesticide or fertilize crops, even if field conditions are not favorable for traditional land-based man-operated spraying equipment. The unmanned aircraft can map out exactly how much pesticide or fertilizer to spray on each acre of the crop to maximize efficiency and minimize product waste. While spraying, the aircraft can also monitor and log current field conditions from an aerial perspective. AI and the IoT system can combine this collected information from field sensors and aircraft sensors and create a detailed live report on current field and crop conditions on-demand. Farmers can then use this collected data to know when and where to make corrections to field soil or where conditions may not be favorable for optimum crop growth.

The IoT has drastically changed and revolutionized how we live our day-to-day lives in areas such as the manufacturing industry, smart-connected cities, and even smart-connected vehicles. Taking all this modern IoT technology and applying it to the agricultural industry, operating on the 5G network, is where the largest impact is made that affects all of us. The agricultural industry can use wireless sensors with the IoT devices paired up with unique communication techniques to analyze and process collected current and historical field and crop information to improve the agricultural industry overall. This process results in less waste, environmental protection, and maximum profits from crop harvests.

Specialized sensors are available for specific agricultural applications, such as soil preparation, crop growth, health status, irrigation equipment monitoring, and insect and pest detection. These can help crop farmers throughout the crop growth stages, from sowing until harvesting, packing, and transportation. Finally, unmanned aerial drones and vehicles for crop surveillance or other favorable applications are important. Unmanned aircraft for crop production is a rapidly growing trend that can be used to optimize crop yield and aerial drone monitoring of field conditions, which can drastically change crop production and how much profit is made. Applying IoT devices and AI technology to the agricultural industry is where the biggest impact will be made.

6.7   AI, IoT, and 5G Security

Almost everything electronic that we see or use in our daily life will need some form of cybersecurity behind it. Even when we are offline just shopping around in the mall, there are IP cameras and many other digital devices. Security specialists who protect them from hacker intervention do not enhance this protection on a frequent and regular basis. The potential vulnerabilities of today's digital world should not cause any paranoia, but digital security basics are worth learning for everyone who uses modern civilization's benefits. Software updates and patches have become more important as technology has progressed and become more sophisticated over the years. They have numerous benefits like obvious security patches and add new features to user devices and other new software. These updates and patches to the IoT devices and AI software are now possible to do at revolutionary speeds, thanks to 5G network technology.

Firstly, what exactly are software updates and security patches? "Patches are software and operating system (OS) updates that address security vulnerabilities within a program or product" (NCCIC 2019). This means that software and firmware developers will often push out updates to provide security fixes and fix potential performance bugs throughout their software. It is also important to remember that hackers will often spoof work-related emails about out-of-date programs or computer software that will either contain a virus or provide a link to a malware-infected program disguised as an urgent "update."

There are no specifically defined standards for software updates and security patches. However, it is a very good practice in the information technology security field to maintain software/firmware updates and security patches. As most know, hackers love security flaws. Therefore, it is essential to keep the latest updates on any device no matter how often it is used. Hackers often write malware and viruses into code, so unprotected users become infected online if they click or download the wrong thing online. Suppose a device is connected to the internet in any way. In that case, it is fair game and vulnerable to hackers at any time, especially if the device is not updated regularly, which hackers often rely on. "These might include repairing security holes that have been discovered and fixing or removing computer bugs" (Symanovich 2019). It is always good to make sure your device runs the latest firmware with the most recent security patches to ensure the most cybersecurity while connected to the internet. This is the easiest step anyone can take to prevent hacker intervention.

Most computers are set to download new updates by default, but the average user is often guilty of clicking "install later" when the new updates window appears and is ready to install. This is an extremely bad habit for anyone to get into. This often happens because some updates and security patches can take longer than usual to install and ultimately disrupt what we are currently working on. Delaying updates far too often could reveal some significant security loopholes in older software/firmware that hackers love to take advantage of. The most recent Equifax data breach where more than 143 million American social security numbers were exposed had a well-known security vulnerability in one of their web applications. There was a fix for this well-known security vulnerability two whole months before the security breach occurred. Still, the Equifax security team failed to update their company software when the update was released for their systems (Davis 2017). This is a perfect example of why you should never delay software updates and security patches when available.

If your device contracts a virus or some form of malware, you have the potential to pass the infection on to other friends, family, and even work-related computers and devices. For example, suppose you forward what appears to be a legitimate email about an online work account to other co-workers or even your work email. In that case, you can infect other computers and devices as that infected email is opened and passed around. It is essential to maintain updates and security patches on your computers and maintain updates on your computer's anti-virus software and spam filters.

The future of device security updates is on the horizon. Updates will likely become fully automated in the future and be processed significantly faster, reducing overall downtime to install security updates and patches. Of course, no one can predict the future, but frequent updates will be vital to surviving an online world without hacker intervention as technology progresses with time. Most software, such as anti-virus programs, have automatic update features. These programs can still only do so much if you never update the device firmware to patch potential security holes. Make your best efforts to habitually check for updates manually on programs and firmwares that do not have automatic update features. Leaving any stones unturned could be a loophole to a network-wide security breach, which can be an extreme hassle for network security admins to resolve.

Businesses are some of the most vulnerable places subject to security attacks. "The 'gold standard' for the implementation of critical patches is 30 days and 90 days for non-crucial patches." (Security 2019). However, 30 days is still more than long enough for cyber attackers to damage when security loopholes are exploited. Unfortunately, many businesses and corporations approach things as "if it is not broke, do not fix it," and this business mentality can be the beginning stages of a virtual network disaster to that business. To a degree, some corporations cannot afford to shut down network operations at any given time to install updates and security patches, although downtime for the installation of network security patches and updates far outweighs any downtime due to a network-wide security breach.

It is vital to understand which software updates are necessary to install and which ones are not quite as vital for installation. It is overall good practice anyway to install any new software, firmware, or driver updates. Only apply automatic updates from trusted network locations (NCCIC 2019). This means only download the latest updates from trusted, reputable sites. Do not attempt to download updates from email attachments containing an "update" file or link to one somewhere on the dark web. Suppose you cannot install trusted updates over a secure network, such as your home or work network. In that case, it is best practice to set up a Virtual Private Network (VPN) connection for a fully encrypted online activity and then download the new updates.

Automatic updates are extremely important. For example, in 2012, the WannaCry ransomware attack hit more than 200 000 computers and networks before a 22-year-old cybersecurity whiz identified and activated a kill switch (ITRC 2012). Microsoft had already released a security patch update several weeks before this known security flaw was exploited. Still, most companies did not have automatic updates enabled, so the known security flaw could be patched. Software developers are often the only ones aware of any new potential security holes in their software. This approach will prevent hackers from being notified of new security holes in software that have already been released to the public, where hackers could push out new viruses and attacks. If you do not update your computers and network-attached devices, everything is fair game for hackers at any given time while online.

Some updates require you to restart your computer to go into effect, and you may not be notified when this is the case (UCSC 2015). Managed networks will often have software updates and patches downloaded and installed automatically. However, suppose they are not periodically rebooted. In that case, some of those important patches may not go entirely into effect, still leaving some network desktops and laptops exposed with open security loopholes that have yet to be patched. Some could argue that this is the network administrator's full responsibility to ensure the complete installation of updates to corporation-owned computers. Still, as an employee using company resources, it would only be appropriate for them to do their part, even if it is just rebooting a computer periodically.

Not only are security updates and patches critical in an online world, but the use of End-of-Life software is hazardous. Using End-of-Life software means that it is no longer supported by its maker (Martins 2018). This means there will be no more software security patches and updates, which means this is a honeypot for hackers! First, using any programs or operating systems beyond their support end date is the same as inviting hackers into the front door. Using software or firmware beyond its support date is never a good idea, especially in any business environment.

Secondly, using any End-of-Life software can also create compliance violations during an Information Technology (IT) audit. The IT department in any business setting must follow well-defined regulations to comply with any future audits. These audits are in place to ensure that large-scale businesses implement the highest security measures possible to reduce or eliminate as many potential security threats as possible. Using such outdated software is a direct violation of any security audit and leaves security loopholes wide open for hackers to come right in.

Thirdly, End-of-Life software can create software incompatibility issues in the future. Even if your local Information Technology Security Team has the know-how to develop security patches for End-of-Life software, there could still be compatibility issues with any other newer software business that may adopt it in the future. As a result, this could cause speed issues, efficiency problems, and/or security problems, just to name a few. These types of issues no business ever wants to come across, especially due to the use of End-of-Life software.

To wrap things up, everything electronic that we either see or use in our daily lives will need some form of cybersecurity behind it. Devices like IP cameras could be turned on us for evil use if the security specialists who protect them from hacker intervention do not enhance this protection regularly. However, it is important to remember that the vulnerabilities of today's digital world should not cause any paranoia. However, basic digital security is worth learning for everyone who uses the benefits of modern civilization and the devices that go with it. Software updates and security patches have become more important as technology has progressed and become more sophisticated over time. These updates have numerous benefits like obvious security patches and add new features to user devices and add other new software. Always keep your devices up to date to help prevent hacker intervention.

6.8 Conclusion

The world of AI, 5G data networks, and the rapidly growing IoT devices are beneficial to us. However, it presents numerous flaws as they are all new and rapidly developing technologies. It is important to note that the 5G network may have better security than the 3G and 4G networks, but it has been said that some of the classic vulnerabilities and security flaws from 3G and 4G networks were directly carried over to the developing 5G network, thus presenting additional security flaws. Both AI and the IoT will benefit from the development of 5G networks where businesses can use such devices, which will be tied to the growing 5G network, and can serve several purposes throughout the business market, among other areas.

When it comes to consumer-based electronic devices, they are certainly on the rise. As technology improves, these devices will consume more bandwidth and data than ever before. The increase in data and bandwidth consumption from newly emerging technologies could include the ability to interpret human speech on-the-fly and identify various patterns throughout data or documents from a mobile device. This data can even adjust business efficiency, increasing overall profits with endless possibilities for automation in manufacturing. This is where the development of 5G data networks come into play. 5G networks will have the bandwidth needs for current and future data-hungry devices in a growing technological world.

AI technology is growing from average scientific simple tools to as far as to use within the professional development community for higher intelligence use. These various organizations can use AI technology to fill the current gap in the data science area, a big game-changer for data science. This also always gives end-consumers the ability to take their business and personal data wherever they go. This is very important in making end-consumers happy while retaining their privacy with their online data.

When it comes to data processing with the help of 5G, AI, and IoT devices, modern technology and its data often demand data management and processing capabilities. This may also include data processing and distributed data stores. All must be included within the data management process to guarantee that support is offered where the received critical data is being stored. 5G network technology will be revolutionary to end-consumers, businesses, and data processing centers worldwide.

References

Aleksandrova, M. (2018, June 10). *IoT in Agriculture: Five Technology Uses for Smart Farming and Challenges to Consider.* DZone. https://dzone.com/articles/iot-in-agriculture-five-technology-uses-for-smart (accessed 22 June 2021).

Anonymous (2018, January 3). *IoT Applications in Agriculture*. IoT for All, https://www. iotforall.com/iot-applications-in-agriculture/ (accessed 22 June 2021).

Biz Intellia (2019, January 1). *A Complete Guide for IoT Based Pest Detection with its Benefits*. Biz Intellia. https://www.biz4intellia.com/blog/a-complete-guide-for-iot-based-pest-detection-with-its-benefits/ (accessed 22 June 2021).

Davis, G. (2017, September 19). *Why Software Updates Are So Important*. McAfee. https://securingtomorrow.mcafee.com/consumer/consumer-threat-notices/software-updates-important/ (accessed 22 June 2021).

Fischer, E. A. (2015). *The Internet of Things: Frequently Asked Questions*. Congressional Research Service. www.crs.gov (accessed 22 June 2021).

GSMA (2018, September 12). *New GSMA Report Highlights How 5G, Artificial Intelligence, and IoT Will Transform the Americas*. GSMA. https://www.gsma.com/newsroom/press-release/new-gsma-report-highlights-how-5g-artificial-intelligence-and-iot-will-transform-the-americas/ (accessed 22 June 2021).

i-Scoop (n.d.) The Internet of Things (IoT) – Essential IoT business guide. https://www.i--scoop.eu/internet-of-things-guide/ (accessed 22 June 2021).

ITRC (2012, June 17). *What are Security Patches and Why Are They Important*. Identity Theft Resource Center. https://www.idtheftcenter.org/what-are-security-patches-and-why-are-they-important/ (accessed 22 June 2021).

Martins, A. (2018, June 27). *5 Risks of Running End-of-Life Software*. Mail. https://www.atmail.com/blog/end-of-life-eol-software/ (accessed 22 June 2021).

Mo, D. (2019, January 1). *Internet of Things (IoT): The Driving Force Behind 5G*. Enterprisetechsuccess. https://www.enterprisetechsuccess.com/article/Internet-of-Things-(IoT):-The-Driving-Force-Behind-5G/c1dvY3UrWTBWS3pwY0pqbEpSMHpIUT09 (accessed 22 June 2021).

NCCIC (2019, November 19). *Understanding Patches and Software Updates*. CISA. https://www.us-cert.gov/ncas/tips/ST04-006 (accessed 22 June 2021).

Security, P. (2019, January 24). *The Importance of Updating your Systems and Software*. Panda Security. https://www.pandasecurity.com/mediacenter/tips/the-importance-of-updating-systems-and-software/ (accessed 22 June 2021).

Symanovich, S. (2019). *Five Reasons Why General Software Updates and Patches are Important*. Norton Security. https://us.norton.com/internetsecurity-how-to-the-importance-of-general-software-updates-and-patches.html (accessed 22 June 2021).

Tesla (2019, January 1). *Software Updates*. Tesla. https://www.tesla.com/support/software-updates (accessed 22 June 2021).

UCSC (2015, September 1). *Install Operating System and Software Updates*. UC Santa Cruz. https://its.ucsc.edu/security/updates.html (accessed 22 June 2021).

7

Intelligent Connectivity: New Capabilities to Bring Complex Use Cases

7.1 Introduction

The term intelligent connectivity describes the combination of flexible technologies; high-speed fifth generation (5G) networks, the Internet of Things (IoT), and Artificial Intelligence (AI). These technologies work in sync with ubiquitous, hyper-connectivity, intelligent connectivity that gives the users contextualized and personalized experiences. This phenomenon will significantly impact people, industries, governments, and organizations, transforming our way of life and work. Intelligent connectivity is the newest phenomenon and promises a revolution in the way things will be done shortly. 5G networks implementation is already ongoing by the mobile operators. This will form the basis of intelligent connectivity. It will drastically improve the network capacity, responsiveness, and output. It will make it possible for the operators to tailor each application's connectivity, increasing AI applications, data analytics, and regulating the IoT (McCarthy 2015). This paper explores intelligent connectivity components, their applications in different fields, challenges, and possibilities.

7.1.1 Artificial Intelligence

Artificial Intelligence (AI) is a branch of computer science that specializes in the invention of intelligent systems. Computer scientist John McCarthy is considered to be the inventor of the term Artificial Intelligence. He had the vision of designing computer systems, computer software, and robots that work while mimicking human intelligence. John McCarthy established AI by studying human thinking, learning, decision, and work process to solve their AI challenges. After that, he used this information to write intelligent codes and systems.

AI uses the principle of exploiting computer system capabilities of speed, accuracy, and efficiency to develop programs that emulate human tendencies. The development of AI is to create specialized expert systems and develop human intelligence into computer systems (Devi, Matthew, and Sandra 2012). It conforms to computer-based intelligence by manifesting cognitive tendencies that the developers associate with other human minds. The different technologies involved in AI encompass natural language processing, machine learning, and deep learning. Cognitive computer systems involve self-adapting systems that use data

Intelligent Connectivity: AI, IoT, and 5G, First Edition. Abdulrahman Yarali.
© 2022 John Wiley & Sons Ltd. Published 2022 by John Wiley & Sons Ltd.

mining, pattern recognition, and natural language processing to mimic the human brain's operations directly. AI has cooperated in numerous areas such as internet search, commerce and trade, entertainment industries, robotics, and content optimization. The prospects of all these technologies are that they become embedded in numerous other technologies to provide independent decision making on behalf of human users through many processes, services, and products. AI has a principal role in information, communication, and technology in traditional telecommunications and digital communication-enabled applications, and has become deeply integrated into many domains of communications, applications, commerce, and content. Key sectors such as customer relationship management have been revolutionized by AI by creating chatbots representing advanced technology for automation. The traditional user interfaces have glaring deficiencies and do not scale well (Nicole and Lee 2015).

The use of chatbots will give brands, businesses, and publishers a solution to AI systems in interactions with their audiences without the need to download applications from the stores and familiarize themselves with the new user interfaces or regularly update and configure the settings. The chatbots provide the users with conversational interfaces that are more customer-friendly (Devi, Matthew, and Sandra 2012). AI is currently undertaking several transformations from silo implementations into universal utility functions in several industries as artificial general intelligence. This ability has become associated with several products, applications, services, and solutions. The mind commerce undertakes AI innovation as a diverse area that includes personalized AI to support and protect the end-users. The IoT is particularly very dependent on AI as it aids in safeguarding assets, supporting analytics, reducing fraud, and enabling automated decision-making (Nicole and Lee 2015).

Artificial intelligence is a science and technology based on disciplines such as computer science, biology, psychology, linguistics, mathematics, and engineering. A major thrust of AI is in developing computer functions associated with human intelligence, such as reasoning, learning, and problem-solving. Out of the following areas, one or multiple areas can build an intelligent system (Nicole and Lee 2015). AI's eventual capability is slowly but surely ushering a phenomenon called "the fourth industrial revolution." In this foreseeable age, the disruptions experienced across much of AI, such as physical, digital, and biological, are all merged into one huge system. This artificial intelligence goal is to build capacity to meet the demand for complex and tough problems.

7.1.2 The Fifth Generation Networks

5G networks provide higher data rates than Fourth Generation Long-Term Evolution (4G/LTE) leveraging directional antennas, millimeter-wave radio frequency, and edge computing solutions (Rappaport and Sun 2013). In addition to higher data transfer rates, the 5G provides ultra-low latency, ideally less than a 1 ms delay, which is needed for some portable or mobile apps and services, for example, haptic internet, virtual reality, industrial automation, and robotics.

The 5G network, unlike 4G/LTE, presents a focused purpose-built technology designed and specifically engineered to facilitate the connected devices and automation systems (Rappaport and Sun 2013). The 5G's prospect positions it as a facilitator and catalyst to the next industrial age, referred to as industry 4.0. There is a clear need to forecast beyond smart factories, intelligent goods, and services towards enterprise as a whole and offer new unique benefits of higher capacity urban wireless application (Rappaport and Sun 2013).

The 5G network is in a bid to improve the IoT. This is uniquely fundamental to most cellular communication providers. It provides a much more robust alternative for the IoT in a wide area networks (WAN) than the current non-cellular one (Gorozu et al. 2014). Other wireless providers/carriers are currently investing in low-power WAN for the IoT. At the same time, they are aggressively planning to provide their IoT with low powered wide area networks (LPWAN) to offer a larger bandwidth (Rappaport and Sun 2013). This higher bandwidth is important for the IoT as it is likely to impact squarely on every virtual industry. It will impact all sectors. The relationship of 5G networks and the IoT is massive (Devi, Matthew, and Sandra 2012). While some of the IoT applications require a very low bandwidth, there is a dire need to invest in 5G as the demand for this technology increases. A larger bandwidth provided by 5G networks will provide the high quality of service (QOS) required in artificially intelligent systems for several IoT value-added services (VAS) (Rappaport and Sun 2013). The 5G network can provide ubiquitous and highly reliable demanding services with almost zero delays (Figure 7.1).

7.1.3 The Internet of Things

The Internet of Things is the concept of connecting several essential items to the internet through sensor tools and devices to accomplish an intelligent recognition and management of networks (McCarthy 2015). The general idea is to have ordinary objects tagged with extra sensory and communication interfaces to make a smart system that is controlled online. The internet's vision is to target a setup where the internet is extended into the physical world, connecting the objects. The IoT allows the communication of essential parameters such as

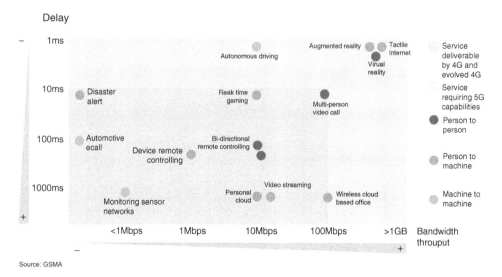

Source: GSMA

Figure 7.1 The most demanding 5G services (GSMA 2019).

the real-time state, location, and environmental conditions of its components (Lily, Chan, and Wang 2013). The IoT component is a wireless sensory network and an additional radio frequency technology used for identification by the user. This idea has been implemented in various departments such as energy efficiency, virtual property office, logistics, barcodes in outlets, mobile phone applications, and tachographs for individual road charging.

The IoT is a network used to connect everything, allowing access to these components remotely anytime and anyplace (Lily, Chan, and Wang 2013). It utilizes sensory components attached to a transmission device, enabling accurate operation, convenient transmission, accurate awareness, and intelligent processing. The use of sensors has enabled objects to become smarter. With an inbuilt networking capability, the objects communicate their immediate state to both the users and allow access to other online services. The internet is wireless sensor technology, micro-sensors, Radio Frequency Identification Chips (RFIC), nanotechnology, connection internet technologies, and artificial intelligent systems. Technology has become smaller, cheaper, and more efficient in energy consumption (Siddique and Tabassum 2015). This has led to more connection with human wants and needs, making the experience ubiquitous. This technology is unrivaled in the fields that utilize remote, automated monitoring, and remote data mining, efficient control, and real-time data interpretation.

The development of the IoT has always been focused on engineering perspectives and focuses on controlling machines to achieve desired results. The technology that has always been employed is Radio Frequency Identification (RFID) tags in conjunction with a global EPC (electronic product code) (Tommi 2015). The RFID is a combination of a minute microchip, which is tagged to a wireless antenna. These tagged objects help a reader to interpret and aggregate the gathered data. The data is then fed into a suitable application, which in turn sends the desired command. The use of the EPC network and standards enable the infrastructure to identify RFID tagged objects. Once the tagged objects' data are gathered, the system simplifies the processing and transmission in real-time (Tommi 2015). All these processes are supported by a wireless sensor network hosted by an energy-efficient multihop Wireless Personal Area Network (WPAN). The RFID systems are minute in size and very economical. They are considered appropriate for use in closed-loop applications such as logistics within an organization.

There are different layers of infrastructure on the IoT. The layers are divided into four layers each. These layers build a sense of the significance of the IoT in businesses, civic and government spaces, and end-user spaces (Siddique and Tabassum 2015). The four layers are:

1) The hardware layer includes the devices where data is produced, e.g. microprocessors, meters, sensors, actuators, and communication hardware.
2) The software layer is the layer that manages all the connected devices. It involves codes that provide the required data integration and interface to other systems (Devi, Matthew, and Sandra 2012).
3) The communication layer is the part of the infrastructure that connects the hardware to the network through a proprietary or open-source communication protocol. It is the route where data are both transmitted and received.
4) The application layer enables the IoT services to be run on smartphones, personal computers, tablets, and other devices. This layer actualizes these technologies' purpose by adding value by making routine jobs easier, efficient, and anticipating the future.

The IoT comprises uniquely recognizable objects plus their virtual representation in a structure that is internet-like. The idea involves the notion that several gadgets and assets around us can be labeled for various special purposes (Gorozu et al. 2014). The technological world is migrating from singular standalone devices into an age where things are connected through the infrastructure of things. This technology has a huge impact on products, services, and remedies across all industries (Siddique and Tabassum 2015).

7.2 Machine-to-Machine Communication and the Internet of Things

Both of these technologies, Machine-to-Machine (M2M) communication and the IoT, refer to the intercommunication between devices to achieve given goals. M2M involves isolated cases of device-to-device signaling and communication. This is usually in a limited geographical space. The IoT is more of a larger scale that works in synergy with vertical software stacks to automate and manage communication between several devices and objects (McCarthy 2015).

Machine-to-machine communication, popularly known as M2M, entails a linear signaling and communication channel operating between different machines to enable them to operate in synchrony in the form of a work cycle. This model is more of a cause-and-effect correlation in which a single signal through action triggers the other connected devices into action. In the technology field, M2M communication is referred to as a subset of the IoT, and others view the IoT as an evolution of M2M communication. Either way, both of these technologies share principles of inter-signaling and communication of different domains in a system. M2M technology is applied in offices, malls, workplaces, and several other places to control electrical appliances such as fans and bulbs through radio frequencies or Bluetooth from smart gadgets (Siddique and Tabassum 2015).

The IoT as a system is a network of multiple devices that communicate using sensors and digital connectivity. These devices work in tandem and enable the users access to a combined network of services accessible over the internet. The devices used by both systems are sensors, embedded systems, actuators, and other connected elements. The IoT tags most of the devices with sensors. These sensors are uniquely identified over the network platform within the internet protocols. The network of these physical machines tagged with sensors, software, and electronics ensure that the devices signal and communicate with each other and exchange data over the internet network (Siddique and Tabassum 2015).

The differences between M2M and IoT include:

1) M2M, the point-to-point communication, is usually embedded within the device hardware at the customer site. In IoT, the devices communicate using internet protocol networks by integrating with different communication protocols.
2) In M2M, most of the devices use cellular and wired networks, while in the IoT, data delivery is done through the middle layer hosted in the cloud.
3) In M2M, the devices do not rely on an internet connection, while in the IoT, the internet is a core principle in its operations.

4) M2M has very limited integration options because the devices must own corresponding communication standards. In the IoT, numerous unlimited options need a remedy capable of managing all the communications (Lily, Chan, and Wang 2013).

7.3 Convergence of Internet of Things, Artificial Intelligence, and 5G

There is an ongoing convergence of three key technologies in the technological field to revolutionize the information and communication technology world. The three technologies are the 5G cellular network, AI, and the internet (Siddique and Tabassum 2015). These technologies have a robust impact in their own right in the information communication and technology field and other major industries that have incorporated the Information and Communications Technology (ICT) departments in the recent past. Combining these three technologies is foreseen to have an endearing impact and create opportunities to enhance the user experiences for communications, several applications, digital components, and trade.

The combination of 5G, AI, and the IoT will usher in a new intelligent connectivity age. Drawing on interviews with mobile operators and analysts, this report describes the exciting services and experiences enabled by intelligent connectivity. It is forecasted that 5G connectivity will reach over a billion people globally by 2025. This will cover approximately 40% of the world population (Horvitz 2014). The intelligent connectivity involving the IoT, AI, and 5G networks will significantly change individuals, industry, and society. This will mark a new area commencement, defined by serious contextualized and personalized technological experiences. Drone technologies connected via the internet will do personal deliveries to homes, and virtual personal assistants will manage them. The three technologies will radically change the world by intelligently connecting the world, making life better (Siddique and Tabassum 2015).

Intelligent connectivity is a combination and coordination of the technologies of AI, 5G networks, and the IoT to accelerate technological innovations to provide new superior and disruptive digital services. The main vision of intelligent connectivity is to gather all digital information from devices, computers, sensors, and detectors found in the IoT. Once the information is gathered, it is processed and contextualized by artificially intelligent systems. Finally, the processed meaningful and useful information is presented to the final consumers. This process occurs through the transition on a large bandwidth network called the 5G network (Horvitz 2014). This connectivity would improve the processes of decision-making in businesses greatly and enable the realization of personalized experiences to the consumers. The main aim is to give a far richer and fulfilling interaction between individuals and their surrounding environment (Devi, Matthew, and Sandra 2012).

AI is becoming increasingly superior and sophisticated due to the great advances in computing power, programmers, and data scientists' expertise, as well as the availability of devices and machine programming languages to develop advanced algorithms. On the other hand, the IoT is becoming the main innovation in the IT world. The 5G network is the third element in a work in progress. Once complete, intelligent connectivity will become a reality (Tommi 2015). The key characteristics of 5G, which is ultra-fast and ultra-low latency connectivity, provide a base for the vision of intelligent connectivity. The connectivity of 5G networks in conjunction with the limitless data collected by the IoT devices and the decision-making and contextualization of AI technologies will revolutionize the capabilities in all industries and sectors and eventually change the world we work and live in (Clark 2015).

7.3.1 The Benefits of Intelligent Connectivity

Intelligent connectivity is primarily used to augment the capability of problems that are difficult because of human limitations. It is meant to make improvements in human duties and build the capacity to solve complex problems. The advantages include:

1) Solving problems that are limited due to human capacities. Usually, boredom and fatigue can interfere with human performance, especially if the job is in a stressful environment and goes on for a long period. Currently, most manufacturing companies have embraced artificial intelligent robots as they are cost-effective and efficient. Issues such as long working hours, stressful environments, and unsafe working conditions have been solved through automated robotics (Chin and Yeoh 2014).
2) AI systems are indisputably preferable for huge data manipulation statistics such as collecting, categorizing, and cataloging information in different working environments. These systems can surpass human understanding and cognition through the process of automating, using artificially intelligent systems, people's intelligent connectivity insights into patterns and relations that would otherwise be hard to recognize (Clark 2015).
3) In medicine, AI has been employed to understand complex pathological pathways, which have been used to develop precise interventions. Predictive models of AI programs have been developed to assist healthcare providers in processes such as triaging, early diagnosis and testing, and prognosis options.
4) Workplace automation leads to an increase in employee output. A large scope of work and leisure activities necessary for winding down has been converged using these intelligent connectivity systems. All this has led to effective artificial intelligence inefficiency and an overall decrease in the overall required work quantity. The results of an artificial intelligence-run job usually have absolute zero error (Clark 2015).
5) Intelligent connectivity systems increase the quality output, simultaneously liberating human energy for creative rather than menial activities.
6) Intelligent connectivity systems have also been employed in leisure activities by meeting interpersonal connections and personal actualization. Social artificial intelligent systems have been developed to help in the care of the elderly and in cooperated creativity tools that engage social and cultural values in an increasingly automated environment (Nicole and Lee 2015).
7) Through forming and predicting complicated interdependent systems, intelligent connectivity can be stretched to provide decision support for different future situations. Artificial systems can form automated protocols for emergency managers such as firefighters, police, and first responders. These systems help this group of managers working in this high-pressure environment to make critical decisions where people's lives are at stake.

7.4   Intelligent Connectivity Applications

There are key areas where intelligent connectivity is expected to make key changes, mainly in transportation/logistics, education, healthcare, entertainment, public safety/security, and industrial and manufacturing operations (Siddique and Tabassum 2015).

7.4.1   Industry

Industries are seriously incorporating the IoT with other key technologies in their command, such as 3D printing, huge data, and streaming analytics. The combination of the IoT and AI automates all of the processes in the industries. Key components, like stock control, supplies, purchase, and human resources can all be controlled and managed by a smart system over the IoT, which provides the basis for communication, control, and automated capture of data while data analytics processes tracts data into meaningful information. AI then automates decision making by engaging machine learning for daily efficiency and effectiveness (Siddique and Tabassum 2015).

Industries such as agriculture, automotive, and healthcare are facing radical changes due to the invention of the IoT, AI, and 5G networks. The technologies are focused on improving the existing processes and augmenting the current infrastructure. The IoT evolves to include the next generation tendencies and procedures. In the agricultural industry, the IoT is paramount in the planning and operations connected through sensors, signaling, and data analytics. They analyze and control conditions in greenhouses, maintaining them at favorable levels for an optimal harvest.

In the healthcare system, the IoT is revolutionizing healthcare providers' detection and prescription abilities. It integrates the entire healthcare plan into a single system accessible to all in a healthcare record system. AI systems can also provide possible diagnoses and prognoses about the results (Siddique and Tabassum 2015).

The IoT can set up smart infrastructure, smart homes, smart buildings, and smart cities. Internet technologies are anticipated to substantially impact the physical infrastructure to improve operational effectiveness and efficiency. One of the objectives of setting up smart cities or buildings is safeguarding assets and establishing value-added services. The intelligent application of the IoT, AI, and 5G networks is key in the expected improvement in process automation departments (Ifr.org. 2016).

In the manufacturing sector, intelligent connectivity is projected to improve output and eliminate human errors. It targets the complete reduction of operating costs and improved working conditions for the employees. This is achieved by the promotion of remote operations to industrial factories. Intelligent connectivity will lower the need for many employees, reducing the wage bill for industries while increasing the flexibility in selecting where to get the production facilities as it would be independent of the geographical availability of skilled expertise.

Intelligent connectivity will enable the automation of industrial processes as well as remote control of industrial robots. The 5G huge bandwidth and ultra-low latency with high-reliability rates will enhance the automation. Machines that learn functional algorithms can utilize signals collected from sensors and high-powered cameras along the supply chain to send an alert signal to the plant operator of inconsistencies or faults in the process. The plant operator can result in a person correcting the anomaly or, better still, it could be done automatically by artificially intelligent systems in real-time. The 5G network would make it possible for remote monitoring from supervisors of all the plant activities. The supervisors can then adjust the intelligent robot actions to perform whatever tasks are assigned to them. The intelligent connectivity would offer both visual and haptic feedback enabled by interlinked tools, for example, touch-sensitive gloves of augmented reality headsets (Ifr.org. 2016).

Intelligent connectivity will enable remote training of new employees, maintenance, and inspection of equipment. Tactically sound internet applications driven by artificially intelligent systems will enable remote inspection, maintenance, and training. Remote monitoring always leads to lower costs and reduced risks, especially in hazardous plants such as mining sites, oil rigs, and nuclear plants (Siddique and Tabassum 2015). These systems can be used in the worker's capacity in building by simulating complex work environments requiring their attention.

In intelligent connectivity, enterprises are concerned with various factors such as efficiency dealing with business operations. The main area to consider is the transition from traditional enterprise resource planning to an IoT-enabled enterprise resource planning (Clark 2015).

7.4.2 Transport and Logistics

The use of intelligent connectivity to provide safer and more comfortable travel is a revolution in this new era (Ifr.org. 2016). The IoT, 5G networks, and AI system signals and communicates the actual geographical positions of vehicles, pedestrians, bicycles, and buildings in real-time, reducing the chances of incidences, accidents, and collisions. The data on weather, road works, traffic, and road surface conditions are relayed in real-time from cyclist helmet or car keys combined with artificially intelligent systems to help road users to choose better routes. The 5G accompanying system enhances the driving experience through monitoring the movement of adjacent vehicles and uses the AI systems to respond appropriately, e.g. apply brakes in emergency cases or call for an ambulance automatically when accidents occur. The intelligent connectivity of the IoT, the 5G, and AI will enable reliable self-driving automobiles such as autonomous trucks that move in platoons and taxis to take people to their destinations safely. The IoT is applying for 5G network status by utilizing Low-Lower WAN on the roads (Clark 2015).

In the transport industry, intelligent connectivity will lead to a much more efficient, increased safety, and faster traffic flow. Big cities have always grappled with traffic snarl-ups. Through the combination of the IoT, AI, and 5G, there would be guaranteed smoother traffic control and flow. This combination will allow driver assistance and traffic supervision systems in a bid to reach their full operating potential (Tan 2015).

In the logistics industry of delivering mail goods and services, artificial connectivity promises improved flexibility and efficiency. Intelligent connectivity guarantees faster and cheaper delivery of goods and services. It incorporates smartphones and other technologies as wearable devices. The vehicles are a principal part of a major convergence of the three technologies: AI, the 5G, and the internet (Tan 2015). Other technologies employed might include cloud technologies, data analytics, and visualization. The technology revolves around car-to-car, car-to-infrastructures, car-to-device, and car-to-pedestrian communication and signaling. Another non-vehicle industry integration has been realized through car-to-home and car-to-grid solutions (Horvitz 2014); the collective term is car-to-everything.

Most importantly, the car-to-car interface is mainly concerned with both public and personal safety. The IoT through signals and communication prevents collision and notifies potential dangers that could affect several road users. The car-to-pedestrian supports the communication and signaling to pedestrians about incoming cars in order to avoid collisions. The car-to-infrastructure prevents collision with buildings, bridges, barriers, and humans. The car-to-everything solutions provide an understanding of which commercial services and applications are invented and supported. All these interfaces are run by special artificial intelligent software (Tan 2015).

By exploiting the low latency of 5G networks, road users, drivers/pedestrians, and the roadside barriers could collect and share data in real-time. Data such as the speed of automobiles, bikes, and pedestrians, the weather, accidents, road service interruptions, traffic load, and other obstacles are collected via the internet. The intelligent traffic monitoring systems would then be used in assisting road users in enabling a smooth flow of traffic. This intelligent connectivity would help vehicles avoid collisions with other vehicles by directing the road users to the best routes to their destinations.

In the coming years, the intelligence community will enable the use of reliable automated self-driven automobiles. The automobiles will be fitted with an AI-based on-board machine that will navigate the streets based on data collected over the IoT by tagged sensors aided by wayside units and other vehicles through 5G networks. This navigation will cover all possible scenarios and situations experienced on the roads by automobiles. These self-driven cars will lead to the emergence of novel mobility-service prototypes similar to technologies as current uber taxi services tailored to driverless public transport. Public transport in this age will be more affordable than the current private or public transport. It will produce saving of money, time, and energy used in human-driven public transport.

The use of the uncrewed delivery vehicle will be made possible by the use of intelligent connectivity. 5G networks will support a large number of terrestrial and aerial uncrewed vehicles. These robots and drones will accurately coordinate deliveries and movements, avoiding accidents with other unmanned vehicles, buildings, structures, and other static objects on their paths. The drones have already been implemented as an efficient means of delivering mail and goods quickly and safely (Siddique and Tabassum 2015).

The 5G networks enable Unmanned Aerial Vehicles (UAVs) to provide affordable, quick, and secure delivery straight into the customers' homes. In coordination with the IoT and AI, the delivery system will be coordinated to fly in large fleets safely and automatically, avoiding collisions with other structures. There is the use of other drones that provide safe and secured connections, authentications, and independent navigation with HD (high definition) video accompaniment and recovery plan protocols in emergency landings (Horvitz 2014). They are particularly very appropriate where the end location is inaccessible due to a lack of road networks caused by rough or challenging terrain or congested traffic. This system has quite a low cost that is lower than a human postman and other courier services (Devi, Matthew, and Sandra 2012).

7.4.3 Healthcare

Health infrastructure has always been limited due to the sensitivity of this sector. These shortcomings provide significant possibilities for intelligent connectivity, the IoT, AI, and 5G networks. The intelligent connectivity enabled services cannot replace the healthcare professionals but play an active role, especially in remote monitoring. The patient can be tagged to monitor symptoms using AI to identify patterns in supporting the patient's symptoms. This is a very empowering role in the healthcare sector. Currently, the company MobiSante 48 has developed a mobile phone-based ultrasound system that enables healthcare workers to perform ultrasound in any location and transmit the images to diagnostics through a secure network over the IoT to give a verdict in the shortest time possible (McCarthy 2015). This model is very appropriate in rural areas where hospitals and doctors may be far away. It should be understood that this system is not to replace access to healthcare. However, it provides a layer of healthcare that comes in handy in previous cases in which patients were either having the resources to access medical care or did not have access.

Intelligent connectivity will help the realization of a more preventive healthcare solution that is more cost-effective. It will allow the healthcare providers and managers to optimize the use of their resources such as machines, time, and pharmaceutical products. Intelligent connectivity will make possible the use of remote diagnosis and surgeries, potentially revolutionizing healthcare access, which is currently limited to the medical specialties in geographical locations. This will decrease healthcare costs, eliminating healthcare tourism in which patients fly to the developed world to receive state-of-the-art healthcare (Clark 2015).

Remote healthcare monitoring and disease prevention have become a reality with the invention of 5G networks. 5G support of many connections will accelerate wearable devices to monitor the users' critical biometric parameters. Artificial intelligent healthcare systems will analyze data from the wearable devices to help establish the current health of the patient and by providing patient-tailored health recommendations and forecasts of potential future issues. Doctors will have a more detailed real-time overview of their patients' medical status, which will empower them to optimize the available resources. It helps to ensure that their clinics and hospitals are always equipped with appropriate quantities of medical devices and drugs.

The possibilities of remote diagnosis and surgical operations have always been a prospect with intelligent connectivity. The expert nature of intelligent connectivity enhanced by high-speed, low-latency, and ultra-high reliability by 5G networks will empower doctors to provide comprehensive medical examinations from a remote location accompanied by powerful audio-visual and haptic feedback (Siddique and Tabassum 2015). This will make it possible to give a diagnosis at any place and at any time. With the capacity of the IoT, 5G networks, and AI, it will be possible for surgeons to perform surgical operations remotely by signaling specialized robots.

7.4.4 Security

The governing of cities and cosmopolitan countries has always been a daunting task for law enforcement. Intelligent connectivity can make cities secure and aid law enforcement in fighting crimes. This is achieved by improving the ease and efficiency of security systems, video surveillance, and emergency responses, such as a fire response. It reduces the cost of operations at these departments (Ifr.org. 2016). Application of intelligent video surveillance and security systems over 5G networks will facilitate many security alarms, cameras, and sensors. These components will relay high-quality real-time video feeds for remote surveillance at police stations in order to assess crime scenes better. Artificial intelligent systems that will automatically analyze the facial expressions, body language, and suspects' movements will help detect and spot offenders in real-time. The system could be used in the prevention of crimes before they can happen. Through the review of past crimes, intelligent connectivity systems can help optimize crime prevention remedies. Utilizing the large amounts of 5G connected cameras in the cities will help coordinate emergencies such as fires, terror attacks, and hurricanes. The cameras could be mounted on fixed installations, moving vehicles, drones, or be body-worn. Remotely controlled automatic robots can then be used to handle cases that could be hazardous to humans, such as fires or collapsed buildings. Drones can be used for surveillance in disaster-hit regions and patrol remote borders to identify illegal immigrants or drug smugglers.

7.4.5 Smart Homes and Personal Assistant

Smart homes are internet-connected homes that give a luxurious lifestyle by automating the home and enhancing entertainment, information, and security. The smart home experiences have extended connected entertainment and office applications. The use of a smartphone could control all the appliances in the home. These domains are connected via the IoT, artificially intelligent systems, and 5G networks. The controlled systems include energy management, security management, office equipment, personal consumer electronics, and communication appliances. Smart home technologies and smart appliances connectivity will transform consumer lifestyles. Chores and asks that were difficult in the past have been made easy. Some of the chores have been turned into fun as the appliances double up as information and entertainment. Major home appliances have become easier to maintain and replace through cloud-based services that transform the appliances, making them easy to use and repair through providing information services.

Intelligent connectivity will also be used as an important solution in the application of virtual personal assistants which will help run personal chores. Powered by the combination of 5G, IoT, and AI, it is much easier and faster to retrieve information, book vocations, plane tickets, make a reservation, and purchase goods and services online.

This involves using independent agents and smart machine technology, which allows the ambient user experience for applications and services. The virtual personal assistants rely heavily on software that provides advice while interacting in a human-like fashion. This intelligent virtual personal assistant's main function concerns answering questions in an advisory role and performing specific actions on behalf of their human owners. The IoT reiterates the need as the machines interact with other components and humans independently (Horvitz 2014).

7.4.6 Wearable Technology

Wearable technology is increasingly emerging as a principal means for communication, infotainment services, military, textile, and other industrial remedies. They provide a new user interface and a convenient means of communication and signaling through the IoT. Wearable technology is forecasted to have a massive impact on the industries. It has been adopted in the clothing, sports, fitness, and healthcare sectors. In the healthcare industry, wearable devices that monitor the basic health indicators such as temperature, pressure, and heart rate have been used to monitor patients. Telemedicine and self-monitoring systems tagged with the IoT devices and AI systems are being implemented by insurance companies to optimize operating costs. The mind trade predicts an evolution from one-purpose wearing devices to wearable technology, which would act as a conduit for the larger universe of objects over the IoT (Ifr.org. 2016). The wearable devices can be employed as:

- Controls for communications and applications such as gesture, motion, and voice.
- The interface between the wireless network and other devices such as the body area network (BAN) and other connections to devices and machines.
- The man–machine interface has become the main part of the ecosystem, mainly the IoT.
- The smart wristbands will link to the world through the three technologies, with 5G networks to the immediate world to the personal work using the BAN. The discoverability of the IoT devices through wearables and wearable controls of the IoT controls is very important. This will ensure new services and products and make automation of tasks achievable and more accessible. Ambient IoT is a view that the IoT will occupy the consumer, creating the need to know what is in the outside world and control what is there with the uttermost control, privacy, and security.

7.4.7 Entertainment

The IoT, 5G networks, and AI are expected to change the design in which we consume entertainment. This intelligent connectivity can deliver 4000 and 8000 ultra-high-definition videos, three-dimensional videos, holograms, virtual reality, and augmented reality applications used in gaming and immersive television. Another fascinating idea is digital services and content for connected stadia for live coverage of sporting events, e.g. World Cups and Olympics. The idea is to have the musical performance broadcasted from the artist's perspective. The audience will be given multiple access to camera angles with the controls to replay, rewind, and overlay information on virtual reality earphones. All this is done from the comfort of one's home or office. Virtual and video games will be immersive and realistic in this era by applying virtual reality and high-definition graphics. The access to fast 5G superfast internet allows gamers to play in any location without carrying the special hardware. Artificial intelligent gaming platforms will provide personalized design games, making them more player relevant. Cloud-based gaming platforms will be made possible through intelligent connectivity (Ifr.org. 2016). This platform will allow the participants to play their favorite video games without the bulky consoles and equipment currently used in the gaming industry. This new experience will be more indulging and immersive by applying augmented reality or virtual reality accompanied by machines with haptic sensors for feedback. The use of hologram displays will provide the consumers with an improved realistic feeling during live sporting events and even music concerts located miles away from their locations. Remote entertainment will be made possible by enjoying sports events and live concerts from the comfort of their homes.

7.4.8 Communication

The IoT, in combination with 5G networks, will revolutionize the communication sector. With improved bandwidth, digital communication will coverer every aspect of communication (Osuwa, Ekhoragbon and Fat 2017). The capture of these aspects, such as subtleties and nuances, will allow people to be present virtually in a remote place. Artificial intelligent system-controlled drones will allow people to make virtual visits to family and friends, transmitting high-quality live 380° images and high-quality audio to the headset of the end-user. With the combination of AI powers hosted by the massive bandwidth 5G networks, there will be an improved real-time transmission of data from sensor networks, greatly improving communication capabilities (Ifr.org. 2016).

7.4.9 Resource Management

Intelligent connectivity has the prospect of improving the resource management capabilities of firms. This will be achieved by relaying real-time data on most parameters, such as water pH, levels of salinity of the soil, and pollution levels. The monitoring of environmental conditions to tackle global issues such as ozone layer depletion and global warming (Knight 2016) can be monitored closely and regularly through systems to formulate remedy options. This is a very critical part of environmental management aspects. Once this information has been relayed through the IoT, artificial intelligent systems can then design the remedies for such critical problems (Ifr.org. 2016).

Intelligent connectivity will reduce environmental pollution by giving humans control of their assets over 5G networks to efficiently manage energy use. This will greatly reduce the emission of greenhouse gases, giving way to new cleaner sources of energy. By employing ubiquitous and reliable 5G networks, the legislators will be empowered to give the public incentives to select green options for transport and recycling waste.

In smart cities, intelligent connectivity can be used in controlling traffic flow and allocating parking spaces over a system that interlinks the automobiles through the IoT and coordinates through the artificially intelligent system a traffic flow that is controlled and optimized, eliminating wastage of time due to uncontrolled traffic (Osuwa, Ekhoragbon and Fat 2017). The application of intelligent connectivity in waste management will have two effects, the simplification of tasks and the reduction of waste. This would effectively reduce pollution. The coordination of waste collection through the control of waste trucks has been made possible through intelligent connectivity.

7.4.10 Agriculture

In agriculture, 5G networks will increase the quality of crops and the overall yields by monitoring the weather and soil conditions. Intelligent systems can also be used to design tailor-made pesticides that target specific pests on the farm. The fertilizers can also be designed using these systems to improve the yields by optimizing the soil conditions. The application of connected and well-coordinated vehicles will improve the distribution of yields and products through optimal routing via intelligent connectivity systems (Osuwa, Ekhoragbon and Fat 2017). The vehicles will also have their conditions maintained at optimal conditions in terms of temperature and humidity while on transportation. This will lead to the products being delivered in an optimal condition, guaranteeing longer market and shelf lives. The management of robust farms will be made easier by deploying many sensors on the farms and powerful drones to give live video feeds in real-time to the farm managers (Ifr.org. 2016).

7.4.11 Education

Augmented reality and virtual reality headsets in education and training are a possibility now with intelligent connectivity. The training of mechanics, medics, engineers, and other professions can learn their trade using AR and VR simulations (Osuwa, Ekhoragbon and Fat 2017). These systems are also applicable in teaching geography and biology trainees about environments and habitats by superimposing images and videos that simulate the real world to virtual reality. The use of these systems has been limited due to the high latency of most internet connections. However, the 5G networks will eliminate these limitations, giving a new radical pathway to approach the education system and enabling remote learning. Digital training will use the techniques of virtual gaming, keeping the students interested. Hands-on skills taught in the schools, such as medical school, engineering, and armed forces will enjoy using this system in a low-pressure environment before employing it in real life. The use of powerful 5G networks and wireless connectivity over the IoT will enable novel forms of hands-on education by enabling students and instructors to use haptic overlay (Osuwa, Ekhoragbon and Fat 2017). The instructors will be able to feel the student's movements as they perform assignments involving motor skills and correct them in real-time and the students will be able to visualize, feel, and hear the trainers' exact movements and instructions.

7.5 Challenges and Risks of Intelligent Connectivity

Researchers have limited reservations on the promise of intelligent connectivity due to short-term and long-term economic shortcomings. The intelligent connectivity challenge is the risk of employment loss, risk of human safety, and security. In addition to this, there are social risks; for example, biased or selfishly manipulated algorithms could create widespread inequalities and discrimination (Siddique and Tabassum 2015).

7.5.1 Economic Risks

Like other technological inventions, intelligent connectivity also disrupts the workforce by altering employment chances and changing job descriptions. Although a viable strategy, research shows that in the next 50 years, 65% of workers will be replaced in the United States of America. This is quite scary as the unemployment rate would soar with the increasing populations as well. Some studies have put the risk at 47% of the jobs as being able to be automated in the coming decade by examining the probable potential automation of job tasks. In a study that focused on the heterogeneity of various occupation tasks, 6% of the jobs were at risk as the nature of several job positions might change over a durable amount of time. To mitigate this potential crisis, a policy has been formulated to prepare the human labor force to complement intelligent connectivity systems. All this has been done through labor force capacity building. On the other side of the coin, however, intelligent connectivity systems create human computation system jobs such as call centers (McCarthy 2015). These new jobs require highly skilled developers; hence capacity building and intelligent connectivity training are required. Just as the industrial revolution replaced the menace of repetitive factory jobs with new engineering jobs, the intelligent connectivity system cognitive revolution will also lead to many opportunities that need unique human abstract reasoning, inventiveness, and knowledge application.

7.5.2 Risks to Human Safety and Agency

Bostrom (2016) categorically warns that autonomous intelligent connectivity systems would shortly adapt to change the revolution's course, eventually overriding their human inventors' intelligence. This threat is called singularity; it occurs when AI becomes superhuman and poses a threat to humanity. However, the scientific congregation believes that the fruits of AI outweigh the risk of singularity. This risk surely bears with its support in equal measure. A recent survey found that 31% of respondents believe that intelligent connectivity systems would be extremely dangerous for humanity, while 52% believe that artificially intelligent systems would benefit humanity (Siddique and Tabassum 2015). The biggest growing concern on the human security front is on the increasing invention and use of remotely controlled weapons known as drones in wars.

Even though drones are not autonomous and are controlled by individuals, they do not choose targets and operate by General Packet Radio Services (GPRS) following a preprogrammed route. These weapons in the hands of the wrong people would bear huge risks and advance terrorist activities. Even though these drones reduce the risk of soldiers engaging in direct battles and increase the geographical reach of their users, the damage they can cause to the innocents can be very costly. The law and policies such as the Geneva conventions are not clear. Autonomous artificial systems can also assist law enforcement in fighting and solving crimes through video evidence fitted on their troopers, body armor, or even drones. The law uses the advancement in pattern recognition done by artificially intelligent systems to detect and prevent criminal activities before or after they occur. The capability of automated surveillance using artificial intelligent systems can challenge security via individual and cultural beliefs of privacy and autonomy. Possible biases can bring this about in AI usage with other numerous risks to surveillance.

7.5.3 Social Risk

The majority of social dangers associated with intelligent connectivity emanate from combining huge information and automated decision-making (Ifr.org. 2016). This concern has been brought to our attention by a recent influx of machine learning, a technique of feeding algorithms to make intelligent predictions about events by analyzing data about relevant past or present conditions. Usually, in cases of with enough comprehensive data, most of the algorithms are sensitive enough to triangulate serious confidential information, e.g. linkage of unrelated pieces of information such as name and year of birth, history of employment, and the existence of a chronic disease. This system would encourage discrimination and segregation by insurance institutions, banks, and hospitals. The information can be used to deny potential patients deemed to be at high risk on dubious ethical and legal grounds. These discriminations will be quite difficult to prove as the algorithms are protected as trade secrets and copyrights (Horvitz 2014). Several data sets are usually incomplete due to the lack or presentation of information from historically sidelined groups; this could result in an intelligent connectivity system with a wide range of biases. One of the studies proved that algorithms of a recruitment software of high-paying jobs targeted men compared to women. In another study, facial recognition software identification capabilities depended on diverse data; the algorithms were nurtured on datasets distributed across all demographics. It was discovered that this software was racially biased as there was an over-representation of most African Americans in the judicial system. The algorithm created from this training was more likely to associate African American faces with a crime.

7.5.4 Secondary Risks

With the invention of increased intelligent connectivity to solve various problems, there are unavoidable secondary problems. Overpopulation could be a secondary problem prompted by intelligent connectivity medical invention systems that improve the human population's life expectancy. The consequent overpopulation shows the risk of viral recombination that could cause the emergence of a deadly virus. The invention of an intelligent connectivity travel system would, in turn, reduce the world into a smaller village, providing a transit route for these deadly viruses. This is just one of the hypothetical scenarios that could be caused by these powerful systems.

7.5.5 Confidentiality and Scalability

The shortcomings of the IoT include confidentiality and scalability. The tagged objects are connected to the internet nodes by structured internet protocols (IP). The RFID (radio frequency ID) tags must cooperate with a TCP (transport confidential protocol)/IP stack and a wireless communication platform to function optimally, with favorable power consumption and appropriate processing power. This brings a major risk, especially in cases of system hacking or breach.

7.6 Recommendations

Intelligent connectivity is expected to take center stage in entertainment, transport, communication, education, commerce, and other key fields when 5G networks are rolled out. The rollout of 5G is projected to be ready in 2021 in China, South Korea, the United States of America, and the United Arab Emirates.

All businesses and companies will be expected to embrace this technology. This is the next big thing in the technological world.

7.7 Conclusion

Intelligent connectivity through the 5G network will revolutionize how we live through innovations that will uplift the world economy. This will be achieved by the exponential expansion of the IoT and AI systems. The prospects at hand would be intelligent transport in self-driving cars, intelligent healthcare systems, intelligent security systems, and many more. Advanced robotics and virtual presence will take center stage, enabling the completion of the "demise" distance. The daily routines will surely change; for example, how we consume entertainment and communicate with our colleagues will be much more fulfilling and accomplished. People will have all their necessary appliances at their fingertips, making the business and public sectors more reliable, effective, and efficient. The 5G network and network slicing will provide the end-users with an extravagant multifaceted service. Cellular connectivity will become the pioneer connectivity for the IoT. Intelligent connectivity will provide both established companies and small business startups with new horizons in information and technology to anticipate customer wants and needs. Intelligent connectivity will help businesses overcome setbacks and challenges. 5G will provide a foundation for businesses to roll out new kinds of products and services that have not been seen before. Intelligent connectivity is surely a principle building component for a sustainable future.

The fusion of AI, 5G, and IoT makes a high-speed, ubiquitous, versatile connectivity that will transform the way we live, work, and socialize.

References

Bostrom, N. (2016). What happens when our computers get smarter than we are? Ted. com.https://www.ted.com/talks/nick_bostrom_what_happens_when_our_computers_get_smarter_than_we_are#t-334532 (accessed March 15, 2019).

Chin, S.J. and Yeoh, C.P. (2014). *Introduction to Fuzzy Logic*, 3e. New York: Prentice-Hall.

Clark, J. (2015). Why 2015 was a breakthrough year in artificial intelligence. http://www.bloomberg.com/news/articles/2015-12-08/why-2015-was-abreakthrough-year-in-artificial-intelligence (accessed: March 4, 2019).

Devi, K.K.A., Matthew, Y., and Sandra, L.A. (2012). Advanced neural network in Artificial Intelligence Systems. *IEEE Trans on Artificial Intelligence Systems* 4 (9): 100–120.

Gorozu, A., Hirano, K., Okawa, K., and Tagawaki, Z. (2014). High-speed data mining technique. *IEEE Trans on Electronics* 10 (17): 10–30.

GSMA (2019). Intelligent connectivity: How the combination of 5G, AI, and IoT is set to change America. https://itig-iraq.iq/wp-content/uploads/2019/05/21494-MWC-Americas-report.pdf (accessed 22 June 2021).

Horvitz, E. (2014). One-hundred year study of Artificial Intelligence: Reflections and framing. https://stanford.app.box.com/s/266hrhww2l3gjoy9euar (accessed: March 15, 2019).

Ifr.org. (2016). IFR Press Release – IFR International Federation of Robotics. http://www.ifr.org/news/ifr-press-release/china-seeking-to-join-the-top10-robotics-nations-by-2020-823/ (accessed March 3, 2019).

Knight, W. (2016). Tech companies want AI to solve global warming. MIT Technology Review. https://www.technologyreview.com/s/545416/couldai-solve-the-worlds-biggest-problems/ (accessed March, 15, 2019).

Lily, D., Chan, B., and Wang, T.G. (2013). A simple explanation of neural network in artificial intelligence. *IEEE Transactions on Control Systems Technology* 247 (4): 1529–5651.

McCarthy, N. (2015) Fear of technology falls with higher income. https://www.statista.com/chart/3723/fear-of-technology-falls-with-higher-income/ (accessed: March 15, 2019).

Nicole, R. and Lee, J.H. (2015). The IoT concepts and design. *International Journal of Engineering* 6 (7): 16–29.

Osuwa, A.A., Ekhoragbon, E.B., and Fat, L.T. (2017). Application of Artificial Intelligence in Internet of Things. 2017 9th International Conference on Computational Intelligence and Communication Networks (CICN). https://www.researchgate.net/publication/323861461_Application_of_artificial_intelligence_in_Internet_of_Things (accessed 22 June 2021).

Rappaport, T.S. and Sun, S. (2013). Millimeter waves mobile communication for 5G cellular. In: *Board of Governors of IEEE Vehicular Technology Society (VTS)*, ISSN No: 2169-3536, Retrieved from: https://doi.org/10.1109/ACCESS.2013.2260813. .

Siddique, U. and Tabassum, H. (2015). Wireless backhauling of 5G small cells. In: *Department of Electrical and Computer Engineering*. University of Manitoba, ISSN No: 1536-1284, Retrieved from: https://doi.org/10.1109/MWC.2019.7306534 .

Tan, C.H. (2015). *Fuzzy Logic and Applications*, 1e. New York: Pearson.

Tommi, J. (2015). Channel models key to 5th generation development. *Microwave Journal* 58 (3): 44–44, 46, 48, 50.

8

IoT: Laws, Policies, and Regulations

8.1 Introduction

With the current technological landscape rapidly changing, the world is being transitioned into the digital age. Crime is no longer just out on the streets but now found mostly on the internet. Every day there are many cases of identity theft and malware infection.

The Internet of Things (IoT) is an increasingly growing topic of conversation in the tech-savvy environment and is more frequent in our personal lives. IoT means linking devices to each other or the internet, making devices communicate, sense, and interact. IoT is spread across every length and breadth of industry, from home appliances to cars, medical devices, personal and industrial electronics, and more interestingly, in insurance and policing.

This technology will significantly impact various markets across the country's economy. There will be cultural changes, societal changes, and economic changes. Agriculture is an example of a financial sector that is set to prosper heavily with IoT devices and will allow farmers to optimize their crop yield. Energy is another sector that will be significantly impacted by the production and delivery of electrical needs. Healthcare and manufacturing will monitor and optimize their operations with long-distance coverage and education with their users. Transportation and infrastructure within smart cities will be able to use these devices to optimize their daily activities. It is the job of society to regulate these devices on how they affect our lives. Information spreading across these devices could be sensitive and must be handled carefully.

Multiple things can become hurdles for developing and deploying IoT devices and systems. The first would be the connectivity issue; currently, we are running out of internet protocol (IP) addresses and are not fully converted to new IP protocols to allow more addresses. Soon we will have built fifth generation (5G) across the United States so it can be utilized more through the markets. This will help with the hurdle of having high enough internet speeds for these devices.

The most significant concern for the deployment of these devices is the cybersecurity risk. These devices can be easily misused and can be used to collect sensitive information. They provide new vulnerabilities within the infrastructure and must be appropriately configured and deployed to ensure they cannot be compromised.

Intelligent Connectivity: AI, IoT, and 5G, First Edition. Abdulrahman Yarali.
© 2022 John Wiley & Sons Ltd. Published 2022 by John Wiley & Sons Ltd.

IoT device connectivity, a subnetwork of the world's universal network transmitting and receiving data and commands, is exposed to a far greater variety and level of threats than earlier products over a closed, private network. There are several potential security threats to an IoT device. The security of each connected node in an IoT network depends on security policies that allow access, cryptography, and tamper resistance. An IoT node or user of that device faces spoofing, tampering, repudiation, information disclosure, denial of service, and elevation of privilege.

With the current pace of growth in IoT, almost a fivefold increase in 10 years, there are also challenges in dealing with device security and user privacy. IoT enters into a world where the devices are everywhere, and they each have a door to the network. There must be authentication for each device to determine who you are and authorization to determine if you even have access. Because of this and the move to whole systems of devices, we must think about the entire system's authentication and not just that of a single device's authentication. Sometimes the problem is in firmware vulnerabilities. If one is running network devices that use parts of other vendor's hardware or firmware, they could create a substantial potential risk for your network. The issue is that users will not properly update their software or firmware as much as they should. This requires being mindful of the hardware, software, firmware, and everything else embedded in a device utilized in production. Any single vulnerability can be a cause for damage.

The following factors are driving IoT technology (Yarali, Srinath, and Joyce 2019):

- The decrease in the cost of processors that have higher capabilities.
- The increase in development and production of sensors.
- Development of cloud storage and big data that allow data storage and analysis.
- The decrease in data-processing cost allows for investment.

Like any other technology, the IoT has a few factors that are hindering progress. They are:

- Security.
- Availability of the internet.
- Production of smaller devices.
- High cost involved in the development of new sensors.
- IoT end-devices often consume a lot of energy.
- IoT end-devices usually have low computing capabilities.
- Low fault rate acceptance in the industry.
- Limited acceptance by society.
- As new IoT devices are manufactured, the old ones have to be discarded. This would lead to a large amount of E-waste generation.

IoT has already captured the attention of the US and EU governments who have formed Congressional data gathering committees, and commissioned reports that will lead to specific policies and regulations to ensure user safety. These proposals and the implementation of laws and regulations can positively and negatively affect the innovation process.

With the increasing complexity of cyber-attacks, the cybersecurity industry must offer protection to more than just the software perimeters and traditional networks. For instance, the most recent DDoS (Distributed Denial of Service) attack on the domain name server provider Dyn (now Oracle) was instigated using IoT implements like printers and Digital Video Recorders (DVRs). The attack managed to bring down renowned companies such as Amazon, Twitter, and Netflix. These companies were taken offline for a considerable time. It was through these attacks that the actual threat of unsafe devices was uncovered in the growing IoT sector. On the global scale, the UK and Australia are among the global leaders in the cybersecurity industry, with the US coming up first, followed by Canada (Stevens 2018). With the cybersecurity sector growing more and more fragmented, the principal prospects are present in four verticals: financial services, government/defense, critical infrastructure, and healthcare. The initiative by the US Government to enhance cybersecurity for critical infrastructure has made the government a considerable spender and supporter of cybersecurity in the country. This translated to a US$19 billion budget for the year 2017. Back in 2015, the financial cybersecurity market in the US was quantified at US$9.5 billion. As such, this made it the largest non-government cybersecurity market. In the period between 2016 and 2020, this same market was projected to go beyond US$68 billion (Stevens 2018).

Multiple agencies monitor the IoT systems; no single agency has complete control of these device regulations. The Federal Communications Commission (FCC) allocates and assigns spectrum bands, while the Department of Commerce, the National Telecommunications, and the Information Administration fulfill that function for federal entities. The National Institute of Standards and Technology creates standards, develops new technologies, and provides the best internet and internet-enabled devices. The Federal Trade Commission (FTC) regulates trade policies and consumer protection. The Department of Homeland Security is responsible for the security of these sectors and the Food and Drug Administration (FDA) and Department of Justice enforce the laws within data. The Department of Energy includes those associated with developing high-performance and green buildings and other energy-related programs, including those related to smart grids. The Department of Transportation (DoT) handles the implementation of various IoT systems and the Federal Aviation Administration (FAA) also utilizes regulations for unmanned aircraft vehicles.

What are some things that could affect the Development and Implementation of IoT? There are multiple things that can become hurdles for developing and deploying IoT devices and systems. The first would be the connectivity issue. We are currently running out of IP addresses and are not fully converted to new IP protocols that will allow more addresses. Soon we will have built 5G across the United States so it can be utilized more through the markets. This will help with the hurdle of having high enough internet speeds for these devices.

The greatest concern for the deployment of these devices is the cybersecurity risk. These devices can be easily misused and can be used to collect sensitive information. These devices provide new vulnerabilities within the infrastructure and must be properly configured and deployed to ensure they cannot be compromised.

This chapter provides some insight into laws and regulations currently imposed on various industries involved in the research and development of IoT. It focuses on the variations of laws and regulations worldwide. The chapter also covers some of the laws being proposed by various governments and how they may affect innovation in IoT.

8.2   Recently Published Laws and Regulations

Statistics prove that numerous IoT devices are under vigorous research and development or released in the market and use. The government is catching up with new technologies to manage challenges in dealing with device security and user privacy.

One such Government organization concerned about the usage of IoT devices, such as automated sensors and control devices within its organization, the Department of Defense (DoD), releases a statement of concern and recommends new policymaking. DoD believes IOT devices provide a great opportunity to strengthen its infrastructure yet IOT is connected to the internet and comes with risks and security concerns.

Lately, United States senators are working on a Bill directed towards security, such as the IoT Cybersecurity Improvement Act of 2017. The United States are also concerned that such bills may inhibit new research and development in IoT; they proposed a couple of bills that enable a committee to overlook developments and encourage IoT developers to adhere to the Development of Innovation and Growth of the Internet of Things (DIGIT) Act.

8.2.1   IoT Cybersecurity Improvement Act of 2017

United States senators Mark Warner, Cory Gardner, Ron Wyden, and Steve Daines, earlier in August 2017, introduced legislation for improving cybersecurity for the IoT. The aim was to provide at least a minimum-security need for IoT vendors, supplying devices to the United States Federal Government. As a whole, this act offers guidelines to vendors and departments of IoT device procurement in the United States Federal Government.

1) Vendors should have provision to receive updates to inhibit any security threat in the future.
2) IoT devices should not contain any pre-saved permanent passwords as this may lead to security vulnerabilities.
3) Since hackers could use some IoT device vulnerability, such as a limited data processing capacity, there should be a process to freeze it, providing necessary guidelines to give protection from any threat.
4) Do not take fraud actions against researchers when they trespass on the Abuse Act and the Digital Millennium Copyright Act and Computer Fraud. They are involved in research to secure and develop production for IOT devices but may trespass on these liability laws (Warner et al. 2017).

8.3   Developing Innovation and Growing the Internet of Things (DIGIT) Act

On August 4, 2017, the United States, Senators introduced the DIGIT Act, which addresses growing IOT devices. The Bill is designed to support the IoT development in terms of laws and regulations inhibiting IoT growth, security concerns inhibiting innovations, and asking the group to manage the spectrum allocation with this new era of interconnected devices. The Bill suggests forming a working group body and guidance they should follow, overlooking the IOT growth and innovation. It was suggested that the working group body should consist of Federal stakeholders for providing recommendations and a report to Congress. Giving one year to the working body to submit its report, this period was suggested since this was a new area of concern and the working body would require this period to gather information in the report's formulation (DIGIT 2018).

In 2018, sometime in November, President Donald Trump signed into regulation the Cybersecurity and Infrastructure Security Agency Act of 2018. This important law uplifted the mission of the previous National Protection and Programs Directorate (NPPD) in the DHS's confines and put in place the Cybersecurity and Infrastructure Security Agency (Singer and Friedman 2014). The CISA constructs the national ability to keep away cyber-attacks and functions with the Federal Government to make available cybersecurity tools, assessment abilities, and incident reaction services to protect the government networks that back up the essential operations of partner departments and organizations (McCarthy 2018). In past years, policymakers have identified the significance of ensuring that the information infrastructure is secure and reacting by growing resources and paying attention to cybersecurity.

In 2020, California and Oregon in the USA introduced new legislation mandating a security measure to be added to all IoT devices (Fernandez 2020).

8.4 General View

IoT gained significant momentum in the enterprise in the year 2016. This momentum will only increase in the future. According to Verizon, businesses are currently viewing IoT as an enabler of sustainability, safety, and economic growth, with most executives either researching or deploying the IoT technology. Enterprises are banking on dramatically growing their businesses, increasing operational efficiency, and delivering an unparalleled experience to partners and customers by digitizing assets through IoT. Unfortunately, this is happening at a slower pace than expected because of an absence of industry-wide IoT standards coupled with security, interoperability, and cost considerations, which make up to half of the executive concerns around IoT. Most IoT projects are either in the concept or pilot phase, not in production. According to McKinsey and Company, companies in the industrial sector are often constrained by long capital cycles, organizational inertia, and a shortage of talented staff who can develop and deploy IoT solutions. Businesses seem to be more focused on simpler use cases to track data and send status alerts. While these projects are easy to deploy and lack data analytic capabilities, they generate quick revenue, and the customers will remain focused on them. This implies that the businesses will not obtain the full value of IoT.

Country growth and betterment come from the innovation of products and services, and IoT provides and helps achieve that. Therefore, any country would surely stay in terms of development and innovation of IoT; however, the fundamental priority of a country lies in the privacy, security, and protection of its citizens.

From two recent bills passed in the Senate, the United States is trying to achieve innovation without compromising even a drop in its security. These two bills are trying to allow innovations by slightly adjusting its laws and regulations to benefit its research and innovation, while not compromising its privacy and safety, by using a specific adjustment made by the government, as discussed below.

8.5 Relaxation of Laws by the Federal Aviation Administration (FAA)

In a press release on June 21, 2017, the Federal Aviation Administration (FAA) simplified its commercial drone rules in the skies. Laws are eased for drone commercial traffic operation, suggesting that commercial drone operation only now needs to pass an aeronautical knowledge test instead of earning a conventional, more expensive pilot's license. With this change, the drone commercial traffic sector experienced increased drone usage from 20 000 to 600 000 from 2016 to 2017, as given in a report from Verizon statistics. This simplification in law will enable more research in investing active involvement times in drones and related technologies. Enterprises will also adopt camera and sensors embedded drone technologies for surveillance. According to Verizon, drones have their maximum use in the industrial inspections sector (Verizon 2017).

8.6 Supporting Innovation of Self-Driving Cars by Government Policies

The future of roads is moving towards automated vehicles. Analysts predict that high end automated vehicles can be safer on roads than human driving.

Recently on the first week of October 2017, further development on the "SELF-DRIVE Act" or Safely Ensuring Lives Future Deployment and Research In Vehicle Evolution Act took place. Various laws and iterative hearings on self-driving laws and regulations are under consideration to make the roads safer and make way for innovation.

The United States Senate Committee has allowed a bill preventing states from proposing its laws for automatic cars. This bill is considered an important step by automakers since it has to deal with only one body, i.e. the National Highway Traffic Safety Administration (NHTSA). This will ease future developments in autonomous vehicles on roads (SELF-DRIVE Act 2017).

8.6.1 Investment by US Department of Homeland Security

Recently in the second week of August 2017, the Department of the United States of Homeland Security invested $750 k for securing the IoT disaster sensors. Metronome software is developing security solutions for strengthening security of IoT sensors and ensures that the sensors are not compromised in any prospective (DHS 2017).

8.6.2 United States Guiding Principles for IoT Security

On November 15, 2016, the United States Department of Homeland Security published its guidelines for securing IoT. It contained procedures to develop IoT security. The central theme behind this article published by the Department of Homeland Security is to appreciate the growth of IoT but to show no compromise on the security aspect. The Department of Homeland Security provides suggestions on how to build secure IoT devices from design, manufacturing, and operating them. These guidelines include:

1) Suggest implanting security at the designing stage of the circuit phase.
2) Keep a check on security by providing constant updates.
3) Maintain proven safekeeping practices.
4) List security risks on possible impact.
5) Maintain transparency on connected devices.
6) Connect to IoT devices with caution.

The report states that most IoT devices previously used the Linux operating system, which is a threat to IoT security. However, using current and up-to-date operating systems can be less or no threat to IoT privacy. These updates ensure updates on firewalls relating to the present security vulnerabilities (US DHS 2016).

8.6.3 The United Kingdom on IoT

In the last week of August 2017, the United Kingdom allowed semi-automated trucks to convey on roads and allocated £8.1 m to trials in platooning. Platooning means up to three wirelessly connected vehicles travelling in convoy, where the lead vehicle controls the acceleration, braking, and steering. All this could happen with a human in a seat to take control in case of an emergency.

I believe that the objective behind allowing this IoT project was to promote and support IoT innovation. This funding for experiments from the government came from the ideology of cutting down on fuel costs and reducing traffic congestion using fully-fledged IoT innovation (*The Guardian* 2017).

The UK government has introduced new mandatory requirements for vendors and IoT components to enhance consumer data integrity and privacy. They hope to raise awareness through cross-company collaboration and encourage manufacturers to consider the security of connected devices at the hardware level. The aim is to promote the best practices by corporations, manufactures, and network administrators to mitigating the security of massive IoT device connectivity.

In May 2019, the UK Government launched a consultation on consumer IoT security (DCMS 2019). The plans, drawn up by the Department for Digital, Culture, Media, and Sport (DCMS), will make sure that all consumer smart devices sold in the UK adhere to the three rigorous security requirements for the IoT (DCMS 2020). These are:

- All consumer internet-connected device passwords must be unique and not resettable to any universal factory setting.
- Manufacturers of consumer IoT devices must provide a public point of contact so anyone can report a vulnerability, and it will be acted on promptly.
- Manufacturers of consumer IoT devices must explicitly state the minimum length of time for which the device will receive security updates at the point of sale, either in-store or online.

8.6.4 United States Department of Commerce

In 2017, on January 12, the United States Department of Commerce published a document on advancing beneficiary growth on internet-connected devices. The document asked for investigations on the pros and cons of increasing IoT, thereby suggesting that by submitting a report the government would lend a supporting hand for research and allow pioneering in this IoT sector. The green paper presents and discusses four areas of IoT (US 2017):

1) Providing required infrastructure. Consider and allocate the necessary spectrum for present and future IoT developments.
2) Taking necessary steps in laws and regulations for promoting IoT growth.
3) Ensuring to maintain standards in IoT connected devices.
4) Allowing the IoT market to grow by providing necessary promotions.

8.6.5 Federal Trade Commission and Creating an IoT Security Solution

The Federal Trade Commission is supporting the innovation and development of IoT connectivity and devices. It has announced an open challenge to the public to gather information on threats and technical details.

A challenge from the Federal Trade Commission is asking consumers to identify and solve home security vulnerabilities. The IoT Home Inspector Challenge is specifically seeking to address the area in IoT that requires up-to-date software in the system.

Every day United States consumers buy innovative products from the market to make their homes smarter and use them for better living, focusing on security, safety, and privacy. The following criteria for functionality are required to win the challenge:

- Recognize connected devices at home.
- Determine the version of software used in those given IoT devices.
- Recommend the latest version that could have been used instead.
- Required assistance in updating the software (FTC 2017).

8.7 Recommendations

Whether regulation and security will hinder or enable IoT innovation remains a matter of discussion. When billions of sensors worldwide are continually acquiring information on their environments, including humans, privacy issues are essential in an IoT world. A majority of the first world have made efforts towards safeguarding customers from illegal consumption of confidential data (Dewri et al. 2017). However, in several cases, the laws are insufficient to meet the high number of new ways individuals are captured and victimized. The EU's recent effort to update the law on copyright is an indicator of the outmoded nature of the laws in many countries.

At the internet's earlier stage, consumers were familiar with tracking software, such as cookies. Since there was a lack of laws regulating cookies on a website to track a cookie's browsing behavior, several firms implemented the practice without considering the user's concerns. The browser responded to the user's concern with tools to regulate usage of the cookies and eradicate them after a session of browsing.

The EU's legislation now restricts how cookies are utilized and what type of information they are permitted to gather on the user (Wang et al. 2016). However, with the increase of mobile technology, which does not require cookies to track the user's behavior, most laws are slowly becoming out of date and insufficient in a world of IoT.

Similarly, the US also depends on outdated regulatory frameworks for new IoT technologies and systems. Though there is no federal law that restricts the gathering and consumption of individual information, the US depends on a patchwork of available state and federal laws to safeguard consumers' privacy (Dupont 2012). Public concern for the Federal Government, specifically the National Security Agency, which is in charge of information collection practices linked to law enforcement and counter-terrorism, indicates the public policy arguments to come.

According to the United States Federal Trade Commission report (2015), it was recommended that best practices for firms should be adopted for consumer information and security. The report further perpetuates the government's disregard when it comes to IoT regulations. The report emphasizes the repeated call of the Commission for robust data security as well as breach notification laws.

Concerns of privacy should also extend to the workplace. Many programs in the marketplace enable employers to track an employee's behavior, mostly based on the personal computer (PC) of the worker. However, IoT permits an employer to fix sensors in almost any corner of an office to monitor employee behavior.

8.8 Conclusion

A clear picture can be drawn from the statements presented so far that the United States government or any country government is concerned about privacy, safety, and security of its country and its citizens and prioritizes this over innovation. This priority might give the researchers and innovative thinkers of IoTs the impression that laws inhibit the growth of the technology and that the government does not provide space for innovative technologies in development. Government, and especially the United States government, as shown from the facts of laws and regulations presented so far, is evidently trying to fund and help in innovation and support the innovators without compromising the privacy, safety, and security of its country and its citizens.

Although security is the biggest concern, enterprises have other demands. Businesses are looking for scalability and simplicity from IoT, and industry-wide technology partners are providing end-to-end services to meet demands. The evolution of IoT platforms that provide industry-specific applications and extensive information analytics are streamlining the enterprise IoT experience. Municipalities are leveraging IoT developments to extend smart city services like smart parking, smart lighting, citizen engagement, and public safety services. From a prediction by the International Data Corporation (IDC), the worldwide base of IoT endpoints can grow from approximately 15 billion at the end of 2016 to a value larger than 82 billion in 2025. Corporations are at the very beginning of uncovering new data-driven revenue sources and delivering enriched client experiences. At present, the majority of the IoT market is focused on the business-to-business market. Apart from predictive maintenance, other popular use cases are inventory management, fleet and asset management, and remote patient monitoring. With enterprises discovering innovative use cases for the devices and the continued availability of simple, low-cost connectivity, this growth of IoT will propel major efficiency and productivity gains.

Regulatory compliance continues to be a driving force behind enterprise IoT adoption. Companies manufacturing drugs in the pharmaceutical sector need to mark packages with an identifier for products, serial number, IoT number, expiration date, and the capability to electronically store and transfer the entire history of transactions with a shipment detailing distribution supply chain. Attempts to stop counterfeit drugs are being made by the US Drug Supply Chain Security Act. This costs the industry anywhere from 75 billion to 200 billion annually and can make up half of all drugs sold in some low-income countries. Yet, increasingly, enterprises are reaping the benefits of IoT beyond compliance capabilities. In the energy sector, a nationwide effort to monitor energy consumption in 2007 under the Energy Independence and Security Act has evolved to install hundreds of millions of digital meters supported by remote reading and other smart grid applications.

The most significant regulatory news is the FAA easing of rules surrounding Unmanned Aerial Vehicles (UAVs) or drones that operated in the previous year. To fly a commercial drone, operators need to pass an aeronautical knowledge test rather than a more expensive pilot's license. The FAA predicted a dramatic increase in drone usage by commercial sectors from 20 000 in 2016 to 600 000 commercial drones by the end of 2017 after this regulatory change was made.

References

DCMS (2019). Department for Digital, Culture, Media & Sport. https://www.gov.uk/government/consultations/consultation-on-regulatory-proposals-on-consumer-iot-security (accessed 22 June 2021).

DCMS (2020). Department for Digital, Culture, Media & Sport, Cybersecurity Center, and Matt Warman MP. https://www.gov.uk/government/consultations/consultation-on-regulatory-proposals-on-consumer-iot-security (accessed 22 June 2021).

Dewri, A., Nguyen, A., Chen, F. et al. (2017). *Cybersecurity & Internet of Things*. Routledge.

DHS (n.d.) S&T Awards Metronome Software $750K to Strengthen Security of First Responder Sensor Systems. https://www.dhs.gov/science-and-technology/news/2017/08/14/news-release-dhs-st-awards-metronome-software-750 (accessed on November 28, 2017).

DIGIT (2018). Developing innovation and growing the Internet of Things Act or the DIGIT Act, S.88 – 115th Congress (2017–2018), Passed 08/03/2017. https://www.govtrack.us/congress/bills/115/s88 (accessed on November 28, 2017).

Dupont, B. (2012). The cybersecurity environment to 2022: Trends, drivers, and implications.

Fernandez, A. (2020). New IoT security regulation: What you need to know. https://www.allot.com/blog/new-iot-security-regulations-what-you-need-to-know/ (accessed 22 June 2021).

FTC (2017). FTC announces Internet of Things challenge to combat security vulnerabilities in home devices. https://www.ftc.gov/news-events/press-releases/2017/01/ftc-announces-internet-things-challenge-combat-security (accessed on November 28, 2017).

McCarthy, D. (2018). Privatizing political authority: cybersecurity, public-private partnerships, and the reproduction of liberal political order. *Politics and Governance*: 5–12.

Singer, P. and Friedman, A. (2014). *Cybersecurity and Cyberwar: What Everyone Needs to Know*. New York: Oxford University Press.

Stevens, T. (2018). Global cybersecurity: New directions in theory and methods. *Politics and Governance*: 1–4.

The Guardian (2017). Semi-automated truck convoys get the green light for UK trials. *The Guardian*. United States. . https://www.theguardian.com/politics/2017/aug/25/semi-automated-truck-convoy-trials-get-uk-go-ahead-platooning (accessed on November 28, 2017).

US (2017). US Department of Commerce releases Green Paper proposing approach for advancing growth of Internet of Things. Washington. https://www.ntia.doc.gov/press-release/2017/us-department-commerce-releases-green-paper-proposing-approach-advancing-growth (accessed on November 28, 2017).

US DHS (2016). Strategic principles for securing the Internet of Things (IoT), US Department of Homeland Security, version 1.0. https://www.dhs.gov/sites/default/files/publications/Strategic_Principles_for_Securing_the_Internet_of_Things-2016-1115-FINAL. . ..pdf (accessed on November 28, 2017).

Verizon (2017). State of the Market Internet of Things 2017, New Jersey, SELF-DRIVE Act, H.R.3388- 115th Congress (2017–2018), Referred in Senate. https://www.congress.gov/bill/115th-congress/house-bill/3388/text (accessed on November 28, 2017).

Wang, G., Gunasekaran, A., Ngai, E.W., and Papadopoulos, T. (2016). Big data analytics in logistics and supply chain management: Certain investigations for research and applications. *International Journal of Production Economics 176*: 98–110.

Warner, M., Gardner, C., Wyden, R., and Daines, S. (2017). Internet of Things Cybersecurity Improvement Act of 2017, S.1691-115th Congress (2017–2018), introduced 08/01/2017. https://www.warner.senate.gov/public/index.cfm/2017/8/enators-introduce-bipartisan-legislation-to-improve-cybersecurity-of-internet-of-things-IoT-devices (accessed on November 28, 2017).

Yarali, A., Srinath, M., and Joyce, R. (2019). A study of various network security challenges in IoT. *Wireless Telecommunications Symposium (WTS 2019)*, NY.

9

Artificial Intelligence and Blockchain

9.1 Introduction

Blockchain and Artificial Intelligence (AI) are two of the most smoking innovation inclines at present. Even though the two advances have unique features creating gatherings and applications, scientists have been talking about and investigating their mix, and they have been found to go amazingly well together.

The expression AI is more established than commonly accepted. PC researcher teacher John McCarthy first authored it in 1955 (Lauterbach, Bonime-Blanc, and Bremmer 2018) and initially characterized AI as "the science and designing of making smart machines." McCarthy was also an educator who started broadly perceived research in the field of AI, on account of early tries with different things such as self-driving autos, basic leadership models, and distributed computing.

AI is about machines and PCs fit to work and respond to circumstances in the equivalent, yet ideally better, route than people. What we are endeavoring to accomplish with AI is to reproduce knowledge. With AI programs, researchers are attempting to influence frameworks to do the following processes:

1) Learn from past encounters to perform better in new circumstances that they have not gone over yet.
2) Draw ends from the accessible information to offer importance to a circumstance.
3) Analyze conditions and events, and have the capacity to decipher them accurately.

Various sci-fi motion pictures have just acquainted us with the idea of AI through menial helpers. These PC-based partners play out the undertakings we request that they do; for example, look into booking, prescribing diversion, and responding to our inquiries.

Siri, Apple's remote helper, is an AI program that is now doing that for us, showing that AI has officially advanced into our everyday lives. From here on, we can anticipate that AI applications will be created to make our lives less demanding and to enable us to redistribute an ever-increasing number of complex routine assignments, such as critical thinking, learning, and redoing different machines we use in our homes (Lauterbach, Bonime-Blanc, and Bremmer 2018).

Intelligent Connectivity: AI, IoT, and 5G, First Edition. Abdulrahman Yarali.
© 2022 John Wiley & Sons Ltd. Published 2022 by John Wiley & Sons Ltd.

9.2 Decentralized Intelligence

Because of its decentralized nature, Blockchain can kill the danger of one gathering imposing a business model of AI and their capacity to control a standout amongst the most dominant and risky advancements known to man.

If we somehow happened to decentralize AI, AI calculations could move toward becoming Decentralized Autonomous Organizations (DAOs). DAOs are associations that can work independently and are decentralized through savvy contracts that are able to pull strings and make decisions without hosting a focal get-together. The clients of DAOs, who comprise its system, choose how DAO capacities work.

Members of a Blockchain arrange to be straightforwardly associated with one another, without experiencing an outsider. Envisage Airbnb as a DAO. Contact between house proprietors and voyagers would be founded on intelligent contracts through which they can execute straightforwardly with one another.

This equivalent model would apply to AI programs running as DAOs. Its brilliant contract structure would educate its learning calculations and the DAO would purchase its information contribution from the market. An undertaking dealing with such a DAO is called SingularityNET, an exceptional learning task unquestionably worth looking at.

Such an AI DAO would work as it is comprised of its keen contracts. It may almost certainly play out the activities that are determined in these eager contracts. Planning these sharp contracts is incredibly mind-boggling, and the accomplishment of an AI DAO will be subject to this engineering structure. Ideally, an AI DAO would almost certainly assume control over advancement sooner or later because it is intended to learn through information to advance itself to be substantially more viable than would be possible through the human structure.

An important note to this is that these shrewd contracts must be planned with the most ultimate safeguard and exactness in order to guarantee that the system remains in charge and not the AI. Like Blockchain applications, nobody is fitting to pull for backdate and tampering, yet a whole system keeps the chains running.

9.2.1 Data Protection

The advancement of AI is reliant on the contribution of data – our information. Through information, AI obtains data about the world and things occurring in it. Mainly, knowledge nourishes AI and, through it, AI will almost certainly consistently improve itself.

On the opposite side, Blockchain is an innovation that considers the scrambled stockpiling of information on a dispersed record. It considers the formation of wholly verified databases that can be investigated by gatherings that have been affirmed to do this (Lauterbach, Bonime-Blanc, and Bremmer 2018). When joining Blockchains with AI, we have a reinforcement framework for a person's delicate and exceedingly profitable individual information. For instance, Spotify utilizes the information we offer to prescribe music dependent on our inclinations. This proposal keeps running on AI, and it is an extraordinary element for Spotify clients, a large portion of whom do not have an issue sharing their utilization information.

Be that as it may, with regards to medicinal or budgetary information, even though accepting suggestions would be amazingly profitable, this information is too delicate to even think about handing it over to a single organization and its calculations. Putting away this information on a Blockchain, which can be reached by an AI using just authorization once it has experienced the correct techniques, could give us the gigantic favorable circumstances of customized proposals while securely putting away our touchy information.

9.2.1.1 Information Monetization

Another troublesome advancement that could be conceivable is joining the two advances in the adaptation of information. Adapting gathered information is a great income hotspot for large organizations, for example, Facebook and Google.

Stage clients make individual information by utilizing their online administrations. This information is then gathered, assembled, put away, and sold to different organizations in the long run. This aspect makes information unfathomably valuable – more profitable than we as clients acknowledge, and we are giving it away for nothing. Data is the new oil and it could turn into our most significant resource sooner rather than later (Pathak and Bhandari 2018).

Blockchain has an influence on making it workable for us to adapt the information we make through commercial information centers. By utilizing Blockchain innovation, we can claim our knowledge and choose how to manage it, rather than outsiders pitching our knowledge to organizations, regularly using unorthodox and shaky methods, because organizations should get it individually. This aspect was preposterous before stringent procedures and managing costly fiat cash exchanges were introduced. Blockchain innovation empowers microtransactions, which is what is required for the exchange of information.

The equivalent goes for AI programs that need our information. For AI calculations to learn and create, AI systems will be required to purchase information straightforwardly from its makers through information commercial centers (Pathak and Bhandari 2018). This aspect will make the whole procedure an unquestionably more reasonable method than is the case now, without tech mammoths misusing their clients.

Such a commercial information center will likewise open up AI for small organizations. Creating and bolstering AI is amazingly expensive for organizations that do not produce their own information. Through decentralized information commercial centers, they would most likely access excessively costly and secretly kept information (Pathak and Bhandari 2018).

9.2.2 Trusting AI Decision Making

As AI calculations end up being more astute through learning, they will turn out to be progressively troublesome for information researchers to see how these projects arrived at explicit resolutions and choices. This aspect is because the AI calculation procedure will most likely be unimaginably complex with a lot of information and factors. However, we should keep auditing conclusions made by AI since we need to ensure that they reflect reality (Marwala and Xing 2018).

There are records of the considerable number of information, factors, and procedures utilized by AIs for their necessary leadership forms. This aspect makes it far simpler to review the whole system.

With Blockchain programming, all means from information passage to conclusions can be watched, which will ensure that this information has not been altered. This builds trust in the conclusions drawn by AI programs. This aspect is a fundamental advance, as people and organizations will not begin utilizing AI applications on the off chance that they work and what data they base their choices on.

The blend of Blockchain innovation and AI is as yet to a great extent an unfamiliar zone. Even though assembly of the two advances has obtained a considerable amount of academic consideration, ventures to this momentous mix are still rare.

When individuals with access to the most high-quality data concerning AI, like Elon Musk, state that AI could, in fact, be the most significant existential risk, giving this capacity to one single substance is, however, not the best. Decentralizing AI and giving it a chance to be planned and constrained by an extensive system through open-source writing of computer programs is presumably the most secure way to deal with this.

Assembling the two advancements can utilize information in a manner that at no other time was thought to be conceivable. Knowledge is a critical element for improving and upgrading AI calculations. Blockchain verifies this information, enabling us to review all mediator steps AI takes to determine the data and allow people to adapt their delivered information.

AI can be unbelievably progressive. However, it must be planned with the most extreme precautions. Blockchain can incredibly aid this. How the exchange between the two innovations will advance is impossible to say. Notwithstanding, its potential for genuine disturbance is there and quickly being created.

In the meantime, Blockchain is another recording framework for advanced data, which stores information in an encoded, appropriated record group. Since data is encoded and disseminated crosswise over a wide range of PCs, it empowers the formation of sealed, compelling databases that can be perused and refreshed by those with authorization.

Although much has been composed from a literary point of view on joining these earth-shattering innovations, real applications are meager at the moment. Be that as it may, I anticipate that this circumstance should change sooner rather than later.

In the following section on applications, three manners are described, which show that AI and Blockchain are made for one another.

9.2.3 AI and Encryption

Information hung on a Blockchain is profoundly secure by its tendency on account of the cryptography, which is intrinsic in its recording framework. This aspect means that Blockchains are perfect for putting away the exceedingly touchy, individual information that can open so much esteem and comfort in our lives when keenly prepared. Consider shrewd social insurance frameworks that make specific findings dependent on our therapeutic sweeps and records. Even basically, the proposal motors utilized by Amazon or Netflix recommend what we may get a kick out of the chance to purchase or watch straight away.

The information encouraged into these frameworks (after being gathered from us as we peruse or communicate with administrations) is exceptionally close to home. The organizations that bargain in it must set up a lot of cash to fulfill information security guidelines.

What is more, expansive scale information breaks prompting the loss of individual information are progressively normal. Blockchain databases hold their data in an encoded state. This aspect implies that only private keys need to remain secret – a couple of kilobytes of information – for the majority of the information on the chain to be secure.

AI also has a bounty to convey to the table as far as security is concerned. A growing AI field is worried about structure calculations equipped for working with or preparing information while still in a scrambled state (De la Rosa et al. 2017). As any piece of an informal procedure, which includes uncovering decoded information, could lead to a security hazard, decreasing these episodes could make things a lot more secure.

Blockchain can enable us to follow, comprehend, and clarify choices made by AI.

Choices made by AIs can, in some cases, be hard for people to understand. This aspect is because they are equipped for evaluating a considerable number of factors autonomously of one another and "realizing" which ones are critical to the general errand it is endeavoring to accomplish. For instance, AI calculations must progressively be utilized to settle whether money-related exchanges are fake and should be blocked or examined (De la Rosa et al. 2017).

For quite a while, however, it will, in any case, be essential to have these choices examined for precision by people. What is more, given the extraordinary measure of information that can be thought about, this can be a mind-boggling undertaking. For instance, Walmart encourages months of value-based information over most of its stores into its AI frameworks, which settle on choices on what items ought to be supplied and where.

When choices are recorded on a data point-by-data point premise on a Blockchain, it makes it far more straightforward for them to be evaluated, with the certainty that the record has not been messed about while the data was recorded and at the beginning of the review procedure.

Regardless of how we can see that AI offers enormous points of interest in numerous fields, if it is not trusted by the general population, at that point, its handiness will be severely constrained. Recording Blockchains' primary leadership process could be a stage towards accomplishing the dimension of straightforwardness and understanding into robot minds required to increase open trust.

AI can oversee Blockchains more effectively than people (or "dumb" traditional PCs). Customarily, PCs have been exceptionally quick yet dumb. Without specific guidelines on the best way to play out an undertaking, PCs cannot complete them. This aspect implies that working with Blockchain information on "dumb" PCs requires many PCs to prepare power because of their encoded nature. For instance, the hashing calculations used to mine squares on the Bitcoin Blockchain take a "beast compel" approach – successfully attempting each mix of characters until they discover one that fits the need to confirm an exchange.

Simulated intelligence endeavors to move away from this animal power approach and oversee assignments in a progressively smart, keen way. Think about how a human master on figuring out codes will, if they are great, turn out to be better and progressively more effective at code-breaking as they effectively decipher an ever-increasing number of codes in their professional capacity. An AI-controlled mining calculation would also handle its activity – albeit as opposed to taking a lifetime to end up as a specialist, it could promptly hone its aptitudes on the off chance that it is encouraged to prepare information.

Unmistakably, Blockchain and AI are two innovative patterns that can turn out to be increasingly progressive when assembled while historic in their own rights. Both serve to improve the other's abilities while likewise offering an open door for better oversight and responsibility.

9.3 Applications

A Blockchain is a decentralized, open computerized record that monitors cryptographic money exchanges in a subsequent request. Blockchains are viewed as problematic to the money-related world because nobody has unlimited oversight over the transactions. Subsequently, many think about this as an increasingly good substitute for physical monetary establishments like banks.

This innovation convention is presently being utilized in the field of human-made brainpower. It permits AI designers to make squares of AI open to different squares of AI and work pairs. While the innovation itself is dynamic, its potential could be parallel to that of the World Wide Web when it previously began.

Blockchain enables clients to share data and complete unknown exchanges. This innovation is picking up publicity. Blockchain offers an open, shared, and decentralized information layer with information access to all partners (De la Rosa et al. 2017). These partners incorporate city governments who utilize this innovation to assess traffic designs, vehicle makers, application engineers, and therapeutic service suppliers who convey customized benefits based on statistic profiles and utilization designs.

While Blockchain has been slanting as of late, most AI-smart associations have bounced into Blockchains to get consistency in their investigations. Experts are interested to recognize what makes Blockchains so unique, and so try an AI confirmation course in order to comprehend it.

9.3.1 The Coordination of Blockchain into AI

Relatively few individuals know the distinction between computerized reasoning and AI. Despite this equivocalness, something is known and expounded on these two fields. The equivalent, be that as it may, cannot be said for Blockchain (Lauterbach, Bonime-Blanc, and Bremmer 2018). Shockingly little is known about this field so we should try to comprehend the idea of Blockchain.

1) Immutability. This alludes to AI's capacity to assess more information and models and, consequently, improve the value of these models. Profound adaptation helps in this specific circumstance and is the consequence of finding when and how whenever given a nitty-gritty daTaset to get collaborations alongside dormant factors.
2) Decentralized. Decentralized units can handle higher measurements and processes, resulting in very high-performance AI systems, for instance, when sharing the data among biological systems or members in a planet-scale environment such as the web. The higher the information sum, the better the models could be.
3) Transparency Blockchain conventions give an alternative obstruction overall open library with outcomes in testing information and models like licensed innovation resources with a copyright guarantee.

The fascinating part is that we can have genuine information that cannot be modified. Consider, for example, the case of AI innovation that gets into Blockchains of information to retrieve data, to find designs, and to create bits of knowledge as per plans.

Most forecasts and examples are increasingly exact compared to the information mining that AI performs, which generally utilizes fragmented, missing information. Also, among Blockchain and AI, the error-prone human components are dispensed with. Working precedents clarify its consistent potential.

Here are the instances of genuine use cases that show what Blockchain and AI can do together.

1) Knowledge mining. New students like Automation bargain from the facts recorded in an engineered database to empower a business to ace neural systems, establishing the framework for more astute AIs and pocket-accommodating information mining and sharing.
2) Better money-related administrations and exchanges. Using the information in Blockchains, AI can assess diverse kinds of advanced items, with socioeconomics relying upon those getting designs while anticipating the kind of items that financial organizations offer.
3) Proven retail. Simulated intelligence can make sense of likenesses that may have been avoided through past AI activities. For instance, AI can discover that buyer exchanges for guttering materials are higher in the late spring.

At that point, a significant box home retailer will increase the stock in those materials. Here Blockchain may demonstrate that the intense interest for stepping stools identify with buys of guttering materials. Blockchain innovation is also being used to approve citizenship in various locales where birth records are absent.

Correspondingly, it can screen the relocation of individuals, gatherings, and the level of psychological oppressor medical problems relying upon those developments. As AI gets this data, expectations become quicker and can assist government offices in settling on better choices concerning movement arrangements and well-being concerns.

9.3.2 Essential Blockchain Benefits

The principal worry of AI is with understanding the concealed examples in Big information bringing about self-sufficient machines. However, Blockchains have the primary problem with accurate records of the board, security, and importance. Information sharing is the principal advantage of Blockchain for AI.

As AI is related to information, Blockchain turns into an entryway that prompts secure information exchange over the web. A large amount of preparation time is saved between the places where the information is developed and assessed. Self-working gadgets have an independent nature; hence, they need security between gadget correspondence, one of the alternate issues that Blockchain can explain. Also, Blockchain guarantees the information confirmation on which AI models depend. The idea of AI models is "Refuse In, Trash Out" – on the off chance that there is any trade-off over information used to build up the model, at that point the model outcomes will not be advantageous.

9.4 How Artificial Intelligence and Blockchain Will Affect Society

A Blockchain is a distributed ledger that is open to anyone and is cryptographically secure. This is done using hashes that continually reference the chain's next block. This means that data can be shared but remains secure because if a hash is tampered with, it will not match all the following blocks. Combined with rules about creating new blocks allows for good security and data integrity. Blockchains see adoption in manufacturing, media and telecom, retail, the public sector, healthcare, and financial services. Many major companies are investing in Blockchains for data integrity. Countries such as Estonia have "e-residents" for their public record-keeping and reference, and India integrates it into all the areas mentioned above.

9.4.1 Banking and Payments

Blockchain enables anybody to trade cash quicker, more effectively, and safely (see bitcoin money); however, numerous banks are now dealing with embracing Blockchain innovation to improve their exchanges.

9.4.2 Cybersecurity

All information is checked and scrambled in a Blockchain utilizing propelled cryptography, making it impervious to unapproved changes and hacks. Unified servers can be truly powerless to information misfortune, debasement, human blunder, and hacking (Salah et al. 2018). Take a look at the numerous hacks we have found in the previous couple of years with Target, Verizon, Deloitte, and Equifax. In a decentralized Blockchain, the circulated framework would permit information stockpiling in the Cloud to be increasingly hearty and to ensure against assaults.

9.4.3 Internet of Things

Today, the Internet of Things (IoT) incorporates vehicles, structures, doorbells, and even coolers implanted with programming, an organized network, and sensors. Be that as it may, because these gadgets work from a focal area that handles correspondences, programmers can access the vehicle you are driving or to your home. As indicated by Kamil Przeorski (CHIPIN n.d.), a specialist in Bitcoin and Ethereum abilities, Blockchain can address these fundamental security concerns since it decentralizes most of the data and information. This aspect is progressively increasingly critical as IoT capacities increment.

9.4.4 Unified Communications

Blockchains can empower quicker, more secure, and increasingly substantial mechanized correspondence. Robotized or advanced correspondence dependent on pre-assembled calculations is, as of now, happening at scale in individual businesses, with instances of these incorporate messages, framework cautions, and call warnings. Matt Peterson, a prime supporter of Jive Communications and an early adopter and excavator of Bitcoin, revealed that while a great deal of correspondence is presently computerized, this sort of communication is by and large non-basic and offbeat (Salah et al. 2018). Blockchains can move the playing field to permit approved and bi-directional interchanges and exchanges. This aspect will significantly upgrade the security and unwavering quality of our communications.

9.4.5 Government

If degenerate lawmakers and long queues at the Department of Motor Vehicles (DMV) give you a migraine, you are not the only one. With Blockchain, we could diminish administration and increment security, proficiency, and straightforwardness. Welfare and joblessness advantages could likewise be all the more effectively confirmed and disseminated, and votes could be checked and verified for authenticity.

9.4.6 Crowdfunding and Donating to Charities

Donating to a noble cause is never an awful thought. Blockchains can help guarantee that your cash gets where you need it to go. Bitcoin-based philanthropies are as of now making trust through brilliant contracts and online notoriety frameworks and enabling contributors to see where their gifts experience a safe and straightforward record. The United Nations' World Food Program is actualizing Blockchain innovation to allow displaced people to buy nourishment by utilizing Iris checks rather than vouchers, money, or charge cards (Salah et al. 2018).

9.4.7 Healthcare

With the majority of the private patient information that medical clinics gather, a safe stage is vital. With Blockchain's appearance, emergency clinics and other human services associations can make a unified and secure database, store critical records, and offer them entirely with approved specialists and patients.

9.4.8 Rentals and Ride-Sharing

Uber and Airbnb may appear decentralized systems. However, the stage proprietors are in complete control of the system and usually take charge of their administration. Blockchain can make decentralized distributed ride-sharing applications and enable vehicle proprietors to auto-pay for things like leaving, tolls, and fuel (De la Rosa et al. 2017).

While Blockchain is still moderately new, and numerous investigations will flop before they succeed, the potential development outcomes are inestimable. Alongside the eight recorded, it will influence retail, vitality to the board, online music, a production network for the board, as well as anticipating, counseling, land, protection, and significantly more (Salah et al. 2018). We could set ourselves up for a future where circulated, self-sufficient arrangements will have a tremendous job – both in our own lives and in business.

9.5 Augmented Reality

Augmented reality is the mix of electronic data with the client's progressive condition.

In contrast to virtual reality, which makes a fake condition, augmented reality utilizes the current situation and overlays new data. Boeing analyst Thomas Caudell instituted the term Augmented reality in 1990 to portray how the head-mounted showcases that circuit testers utilized when collecting confounded wiring bridle worked. One of the leading business uses of Augmented Reality (AR) innovation was the yellow "first down" line that started showing up in broadcast football match-ups at some point in 1998. Today, Google glass and heads-up presentations in vehicle windshields are maybe the most notable purchaser AR items. The innovation is utilized in numerous businesses, including therapeutic services, open well-being, gas and oil, the travel industry, and advertising (De la Rosa et al. 2017).

Augmented reality applications are written in extraordinary three-dimensional (3D) programs that enable the designer to tie liveliness or relevant advanced data in the PC program to an Augmented reality "marker," in fact. When a processing gadget's AR application or program module gets computerized data from a known marker, it starts to execute its code and layer the right picture or pictures.

AR applications for cell phones frequently incorporate a worldwide situating framework, Global Positioning Systems (GPS), to pinpoint the client's area and its compass to distinguish gadget introduction. The military's modern AR programs for preparing may incorporate machine vision, object acknowledgment, and signal acknowledgment innovations.

9.5.1 Augmented Reality in the Production Context

Augmented reality, which improves the physical world with computerized information and pictures, could make mechanical fixes simpler. Augmented reality adds advanced symbolism and information to enhance this present reality's perspectives, giving clients more data about their surroundings. That is a stage past virtual experience, which endeavors to recreate reality. With their green screens and built-in cameras and movement sensors, cell phones, and tablets are prominent stages. Head-mounted presentations keep on rising, particularly where sans hands activity is necessary.

Gee-virtuoso shopper utilizes – for example, filtering objects with a cell phone to pull up item specs and costs – snatch tech-news features, yet mechanical applications are not elusive. The unpredictable or high-chance field is a typical use among early adopters: hold a tablet over an oil-pipeline valve – schematic floats over the nuts that need fixing and show how they should arrange framework tells the central station the activity was finished. Juniper Research predicts augmented reality will become 10 times by 2019, to $2.4 billion in income (De la Rosa et al. 2017).

A branch of the purported IoT – sensors are fundamental for catching client developments and essential information – augmented reality is coming more from nerdy new businesses than built-up players; however, Intel, Microsoft, and Qualcomm have extended and are under way. Juniper expects organizations to do heaps of customization to make innovation work for them; it also refers to an absence of security and protection guidelines. Then afterwards there is word related to well-being. A laborer could locate an augmented view acting as a burden, and after that there is a trip-reality method to remind us that it is a manager.

9.5.2 How Augmented Reality Works

Augmented reality is live. For it to work, the client must almost certainly observe this present reality as it is at present. AR controls this current reality space the client sees, modifying the client's view of the real world. In one AR stage, the client watches a live chronicle of this present reality with virtual components forced over it. Loads of games use this kind of AR; the watcher can watch the diversion live from their very own TV yet see the scores overlaid on the amusement field (De la Rosa et al. 2017).

Another AR type enables the client to check out their condition typically and continuously, yet through a showcase that overlays data to augment the understanding. A case of this is Google Glass, a gadget that seems much like an ordinary pair of glasses. However, it incorporates a little screen on which the client can see GPS bearings, check the climate, send photographs, and perform in numerous different capacities.

When a virtual item is set between the client and this present reality, object acknowledgment and PC vision can enable the article to be controlled by genuine physical materials and allows the client to communicate with the virtual components.

For instance, some versatile retailer applications enable customers to choose a virtual form of something they are thinking about buying, for example, a household item, and view it in the original space of their home through their telephone. They can see their real lounge room, for instance. However, the virtual love seat they have picked is presently noticeable to them through their screen, giving them a chance to choose if it will fit in that room and the off-chance they like its appearance inside that room.

Another precedent enables the client to filter items or unique codes (for example, Universal Product Code (UPC) images) that utilize AR to demonstrate to the client more data about a physical object before they get it, see surveys from different purchasers, or check what is inside their unopened bundle.

9.5.3 Marker and Marker-Less AR

When object acknowledgment is utilized with augmented reality, the framework perceives what is being seen and afterwards employs that data to connect with the AR gadget. When a particular marker is evident to the device the client can cooperate in order to finish the AR experience.

These markers may be QR codes, sequential numbers, or other articles that can be disengaged from their condition for the camera to see. When enrolled, the augmented reality gadget may overlay data from that marker straightforwardly on the screen or open a connection, play a sound, and so on. Marker-less augmented reality enables a framework to utilize an area or a position-based article to stay focused, similar to the compass, GPS, or an accelerometer. These sorts of augmented reality frameworks are executed when a city is vital, such as a route AR.

9.5.4 Layered AR

This type of AR utilizes a gadget used to perceive a physical space and virtual overlay data over it. It is how one can attempt virtual garments, show route ventures before a journey, check whether another household item will fit in your home, put on fun tattoos, and the sky is the limit from there (Lauterbach, Bonime-Blanc, and Bremmer 2018).

9.5.5 Projection AR

This aspect may appear at first to be equivalent to layered or superimposed augmented reality. Yet it is diverse in one explicit way: good light is anticipated on to a surface to mimic a physical item. Another approach to consider projection AR is as a multidimensional image.

One explicit use for this augmented reality may be extending a keypad or console legitimately on to a surface, enabling a client to type utilizing the anticipated virtual console.

There are numerous points of interest in utilizing augmented reality in zones like a drug, the travel industry, the work environment, support, promoting, the military, and others.

9.5.6 AR in Education

It may very well be less demanding and progressively amusing to learn with augmented reality within certain faculties, and there are vast amounts of AR applications that can encourage that. A couple of glasses or a cell phone can be all one has to become familiar with physical items, similar to works of art. One example of a free AR application is SkyView, which enables one to point a telephone at the sky or the ground and see where stars, satellites, planets, and groups of stars are situated at that minute, both during the day, around evening time, and from the other side of the earth.

Skyview is viewed as a layered augmented reality application that utilizes GPS. It demonstrates this present reality, similar to trees and other individuals. It also uses the location and the current time to train someone where these articles are found and to give more data about them. Google Translate is another case of an AR application valuable for learning. With it, one can examine a message in a language one does not comprehend, and it will interpret it continuously (Lauterbach, Bonime-Blanc, and Bremmer 2018).

9.5.7 AR in Navigation

Showing route courses against a windshield or through a headset conveys augmented guidelines for drivers, bicyclists, and different voyagers, so they do not need to look down at their GPS gadget or cell phone to see which street to take ahead. Pilots may utilize an AR framework to show straightforward speed and height markers legitimately inside their observable pathway for much the same reason. Another utilization for an AR route application may be to overlay an eatery's appraisals, client remarks, or menu things directly over the structure before one heads inside. Likewise, it may demonstrate the snappiest course to the closest Italian eatery as one strolls through an unfamiliar city (De and Bourdot 2018).

GPS AR applications like Car Finder AR can be utilized to locate where you left your vehicle. A holographic GPS framework like WayRay (used to develop strong holographic AR tools) may overlay headings directly out and about before you.

9.5.8 AR in Games

There are bunches of AR recreations and AR toys that can consolidate the physical and virtual world, and they come in a wide range of structures for heaps of gadgets. One easily understood model is Snapchat, which gives clients a chance to overlay fun veils and plans on their appearances before communicating something specific through their cell phones. The application utilizes a live form of one face to put a virtual picture over it.

9.6 Mixed Reality

Mixed reality (MR), as the name indicates, blends actual and virtual situations to shape a crossover reality. MR utilizes components of both virtual simulation and augmented reality to make something new. It is hard to classify MR as anything besides augmented reality. It works by overlaying virtual components legitimately on to this present reality, giving someone a chance to see both in the meantime, particularly like AR. One essential concentration with mixed reality is that the articles are tied down to good physical items associated with progressively. This aspect implies that MR could enable virtual characters to sit in the rear seats in a room or for the virtual downpour to fall and hit the good ground with life-like material science.

MR lets the client consistently exist in both a genuine state with the definite articles around them and the virtual world with programming rendered objects cooperating with certifiable items to make an utterly vivid encounter. The Microsoft HoloLens exhibition is an actual case of what is implied by mixed reality.

9.7 Virtual Reality

Virtual reality (VR) makes it conceivable to encounter anything, anyplace, whenever. It is the most vivid kind of real innovation and can persuade the human mind that it is at a place, although it is not. Head-mounted showcases are utilized with earphones and hand controllers to give an utterly vivid encounter. With the most significant innovation organizations on Earth (Facebook, Google, and Microsoft) putting billions of dollars into virtual reality organizations and new companies, augmented reality's eventual fate is set to be a mainstay of our regular day-to-day existence.

A realistic 3D picture or fake condition is made with a blend of original equipment and programming and displayed to the client. Any questions are suspended and acknowledged as a legitimate domain in which it cooperates within a genuine or physical way.

Complete inundation implies that the substantial experience feels so genuine that we overlook a virtual-fake condition and start cooperating with it as we would typically in reality. In an augmented experience condition, a manufactured world could conceivably mirror the properties of a valid domain. This implies that the virtual experience condition may reenact a regular setting. For example, strolling around London's roads may surpass the limits of physical reality by making a world in which the physical laws overseeing gravity, time, and material properties never again hold (Vermesan and Bacquet 2017).

9.7.1 Virtual World

A virtual world is a three-dimensional condition regularly, yet not really, acknowledged through a medium (for example, rendering, show, etc.) where one can associate with others and make questions as a feature of that communication. In a virtual world, visual viewpoints are receptive to development, and cooperation impersonates those accomplished in reality (Vermesan and Bacquet 2017).

Augmented reality drenching is the view of being physically present in a non-physical world. It envelops the essence's feeling, which is where the human mind trusts that it is at some place; it is honestly not and is cultivated through simply mental and physical methods. The condition of complete submersion exists when enough faculties are initiated to make the impression of being available in a non-physical world. There are two basic kinds of inundation, mental immersion and physical immersion.

9.7.2 Mental Immersion

Mental immersion is a profound mental condition of commitment, with the suspension of disbelief and is in a virtual situation.

9.7.3 Physical Immersion

Physical immersion is an exhibited real commitment in a virtual domain, with the suspension of doubt that one is in a virtual situation.

9.7.4 Tangible Feedback

Virtual reality requires, however, many of our faculties as could reasonably be expected to be mimicked. These faculties incorporate vision (visual), hearing (aural), contact (haptic), and that is only the tip of the iceberg. Legitimately invigorating this sense requires substantial criticism, accomplished through incorporated equipment and programming (otherwise called data sources). Instances of this equipment and information sources are discussed below as critical parts of a virtual experience framework, incorporating head-mounted presentations (HMPs), unique gloves or hand extras, and hand controls.

9.7.5 Intelligence

The communication component is urgent for virtual reality encounters to give clients enough solace to draw in with the virtual condition normally. If the virtual situation reacts to a client's activity characteristically, submersion energy and faculties will remain. On the off-chance that the virtual situation cannot respond speedily enough, the human mind will rapidly see, and the feeling of inundation will reduce (Ma et al. 2012). Virtual condition reactions to the association can incorporate how a member moves around or changes in their perspective, by and large, through their head developments.

9.7.6 Types of Virtual Reality

A few classifications of virtual reality advancements exist, which are bound to develop as this innovation advances. The different sorts of virtual reality contrast in their inundation dimensions and augmented reality applications and use cases. We will investigate a couple of the distinctive classes of augmented reality later.

Non-vivid reproductions are the least vivid execution of augmented reality innovation. In a non-vivid reproduction, just a subset of the client's faculties is invigorated, considering fringe attention to the reality outside the augmented experience re-enactment. Clients go into these 3D virtual conditions through an entrance or window by using standard high goal screens controlled by handling power commonly found on ordinary work area work-stations (Jung and Tom 2018).

9.7.7 Semi-Immersive

Semi-vivid recreations give a progressively vivid encounter, in which the client is some-what yet not completely submerged in a virtual situation. Semi-vivid recreations intently look like and use a large number of similar advancements found in flight reenactment. Elite graphical processing frameworks control semi-vivid re-enactments regularly and then combine with comprehensive screen projector frameworks or various TV projection frame-works to appropriately animate the client's visuals (Ma et al. 2012).

9.7.8 Completely Immersive

Completely vivid recreations give the most vivid usage of augmented reality innovation. In an entirely vivid reproduction, equipment, such as head-mounted shows and movement recognizing gadgets, is utilized to invigorate most clients' detections. Utterly vivid re-enactments can give practical clients some encounters by conveying a full field of view, high goals, augmented update rates, invigorated rates, and abnormal amounts of difference in a client's head-mounted display (HMD) (Jung and Tom 2018).

9.8 Key Components in a Virtual Reality System

9.8.1 PC (Personal Computer)/Console/Smartphone

Virtual reality content, which clients see within an augmented experience headset, is simi-larly vital to the headset itself. Explanatory processing power is required to control these natural 3D conditions. This aspect is the place where a PC (Personal Computer), comforts, and cell phones come in. They go about as the motor to control the substance being delivered.

9.8.2 Head-Mounted Display

A head-mounted showcase (also called an HMD, headset, or goggles) is a kind of gadget containing a presentation mounted before a client's eyes. This presentation generally covers the client's full field of view and shows virtual reality content. Some virtual simulation head-mounted showcases use cell phone shows, including the Google Cardboard and Samsung Gear VR. Head-mounted presentations regularly likewise go with a headset to accommodate sound incitement.

9.8.3 Information Devices

Information gadgets are two classifications of parts that give clients a feeling of drenching (for example, persuading the human mind to acknowledge a fake domain as genuine). They provide clients with a progressively standard approach to explore and collaborate inside an augmented experience condition.

9.8.4 Augmented Reality versus Virtual Reality

Augmented Reality (AR) and Virtual Reality (VR) are introduced using top-notch 3D video and sound. The two advances originate from a similar thought of inundating clients with a digital domain. Be that as it may, while VR is vivid, AR mainly overlays virtual articles over this present reality. It utilizes regular gadgets, cell phone or a tablet, and sensors and market to recognize physical item situations and afterwards figure out where to put virtual ones.

Even though the augmented reality is still in its earliest stages, it has been around for some time now. A Survey of AR by Ronald T. Azuma that goes back to 1997 broadly expounds on AR's conceivable uses. The creator recognized something like six classes of potential use: medicinal representation, support and fix, explanation, robot way of arranging, excitement, and military flying machine route and focus (Jung and Tom 2018).

9.8.5 Benefits of Augmented Reality

Even though not at its full blossom, augmented reality (AR) has a great deal to offer. Because of its highlights, AR is viewed as more speaking to the market than augmented reality.

As per Digi-Capital's ongoing report, AR applications can achieve 3.5 billion introduced bases and up to $85–90 billion inside five years. In the interim, VR's numbers are 50–60 million imported bases and $10–15 billion.

The motivation behind AR is substantially more useful due to its universality, while VR is increasingly engaged. VR's primary strong point is how it inundates a client into virtual reality, making it a unique device for gaming or 3D films. As per the report, AR can address cell phones and tablets as they both tear up and develop. The potential outcomes and fields of augmented reality applications are incredible.

9.9 Augmented Reality Uses

Gradually yet unquestionably, augmented reality is changing the state of the business. Tractica guessed that by 2019 an introduced base of effectively utilized augmented reality applications would develop to more than 2.2 billion apps. Augmented reality can be connected to different businesses. A standout amongst the most intriguing cases originates from the accompanying businesses.

9.9.1 Retail

In retail, augmented reality (AR) has bunches of chances. One has to choose whether it will be a coming up or out-of-store involvement. The main chance implies that clients will cooperate with AR inside the dividers of the store. This could be virtual fitting rooms to enable clients to choose the size or the shade of an item. Out-of-store experience implies that clients do not need to leave their homes to have an encounter like Converse, the Sampler application that permits clients to attempt to pick a couple of shoes that is a most loved model. EBay Inc., as of late, reported that it is dealing with an AR pack to make shopping increasingly fun and productive. For example, it will permit dealers to select the container's correct size for an item by overlaying a picture of a case overstock (Arnaldi, Guitton, and Moreau 2018).

9.9.2 Real Estate

Since the internet is the central spot where purchasers and leaseholders search for new homes, AR has a great deal to offer for the land. It can enable clients to encounter houses unexpectedly, channel the ones they like or do not want, and spare some time for customers and real estate brokers. It is an incredible instrument for development laborers also. They breathe life into the outlines and pictures for customers to perceive how their planned new home may look.

9.9.3 Interior Design

AR-enabled inside plan applications are here to help settle on a correct choice about another household item's size and style. A standout amongst most mainstream precedents originates from a Swedish retail mammoth IKEA and its IKEA Place AR application. It settles on purchasing choices simpler by empowering them to "attempt on" their pieces in one room and take photographs and recordings of the outcome. It is precise to the point that one can even observe the surface of the furnishings.

9.9.4 Tourism and Maps

Although relatively new for the travel industry, AR has become increasingly popular and has many benefits such as physical location enhancement, gaming apps, and wall map compatibility in store for companies and hotels. There are many scenarios and applications of AR usage in museums and galleries, giving visitors more information. Multiple images can be turned into three-dimensional animation, and visitors can download an app and interact with it. Galleries that permit data about the displays have introduced AR technology to present a new dimension to their old displays. With the Skin and Bone app, it is possible to superimpose many skeletons to reconstruct the creatures. China is among the nations that handle AR technology to connect with shows and draw in travelers. Road signs guide and give assistance to explore and investigate urban areas, lodging visits – the sky is the point of confinement. With technological advancement in Blockchain, Robots, and IoT, we will see many applications within the travel industry evolve.

9.9.5 Training and Education

Bringing AR innovation into a study hall can make the practice all the more captivating, intuitive, and even the most exhausting subject somewhat fun. By downloading and getting to applications on their telephones, understudies can get progressively limited data or well-ordered directions and superior comprehension of the subject.

9.9.6 Healthcare

One of the enterprises that can profit from augmented reality is social insurance. From helping patients recognize and portray their side effects better, with applications like EyeDecide that can demonstrate an impact of, for example, a waterfall on the human eye and along these lines helps a patient comprehend the side effects. Either or then again, this is valuable to medical staff in making it simpler to discover veins or assisting specialists in using strategies – they all appear extraordinary methods for exploiting augmented reality.

9.10 Applications of Virtual Reality in Business

Virtual Reality (VR) may have begun life as a specialty item in the gaming business, yet its advantages have now moved into the more extensive business circle. With VR, organizations can make consistent decisions with life recreations in hazard-free, practical ways. The uses of VR and AR are restricted by our creative energies. While the innovation still has some of the best approaches before it hits the standard, here are five essential business applications for VR used at present.

9.10.1 Training

Preparing is a standout amongst the most imperative utilizations of VR. In 2017, Walmart collaborated with a VR maker to strive to plan representatives for its Black Friday deals. Submerging representatives in an exact situation of long lines and groups are ideal for setting them up for not regular occasions (Kalawsky 2014). It additionally expels the need to irritate ordinary business activities for preparing purposes. In a progressively unique case of VR preparation, Oculus Virtual Speech enables clients to rehearse their open talking aptitudes in a reproduced situation. Speakers can transfer their introduction slides to the virtual room, experience diversions, and constantly criticize their conveyance. In the therapeutic part, VR empowers therapeutic services experts to rehearse in a hazard-free condition that would be inconceivable in reality. Oculus worked with the Children's Hospital of Los Angeles (CHLA) to prepare staff for high hazard pediatric injury cases (Kalawsky 2014).

9.10.2   Retail

Retail offers the absolute most expressly business uses of VR. In physical shops, VR heats mapping innovation. For example, from Yulio VR tracks, a customer's look comes up, giving a point-by-point example of which regions or items will pull in their consideration. This aspect empowers retailers to test and refine their presentations, signage, and store format to expand shopper experience and spending. VR likewise allows customers to investigate items in a real existence way. In 2016 Ikea propelled its VR Kitchen Experience in Australia to enable clients to find a kitchen and includes an envision of how they would feel with it in their own home. As LEK's 2017 review counseling indicated, around 70% of early tech adopters were anxious to utilize AR and VR innovation for shopping purposes. VR stores are never swamped, have profoundly mindful aides, and encourage a very customized shopping knowledge.

9.10.3   Construction

The utilization of VR in development has a large group of advantages. VR stages, for example, those given by Iris VR, empower planners to walk customers through their structures before they have been fabricated, providing imperative open doors for input and change. The capacity to investigate development designs in a 1 : 1 scale through VR likewise crosses over any barrier between this present reality and a creator's creative energy, giving them a chance to envisage their structures' full-scale impact. VR portfolios have likewise developed as a path for planners to grandstand their work to forthcoming customers. Innovation makes it simple to transform paper plans into 3D PC models, and afterward into vivid VR reproductions. Investigating building structures through VR causes potential customers to be more likely to comprehend a draftsman's work.

9.10.4   Data Representation

Information representation has made some fantastic progress since the time of the pie diagram. Augmented and VR makes it conceivable to show information in 3D shows, which would then be communicated dynamically. Established in 2016, the US organization Virtualitics has made a virtual stage that blends AI, Big Data, and Mixed Reality to offer point-by-point and connect with information representation strategies (Kalawsky 2014). In the Virtualitics stage, clients see, break down, and work cooperatively on their information in their own VR space. Such a customizable methodology ensures that the information examination satisfies the necessities of individual organizations. The original introduction of information through VR is a critical advance in changing bits of knowledge into business activities and observing potential anomalies that should be tended.

9.10.5 Manufacture

VR has an essential job in the assembling business because of its one-of-a-kind applications in the plan and prototyping process. For example, producers, such as aviation goliaths Boeing and Airbus, utilize the innovation to wipe out the requirement for costly, full-scale models of their planes. Since 2007, Airbus has employed VR innovation RAMSIS (Realistic Anthropological Mathematical System) to reproduce a lodge inside plan. With a specific spotlight on ergonomics, RAMSIS empowers Airbus to amplify the space inside flying machine lodges and improve client comfort. In the meantime, it checks variables, for example, the simplicity of part upkeep and establishment. In the small space of flying machines, slight changes can have extensive effects. VR's vivid experience encourages producers to take a far-reaching view on modifications, including essential well-being highlights, for example, the reachability of breathing apparatuses and life jackets.

9.11 The Future of Blockchain

In improving the web, one can point to milestone occasions that can separate the procedure into stages. Among these imperative milestones is the production of the main PC in the 1960s, the improvement of the electronic mail framework during the 1970s, the formation of Ethernet later, the Internet's start during the 1990s, and the principal programs making and web search tools a decade later. Following every one of these trademark improvements, the web changed drastically. Each progression was vital in making the web that we know and depend on today.

Likewise, it is conceivable to think back on Blockchain's improvement and partition it into stages separated by significant advancements and developments. Blockchain innovation has just been in presence for a small amount of the time that the web has existed, so it is almost certain that there will be important advancements to come. However, even now, specialists have started to partition Blockchain's historical backdrop into somewhere around three critical stages.

While the thoughts that would go into Blockchain were whirling around in software engineering networks, it was the pseudonymous designer of bitcoin, Satoshi Nakamoto, who sketched out the Blockchain, probably being aware of it in the white paper for BTC. Along these lines, Blockchain innovation started with bitcoin. As per a Coin Insider, "numerous enthusiastic designers around the globe still think about that Blockchain innovation may be flawlessly fit" for this computerized cash and for propelling the objectives of advanced monetary forms all the more comprehensively.

In the most punctual stages, Blockchain sets up the essential reason for a standard open record underpinning digital money arrange. Satoshi's Blockchain concept makes utilization of 1 megabyte (MB) squares of data on bitcoin exchanges. Squares are connected through a multiple cryptographic confirmation process, forming a changeless chain. Indeed, even in its most regular appearances, Blockchain innovation set up many of the focal highlights of these frameworks, which remain today. Undoubtedly, bitcoin's Blockchain remains, to a great extent, unaltered from these earliest endeavors.

As time went on, engineers started to trust that a Blockchain could accomplish more than just record exchanges. For example, authors of Ethereum (a global, decentralized platform for money and new kinds of applications) believed that advantages and trust understandings could likewise profit by the Blockchain executives. Along these lines, Ethereum speaks to the second-age of Blockchain innovation.

The significant development realized by Ethereum was the coming of brilliant contracts. Typically, settlements in the standard business world are overseen by two separate elements, some of which have different factors aiding the oversight procedure. Brilliant agreements are those that are self-overseeing on a Blockchain. They are activated by an occasion like the death of a lapse date or accomplishing a specific value objective; accordingly, the brilliant contract oversees itself, making changes as required and without the contribution of outside elements.

Now, numerous experts trust that we are still spending billions towards the undiscovered capability of block chain contracts. In this manner, regardless of whether we have genuinely proceeded onward to the resulting phase of Blockchain advancement, it is easily proven to be wrong.

One of the pressing issues confronting Blockchain is scaling. Bitcoin stays vexed by exchange, preparing times, and bottlenecks. Numerous new computerized monetary standards have endeavored to reconsider their Blockchain to suit these issues, but with changing degrees of progress. Later on, a standout amongst the most immediate improvements making ready for Blockchain innovation going ahead will probably have to do with adaptability.

Apart from this, new utilization of Blockchain innovation is being found and continuously executed. It is hard to state precisely where these advancements will lead the change and the digital money industry in general. Supporters of Blockchain will probably find this unfathomably energizing; from their point of view, we live in a minute with an epochal innovation that is proceeding to develop and unfurl (Shivakumar and Sethii 2019).

Blockchain innovation has turned out to be prevalent because of its active selection of digital currencies like bitcoin. This dispersed computerized record has numerous favorable circumstances. It can keep the records of everything being equal or cash exchange made between any two gatherings in a safe, unchanging, and straightforward way. A year ago, the idea of Blockchain began to catch open consideration. Specialists anticipated Blockchain innovation would be actualized for different enterprises and expect that Blockchain's eventual fate is to upset common business forms. In any case, Blockchain's advantages and disadvantages demonstrate that it is not as simple to do as it appears.

A year ago, we saw an expansion in subsidizing Blockchain new businesses. Be that as it may, similar to any innovation, Blockchain is as yet juvenile in its usage, so it can meet speculators' desires. Subsequently, numerous Blockchain new businesses can be viewed as only an exercise in futility and cash. False beginnings in Blockchain sending could lead to fizzled advancements, imprudent choices, and even total refusal of this creative innovation.

Without a doubt, Blockchain innovation will later influence each part of organizations, yet this is a regular procedure that requires time and persistence (Pathak and Bhandari 2018). Gartner predicts that most customary organizations will watch out for Blockchain innovation; however, they may not design any activities, sitting tight for more instances of any changes best uses.

The explanation behind this is that customary ventures require more change for a Blockchain arrangement than have recently showed up in organizations. Gartner indicated that just 10% of conventional organizations would accomplish any extreme change with Blockchain advances by 2023.

9.12 Blockchain Applications

Unlike other conventional organizations, the banking and fund ventures do not have to provide radical change when embracing Blockchain innovation procedures. After it was effectively connected for the digital currency, money-related organizations started honestly to consider Blockchain selection for current financial activities. For example, in 2016, ReiseBank AG in Germany finished momentary installments between two of its customers on a cross-fringe premise, utilizing Blockchain innovation in around 20 seconds. As to the late PWC report, 77% of financial organizations were relied upon to receive Blockchain innovation as a feature of an underway framework or procedure by 2020 (Shivakumar and Sethii 2019).

Even though the idea of Blockchain is straightforward, it will bring vital investment funds for banks. Blockchain innovation will enable banks to diminish extreme organization, direct quicker exchanges at lower costs, and improve its mystery. Gartner's Blockchain expectations are that the financial businesses will infer 1 billion dollars of business esteem from utilization of Blockchain-based digital forms of money by 2020.

Additionally, Blockchain can propel new cryptographic forms of money that will be managed or impacted by financial arrangements. Like this, banks need to lessen the upper hand of independent digital forms of payment and accomplish more prominent power over their fiscal strategy. The Australian Securities Exchange also wanted to utilize another Blockchain-based framework to deal with the Australian commercial market towards the end of 2020.

9.12.1 National Cryptographic Money

Russian President Vladimir Putin was the primary person who proposed to issue "Crypto Rouble," a national digital currency. It is inescapable that administrations should perceive the advantages of Blockchain-determined monetary forms. At the ascent of bitcoin, governments communicated their distrust regarding the specific utilization of digital forms of money. Be that as it may, they needed to stress when Bitcoin turned into tradeable cash that could not be constrained by any legislature.

Albeit a few nations like China still boycott bitcoin trades, we ought to expect that administrations will acknowledge the Blockchain-based money in 2018 in light of its possible favorable circumstances for open and likely administrations. Before that year, Venezuela has just propelled its national digital currency petro (Petromoneda), supported by the nation's oil and mineral stores. Venezuela's legislature trusts that this digital currency will permit bypassing the US authorization and draw global funds to the government. By 2022, Gartner predicts that something like five nations will issue national digital money (Pathak and Bhandari 2018).

9.12.2 Blockchain into Government

The possibility of the conveyed record is additionally extremely alluring to government experts that need to administrate exceptionally substantial amounts of information. Every office has a different database, so they always need to require data about occupants from one another. In any case, the execution of Blockchain advances for compelling information to the executives will improve such offices (Shivakumar and Sethii 2019).

Estonia has officially executed Blockchain innovation on the administration level. Practically all open administrations in Estonia approach X-Road, a decentralized advanced record that contains all inhabitants and residents' data. The innovation utilizes a propelled encryption innovation and incorporates two-factor confirmation, empowering individuals to control their information and ensure security. As per Gartner, by 2022, over a billion people will have a little information about them put away on a Blockchain, yet they may not know about it.

9.12.3 Blockchain Specialists

Regardless of Blockchain being on the highest point of its prevalence, the activity advertises the absence of Blockchain specialists. Upwork, an internet outsourcing database, has a quick expanding interest in individuals with specific recent "Blockchain" abilities. While innovation is new, there are a predetermined number of Blockchain engineers. On the off chance that one enters the business with some involvement in Blockchain innovation, it will work well. In any case, there is a hazard that a Blockchain startup that procured one may need to shut down soon, given an absence of financing. Numerous individuals would like to stop their present place of employment to work for a Blockchain venture. Along these lines, extreme interest in experienced Blockchain designers will likewise be one of the Blockchain patterns in the future.

9.13 Blockchain and the Internet of Things

The International Data Corporation (IDC) reports that numerous IoT organizations are thinking about Blockchain innovation in their answers. In this manner, IDC expects that almost 20% of IoT organizations will empower Blockchain benefits in the future. The purpose behind this is that Blockchain innovation can give a protected and versatile system for correspondence between IoT gadgets. While current security conventions previously seemed, by all accounts, to be powerless when executed to IoT gadgets, Blockchain has effectively endorsed its high protection from cyber-attacks.

Moreover, Blockchain will enable brilliant gadgets to make mechanized smaller scale exchanges. Because of its dispersed nature, Blockchain will direct transfers quicker and be less expensive. IoT gadgets will use brilliant contracts, which will be considered as the understanding between the two gatherings.

9.14 Law Coordination

Other than cryptographic money, Blockchain innovation benefits us with another significant probability, for example, "keen gets." The principal thought of savvy arrangements is its scheduled execution when conditions are met. For example, conveying products after the installment has been obtained. In any case, different states of agreements ought to likewise be consequently directed. Hence, Insurers AIG is presently guiding a Blockchain framework that permits making complex protection arrangements.

One ought to likewise remember that brilliant contracts are decentralized and are not managed by any specialist. Be that as it may, what should parties do if there should be any contradiction? Members of savvy contracts more often than not consent to be bound by guidelines, yet consider the possibility that a question shows up between gatherings from various nations. Presently, it is not clear how authoritative questions ought to be settled. In this way, the standard of law should be implemented into brilliant contracts sooner rather than later to determine any issue between the gatherings.

Blockchain, later on, will change business forms in numerous enterprises. However, its appropriation requires time and endeavor. In any case, soon we can expect that legislatures will at long last acknowledge Blockchain advantages and start to utilize it for improving money-related and open administrations. Even though some Blockchain new businesses will come up short, individuals will understand information on the most proficient method to utilize this innovation. Blockchain will animate individuals to secure new abilities, while customary business should re-examine their procedures. In the near future, we should see more instances of fruitful execution of Blockchain innovations.

9.15 Collaboration for Blockchain Success

Close joint effort keeps on being the total need for Blockchain achievement. The closer the collaborative effort among engineers and business associations, the better the outcomes that arise. What is more, the closer everyone works with shoppers, the more probable the result will be something alluring to them.

The instruments to interface with it are generally planned for designers. Making encounters for customers is hard and enabling purchasers to connect with it straightforwardly can be much harder.

Each activity on an open Blockchain requires an exchange charge in cryptographic money. It is a little expensive. However, it is more noteworthy than zero. That was worthy when Blockchains were utilized exclusively for budgetary exchanges. However, the present use cases have extended to incorporate complex trades with savvy gets that may have nothing to do with cash exchanges.

Tackling this issue requires a specialized aptitude from the designer network and a clear comprehension of client experience, which will pull in customers to utilize the Blockchain. In addition, there is a potential answer – all the more vitally, it has been shared. Somewhere down in an ethereal GitHub vault lies a solution that could permit specialist co-ops to pay for mining costs without influencing the exchange's uprightness.

Shoppers will never again need digital money to invest, conveying us more like a client experience that customers will perceive. This attention to talk and sharing is the way to the future accomplishment of this innovation.

Designers, obviously, definitely know this. It is truly energizing that the organizations that remain to pick up the most from this innovation's utilization know it as well. They are reconsidering how they work: instead of building up their administrations in shut, exclusive storehouses, they are also tossing open their ways to engineers and different pioneers to construct what is to come.

Associations facilitate gatherings, round-tables, board discourses, and hackathons to make the crucial associations and pool assets together. Organizations are producing associations with engineer networks.

This aspect is the exciting virtuoso of Blockchain: it supports cooperation. Just as designers, organizations need to contribute their thoughts and empowering advances all together for them both to succeed. We saw the advantages of this methodology for ourselves at Thomson Reuters not long ago, when we facilitated a hackathon with Ethereum to test our empowering innovation BlockOne ID, which we at that point placed online in beta for further improvement. It is an administration that causes engineers to perform perseverance on their clients – another perceived test when purchasers straightforwardly interface with Blockchain – and the consequences of this methodology have been empowering (Vermesan and Bacquet 2017).

Engineers have been exceptionally positive. They disclosed to us they valued a solid brand attempting to empower them, to enable them to deliver an issue near both of our souls. They have met people's high expectations and connected creatively with our mutual reason: to make the Blockchain work for associations and their clients.

References

Arnaldi, B., Guitton, P., and Moreau, G. (2018). *Virtual Reality and Augmented Reality: Myths and Realities*. Wiley-ISTE.

CHIPIN (2019, November). Meet the boss – exclusive interview with experty CEO kamil przeorskiv. https://www.chipin.com/experty-ceo-kamil-przeorski-interview/ (accessed 22 June 2021).

De, P.L.T. and Bourdot, P. (2018). *Augmented Reality, Virtual Reality, and Computer Graphics: Proceedings of the 5th International Conference, AVR 2018*, Otranto, Italy (June 24–27, 2018).

De la Rosa, J.I., El-Fadki, A., Torres, V., and Amengual, X. (2017). Logo recognition by consensus for enabling blockchain implementation. In: *Recent Advances in Artificial Intelligence Research and Development: Proceedings of the 20th International Conference of the Catalan Association for Artificial Intelligence*, Deltebre, Terres de l'Ebre, Spain, (October 25–27, 2017), 257–262. IOS Press.

Jung, T.H. and Tom, D.M.C. (2018). *Augmented Reality and Virtual Reality: Empowering Human, Place, and Business*. Springer International Publishing AG.

Kalawsky, R.S. (2014). *The Science of Virtual Reality and Virtual Environments: A Technical, Scientific, and Engineering Reference on Virtual Environments*. Wokingham, England: Addison-Wesley.

Lauterbach, A., Bonime-Blanc, A., and Bremmer, I. (2018). The Artificial Intelligence imperative: A practical roadmap for the business. https://www.amazon.com/Artificial-Intelligence-Imperative-Practical-Business/dp/1440859949 (accessed 22 June 2021).

Ma, D., Gausemeier, J., Fan, X., and Grafe, M. (2012). *Virtual Reality & Augmented Reality in Industry*. Springer Retrieved from: https://www.google.com/books/edition/Virtual_Reality_Augmented_Reality_in_Ind/h3BphcV7oRkC?hl=en&gbpv=1&dq=Virtual+Reality+and+Augmented+Reality+in+Industry&printsec=frontcover#spf=1607324844826.

Marwala, T. and Xing, B. (2018). Blockchain and Artificial Intelligence. *SSRN Electronic Journal* Retrieved from: https://www.researchgate.net/publication/323164794_Blockchain_and_Artificial_Intelligence.

Pathak, N. and Bhandari, A. (2018). IOT, AI, and Blockchain for.NET: Building a next-generation application from the ground up.

Salah, K., Habib ur Rehman, M., Nizamuddin, M., and Al-Fuqaha, N.A. (2018). Blockchain for AI: Review and open research challenges. IEEE Access. PP. 10.1109. https://www.researchgate.net/publication/330010876_Blockchain_for_AI_Review_and_Open_Research_Challenges_Top_of_Form (accessed 22 June 2021).

Shivakumar, S.K. and Sethii, S. (2019). *Building Digital Experience Platforms: A Guide to Developing Next-Generation Enterprise Applications*. Apress Retrieved from: https://www.google.com/books/edition/Building_Digital_Experience_Platforms/FBOGDwAAQBAJ?hl=en&gbpv=1&dq=Building+digital+experience+platforms:+A+guide+to+developing+next-generation+enterprise+applications.&printsec=frontcover#spf=1607324639139.

Vermesan, O., and Bacquet, J. (2017). *Cognitive Hyperconnected Digital Transformation: Internet of Things Intelligence Evolution*. River Publishers. https://www.google.com/books/edition/Cognitive_Hyperconnected_Digital_Transfo/nPIxDwAAQBAJ?hl=en&gbpv=1&dq=Cognitive+Hyper+connected+Digital+Transformation:+Internet+of+Things+intelligence+evolution.&printsec=frontcover#spf=1607324519942.

10

Digital Twin Technology

10.1 Introduction

Current globalization trends demand complex and advanced information and communication technology systems. Information Technology (IT) systems have become the basis of basic operations in the world (Boschert and Rosen 2016). These demands have led to the advancement of digital infrastructure applied in research and production processes. The demands require new infrastructures such as networking of all devices, mobile devices, cloud infrastructure, data analytics algorithms, and collective cloud services. This chapter explores the Digital Twin concept and how it is interrelated to other technologies.

Digital Twin technology involves creating virtual simulation models of technical and physical assets that are untouched but maintained and changed by the information within a physical object (Botkina et al. 2018). These models are quite dynamic and receive real-time readings of information from sensors of physical assets, sensors of control devices, and the general environment. The models also take into consideration historical information obtained to adjust the parameters of the physical asset.

The models need to be dynamically updated in the Digital Twin concept to function correctly (Hribernik, Wuest, and Thoben 2013). The systems update the measurements in real-time and are regularly updated on the new and old data using Machine Learning (ML) algorithms. The system's goal is to achieve the physical object's optimal operational capabilities through regular and dynamic updates. When experts create the Digital Twin models, the physical object utilizes partial differential equations. The partial differential equations are traditionally constructed in combination with integral equations that employ the finite method. It should be noted that the finite element method objects to the changes in the Digital Twin model's characteristics without the input of an expert during maintenance of the changing object. This is because the model does not permit the dynamic addition of novel data, adjusting the sizes, and the number of grids involved in tracking changes that happen in the physical asset.

The Digital Twin system (see Figure 10.1) needs to continually learn and change its mode of operation based on inputs and updates by using methods such as Artificial Intelligence (AI), Machine Learning (ML), and Neural Networks. These dynamic Digital Twin models enable the projection of technical objects into the digital platform. This model ensures the

Intelligent Connectivity: AI, IoT, and 5G, First Edition. Abdulrahman Yarali.
© 2022 John Wiley & Sons Ltd. Published 2022 by John Wiley & Sons Ltd.

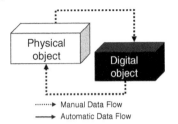

Figure 10.1 Digital Twin model (Boschert and Rosen 2016).

possibility to utilize these systems in order to optimize operations of the physical assets through automatic monitoring of technical aspects, fault aspects, and prediction of the future status of operations (Hribernik, Wuest, and Thoben 2013).

10.2 The Timeline and History of Digital Twin Technology

The concept of the Digital Twin is a concept evolving from other technologies. The technology has its roots in other technologies such as system simulation, three-dimensional (3D) modeling, geometric digital prototyping, and functional and behavioral prototyping. It is not an exclusively new invention. There is no single inventor or expert who can claim development of Digital Twin models (Boschert and Rosen 2016). Currently, there has been increased popularity of Digital Twin technology. The popularity reflects mainly on the inevitable future dependence on this technology in most economies and applications. The technology links both the virtual and physical worlds, and the two models are becoming integrated to great effect and advantage.

The concept has been popularized by Grieves' conception of virtual and physical products (Grieves 2014). The National Aeronautics and space exploration, popularly known as NASA, has also brought about numerous Digital Twin technology contributions. The Air Force Research laboratory has also perfected the concepts through research and contributions. The Digital Twin technology has solved several IT shortcomings and inadequacies, such as data acquisition, computer performance, algorithms, and digital descriptions. Siemens industries were the first industry player to apply Digital Twin technology in 2016.

There are currently tremendous research efforts on Digital Twin technology, with most industries devoting funds to research. The interest in Digital Twin has grown exponentially. Digital Twin models on the shop-floor have been explored (Tao et al. 2019a,b). The research focuses on the characteristics, operation mechanisms, key technologies, and Digital Twin composition on the shop-floor. The research provides theoretical support for the use of Digital Twins in the field of manufacturing. In its conclusion, the research gives recommendations on prospects and further application opportunities. Tao et al. (2019a,b) further explored the extended applications of three-dimension models and data and service models in order to improve the models.

Over the years, several experts have tried to define the Digital Twin concept, with two prominent definitions given by Grieves and another by NASA. The National Aeronautics Space explorations define the Digital Twin as an integration of multiphysics and probabilistic and multiscale simulation of a vehicle or system that employs the most appropriate physical models, updates sensors, and fleets history that mirror the operations of a corresponding twin. On the other hand, Grieves (2014) defined a Digital Twin as having three main operational parts: the physical asset in real space, the virtual products in virtual space, and the connection of information that links the physical and virtual entities. The definition of the Digital Twin is described in three categories. It involves a virtual entity that mimics the physical entity in the digital form to simulate the physical asset (behavior monitoring its status, complexities both internal and external), a reflection of system performance (detecting malfunctions), and predicting future trends. This three-dimensional model of a Digital Twin by Grieves is the most popular definition.

Continuous upgrading and expansion of Digital Twin technology requirements have led to new demands and trends. The most significant step has seen its use in civilian industries compared to before, which only applied to NASA and Military research (Grieves 2014). The popularity of Digital Twin has seen its application in several fields with different users and different demands. The combination of Digital Twin and other technologies such as the Internet of Things (IoT) has provided favorable cyber–physical interaction and data integration (Grieves 2014).

10.3 Technologies Employed in Digital Twin Models

Through the fusion of technologies in an intelligent connectivity platform for an up-to-date model of an actual physical asset, Digital Twin creates a virtual simulation model of a component, or a system of systems of statistical and physics-based methods that can update and represent the current assets of the operating environment.

10.3.1 Cloud Services

The Digital Twin models employ complex programs and algorithms (Boschert and Rosen 2016). As this model is dynamic, it needs to be hosted by powerful computers with large data at stake. Therefore, it is recommended that cloud services should be utilized to undertake and maintain models and programs in a common source computing environment. The cloud services provide convenient network services and demands to the general computing resources, including storage space, servers, applications, and software services. The services and resources are promptly used and released conveniently, incurring minimal operation costs (Hribernik, Wuest, and Thoben 2013).

There is a technological possibility of implementing the Digital Twin models for a set of machines and assets in cloud environments. The cloud environment's computing environment employs supercomputers and provides infrastructure-level services that allow the installation of platform software and platform-level services to host essential software.

10.3.2 Cyber-Physical Systems

The Digital Twin model has to implement technical state monitoring, diagnostics, and trends (Grieves 2014). The physical asset needs to interact with its virtual twin over the Internet using TCP/IP protocols. A class of cyber-physical systems does the connection.

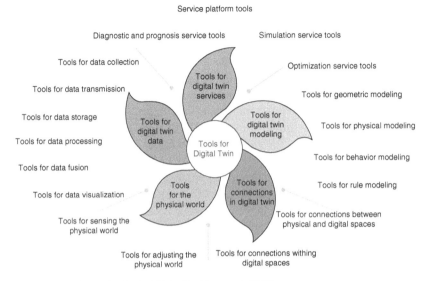

Figure 10.2 Tools for Digital Twin (Botkina et al. 2018).

The cyber-physical systems are technical systems that utilize global networks with corresponding protocols that interact internally with digital counterparts. The cyber-physical system's primary role is done by the sensors, which act as measurement instruments that relay meaningful data into the computing systems. There are various sensors used as measurement gadgets, from elementary ones to more complex and integrated ones. The sensors are installed in the wireless networks and measuring systems accompanied by a fault-tolerant wireless transmission, which is self-organizing, efficient, and adaptive. The cyber-physical systems employ current technology such as the Internet of Things (IoT). This technology complements the internet of people who can build technological research and operational processes while significantly reducing human participation, leading to absolute automation. The IoT is critical in developing the paradigm of transferring calculations from data centers, cloud computing, and the interaction of physically distributed devices. This approach is called foggy calculations (Hribernik, Wuest, and Thoben 2013). Figure 10.2 depicts examples of the service platform for Digital Twin (DTW).

10.4 The Dimension of Digital Twin Models

With three basic components of the real environment physical systems, the digital environment state and data linking these two states, Digital Twin is based on a five-dimensional model. As an enabling technology, Digital Twin is expected to become an integration of industry 4.0 for more widespread coverage, especially in IoT for manufacturing, healthcare, smart city to improve safety, cost saving, and new products.

10.4.1 Digital Twin Data

This is a crucial driver of Digital Twin models. Digital Twin engages a multitemporal scale, heterogeneous, multisource, and multidimensional data (Botkina et al. 2018). The data obtained from these physical entities, such as static attribute data or dynamic conditions, is key to running the Digital Twin models. Some of the user data is generated by the virtual twin, which reflects the results of the simulation. A certain amount of data is extracted from services. The data achieved from services mostly describes execution and invocation services. Another set of data is provided by domain experts from their pool of knowledge of the system, usually achieved by studying past or historical data (Botkina et al. 2018). Lastly, some of the data is known as fusion data and is acquired from integration of all the data types listed above.

10.4.2 Services in Digital Twins

Service is a key aspect of Digital Twins. There is an insurgent need for product-service integration in several aspects of modern life. Organizations and businesses are starting to take into consideration the importance of service-product integration. Service is essential in Digital Twin models in light of the paradigm of everything-as-a service (Grieves 2014). Digital Twin models give the users application services such as simulation, monitoring, verification, optimization, prognosis, and optimization. The services are mostly utilized in healthcare applications. Third-party services such as algorithm services, data services, and knowledge services are fundamental in building functional Digital Twin models. Also, Digital Twin operations need constant and continuous support of numerous platforms that accommodate a model building, service delivery, and customized software development.

10.4.3 Connection in Digital Twins

The virtual representatives are connected to their physical counterparts dynamically to facilitate advanced simulation, analysis, and operations (Grieves 2014). There are connections between physical assets, virtual models, services, and data to enable information to flow through the entire system. There are six known connections in Digital Twin models. They are the connection between physical assets and virtual assets (CN_PV), the connection between virtual models and data (CN_VS), the connection between virtual model and data (CN_VD), the connection between physical assets and data (CN_PD), the connection between physical entities and services (CN_PS), and the connection between services and data (CN_SD). The connections ensure ample collaboration between the four parts of the Digital Twin (Grieves 2014).

10.4.4 Physical Assets in Digital Twins

These are the machines or objects of interest. Digital Twin creates the virtual models of these physical entries in a bid to stimulate their manner of operations. The physical entities are the foundation of Digital Twin technology. It can either be active processes, devices, products, physical systems, or an organization. The Digital Twin models implement actions according to physical laws and deals in their environments. The physical entities can be divided into three levels: the unit level, the system level, and the product level.

10.4.5 Virtual Entities in Digital Twins

These are the faithful replicas of the physical entities (Grieves 2014). They simulate the geometries, behaviors, dimensions, properties, and rules of the corresponding physical entity. They employ the three-dimensional geometric models that describe the physical asset in terms of structural relation, tolerance, size, and shape, and also mimic the physical-based properties such as wear, speed, and force. The physics models simulate the physical aspects of the entities, such as fracture, wear, tear, deformity, and corrosion. The behavior models (see Figure 10.3) mimic the actual behaviors, such as performance, state transition, and coordination by considering these entities' responding tendencies against changes in the asset's external environment. The virtual entity enables Digital Twin entities to evaluate, judge, and make autonomous decision-making by following commands deduced from historical data.

Digital Twin technology is a high-tech system that processes a large amount of data. The data in question is collected over devices and tends to be descriptive, using color, height, weight, temperature, cost, etc. The data collected gives the readers a feel of what, when, and how (Jain et al. 2019). The system uses data analytics to explore the data and has an

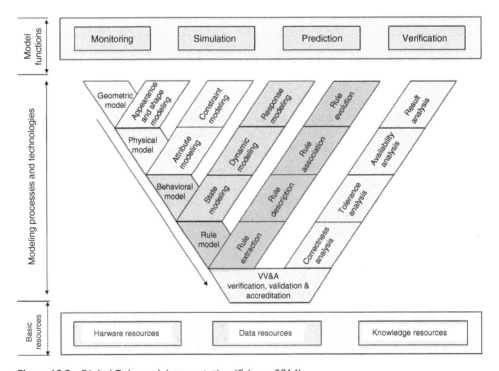

Figure 10.3 Digital Twin model presentation (Grieves 2014).

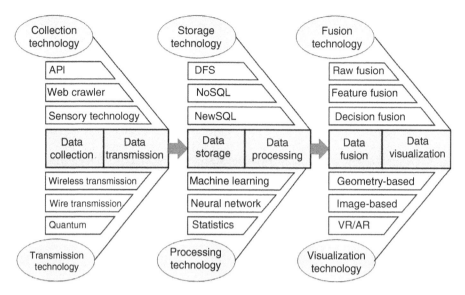

Figure 10.4 Enabling technologies of Digital Twin modules (Hribernik, Wuest, and Thoben 2013).

output that makes sense; for example, the cause of a malfunction in a machine. Digital Twin gives a virtual imitation of a process, product, or system that enables the users to improve the process virtually to avoid shortcomings. The technology utilizes several IT concepts such as the IoT, ML, and Data Analytics. Digital Twin technology utilizes these technologies to create digital simulation models that are as adaptive as their actual counterparts.

The simulations utilize real-time updates and repeated constant learning from several sources in the physical object. The data presents the status and working conditions of the asset (Grieves 2014). The system has sensors installed to collect real-time data to present the current situation of the physical object. Usually, the data is collected through the IoT technology and is then gathered, analyzed, and processed in predictive analytics through the Digital Twin system to improve the physical asset's performance levels. This optimizes maintenance of the physical assets (Jain et al. 2019).

Digital technologies provide a needed interface that empowers users to connect past experiences, analyze situations, and predict their assets' future trends. The source of data used in Digital Twin systems (Figure 10.4) contributes to the system's learning curve by using machine learning. The system models learn continuously from gathered information from sensors in the machines as well as from assets, processes, usage, experts, and other necessary sources (Jain et al. 2019).

10.5 Digital Twin and Other Technologies

A Digital Twin is an integration of numerous technologies to include the IoT, Digital Twins and the IoT, connectivity, Data Analytics, ML, and Artificial Intelligence (AI).

10.5.1 Digital Twins and Internet of Things

The IoT is the concept of connecting several essential items to the internet through sensor tools and devices to accomplish an intelligent recognition and management of networks (Kiritsis 2011). The general idea is to have ordinary objects tagged with extra sensory and communication interfaces to make a smart system that is controlled online. The vision of the IoT is to target a setup in which the internet is extended into the physical world connecting the objects (Kiritsis 2011). The IoT allows the communication of essential parameters such as its components' real-time state, location, and environmental conditions. These are key fog Digital Twin modules. The IoT components comprise a wireless sensory network and an additional radio frequency technology used for identification by the Digital Twin user (Kiritsis 2011). This idea has been implemented in various departments such as energy efficiency, a virtual property office, logistics, barcodes in outlets, mobile phone applications, and tachographs for individual road charging. The emergence of IoT has enabled making Digital Twin technology possible (Jain et al. 2019).

The IoT devices have been improved over the years, with the Digital Twins taking great pride in using the system as sensors to transmit data (Kiritsis 2011). The devices applied currently take only minutes to install and are less complex objects giving cost-effective solutions to companies. A Digital Twin is employed in the prediction of incomes using variable data from IoT sensors. In combination with AI software, Data Analytics, the Digital Twin modules, and the IoT optimize its functionality. It helps experts decide and figure out the Digital Twin modules (Hribernik, Wuest, and Thoben 2013).

10.5.2 Digital Twins and Artificial Intelligence

Digital Twin models employ the use of AI in automating their actions. The virtual entities employ AI software in the automation of their functions through mimicking human intelligence. AI is a science and technology-based on disciplines such as computer science, biology, psychology, linguistics, mathematics, and engineering (Hribernik, Wuest, and Thoben 2013). The main branch of AI applied in a major thrust is developing computer functions associated with human intelligence, such as reasoning, learning, and problem-solving. Out of the following areas, one or multiple areas can contribute to building an intelligent system. The eventual capability of AI is slowly but surely ushering a phenomenon called "the fourth industrial revolution." In this foreseeable age, the disruptions that are experienced across a large range of AI, such as physical, digital, and biological, will all be merged into one huge system. This AI goal is to build capacity to meet the demand to solve complex and tough problems (Jain et al. 2019).

10.5.3 Digital Twins and Analytics

The data collected by IoT sensors is massive. Digital Twin applies analytic algorithms in the management of these data. In certain cases, data representation is completely complex, comprising several finite state machines that can potentially contain numerous discrete states. Due to this complexity, Digital Twins have to be built accurately by machine learning algorithms. Once coded, these algorithms facilitate accurate diagnostic, optimization, and predictive software (Jain et al. 2019). The use of chatbots will give brands, businesses, and publishers a solution to AI systems in interactions with their audiences without the need for them to download applications from the stores and familiarize the new user with interfaces or regularly update and configure the settings. The chatbots provide users with conversational interfaces that are more customer friendly.

Computer analytics technology is currently undertaking several transformations from silo implementations into universal utility functions in several industries, especially in the Digital Twin. This ability has become associated with several products, applications, services, and solutions. Mind commerce undertakes computer analytics innovation as a diverse area that includes personalized AI to support and protect the end-users (Jain et al. 2019). The IoT particularly is very dependent on AI as it aids in safeguarding assets, supporting analytics, reducing fraud, and enabling automated decisions in data analytics.

10.5.4   Digital Twins and Connectivity

Due to the transmission of large data between the virtual and physical assets in a Digital Twin, it is important to install a great network (Abramovici, Göbel, and Dang 2016). The fifth generation (5G) network is a novel technology that is surely a game-changer in cellular communication service providers and Digital Twin application implementation. This network will support millimeter-wavelength radio frequency in addition to the evolution of Long Term Evolution (LTE). LTE is considered to be an integral part of the 5G heterogeneous networks (Jain et al. 2019). There are elaborate plans by the communication device providers to commission the 5G network equipment at Base Transceiver Stations to enable Mobile Edge Computing (MEC), enabling distributed computing, and transforming the base transceiver stations into scattered data centers. The combination of 5G networks, the IoT, and AI will change the wireless carrier operations and facilitate enhanced services, new technological applications, and new business models for the mobile network providers.

The demand for fast and heavy data in the application has increased in the age of mobile phones in Digital Twin applications (Abramovici, Göbel, and Dang 2016). Applications of the internet in telecommunication industries require quicker and more data connections. These demands have prompted many industry stakeholders in the telecommunication industry to come up with a next-generation network, called the 5G network. This technology is key to the transformation in the construction of mobile and network technology. The principal purpose of developing such a superior network was to address the ever-increasing demand for cellular data usage. Figure 10.5 depicts a sample Digital Twin connectivity.

10.5.5   Digital Twins and Machine Learning

Machine Learning (ML) is a sub-field of AI that focuses on how a computer system can master a more efficient way to perform its function without a predetermined program that directs it to execute commands in a specific way (Abramovici, Göbel, and Dang 2016). This is key in Digital Twin models to help in simulations and predictions after analysis of data inputs. AI currently has not been developed entirely to tackle Digital Twin modules. Most of the current solutions are restricted mainly to ML, which aims to develop systems that are dynamic with "cognitive" abilities, as the name suggests. Unlike contemporary programs

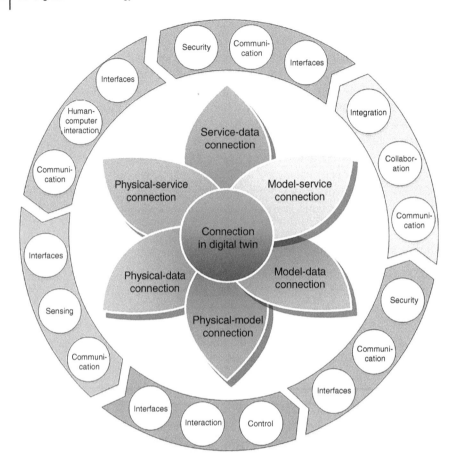

Figure 10.5 Digital Twin connectivity (Zhang et al. 2019).

that are static, ML systems are somewhat dynamic. ML utilizes an integration of several fields, including data mining, statistics, and mathematical algorithms. This is the primary mode of operation of the Digital Twin.

ML systems have algorithms that make conclusions and decisions to find solutions to problems by referring to past models based on sample inputs that mimic real-life situations. This is directly translated to Digital Twin modules. Virtual entities are dynamic and change their vectors and appearances from time to time; hence ML provides a platform to record the events appropriately. ML algorithms are designed to identify breaches promptly in real-time (Zhang et al. 2019). The ML then executes decisions assisted by intelligent systems to isolate the physical asset issue before it halts operations in a matter of seconds. This prompt action prevents system breakdown from preventing other devices connected in the network from breaking down. In ML and AI applications, the biggest relevant challenge is identifying needed patterns and recognizing a deviation from the expectation to constitute a breakdown. Once this identification is done, the AI can then be used to restore normality (Zhang et al. 2019). It is important to note that not all deviations from normality are abnormal; ML should classify these deviations accordingly. Wrongful classification can

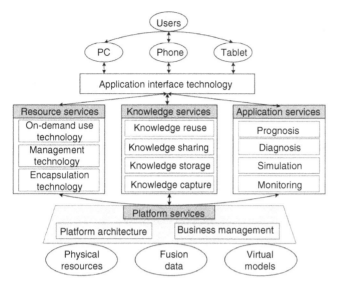

Figure 10.6   Enabling technologies of Digital Twin (Zhang et al. 2019).

cause huge problems by generating false positives and might lead to unnecessary break-downs. The AI must be well-coordinated to give the best results (Botkina et al. 2018). The enabling technologies of a Digital Twin are shown in Figure 10.6.

10.6   Digital Twin Technology Implementation

The implementation of the Digital Twin system requires practicality. The process may initially seem easy to implement and straightforward, but it involves several intricate plans and expertise. Organizations wanting to implement the technology need to consider the infrastructure, broad attitude, policies, human resources, budget, and other compulsory requirements. There are several fundamental steps when implementing a Digital Twin system.

In the case of a chief engineer remotely monitoring the construction of a multistorey building, constantly tracking issues regarding materials, measurements, processes, and technology from the comfort of his home away from the site, the only possible way to do this is by using a Digital Twin system. The engineer's Digital Twin is a virtual representation of the building and the processes being carried out in the construction site. The system includes the virtual model of the physical object, information from the object, special one-to-one correspondence to the asset, and access to monitor the asset (Zhang et al. 2019). The system employs data and intelligence software for monitoring the structure, trends, context, and behavior of the asset and offers an interface that allows the operator to understand the present and past trends and deduce future trends from the processed information.

Digital Twin pairing allows both the virtual simulation and actual asset to relay data enabling analysis and monitoring to foresee shortcomings and work on them even before they occur. This prevents downtime, develops new opportunities, and allows planning using simulations (Abramovici, Göbel, and Dang 2016).

The technology drives innovation and performance to optimal levels. Digital Twin technology is a key product for technicians used to monitor, analyze, and predict their assets' potential, usually available at their fingertips. The technology is viewed to be the next breakthrough and is forecast by a specialist that in 2028 companies that employ Digital Twins in their operations will experience significant growth in cycle time and critical responses. Over the coming years, many organizations will employ Digital Twin technology to optimize their assets and operations. Through this technology, the physical world simulations have opened new collaborations and opportunities between the physical world product experts and data analytics scientists who translate a large amount of data and give understandable conclusions (Botkina et al. 2018).

The technology helps organizations enhance the customer experience positively by better understanding their needs, improving existing products, improving services, improving operations, and helping in driving innovation of novel ideas and businesses. There is a virtual copy known as the twin running in the powerful cloud for every physical asset and transmits rich data with high-tech ML and AI. The technology ensures those companies that embrace it have a competitive advantage over the others; the system can cut off over 50% of the product cost and production time. These companies can integrate smart parts into current and new products and then connect them to a central cloud location fixed with big-data, in-memory, and analytics to grasp sensor data that enhance the business and contextual data (Zhang et al. 2019).

The system constantly analyzes the transmitted data and identifies weak links that need improvement. These digital insights create new services and products that immensely improve the organization's performance (Zhang et al. 2019).

10.7 Benefits of Digital Twins

Digital Twin technology has numerous benefits. The technology provides real-time mirroring for engineers to simulate the operations of highly complex assets in order to successfully predict and prevent malfunctions and breakdowns (Zhang et al. 2019).

Digital Twin maturity models are systems dependent on the credibility of sensor-generated data from the physical machine and its habitat or environment. This model illustrates that the virtual model slowly improves as more information is gathered from the physical asset and its environment. The historical data and real-time data are recorded and analyzed by AI to assess the assets' current condition and state.

One of the biggest benefits of Digital Twin is in providing a complete outlook of a project to the users at different stages of its development. The central source of data from the asset empowers organizations to build strong collaboration between the different departments and even without the organization (Zhang et al. 2019).

Digital Twin technology has been proved to drastically reduce product development cost and time by approximately 50%. This lowers the cost of production tremendously. Digital Twin systems have made it possible to coordinate chain businesses in different locations in real-time. There is improved coordination between different departments through the implementation of development cycles, both externally and externally. It helps coordinate suppliers, product design departments, production, manufacturing, sales, repair, and maintenance of complex systems (Botkina et al. 2018).

Digital Twin technology enhances accuracy in decision making, eliminating guesswork. It is used to determine the best option in the servicing of physical assets. Digital Twin technology is key for organizations centered on physical assets. The organizations focus on combining Digital Twins with traditional operational technologies; this hybrid enables them to have easy access to the hybrid system of intelligence and knowledge on their assets and processes, eventually ensuring an optimal operating business environment. In the future, newer markets will arise to utilize more result-oriented applications that are more versatile.

Digital Twin technology ensures that customer feedback is considered as a valuable input in making organization demands. Consumers influence the business strategies employed by managers to improve their experience. Businesses are looking to enhance the experiences of their customer base to retain them and target new customers. The enterprises employ Digital Twin systems focusing on customer behavior and reactions. The feedback from these applications is then used to make changes that boost services according to customer needs.

Digital Twin technology has revolutionized planning. It helps managers find an optimal set of solutions that help maximize key performance aspects and provide forecasts for future long-term business plans. NASA has demonstrated that this benefit explores the deployment of spacecraft or scientific devices that relay data to Earth on 3D real-time visualization.

In general, Digital Twin technology reduces operational cost, extends the operational life span of assets and machines, reduces time-to-market, ensures efficient control of production, and ensures assessment of systems and future trends. It also optimizes operability, preventive maintenance of assets, and continuous refinement of products and production models (Zhang et al. 2019).

10.8 Application of Digital Twins

Over the years, the Digital Twin concept has been forecasted to have extensive applications in society's various departments. The concept is rapidly growing in application and inventions in the technology field due to the robust advancement and actualization of the IoT and AI. The application could include manufacturing, sports healthcare, and digital cities (Zhang et al. 2019).

10.8.1 Manufacturing

The concept of Digital Twins is very popular among large-scale manufactures and producers. These firms' management is always interested in tracking and monitoring products, employees, and assets (Tao et al. 2019a,b). The task of manufacturing, if not automated, can be very daunting. The concept of Digital Twins is necessary for the manufacturing setup. Digital setup enables tracking and monitoring and saves money and time, which is a key consideration in lowering the cost of production. Internet connectivity is the principal driver of Digital Twins (Tao et al. 2019a,b). The complete utilization of the Digital Twin concept is expected to be in full operation in manufacturing by the fourth industrial revolution.

The Digital Twin concept gives the manufacturers real-time reports and status on machine system performance, defects, and status. The system also gives reports on production line feedbacks. The technology gives the managers the privilege of predicting trends in real-time, making them more prepared to overcome the challenges in a timely and appropriate way. Digital Twin systems enable the exceptional performance of the electronic machines employed in manufacturing and, of course, greater connectivity is enabled (Tao et al. 2019a,b). Manufacturers develop AI algorithms that enable greater accuracy and efficiency. Digital Twins ensure manufacturing is largely efficient as it can store large volumes of data essential for the output and prediction analysis. Also, Digital Twin enables testing of the products, including a real-time supported system with feedback and output that is priceless.

In manufacturing, Digital Twins are applied as a virtual copy of the final product or machine developed simultaneously. Information of the true asset is transmitted into the virtual copy for simulation and testing of novel ideas before the real manufacturing commences (Tao et al. 2019a,b).

In the automobile industry, Digital Twins have been applied by Tesla to design and run electric cars. Digital Twin is utilized for simulation and data analytics of the engine and other car parts in its monitoring and running. AI algorithms improve the precision of testing. It can undertake data analytics in real-time on Tesla automobiles and predict the status of various components both currently and for the future (Tao et al. 2019a,b).

In the construction industry, the concept of Digital Twins is being employed extensively. Architectures and engineers use Digital Twins to accurately and precisely develop the plans for massive structures, from storey buildings, bridges, tunnels, and even cruise ships. Smart city buildings have utilized Digital Twin systems in design, development, and daily running. They also provide a platform for real-time monitoring and prediction. The application of Digital Twin in the construction industry in data analytics can provide more accurate data, which is core in predicting and maintaining structures and buildings.

The predictions and adjustments are then done virtually through effective simulation before implementing the readjustments physically (Tao et al. 2019a,b). Through simulation using Digital Twins, the engineers and architectures can accurately predict situations and correct them before implementing the projects. This simulation has seen engineers move from the static copy of plans and blueprints to 3D models that are more current and easier to read. The static blueprint models serve a purpose but can also provide real-time parameters limiting the design's predictability and learnability (Tao et al. 2019a,b). The technology of Digital Twin enables the engineers to learn and monitor the designs at the same time. It also allows the application of machine and deep learning codes.

10.8.2 Healthcare

Similar to manufacturing, the Digital Twin application is key to the growth of high-tech healthcare systems. The transformation of healthcare systems in terms of growth and development has been quite unforeseen (Tao et al. 2018). Impossible procedures are slowly becoming possible with AI and the IoT in diagnosis, prognosis, and treatment. With the IoT, devices are now affordable and easy to implement due to the rise in connectivity. The new advancement and ease in connectivity have given rise to increased growth of potential applications of Digital Twin in the patient car (Tao et al. 2018).

Researchers are currently using Digital Twin systems to undertake novel drug trials for side effects, efficacy, safety, dosage, and efficacy. This simulation will eliminate the need to use human beings and animals as experimental subjects (Tao et al. 2018).

Currently, Digital Twins are employed by surgeons to plan and execute complex surgical procedures. The surgeon's training has previously been done on cadavers or animal models. Digital Twin technology has improved this through real-time simulations that project the specific patient situation. Researchers as well exploit Digital Twins to study their hypotheses with real-time simulations of their models in different environments (Tao et al. 2019a,b).

In the coming years, the body will be fitted with a Digital Twin system that gives a real-time analysis of its vitals to physicians. The technology combined with AI algorithms has been utilized to create smarter decisions and predictions (Tao et al. 2018). Most applications currently aid in ongoing patient care and treatment but are not directly involved in individual patient care.

The majority of the applications of Digital Twin management systems are still at the developmental stages overall; the projected use includes bed management, ward management, and entire hospital appliances (Tao et al. 2018). The privilege to use these simulations in real-time is critical to healthcare officials as they can be the narrow difference between life and death. In combination with AI, Digital Twins can predict malaise and disease based on information that is relayed in real-time or from the patient's historical data (Tao et al. 2018).

In healthcare, Digital Twin ensures safety by virtualizing a hospital system to assess the safety of tests and environments. The technology is applied in testing the impact of proposed changes in the healthcare systems (Abramovici, Göbel, and Dang 2016). The quality of healthcare delivered to patients can also be greatly improved. Surgeons can perform rehearsals of complicated surgeries in virtual organs before doing it on actual patients.

Digital Twin is applied in the predictive maintenance and repair of hospital equipment by lowering their stalling due to abrupt breakdowns. Predictive maintenance is used in both hospital equipment and by manufacturers as well, making them more adaptable and precise. The advancement of AI, the IoT, and Industry 4.0 facilitates the Digital Twin concept in healthcare.

Healthcare is very dependent on research. Biomedical scientists have employed Digital Twin technology to identify gaps that require research (Tao et al. 2018). These insights empower medical scientists to have a wide horizon of thought in helping to achieve medical solutions through predictive maintenance of research, aspects to analyze results, and a discovery (Tao et al. 2018).

10.8.3 Smart Cities

This is one of the most ambitious applications of Digital Twin to be invented. It is expected to have a dramatic effect on the running of metropolitan areas. This dream is almost being achieved due to fast connectivity and the invention of the IoT. The world is becoming increasingly urbanized, which has led to an increased need for more connected communities in this digital era. These needs make Digital Twin technology a necessary solution. With the massive data collected from IoT sensors installed in city objects, the researchers aim to create advanced AI algorithms.

The Digital Twin is employed to capture spatial and temporary implications to ensure urban sustainability. A practical example is virtual Singapore, an ongoing government project for a smart city Singapore initiative. It is the first world initiative to build the first smart city with a digital economy.

Advanced and fast connectivity is a major determinant of launching successful smart cities. This connectivity affects major core services within the smart cities, and is employed in policing and crime-fighting. The entire police department is connected to these systems to monitor real-time criminal events. The system is also employed in traffic management to help alleviate costly traffic snarl-ups and jams. The traffic cameras would record events and trends; the data is used to code AI algorithms to manage better traffic and environmental hazard emissions in the road network.

The Digital Twin system is involved in the management of roads, logistics, buildings, public services, people, and the power grid. These services are performed using sensors and IoT devices fitted with different kinds of future-proofing. Digital Twin is currently being employed in the management and running of current small cities. The systems play beneficial roles in planning for the cities as well as other energy-saving solutions for sustainability. The data collected by IoT offers excellent solutions on the modalities of resource distribution and usage.

10.8.4 Space Exploration

Space scientists have explored Digital Twin technology. The virtual twin implanted in habitable planets contains limited data sources, such as the device's pressure, temperature, and state. The virtual twin is responsible for capturing its state's principal metric parameters using low power and a resource-constraint physical asset. For example, a connected light bulb sends signals on its power consumption rate.

The application of Digital Twin technology is heavily dependent on power and proof of connectivity development. This ensures the rapid development of device-to-platform performance. The device-to-device functionality houses enough information to create derivative information for further complex analysis and use. This kind of Digital Twin possesses entire measurable and meaningful information sensors from a physical asset. A practical example occurs when temperature and pressure measurements are not synced; the AI would employ linear regression algorithms to identify correlation with the asset's health. This type of system is most suitable when the asset in question is neither power nor data constrained. Such a system utilizes both data and prototyping characterization stages in IoT development. This enhanced form of Digital Twin empowers the data from the installed sensors on the asset with derivative data, federated data sources, intelligence data, and correlated data from ML and AI algorithms.

10.8.5 Business

Digital Twin technology can be employed far and wide, especially in businesses. The most common application is to improve the customer experience through performance tuning. Secondly, it is key in asset management, especially in machine maintenance. The Digital

Twin system's maintenance of assets is done by gathering and analyzing performance data accumulated over time under fluctuating conditions. This application has been employed in the automobile industry. A practical example is applying Digital Twin in car engines that can be visualized in the virtual asset to manage maintenance like identify car components that are about to wear out completely. In businesses, Digital Twin is used to integrate the system's data to allow visibility into the current and future asset states and process the needed remedial business decisions.

10.9 Challenges of Digital Twins

Digital Twin technology runs in tandem with IoT and AI technology and hence shares challenges (Grieves and Vickers 2016). These challenges should be mapped out first before finding amicable remedies. Several common challenges are found in the IoT as well as data analytics. Challenges in these sub-technologies directly affect Digital Twins and should be mapped out for possible solutions. The common challenges are discussed below.

10.9.1 Privacy and Data Security

The industry of information and technology has grappled with data security issues (Grieves and Vickers 2016). In Digital Twin technology, a privacy and data security challenge is obvious due to the robust amount of data used. Some of the data fed to these systems are quite sensitive, and if they fall into the wrong hands could lead to financial and other losses (Kobara 2016). On the bright side, this challenge has operational remedies; the system must follow the latest and current updates of security and privacy regulations. Building user trust in these systems is also a significant challenge for Digital Twin implementation. The end-users should be able to trust their personal information to have confidence in using the system (Kobara 2016).

10.9.2 Infrastructure

The current information technology (IT) infrastructure is a limitation to the demands of the Digital Twin system. This is quite common in the other technologies, IoT and AI. The technology requires IT infrastructures that would allow for the successful implementation of data analytics and IoT to facilitate effective operations of Digital Twins. Lack of such infrastructures that are well interconnected becomes an impediment to the implementation of Digital Twins, making it hard to achieve objectives.

10.9.3 Data

This is the second most common impediment to successful implementation of the Digital Twin concept (Grieves and Vickers 2016). The success of a Digital Twin is dependent on the accuracy and precision of data input. The data should be of high quality, free from noise interference, and with a constant and uninterrupted data stream. If the data is inconsistent and inadequate, the Digital Twin system will underperform and give erroneous output. IoT usually feeds the data, which should be of high quality and in the right quantity. Quality data is critical for the planning and analysis of device utilization. It is vital in recognizing the appropriate data signal collected and applied for efficient use in the system (Kobara 2016).

10.9.4 Trust

This is one of the most difficult challenges to mitigate. The concept of trust involves both the technology providers and the end-user (Grieves and Vickers 2016). The Digital Twin technology ought to be well explained at the foundation stage to make the end-users and the providers understand the benefits, risks, and challenges of using the technology. This education aims to overcome the trust issues arising from sharing sensitive data. When the organization and the users understand one another, trust in using the Digital Twin system prevails (Kobara 2016) and inevitably trust grows. In a bid to build trust, the Digital Twin technology should enlighten the users on the measures taken to ensure privacy and data security (Grieves and Vickers 2016).

10.9.5 Expectations

Understanding the population's expectations is a huge advantage and a driving force to Digital Twin technology (Grieves and Vickers 2016). The expectations should be managed through more education and understanding. Big technology companies are currently implementing technology, but care should be taken to manage and highlight expectations. There is a need to build strong foundations for the IoT networks and better understanding of the information needed for analytics to ensure organizations implement Digital Twin technology (Grieves and Vickers 2016). The users should understand that Digital Twin technology is solely meant to solve all the current problems. Both the negative and positive expectations should be well documented to ensure the appropriate measure is taken when developing Digital Twin systems.

References

Abramovici, M., Göbel, J.M., and Dang, H.B. (2016). Semantic data management for the development and continuous reconfiguration of smart products and systems. *CIRP Annals – Manufacturing Technology* 65 (1): 185–188.

Boschert, S. and Rosen, R. (2016). Digital twin – the simulation aspect. In: *Mechatronic Futures* (eds. P. Hehenberger and D. Bradley). Berlin/Heidelberg: Springer.

Botkina, D., Hedlind, M., Olsson, B. et al. (2018). Digital Twin of a cutting tool. *Procedia CIRP* 72: 215–218.

Grieves, M. (2014). *Digital Twin: Manufacturing Excellence through Virtual Factory Replication*. White paper. Melbourne, FL: Florida Institute of Technology.

Grieves, M. and Vickers, J. (2016). Digital twin: mitigating unpredictable, undesirable emergent behavior in complex systems. In: *Trans-Disciplinary Perspectives on System Complexity – New Findings and Approaches* (eds. F.-J. Kahlen, S. Flumerfelt and A. Alves). Berlin/Heidelberg: Springer.

Hribernik, K., Wuest, T., and Thoben, K.-D. (2013). Towards product avatars representing middle-of-life – Information for improving design, development, and manufacturing processes. *IFIP Advances in Information and Communication Technology* 411: 85–96.

Jain, P., Poon, J., Singh, J.P. et al. (2019). A digital twin approach for fault diagnosis in distributed photovoltaic system. *IEEE Transactions on Power Electronics* 35 (1): 1.

Kiritsis, D. (2011). Closed-loop PLM for intelligent products in the era of the Internet of Things. *Computer-Aided Design* 43 (5): 479–501.

Kobara, K. (2016). Cyber-physical security for industrial control systems and IoT. *IEICE Transactions on Information and Systems* E99.D: 787–795.

Tao, F., Zhang, M., Liu, Y., and Nee, A.Y.C. (2018). Digital Twin driven prognostics and health management for complex equipment. *CIRP Annals Manufacturing Technology* 67 (1): 169–172.

Tao, F. and Qi, Q. (2019a). New IT driven service-oriented smart manufacturing: framework and characteristics. *IEEE Transactions on Systems, Man, and Cybernetics: Systems* 49 (1): 81–91.

Tao, F., Zhang, M., and Nee, A.Y.C. (2019b). *Digital Twin Driven Smart Manufacturing*. Elsevier–Academic Press. ISBN: 9780128176306.

Zhang, Z., Wang, X., Zhu, X. et al. (2019). Cloud manufacturing paradigm with a ubiquitousrobotic system for product customization. *Robotics and Computer-Integrated Manufacturing* 60: 12–22.

11

Artificial Intelligence, Big Data Analytics, and IoT

11.1   Introduction

Data is integral to the development of products and the growth of industries. Metrical data enables the segmentation of information. Vast amounts of information are collected and transcribed from the internet for analysis and product development. The value of big data includes monetary assets such as money and value in the usage of information itself. Data can be collected involuntarily or voluntarily, which raises both ethical and legal issues. Data can be sold for marketing purposes and utilized as analysis tools to strengthen business performance. Various forms of data include specification metrics on performance, demographic, and personal characteristics of people in the population. No matter how the data is gathered, willingly or unwillingly, the value can be derived from the information in many ways.

People can communicate from continent to continent, in seconds, because of the telecommunications industry's technologies. With each communication form comes standard principles that establish the origin of such communication. Each sector has service providers who have the capabilities to identify each communication. These bits of identifying data are sometimes collected, organized, and analyzed for marketing and enterprise optimization. Massive amounts of data are collected by large companies for which consumers rely on for various purposes. The information then becomes a profitable target for companies because of the value it holds for these organizations.

Sensors acquire information that can be sent to a cloud. Once information is in the cloud, information can be categorized, analyzed, and designed for future implementations. While data security while traveling to and from the cloud could be strengthened, access to devices and the cloud can be made secure with encryption methods and device authentication. For Internet of Thing (IoT) devices, data is transmitted to the cloud with long-haul transmissions. In IoT devices, five layers control the data flow and function of the device. The layers are:

1) The device itself, which is designed for a purpose or a function.
2) Sensors and actuators allow the product to monitor the environment and command device functions.

Intelligent Connectivity: AI, IoT, and 5G, First Edition. Abdulrahman Yarali.
© 2022 John Wiley & Sons Ltd. Published 2022 by John Wiley & Sons Ltd.

3) The controller uses short-haul communications to convert analog to digital signals and transmit them to the agent.
4) The agent is the fourth layer and decides what data to send to the cloud.
5) Long-haul communication is the sending of data to the cloud. It can be performed using cellular, satellite, WiFi, Ethernet, and sub-gigahertz options LoRa or SigFox (Biron and Follet 2016, pp. 22–27).

With the introduction of faster and smaller computer hardware and better programming practices that use this new power, the widespread use of Artificial Intelligence (AI) and the IoT are becoming a reality. AI can be defined as the growing body of computational techniques relating to computer systems capable of performing tasks that would otherwise require human intelligence. Many people's modern assumption is that AI is always a sentient computer, but, in reality, AI applications are integrated into many people's lives. AI has given way to many breakthroughs within many scientific and analytical fields that have benefited people worldwide. The IoT is a network of different hardware that can collect information, process information, and communicate it to other systems (Internet of Things 2001). The term "things" refers to any device that can do these three things. What is distinctive about these devices is using sensors and other hardware to input data into the computer to be processed and communicated. Smartphones are not generally considered "things" within IoT, but many now have sensors installed so they are now being considered more often as "things." This subject is becoming more critical within our markets, and our understanding of it must be profound. IoT will have many objects and many different brands of objects that will be connected to other devices. This creates concern in ensuring that these users understand how these devices work.

IoT has changed how society works and how we, as humans, can connect to the technology that serves our needs. IoT includes many technologies that come in all shapes, sizes, and usage, and can be in any environment such as a kitchen appliance and have even been integrated into cities. This connectedness between people and technology has shown great promise even in its modern infancy stages and will continue to innovate the way people live and operate. With the complete implementation of IoT in society, AI has also been widely implemented as a management system (Vaghela 2019). It helps aggregate all of the data received from these devices. There are many misconceptions about AI and IoT that have been propagated through media and digital illiteracy, and this paper will help alleviate some of them.

11.2 Analytics

Analytics is the unveiling, interpretation, and transmission of data patterns that are meaningful. Analytics is applicable where recorded information in statistics, operation research, and computer performance shows or quantifies an organization's performance, businesses, or institutions. The data revolution has analyzed data regarding types, kinds, in various stages of the analysis. The main aim of data analytics is to offer businesses a variety of solutions towards the success of the business regarding smart decision-making for a better business outcome. Data analytics enables the company to gather knowledgeable information that gives the business a competitive power edge.

Big data analytics cannot just be considered as the only blanket strategy but can also be categorized into various types. The most dominant types of analytics are descriptive, prescriptive, and predictive, which enable the organizations to make the most out of their big data (DeZyre 2016). We first look into details of these analytic types and then focus on how we can apply these strategies to transform the data analytics in big data handling organizations.

11.2.1 Predictive Analytics

Analyzing the trends and the past data pattern can tell the business accurately about what could happen shortly, and this sets realistic objectives, restraining expectations, and planning of the business. This analytic enables the company to study data and determine "what could happen ahead using the past patterns and trend performance." The organization gathers data and compares it with the other customer user behavior datasets and a webserver to obtain a real picture through this type of analytics. Companies can foresee the future growth of their business if they maintain the trend. This analytic provides recommendations and answers to questions non-answerable by business intelligence (BI). It helps to foresee the chances of future outcomes through machine learning and in statistical algorithms. However, the accuracy level is not 100% genuine since it applies the concept of probabilities. The algorithm predicts by taking the data and filling in the missing one by guessing. The data is drawn from history present in CRM (customer relation management) systems, POS (point of sale) system, ERP (enterprise resource planning) system, and HR (human resource) systems to obtain a pattern and relationship of the dataset's variables.

11.2.2 Prescriptive Analytics

Here the big data might be good enough to rely on when predicting the winning of exact lottery numbers, but it shows the problem and explains its occurrence. The organization can use data-found and data-back factors to prescribe business challenges leading to realization. This process predicts the outcome likely to occur and the likelihood of such results maximizing crucial business metrics. It incorporates the simulation of what an organization does to optimize for the best outcomes. Prescriptive analytics is a general combination of business rules and mathematical models where the data can be external (social media data) and internal (within the organization). Under prescriptive analytics, the business rules are best practices, preferences, and related constraints, while the mathematical models include machine learning, operation research, statistics, and language processing. This type of analytic is complex. Therefore, most organizations do not use it in daily business since it is difficult to manage.

11.2.3 Descriptive Analytics

Descriptive analytics is the type that 90% of companies use, which analyses incoming data in current time and historical ones to determine the future. It singles out the reason behind the success and the failure of the past operation of the business. The organization/business will derive the data from past events to understand future outcomes. Descriptive analytics is based on aggregate database functions that require mathematical knowledge of summarizing the metrics, like percentage index and average response time. Notably, the business can get the results from the web server by using the Google analytic tool, which can help it to understand what happened previously and validate whether the promotional campaign was successful.

There are different ways to transform the analytic strategy into a favorable business environment for most businesses (Kitchin 2014). Firstly, we consider the reason why organizations need an analytical approach. Analytics do foster the quality, actionable, and timely insights that enable leaders to make informed decisions that are considered to be better. The analytics functions are mostly centralized divisions of the expert in science by supporting the internal team, BI, providing reports, dashboards, and advanced data products. When a clear strategy is absent, the analytic world's quick changes can wrongly lead the entire team, resulting in an expensive test and tedious integration, costing valuable executive time.

Traditionally, reporting started with finance and accounting departments. Now, these departments have moved to the digital way. Big data analytics is an area of multidisciplinary expertise and knowledge of finance; technology and marketing are the essential factors. Notwithstanding, an excellent analytic strategy is the one that needs to enable data-driven culture for identification of any significant change in the business.

Data analytics have created a data-driven culture. Any industry can adopt the culture in areas that rely on data, such as engaging the internal clients or any other analytic projects delivery. The culture driven by data can also audit the analytical tools, overload, clean duplication, and report catalog. It can also monitor the business's crucial sign, creating dashboards in the system for a transparency culture. Data-driven culture also enables story-telling visual systems that instill the analytics across the organization. This culture also can develop consultative and insightful research led by withstanding methodology (Moe 2013).

Analytic strategies have supported business transformation through the provision of thought leadership in analytical strategy and solutions. It can also be a result of developing a relationship with business leaders and understanding their needs. The organization can also transform the business by developing skills and aligning old priorities to the current organization's needs. Also, enabling the quality control systems, audit, and compliance tools can result in business transformation (Wang et al. 2016). Analytics can also be transformed by developing talent through recruiting, developing, and retaining a diverse, world-class executive team. The skill can also be developed by encouraging a trust culture that rewards deserving behaviors. Developing tools for learning that supports the clients internally and externally can also contribute to talent development, with identification of opportunities for data points across the physical and digital customer journey.

Lastly, the business can encourage innovations through the identification of external trends to relay strategic decisions. Innovation can also be driven by educating the team about data creativity usage and analytics to solve business challenges. Encouraging a data-driven innovation culture by incorporating external speakers is another contributing factor. Creation and testing of new ways to transform current practices enable the business to drive innovation.

Additionally, there are substantial case studies where this transformation has been put in place. For example, in the banking industry, Deutsche Zentral (DZ) banks improve their profitability while lowering their risk by leveraging real-time actionable insight. They deliver a single-point truth for regulatory and financial reporting and one source of analytical Systems, Applications, and Products (SAP) (for managing business operations and customer relations). It simplifies logistics, finance, supply chain management, and inventory management, with quick implementations and quick results. Cisco identified Qlik (provider of Qlik view and Qlik sense, BI and visualization software) as the potential partner in the technology industry after the self-service solution for actionable insights, therefore identifying $100 million in support renewals in approximation and $4 million cost savings.

To be a champion in data analytics, one should assess how your data suits the business needs to call for action to develop a culture of change in the management and unveiling all the needed actions. Management should be willing to review strategic objectives and organizational goals to accommodate data analytics.

11.3   AI Technology in Big Data and IoT

Big Data is a massive market in modern times that includes many jobs and industries, including healthcare, sales, stocks, and many more. Big Data (1996) can be defined as "an accumulation of data that is too large and complex for processing by traditional database management tools." Taking the definition of Big Data into consideration, AI may be one of the most significant breakthroughs for the data industry. Big Data can come in any form imaginable. Still, there is always one problem in the traversal: it is physically impossible for humans to take advantage of it efficiently. AI has given way to traversal problems by cataloging and taking advantage of the massive amounts of data generated by these industries efficiently and accurately. This data has to have a source, and this is where the effect of IoT comes into play with Big Data. With the massive amounts of tech being connected to the internet, massive amounts of data are generated.

One of the largest and most sought-after commodities in modern times pertains to Big Data, which is user data. This user data application is limitless and has created massive markets that generate copious amounts of revenue. Social media is the most prominent example of user data aggregation in modern times, with Facebook brandishing 2.306 billion users in Q1 in 2020 alone.

Figure 11.1 shows the massive growth of the social media industry, which has exploded since its creation, requiring new and innovative ways of managing incoming data. With this many users who can create an endless amount of personal data, Facebook has implemented AI in many ways. Facebook's implementation of AI also starts the conversation of ethics within AI and Big Data. AI has been used by Facebook to take user data about web browsing and uses it to market products to users. Even products and searching habits that do not pertain to Facebook are used as marketing advantages, which helped generate revenue. With the abilities given to the Big Data industry by AI, society has seen great jumps in data-driven enterprises, but society has also seen their data abused. Overall, AI has streamlined and single-handedly made the Big Data industry possible through its traversal and aggregation abilities.

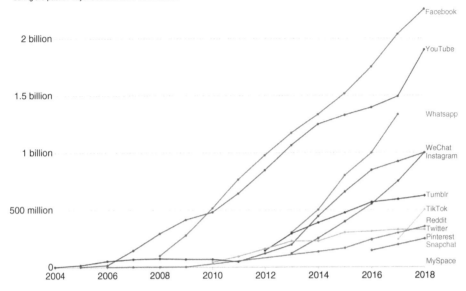

Number of people using social media platforms, 2004 to 2018

Estimates correspond to monthly active users (MAUs). Facebook, for example, measures MAUs as users that have logged in during the past 30 days. See source for more details.

Figure 11.1 The number of monthly active Facebook users worldwide 2008–2020 (Ortiz-Ospina, 2019).

11.4 AI Technology Applications and Use Cases

The applications and use cases surrounding AI are limitless and can be implemented in any industry. The most prominent use case for AI at this time is individually inspecting pieces of Big Data. One of the most promising applications for AI is in the field of healthcare and health research industries. Health research has been shown to create massive amounts of data, of which AI can traverse and return pertinent information. Examples of this are AI looking at the human genome, which has 3 billion base pairs, and determining new medicines or health treatments (Wikipedia 2020a). The use cases for AI within the medical field do not stop at Big Data traversals and extend to AI-assisted robotics. AI-assisted robotics can analyze past surgical procedures and their outcomes, which allows them to guide surgeons on new or better practices. These robotics have led to a 21% reduction in a patient's hospital stay after a surgery that used them (Singh 2019). Another use within the medical industry that is taking advantage of AI is image analysis while researching and performing surgery. This imagery analysis allows for a much quicker analysis, and AI can find things that humans just cannot discern, especially in a surgical situation. Overall, whether it is data analysis, surgery assistance, or imagery analysis, AI is being implemented in the healthcare field in very innovative and helpful ways (Marr 2019).

Another industry that AI has been heavily involved in is the predictive market industries such as insurance, finance, and the stock market. AI can run many iterations of calculations quickly, especially with the modern breakthroughs with computational hardware. A significant portion of insurance boils down to risk analysis, and AI is a significant component for accurate risk analysis models. These risk analysis models are also used heavily in the financial industry. In both cases, AI is used to run many iterations of predictive algorithms that help these industries make informed decisions, whether that means to insure someone or to lend to someone. The applications within finance and banking using AI are endless, and the graphic in Figure 11.2 helps to show this.

This graph shows some of the most prominent uses for AI in the financial industry and how they affect the banking environment. One of the biggest benefits offered in the graph is automating existing processes that would have been completed by human workers. These processes are not only sped up but they are also now completed with accuracy, and a lot of money is being saved. The money-saving qualities alone make the overhead cost of automating processes using AI pay for itself in the end. This image shows the top reasons why banks should implement AI and offers a way that through helping with decision-making, customer interactions can be streamlined and employees can he helped to be more effective at their jobs. Figure 11.3 shows the applications of AI in different areas of banking.

Another primary AI application has been in IoT technologies such as smart cities (Figure 11.4) and smart houses. These smart cities use AI technology to create a safer, more intelligent, and more intuitive environment. An example of AI being used in smart cities to make them a safer environment is facial recognition. This technology takes advantage of image analysis, which can match a person's face from an image or video, allowing law enforcement to find criminals. Another big advantage of AI within a smart city is the ability to track and help traffic control. AI can help track traffic patterns, which

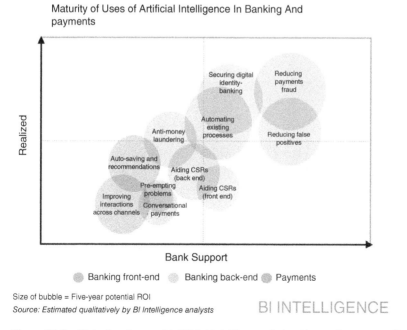

Figure 11.2 Maturity of uses of Artificial Intelligence in banking and payments (Redbytes 2019).

AI AND BANKING
FEAR NOT

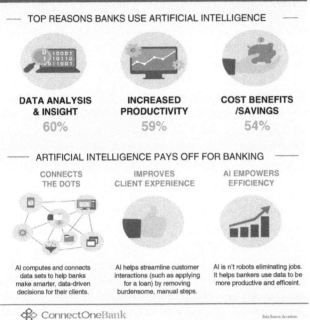

Figure 11.3 AI and banking fear not (Sorrentino 2018).

TOP REASONS BANKS USE ARTIFICIAL INTELLIGENCE

DATA ANALYSIS & INSIGHT	INCREASED PRODUCTIVITY	COST BENEFITS /SAVINGS
60%	59%	54%

ARTIFICIAL INTELLIGENCE PAYS OFF FOR BANKING

CONNECTS THE DOTS	IMPROVES CLIENT EXPERIENCE	AI EMPOWERS EFFICIENCY
AI computes and connects data sets to help banks make smarter, data-driven decisions for their clients.	AI helps streamline customer interactions (such as applying for a loan) by removing burdensome, manual steps.	AI is n't robots eliminating jobs. It helps bankers use data to be more productive and efficeint.

ConnectOneBank

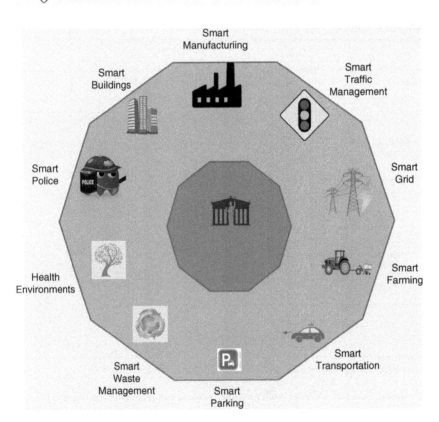

Figure 11.4 Smart city cases for AI-powered IoT-enabled technology (Packt 2019, August 9).

can help traffic controllers route cars in less congested areas and get residents to their intended locations faster. Although not completely related to the city, another component of AI tech that will help with traffic congestion will be self-driving vehicles. The age of human driving will soon be phased out with advanced AI software, such as the software used for Tesla's self-driving vehicles. Many other technologies are being implemented into smart cities, and each one of them is taking advantage of AI in some way. This image in Figure 11.4 shows some of the smart cities' components and how many things it will affect.

11.5   AI Technology Impact on the Vertical Market

When discussing software, the vertical market can be defined as software to address any given business needs within a discernable vertical market; software is created for a specific business or industry and is made to satisfy a particular need (Wikipedia 2020b). The vertical software market is vast and includes many heavy-hitting companies that have made huge profits filling the needs of any industry that uses the software. The image in Figure 11.5 conveys the massive amount of companies that serve the software need in the vertical and horizontal markets and the wide variety of sectors supported.

AI is being implemented into the software through algorithms and automated processes embedded in the code. AI affects the vertical market for many reasons by making software smarter, faster, and worth more. These factors change the way companies decide which software and which company to choose when looking for a software designer. Another effect of AI being introduced into the vertical market is the efficiency at which the receiving company can perform within their market. How the vertical

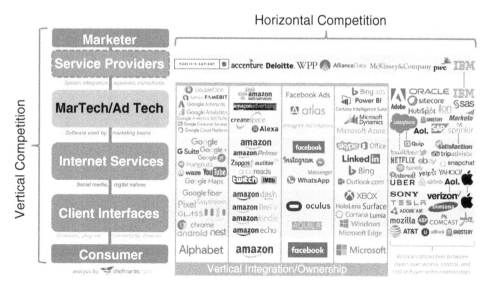

Figure 11.5   Vertical and horizontal competition (Brinker 2016).

market is affected can come back to the use cases and applications of AI. There is probably not a major industry in the world that is not taking advantage of the capabilities of AI. Overall, the vertical market is reliant on efficient software that can be achieved by implementing AI.

11.5.1 AI Predictive Analytics in the Vertical Market

Predictive software has revolutionized many industries and has given them insight into the future while giving companies the ability to make educated decisions. AI is now being implemented into this predictive software to get a leg up with potential customers or decision making. When considering customers, AI is now gaining the ability to make non-logical decisions so that the predictions created can be more human-like. Non-logical decision making allows for a more accurate outcome when predicting what a customer will do, because many factors other than logic go into human decision-making. The vertical market can take advantage of this AI-driven predictive analysis in many ways by predicting new market trends. Predicting market trends can be driven by AI technology through the use of Big Data analysis and by using social media trends to predict potential changes in markets. Predictive analytics can be implemented in any industry that relies on the future and success by guessing. These industries are very

Figure 11.6 Deploying predictive analytics (Just 2017).

diverse and different, but all contain some form of prediction aspect that takes advantage of AI. The image in Figure 11.6 helps to illustrate the diverseness of these industries.

11.6   AI in Big Data and IoT Market Analysis and Forecasts

AI is currently being used by social media hosts and marketers to analyze Big Data, which can help forecast future market changes and market trends. Using the information gained from this AI analysis, software companies can make educated decisions based on the future market. AI can also help influence market trends by noticing a future trend as a company can put more resources into marketing it. Big Data is a big component in market analysis and forecasting because Big Data is composed of user data. Users make up modern markets, so using AI to traverse users' internet data allows companies to forecast what may soon be popular. Overall, Big Data and AI are changing how marketing operates and how analyzing users' data makes forecasting more accurate. In the current usage of AI in marketing analysis and forecasting, these areas, shown in Figure 11.7, are the most likely areas to be taken advantage of by companies.

11.7   Conclusion

In conclusion, AI is changing many ways of life, including IoT, Big Data, and prediction analysis. AI is making processes for everyone more efficient and accurate while becoming more worthwhile price-wise. AI will continue to change the way humans live their lives while also helping to bridge the gap between people and technology.

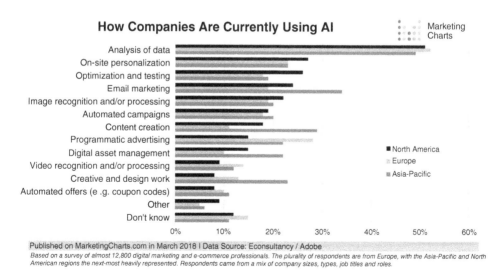

Figure 11.7   How companies are currently using AI (Vaghela 2019).

References

Big Data (1996). The Merriam-Webster.Com Dictionary. https://www.merriam-webster.com/dictionary/big%20data (accessed 22 June 2021).

Biron, J. and Follet, J. (2016). *Foundational Elements of an IoT Solution: The Edge, The Cloud, and Application Development*, 1e, 22–27. Sebastopol, CA: O'Reilly Media.

Brinker, S. (2016). 5 disruptions to marketing, part 3: vertical competition. https://chiefmartec.com/2016/12/5-disruptions-marketing-part-3-vertical-competition/ (accessed 22 June 2021).

Clement, J. (2020). Statista. https://www.statista.com/statistics/264810/number-of-monthly-active-facebook-users-worldwide/ (accessed 22 June 2021).

DeZyre (2016). Types of analytics: descriptive, predictive, prescriptive analytics. https://www.dezyre.com/article/types-of-analytics-descriptive-predictive-prescriptive-analytics/209 (accessed 22 June 2021).

Internet of Things (2001). The Merriam-Webster.Com Dictionary. https://www.merriam-webster.com/dictionary/Internet%20of%20Things (accessed 22 June 2021).

Just, E. (2017, May 4). The top three recommendations for successfully deploying predictive analytics in healthcare. https://www.healthcatalyst.com/deploying-predictive-analytics-healthcare (accessed 22 June 2021).

Kitchin, R. (2014). *The Data Revolution: Big Data, Open Data, Data Infrastructures, and Their Consequences*. Sage.

Marr, B. (2019, May 13). How is AI used in healthcare – 5 powerful real-world examples that show the latest advances. Forbes. https://www.forbes.com/sites/bernardmarr/2018/07/27/how-is-ai-used-in-healthcare-5-powerful-real-world-examples-that-show-the-latest-advances/#36452535dfbe (accessed 22 June 2021).

Moe (2013). Six steps to a business-driven analytics strategy – Hidden insights. https://blogs.sas.com/content/hiddeninsights/2013/10/13/six-steps-to-a-business-driven-analytics-strategy (accessed 22 June 2021).

Ortiz-Ospina, E., (2019). The Rise of Social Media. Our World in Data, Sept 18, 2019. https://ourworldindata.org/rise-of-social-media.

Packt (2019). Artificial Intelligence for smart cities. https://becominghuman.ai/artificial-intelligence-for-smart-cities-64e6774808f8 (accessed 22 June 2021).

Redbyte (2019). Impact of AI in the banking sector UK. https://www.redbytes.co.uk/ai-in-banking-sector/ (accessed 22 June 2021).

Singh, A. (2019). *How AI is improving predictive analytics*. MarTech Vibe Retrieved from: https://www.martechvibe.com/insights/staff-articles/how-ai-is-improving-predictive-analytics/.

Sorrentino, F. (2018). AI and banking: ditch the fear, embrace the data. https://blogs-images.forbes.com/franksorrentino/files/2018/02/CNOB-AI-content-2.23-1200x1800.jpg (accessed 22 June 2021).

Vaghela, Y. (2019). The future of AI and project management. https://project-management.com/the-future-of-ai-and-project-management/ (accessed 22 June 2021).

Wang, G., Gunasekaran, A., Ngai, E.W., and Papadopoulos, T. (2016). Big data analytics in logistics and supply chain management: Certain investigations for research and applications. *International Journal of Production Economics* 176: 98–110.

Wikipedia contributors (2020a, July 20). Human genome. Wikipedia. https://en.wikipedia.org/wiki/Human_genome (accessed 22 June 2021).

Wikipedia contributors (2020b, April 21). Vertical market. Wikipedia. https://en.wikipedia.org/wiki/Vertical_market (accessed 22 June 2021).

12

Digital Transformation Trends in the Automotive Industry

12.1   Introduction

Integration of the Internet of Things (IoT) and Artificial Intelligence (AI) has led companies to develop new digital experience strategies within their automotive field. The increased demand for these "digital" experiences has pushed companies to develop better means of internet-connected automotive products and provide better services towards their customer base. Connectivity between automotive devices is oriented to provide users with a more convenient experience. Since the customer base demands a more convenient and digital experience, this has forced companies to invest and develop different models to satisfy their demands.

Data collection on these automotive devices allows for companies to provide better services. The integration of IoT devices/sensors dramatically drives down the cost and provides an engaging experience for their consumers. AI and IoT devices can be implemented into "smart" factories that drive down production costs and automate the production process. AI will seek to manage and schedule tasks as well as reduce the rate of mistakes or defects. Since implementing IoT and AI would provide significant benefits, companies will reduce the centralized factories to where factories will be diversified and specialize in specific manufacturing. IoT connectivity will allow companies and consumers to provide "predictive maintenance" where sensors collect the necessary data and report issues to the company or the consumer. Companies will collect the necessary data from consumer vehicles to assess risks or provide improvements to their products.

Predictive maintenance will be achieved through the use of IoT tools. Gone now is the time of guessing what is and is not wrong with your vehicles. With sensors collecting data, it will be easier to evaluate the risk of malfunction. These sensors form a self-diagnostic system for your car. With these sensors, it will be possible to predict problems before they can occur and greatly reduce the amount of traveling malfunctions by sending alerts when certain conditions are met to indicate an incoming issue. Repairs will also take tech-savvy technicians to perform the proper software fixes and open the door to better remote services for software. Trucking businesses will especially benefit from this, keeping more trucks on the road for longer times.

An example of a predictive maintenance system technology is the Michelin tire monitoring program. Information technology (IT) intakes data about various conditions, like road conditions, to predict the tire's life span and send alerts when the condition hits a certain point. Trucking fleets benefit in a plethora of ways outside of just early alerts for mechanical issues. With the ability to maximize fuel efficiency and truck safety, trucking is more cost-effective. It is even possible to monitor cargo conditions that are very important for items that require certain temperatures to remain viable or need to stay within certain safety parameters like oil or acidic materials.

The automotive industry is still relatively product-centered. However, it has begun shifting to a more data-driven model. These companies are still needed to provide a good product to the market, aka a car. Yet they are integrating new electronic technology into their automotive. They integrate these new forms of technology that collect data and connect to the internet, and they need the means to process, analyze, and react to that data. In simple terms, these companies are becoming data-driven because of the market need for internet-connected things. Furthermore, these companies now need to function almost as a service provider since heavy data collection for predictive maintenance and vehicle analytics becomes necessary in this current technological climate.

The data-driven model becomes even more prevalent due to IoT and AI beginning to see implementations within automotive manufacturing. A constant data flow between these interconnected manufacturing devices provides how a company can shift and adjust it by analyzing its manufacture. Known bugs or reports of issues can be relayed to these smart facilities for AI to adjust according to the presented issues. In this current market, data collection becomes necessary for companies to provide a better and more convenient product for their consumers. At this point, automotive companies essentially blend the product-centered and data-driven models into a single business model. However, it is not exactly a single business model; rather, it is a state in which two models are integrated so that these businesses can remain viable.

If the fusion of AI, IoT, and Big Data continues to be implemented further, company supply chains will continue to get faster and reduce product deficiencies. This type of integration is a massive investment, and I doubt many will completely make the full commitment to it. However, I believe it comes down to the implementation cost. This would require companies to remove old production methods and replace them with new methods without having these new methods completely tested. However, I would argue that this fusion would almost outweigh the implementation costs required. If the statistics are correct and well tested, companies will need to start integrating these smart factories to remain competitive within the market. Reducing costs for manufacturing and reducing defects will allow these types of automotive companies to increase profit margins.

The fusion of AI, IoT, and Big Data will only continue to be more and more necessary for automotive companies that implement smart technologies within their products. These smart vehicles and factories will need the means to support the massive amount of data collected from their internet-connected devices. If the automotive industry continues to integrate these new technologies, they will need to shift/balance their business models between product-centered and data-driven models.

12.2 Evolution of the Automotive Industry

The landscape of the automotive industry had been homogeneous before IT came into the industry. For instance, the players' types were limited; they were mainly automotive manufacturers, such as Toyota and Ford, and Operational Equipment Manufacturers (OEMs), such as Bosch. Moreover, the business models were based on a product-centric approach. TeleTech's report describes that the automotive industry is well known for being product-centric and emphasizing sales volume (TeleTech 2014). However, the product-centric business model and the industry's landscape have been drastically changed at high speed. This is because various kinds of information technologies have come into the industry. Especially, technologies of the IoT, Big Data, and Machine Learning (ML) have affected the industry. Kolar and Lindström (2018) mention that "Digitalization and servitization change many industries such as the automotive industry." Furthermore, Koushik and Mehl (2015) argue that digitization of the formerly analog world of the automobile forces OEMs and dealers to rethink their traditional strategies and business models. Due to these technologies, the future of the car has changed. The car of the future is electrified, autonomous, shared, connected, and yearly updated. Figure 12.1 is a brief explanation of the five terms also known as "eascy"? It will emit fewer exhaust fumes and noise into its environment because it is electric. It will take up less personal time and space because it moves autonomously. It will be more accessible because users will not need a driving license to use it. It will be more affordable because it will no longer have to be bought outright but can instead be paid for in small amounts per-use (Kuhnert and Stürmer 2018).

Besides technological advances, other car trends will affect the automotive industry's change, such as car usage, having fewer cars among young people and people living in urban areas, and a low rate of growth of vehicle unit sales. Firstly, the usage of cars is expected to change as time passes (see Figure 12.2): "until recently, customers have mostly picked a single car to fulfill an array of requirements" (Wyman 2019). People have bought cars for various reasons so far, such as commuting, trips, and status. However, the majority of people will be "mobilized" who simply want to get from point A to B and are not emotionally involved in cars (Wyman 2019). For example, a family might want to rent a car to go from their house to their destination by paying only money needed for the trip.

Secondly, there is a change in owning cars among young people and people living in renting areas. A census shows that driver licensing among young people has continued to

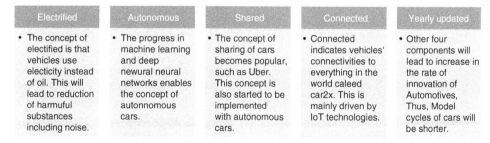

Electrified	Autonomous	Shared	Connected	Yearly updated
• The concept of electified is that vehicles use electicity instead of oil. This will lead to reduction of harmful substances including noise.	• The progress in machine learning and deep newural neural networks enables the concept of autonnomous cars.	• The concept of sharing of cars becomes popular, such as Uber. This concept is also started to be implemented with autonomous cars.	• Connected indicates vehicles' connectivities to everything in the world caleed car2x. This is mainly driven by IoT technologies.	• Other four components will lead to increase in the rate of innovation of Automotives, Thus, Model cycles of cars will be shorter.

Figure 12.1   The car of the future is electrified, autonomous, shared, connected, and yearly updated (Kuhnert and Stürmer 2017–2018).

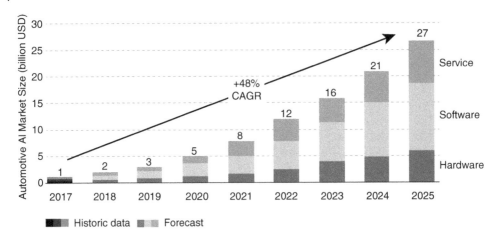

Figure 12.2 The global market of AIC automotive systems (Intellias 2020).

decline (Dutzik, Inglis, and Baxandalin 2014). Furthermore, today's young people drive less than previous generations of young Americans, even when economic and other factors linked to vehicle ownership or driving are taken into account. More of today's people living in urban areas have other kinds of transportation and so tend to have fewer cars. Tomer shows that "7.5 million households do not have access to a private automobile, and over 90% of households in large metropolitan areas live in neighborhoods with access to a transit service of some kind" (Tomer 2011). Thirdly, there is a trend that the growth rate of vehicle unit sales is going down. Although the sales of cars keep growing, the rate of growth is going down. An article published by McKinsey & Company argues that overall global car sales will continue to grow, but the annual growth rate is expected to drop from 3.6% to around 2% by 2030 (Gao et al. 2016). Thus, due to these factors, which are new to the automotive industry, the industry is currently changing to follow the new attitudes towards cars.

In terms of business perspectives, there will be a change in the revenue pool of businesses in the automotive industry due to new technologies introduced earlier. Currently, in the automotive industry, the main revenue resource is creating cars and selling them. However, the situation also will alter in the future: "the automotive revenue pool will significantly increase and diversify toward on-demand mobility services and data-driven services" (Gao et al. 2016). Therefore, the ways to make revenue from cars will change drastically in the future. Figure 12.2 shows the global market of AI automotive systems.

It is said that this change will "create up to $1.5 trillion – or 30 percent more – in additional revenue potential in 2030, compared with about $5.2 trillion from traditional car sales and aftermarket products/services, up by 50 percent from about $3.5 trillion in 2015" (Gao et al. 2016). Similarly, PwC argues that profitable mobility services will compensate for declining vehicle sales share. Mobility as a service (MaaS) will account for 22% of automotive industry revenue by 2030 and 30% of profits, compared with 38% of revenue and 26% of profits for new car sales (Viereckel et al. 2018). This is because, due to the incorporation of IoT technologies in cars and any devices around people, they can create huge data. Businesses can provide services in many ways by scrutinizing the data, such as providing personalized services via digital platforms in cars.

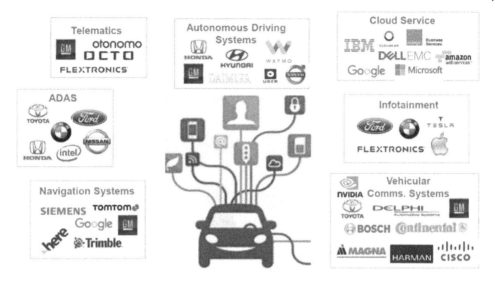

Figure 12.3 Connected car leadership landscapes (EQUINX in Harrison and Mertens 2019).

These technologies, usage of cars, and revenue resources in the automotive industry are destroying the traditional automotive industry. A report argues that "the global automotive industry is about to enter a period of wide-ranging and transformative change" (Mohr et al. 2013). The transformation is visible when seeing the players in the current industry. For instance, Accenture's report mentions that "nontraditional players such as Google and Uber attempt to drive market disruption" (Calderwood et al. 2016). As mentioned, there are already non-traditional players in the industry. Some companies provide connectivity, create an ecosystem of connected cars and self-driving cars, and make IoT platforms (Figure 12.3). Thus, the entrance of new technologies in the automotive industry and the change in car usage causes the industry's transformation, including the car's technological future, revenue pool, and players in the industry.

Moreover, the business model is also changing because of this transformation, discussed in the next section. Of course, some AI and IoT implementation issues around self-driving cars need to be addressed and solved. ML algorithm obscurity, lack of agile techniques to apply to AI algorithm development, difficulty to tackle errors, simulation complexity of data volume, and marketing time and cost are some of the self-driving issues (Intellias 2020).

12.3   Data-Driven Business Model and Data Monetization

With the development of the IoT concept and the technology created from it, manufacturers in the automotive industry have begun to transform their business model and operations. Using IoT, automotive manufacturers will be able to address consumer needs with greater precision and create more personalized experiences with their products and services. On the business side of this transformation, it will be possible to transition to automated manufacturing plants – or smart factories. In these factories, the primary workforce will consist of robots controlled by an on-site wireless network spanning the factory's breadth thanks to the rise of high-speed communication standards such as fifth generation (5G). Combined with AI, robots connected in a network with IoT devices will learn from collected feedback and become more self-sufficient. In addition to optimizing production on the factory floor, this combination, referred to as "Intelligent Connectivity," will eventually include the robotic workforce learning how to create schedules and optimize workflow. In turn, this combination of skilled human laborers and learning robots can optimize production quality while keeping manufacturing costs down.

Most aspects of the automobile industry have been revolutionized by IT. The connectivity of end-users with applications in the automobile has become an essential feature set. Predictive maintenance is a digital technology that is part of the IoT that reports on the vehicle's performance. Protection and data security are implemented in vehicle software as well. MaaS such as Uber and Lyft have also helped to transform the automotive industry. There are even online sources for buying automobiles, such as Auto Trader and Car Gurus. Elon Musk, the CEO (Chief Executive Officer) of Tesla, predicts that autonomous driving will become the norm. Using Global Positioning Systems (GPSs), sensors, cameras, connectivity, and algorithms, cars will be able to navigate safely to your destination. This will potentially save hundreds of thousands of lives and close to one trillion dollars.

MaaS provides great advantages regarding ridesharing and connected living. These ridesharing services give customers a huge advantage by removing the expense of maintenance, licenses, and vehicle purchasing. Even the large manufacturers are getting into the ridesharing market. Partnering and investing in ridesharing companies is how several automotive industries, such as Fiat partnering with Google, are breaking into the market of mobility as a service. In contrast, others are pioneering mobility as a service themselves, like Volkswagen.

Information technology also improves the supply chain and manufacturing of the automotive industry. Digitizing the connected supply chain has lowered costs, and has accelerated design, manufacturing, and delivery, streamlined by smart technology. Automotive plants are 75% automated, which provides consistency and lower overall costs.

There are some challenges with the digital transformation of the automobile industry. Business and manufacturing automation requires new business models and new ways of working. Automotive companies must continue to offer the same safety standards, quality, and performance while maintaining profitability.

The digital transformation can improve product development for large OEM manufacturers. Engineers spend up to 70% of their time searching for information and only 30% of their time performing engineering duties. With more accurate information available in real-time, engineers can spend more time being creative and innovating. Another problem that IT resolves is warranty issues. Companies discovered that 80% of warranty issues were already resolved but did not know without updated information. The digitization of the automotive industry is just one example of how IT is transforming business. Automation of business and manufacturing processes is becoming the status quo across most industries.

12.3.1 Big Data

In the automotive industry, the data-driven business models will be crucial, as discussed in the previous section. The main driving force behind this change is the emergence of Big Data in automotive fields and any kinds of fields, such as smartphones and smart appliances. The amount of data and the computation technologies applied to the data are also significantly increasing at the same time as IoT technologies are embodied in things around people. This situation indicates that businesses in automotive industries can provide more personalized services by integrating data they collected from cars and other areas, such as your house's smart alliances. Therefore, since big data is the core of personalized data-driven services, it is worth seeing what exactly is Big Data and what is happening in the field.

Although there are various definitions of big data, the widely known definition is IBM's definition (O'Leary 2013). According to the firm, Big Data is defined as four Vs: volume, variety, velocity, and veracity (Zikopoulos et al. 2013). Values and volatility are also two important factors to consider when it comes to data sustainability.

Volume. Volume of data simply refers to the amount of data. O'Leary mentions that data produced by IoT is one of the examples of Big Data (O'Leary 2013). The volume of data is increasing now at a rapid speed; "the volume of data continues to double every three years as information pours in from digital platforms, wireless sensors, virtual reality applications, and billions of mobile phones" (Henke, Bughin, Chui, et al. 2016). There are two reasons for this situation. Firstly, the number of IoT devices is increasing. Since cars also now have connectivity and many sensors in them, they can be said to be big contributors to the increase of data. Secondly, there are advancements in sensors. Currently, the present sensors can create more information compared to older sensors.

Variety. Variety refers to attempting to get all kinds of data to analyze situations or make decisions. There is no doubt that the variety of data is now also increasing. This is because many things in society can have connectivity and many kinds of sensors. For instance, smartphones can send many kinds of data, such as geography and phone usage. Moreover, cars can also create a variety of data since they have many types of sensors. Especially, the types of data produced from autonomous cars will be huge: geography, degree of congestions on streets, conditions of roads, and so on.

Velocity. The velocity of big data is about the speed of how long it takes for data to arrive at businesses and for them to process and understand data (Zikopoulos et al. 2013). Due to advancements in telecommunication and data analytics fields, the velocity also increases. For instance, the emergence of 5G enables cars to transmit the data they collected at high speed for the data to be analyzed or processed. Moreover, machine learning enables people to analyze at high speed and visualize results from the analysis for humans to understand.

Veracity. This refers to how trustful data is. All of the data collected and analyzed should be of high quality to create a machine learning that produces reliable results, so it is crucial to eliminate low quality and deceitful data before analyzing big data. Since edge computing, data processing "at or near the source of data generation" (Meulen 2018), it started to be employed to do tasks, such as getting rid of garbage data, damaged data, and deceitful data, before analyzing the veracity of data, which is also increasing.

12.3.2 Product Development

With all these new disruptions, there are new and interesting opportunities presented in the development of products. Despite the challenges presented by technological advances, the benefits digitalization presents to the automotive industry far outweigh the challenges.

Originally automotive industries followed a rigid cycle. They would install and update the technology every year with their new models in a structured and disciplined method. However, these days the cycle has been broken as new technologies are constantly emerging and harnessed for new models. This results from a move from the original cyclical nature of the automobile industry to more Mobility as a Service mindset for the industry.

This shift in views from a basic cyclical business model to mobility as a model has also created new business models. It has put development teams into a tough spot as they mix and match old and new demands to create new products. The old-style was a model that was developed, engineered, and constructed, and then shipped out to dealers. However, these days the cycles happen much faster, so companies have to keep up with the constant introduction of new tech.

Product development in an intelligent enterprise addresses how to strike that crucial balance of constant innovation and efficiency. Engineers spend more time looking for information to do their work than they spend engineering new products. By stream lining, the process of finding relevant information companies could remove some stress from production. There is also the issue of warranty solutions being shared efficiently with other sections of the company. Thanks to today's innovations, companies can share information better and provide a streamlined means of finding relevant information. Of course, none of this could be possible without finding workers with the proper tech and engineering skills to provide viable ways of accomplishing these goals.

Due to the automotive industry changes, the business models in the industry are shifting to data-driven business models. This is because, due to the cars' connectivity and any devices, and big data created from them, businesses can utilize the data. Moreover, as discussed earlier, industry revenues will not only come from the sales of cars. The potential profitability of car data monetization is large. A report from McKinsey & Company indicates that "the overall revenue pool from car data monetization at a global scale might add up to USD 450–750 billion by 2030" (Bertoncello et al. 2016). Therefore, it is no longer possible for players in the industry to make huge revenues, relying on only manufacturing products. "As a consequence of emerging data sources and analytics, data-driven business models are set to become the key value driver in the automotive industry" (Horn and Schumacher 2018).

Although there is no rigid definition of data-driven business, the core idea is that businesses' services are based on data they collect. The business model industry players are of three types: Data Harvesting, Data Matching, and As a Service (Seiberth and Gründinger 2018). Data Harvesting is where data collected is utilized for product innovation and optimization. Since current cars create a huge amount of data, vehicles can now capture and share data, including geolocation, vehicle performance, driver behavior, and biometric data (Hood et al. 2019). Automotive companies can optimize their products, such as Tesla Model S car's software update that improved and optimized the product. The higher stage of Data Harvesting is Data Matching. This enables the contextualization or matching of information using a digital platform, focusing on process innovation. Process innovations indicate that data is used to optimize the processes of providing services. For instance, Uber is one of the examples of Data Matching. This is because Uber provided a platform for ridesharing and created an algorithm that enables the business to match customer needs. The company eventually made taxi services better so that the customer needs are matched to the services more than traditional taxi services. The highest type of data-driven business is As a Service model, which is also called an outcome-based model. This business model is currently becoming popular in any field as there is a term, "anything-as-a-service" (Groene et al. 2016). Seiberth and Gründinger (2018) argue that "As-a-Service or outcome-based models transition companies from selling a product through a single transaction to providing a service with a guaranteed outcome, often usage-based or in a gain/risk share model. Therefore, in this service model, the businesses will sell their results created from their products. For instance, there are cloud computing services, which "provide IT as a service over the internet or dedicated network delivery on demand, which are payment based on usage" (Dell n.d.). In the automotive industry, there could be "Car-As-a-Service." For example, Daimler, an automotive company, lunched a subscription service of its car, which is called "Mercedes me Flexperience." This enables the customers to rent cars at fixed monthly fees, including insurance, tax, tires, maintenance, and warranty repairs (Daimler 2019). Thus, the company does not sell its cars but sells them as a service. These three types of data-driven businesses cannot be realized without analyzing big data and IoT technologies that create the data. The data can enhance the launch of services or creators classified into one of the three types. For instance, it is possible to further make the service of "Mercedes me Flexperience" better by removing the fixed cost and costing users based on how much the users use the cars based on data the cars produce. Thus, it can be argued that the data enables businesses to personalize their services for users.

12.4   Services of the Data-Driven Business Model

It was discussed that the four components that define Big Data are currently increasing, and the automotive industry is now entering into data-driven business models. Moreover, with regards to automotive manufacturers, the era when they only sold their products has ended. This is because today's sensor technologies implemented in cars enable the firms to see customers' use of cars. They can also see a whole view of customer behaviors other than cars because they can see them from data generated from things around the customers. A report published by DellEMC argues that car manufacturers can get an overall image of customers by connecting the many different touchpoints throughout the complete buying cycle, analyzing each individual's actions and gaining an in-depth understanding of typical customer behavior in all aspects and customers (DellEMC 2017). The variety of services will also increase because businesses in the automotive industry can use car data and utilize data from other devices, such as smartphones, if allowed to do so. They can then create new services by integrating and analyzing the data, which enables them to have a deep understanding of customers. In other words, the services will be more personalized due to the deep understanding based on data.

Seiberth and Gründinger think that the seven core service categories of the car industry's data-driven services are Mobility Services, Customer Experience, Connected Car Services, Safe Guarding, Digital Life, IoT, and Bottom-Line Savings. Although there are only seven categories of data-driven services in the automotive industry, many types of services will be created, classified into Data Harvesting, Data Matching, and As a Service. For instance, in terms of mobility service, MaaS will be classified into mobility service and as a service data-driven service. "At its core, MaaS relies on a digital platform that integrates end-to-end trip planning, booking, electronic ticketing, and payment services across all modes of transportation, public or private" (Goodall et al. 2017). The platform offers the best combination of transportation by evaluating customer's information, such as their locations and their needs, and data from the transportations, such as cars' locations. This service will start to be implemented in cities where there are many types of transportation, and the population in urban cities is growing (Goodall et al. 2017). Therefore, players in the automotive industry must fit their business models for the data-driven services to make a profit from them. The automotive industry services will be diversified because the players have many choices of selecting data to reach their business goals. Furthermore, the players must deal with many data-driven services or focus on some services by changing their business models and especially traditional payers in the field must change their strategies from their traditional product-centered approach.

12.5 Values of New Services in the New Automotive Industry

Although services in the new automotive industry will be diversified, it is possible to claim that the services' fundamental value will be the same: increasing efficiency. Data-driven businesses can personalize services based on collected data businesses. Personalization of services is already seen in normal lives. For instance, there are many music streaming services, such as Apple Music and Spotify. They suggest certain songs based on what users have listened to and compare them with others who have similar tendencies. That is, those apps personalize music recommendations by analyzing the data they collect from their customers. Personalization raises efficiency when businesses meet their customers' demands. This trend will be the main factor in any industries including the new automotive industry since people want that kind of service. A report from IBM argues that consumers currently "seek information and value that are personalized and relevant" (IBM 2015). Personalization will be shown in many ways in the automotive industry. For instance, infotainment in cars can be personalized by using existing data from smartphones or apps and interpreting data about the owners' car usage, such as locations where they often visit. MaaS is also one type of personalization because it can provide the best service that customers want, most based on the input, such as pricing they prefer and whether they want to arrive at their locations earlier or not, and locations and transport rotations. Furthermore, personalization in the automotive industry's data-driven services and infotainment in various forms where service providers can collect a variety of information from various sources, not only cars but also other devices, can achieve their personalized service goals. Therefore, because personalization can increase the probability that the services can meet the customers' expectations, the efficiency of interaction between customers and services in the new automotive industry will go up.

12.5.1 Consumer Trust

It has been discussed that services in the new automotive industry are driven by data collected from cars and other data sources. This form of service can increase efficacy between users and players in the industry by personalizing their services. However, since the services are based on user data, there must be a concern around privacy. As the industry's transformation continues, concern about the privacy of the data happens from consumers and businesses. For example, 56% of executives believe that connected car security and privacy are important factors informing them (Halmos and Golding 2019). In addition, Halmos and Golding argue that 62% of consumers said they would consider one brand over another if it had better security and privacy by using its unpublished data on its survey. Moreover, Colbert argues that "Connected vehicles (CVs) and Autonomous Vehicles (AVs) pose novel ethical and legal challenges that industry and governments must immediately address, particularly about privacy and data protection" (Colbert 2018).

The automotive industry is the second most data-driven industry in recent years, thanks to technological developments. As the name would suggest, Smart Cars are functional, but early examples of how combining automobiles with the latest in consumer GPS navigation and wireless communication technology while not necessarily having all the hardware and software necessary to leap to an AV. Even so, to function at the capacity desired by consumers, large amounts of data are periodically communicated between the vehicle and the driver and any cloud platform that helps the vehicle's onboard computer(s) perform their tasks. To do this, the environment in which this software operates must have security measures in place, and these measures need to be as robust as possible. Suppose a hacker manages to get access to a consumer's vehicle data. In that case, they would be able to learn where they go, what routes they travel on, possibly even turn their vehicle into a mobile host for viruses. Protection and data security become a very important subject, as it is the second-most data-driven industry. The cars collect data about all sorts of things. Driving patterns, routes, traffic, and all of this data needs to be protected. Automotive makers have been searching for newer advancements in security to back their security for the data collected by their cars. Some cars can even use Artificial Intelligence that can learn their driver's preferences while driving and typical driving behaviors.

A lack of security can result in dangerous, compromised vehicles becoming possessed by malicious code and posing a safety threat for everyone nearby. Some apps that suffer from vulnerabilities are the popular OnStar RemoteLink iOS for vehicles. As convenient as the app can be for drivers, hackers could use it as a playground for testing out ideas. General Motors suffered a catastrophic hacking incident when hackers took over several vehicle functions in some of their vehicles and wrought havoc.

The privacy issue of data created from cars is an important problem to solve before the automotive industry players launch their services in public. There are many aspects that businesses must deal with when implementing data-driven businesses. For instance, a player who attempts to implement car-sharing services must define how to use data that it gets from the cars. By car-sharing, the service can collect a great amount of data from each customer. If the data is leaked, there is a possibility that third parties could maliciously use the data.

Moreover, it is necessary to discuss the rights of the data collected. In data-driven services, data collected is often processed or analyzed. It must then be determined whether possession of the data belongs to the customers or the service providers after the analysis. Therefore, since this privacy problem is directly related to consumer trust, players in the new automotive industry must prepare for the issue. However, there is good news that people are willing to share their data for the services of connected cars. A report from

McKinsey & Company argues that customers showed a higher willingness to share data and to pay for time-related use cases such as networked parking, allowing them to save valuable time in city centers, often looking for available parking spots (Bertoncello et al. 2016). Since the company's survey focused only on three countries, Germany, the US, and China, it is skeptical that there is the same trend in the world. However, it could be said that as technologies spread into people's lives, the attitude towards sharing data for better services becomes easier. Therefore, in terms of consumer trust, it could be argued that players in the new automotive industry pass a certain stage where consumers are willing to share their data. However, to maintain the trust, the players must deal with privacy issues around the data.

12.6 Conclusion

In conclusion, the automotive industry has been at the forefront of technological development, alongside other industries where information exchange is critical. In particular, the last few years have seen a shift from a focus on product development to developing and improving services. This shift can be observed not only among automotive manufacturers but businesses that are wholly dependent on vehicles to operate, whether it is transporting goods or a consumer from their house to the other side of the city in which they live.

There is no doubt that the integration of the IoT and AI in the Automotive Industry would boost its economic growth. This is why there is a demand for the integration of AI and IoT in the automotive industry and development to produce new business models and smart ways of working that could make more progress in the industry and reduce costs, human effort, and the manufacture of consumer-friendly cars. The use of digital technology in the industry reduces the expenses and human effort made in the hectic manufacturing process. The vehicles manufactured are also much more reliant and error-free due to the heavy work being done by robots. However, all the facilities mentioned above are still in their progress level and will soon be provided in the upcoming cars and other vehicles. IoT and AI have made industries more connected to the consumers and get their feedback to improve their vehicle design, development, and manufacturing process in order to bring a better product in the industry. It has also brought some challenges in the industry. Privacy of the consumers could be nominated as one of the major challenges for the automotive industry. It is important to keep in mind that many of the effects that IoT and AI have on the automotive industry stem from the consumers themselves. Many of these customers practically demand full connectivity in the products they purchase, which includes numerous industries outside the automotive scope. This demand results in more than 100 million lines of code per connected vehicle. For the digital transformation to connected vehicles to occur, several key features must be in place. Currently, most consumers do not understand general maintenance on a car. Over the years, vehicles have installed technical devices in their cars to monitor different variables involved with an automobile operating at a normal level. Some examples of these devices include tire sensors, engine health monitors, oil level sensors, and gas lights. The technology being developed and the increased connectivity level will allow cars to be connected to the internet. While operating on the internet, these sensors can then communicate with other systems to help calculate whether there are problems with the vehicle. If a car is completely electrical and powered by a computer, instead of going to the mechanic to fix your car, you will eventually be able to call a help desk. This will help the supply chain industry and the automobile industry with designing systems to increase their efficiency.

These technologies also generate consumer data in an amount that has never been considered. Each vehicle can collect huge amounts of data points on the consumer. This data generates the problem with understanding how to protect all this consumer information. Consumer interests must be put before all else, and each automotive business must consider this.

Consumers have more knowledge about vehicles than ever. Each consumer can go into an auto lot and know exactly the make and model that they want. There are now car dealerships that work entirely online and will deliver cars to you that you purchase.

The amount of data being collected from these smart vehicles generates the ability to use autonomous driving. This consists of a car that can travel on roadways without a human driver. The technologies on these vehicles are vast and range from cameras to laser sensors. There is currently fear within the truck driving industry that many truck drivers will lose their jobs if autonomous driving succeeds. These vehicles have the chance to be present in incredibly safe driving conditions.

Consumers still dictate what type of products they want and what will be produced in the end. Each business will have to incorporate a new business model to meet the needs of this technology and to fit the needs of their consumers. Their business models will need to be agile because of the ever-changing technological trends. An agile business can adapt to change and build the business around changing and adapting to the newest trends. This model also has an entirely new data set to utilize and to understand what their consumers want. Instead of focusing on marketing strategies that get results on what type of equipment they need to add, these businesses will be able to determine their consumer needs by utilizing the data collected from the consumer.

References

Bertoncello, M. et al. (2016). Monetizing car data. McKinsey & Company [online document]. https://www.mckinsey.com/~/media/McKinsey/Industries/Automotive%20and%20 Assembly/Our%20Insights/Monetizing%20car%20data/Monetizing-car-data.ashx (accessed December 17, 2019).

Calderwood, J. et al. (2016). World Economic Forum White Paper on Digital Transformation of Industries: In collaboration with Accenture, World Economic Forum [online document]. http://reports.weforum.org/digital-transformation/wp-content/blogs.dir/94/mp/files/pages/ files/wef-dti-automotivewhitepaper-final-january-2016.v1.pdf (accessed December 17, 2019).

Colbert, C (2018). Privacy under the hood: towards an international data privacy framework for autonomous vehicles [online document]. https://conferences.law.stanford.edu/werobot/ wp-content/uploads/sites/47/2018/02/Privacy-Under-the-Hood-Towards-an-International-Data-Privacy-Framework-for-Autonomous-Vehicles.pdf (accessed December 17, 2019).

Daimler (2018). A Mercedes-Benz for every occasion Mercedes Me Flexperience, Daimler [online document]. https://www.daimler-mobility.com/en/solutions/renting/mercedes-me-flexperience/ (accessed December 17, 2019).

Dell EMC (2017). Connected cars [online document]. https://www.dellemc.com/content/dam/uwaem/production-design-assets/en-gb/ConnectedCIO/pdf/ConnectedCars-Readonline-min.pdf (accessed December 17, 2019).

Dell Technologies (n.d.). Cloud Computing Services, Dell Technologies [online document]. https://www.dellemc.com/en-us/glossary/cloud-computing-services.htm (accessed December 17, 2019).

Dutzik, T., Inglis, J., and Baxandall, P. (2014) Millennials in motion changing travel habits of young Americans and the implications for Public Policy, [online document]. https://uspirg.org/sites/pirg/files/reports/Millennials%20in%20Motion%20USPIRG.pdf (accessed December 17, 2019).

Gao, P., Kaas, H., Mohr, D., and Wee, D (2016). Automotive revolution – perspective towards 2030 [online document]. https://www.mckinsey.com/industries/automotive-and-assembly/our-insights/disruptive-trends-that-will-transform-the-auto-industry/de-de (accessed December 17, 2019).

Goodall, W., Bornstein, J., Fishman, T., and Bonthron, B (2017). The rise of mobility as a service. Deloitte [online document]. https://www2.deloitte.com/us/en/insights/deloitte-review/issue-20/smart-transportation-technology-mobility-as-a-service.html (accessed December 17, 2019).

Groene, F., Herdé, B., Phaneuf, D., and Stürmer, F. (2016). Zero infrastructure – anything-as-a-service: How CSPs can harness the full power of the cloud, PwC [online document]. https://www.pwc.fr/fr/assets/files/pdf/2016/01/pwc_communication_review_zero_infrastructure_janv2016.pdf (accessed December 17, 2019).

Halmos, G. and Golding, J. (2019). Securing privacy for the future of the connected car, IBM [online document]. Available at: https://www.ibm.com/downloads/cas/D8LEB3AQ (accessed December 17, 2019).

Harrison, L. and Mertens, K. (2019). Connected car reigns at the Detroit auto show. https://blog.equinix.com/blog/2019/01/15/connected-car-reigns-at-the-detroit-auto-show/(accessed 22 June 2021).

Henke, N., Bughin, J., Chui, M., et al. (2016). The age of analytics: Competing in a data-driven world. [online document]. https://www.mckinsey.com/business-functions/mckinsey-analytics/our-insights/the-age-of-analytics-competing-in-a-data-driven-world (accessed December 17, 2019).

Hood, J. et al. (2019). Monetizing data in the age of connected vehicles Deloitte [online document]. https://www2.deloitte.com/us/en/insights/industry/automotive/monetizing-data-connected-vehicles.html (accessed December 17, 2019).

Horn, H. and Schumacher, S (2018). *The IBM Automotive Playbook*, IBM [online document]. https://ai-monday.de/wp-content/uploads/2019/03/Automotive_Playbook_sneakpeek.pdf (accessed December 17, 2019).

IBM (2015). Automotive 2025: Industry without borders engage with consumers, embrace mobility and exploit the ecosystem [online document]. https://www.ibm.com/downloads/cas/4JEQ0DN1 (accessed December 17, 2019).

Intellias (2020, February 24). Automotive industry: Is it worth the effort? https://www.intellias.com/adoption-of-ai-in-the-automotive-industry-is-it-worth-the-effort/ (accessed 22 June 2021).

Kolar, E. and Lindstöm, L. (2018). Future business model for OEMs in the automotive industry business model. Adaptation based on the role an OEM takes in a future business network, Chalmers University of Technology [online document]. https://pdfs.semanticscholar.org/bfb7/22bf9ede0e3eb68de29629a2b1e04132ca80.pdf (accessed December 17, 2019).

Koushik, S. and Mehl, R (2015). The automotive industry as a digital business, NTT DATA Deutschland GmbH [online document]. Available at: https://emea.nttdata.com/fileadmin/web_data/publications/nttdata_Management_Summary_Online_Version_engl_vs2_cj.pdf (accessed December 17, 2019).

Kuhnert, F. and Stürmer, C(2017–2018). Five trends transforming the automotive industry, PwC. [online document]. https://eu-smartcities.eu/sites/default/files/2018-03/pwc-five-trends-transforming-the-automotive-industry.compressed.pdf (accessed December 17, 2019).

Meulen, R (2018). What edge computing means for infrastructure and operations leaders [online document]. https://www.gartner.com/smarterwithgartner/what-edge-computing-means-for-infrastructure-and-operations-leaders/ (accessed December 17, 2019).

Mohr, D. et al. (2013) The road to 2020 and beyond: What's driving the global automotive industry, McKinsey & Company [online document]. https://www.mckinsey.com/~/media/mckinsey/dotcom/client_service/Automotive%20and%20Assembly/PDFs/McK_The_road_to_2020_and_beyond.ashx (accessedDecember 17, 2019).

O'Leary, D.E. (2013). Artificial intelligence and big data. *IEEE Intelligent Systems* 28 (2): 96–99. https://doi.org/10.1109/MIS.2013.39.

Seiberth, G. and Gründinger, W (2018). Data-driven business models in connected cars, mobility services & beyond, Accenture [online document]. https://www.bvdw.org/fileadmin/bvdw/upload/publikationen/connected_mobility/20180418_data_driven_business_models_Seiberth_Gruendinger.pdf (accessed December 17, 2019).

TeleTech (2014). Placing customer centricity in the driver's seat of the automotive industry, TeleTech [online document]. https://www.ttec.com/sites/default/files/white-paper-placing-customer-centricity-drivers-seat-automotive-industry_0.pdf (accessed December 17, 2019).

Tomer, A (2011). Transit access and zero-vehicle households. Metropolitan Policy Program at Brookings [online document]. https://www.brookings.edu/wp-content/uploads/2016/06/0818_transportation_tomer.pdf (accessed December 17, 2019).

Viereckel, R. et al. (2018). The 2018 Strategy & Digital Auto Report [online document]. https://www.strategyand.pwc.com/de/de/studie/digital-auto-report-2018.pdf (accessed December 17, 2019).

Wyman, O (2019). Building the Automotive Industry of 2030 [online document]. https://www.oliverwyman.com/content/dam/oliver-wyman/v2/publications/2019/jun/AutomotiveManager2019/Oliver_Wyman_Automotive_Manager_Coverstory_web_final.pdf (accessed December 17, 2019).

Zikopoulos, P. et al. (2013). *Harness the Power of Big Data*. McGraw-Hill.

13

Wireless Sensors/IoT and Artificial Intelligence for Smart Grid and Smart Home

13.1 Introduction

The United States electricity generating and distribution infrastructure is undergoing dramatic changes. Historically, the industry has been driven by the production and supplier side. Large baseload plants (mainly coal and nuclear) have maintained enough supply to handle the normal requirements with excess capacity available on demand. Recently, interest in renewable energy has greatly increased, leading to more wind farms and solar plants. While these comprise only a very small fraction of the nation's total electrical generation capacity, their contribution is expected to grow in the coming decades. However, if these energy solutions are ever to have a major impact, several technological challenges must be met and solved. Among these are efficient, large-scale energy storage solutions and an extensive, responsive communications network to control the entire power grid.

The buzz phrase for this updated and improved electrical system is "the Smart Grid." The Smart Grid is intended to operate this network of generators and distributors of power more efficiently with automatic control and operation of the various systems in response to user needs and power availability. The Smart Grid will acquire and process real-time data as each consumer is using the power, which will allow utilities to increase the distribution network's stability with variable tariffs according to the time of day. This will reduce fluctuation, allowing the overall electrical grid to achieve a more constant load throughout the day and efficiency by remote maintenance and the grid's operation.

The reality is that there is no defined standard or picture of what the Smart Grid is. It is an emerging technology whose full purposes and requirements will only become clearer as the marketplace drives it. Will wind and solar become a major factor in electricity generation, entailing the grid's need to balance the load to deal with their discontinuous supply? If so, is there money available to build new high-voltage lines to transport this product from their sometimes remote locations to the nation's population centers? Will the public embrace electric cars, further taxing the electricity supply? Will viable energy storage solutions come to fruition? These factors will play a role in determining whether the Smart Grid is implemented and what it will look like. As the grid moves forward, several questions have yet to be answered on the communication front. What and how much data is needed?

Intelligent Connectivity: AI, IoT, and 5G, First Edition. Abdulrahman Yarali.
© 2022 John Wiley & Sons Ltd. Published 2022 by John Wiley & Sons Ltd.

What will be the required bandwidth needed for communication? Will the industry settle on a particular technology or protocol?

Presently, there are projects in place or ongoing throughout the US to install smart meters on customer premises, which will replace the old electric usage meters, which simply recorded the total usage for a given period (typically one month). At a minimum, these smart meters will allow the utility to obtain readings automatically through several possible communication channels. However, this is simply the first step in the Smart Grid process. Eventually, these meters are expected to provide constant, real-time data back to the utility to monitor usage rates, detect problems, and adjust the grid accordingly (INL 2009).

This change is simply an intermediate step as a Smart Grid's true power lies in two-way communication between the utility and the customer. Ideally, the customer will be sent information through the smart meter providing items such as power rate pricing, which fluctuates based on the day and usage rates. The smart meter may communicate directly with appliances such as a washer and dryer, the stove and refrigerator, the heating and air unit, and the electric car's charging station.

Communication on the Smart Grid can be divided into two primary sections – short-range communication such as a home area network (HAN), which connects the home's varied devices to its smart meter, and the longer-range transmission that is necessary to span the distance from the utility to the customer. A Smart Grid requires further communication between the interconnected utility generators and suppliers, but that is beyond this chapter's scope. Ensuring security in each of these networks (which may each have different media) will be required as all of them must work together for the Smart Grid to function properly.

Many of the communication and security components are common between these energy subsystems. Supervisory Control and Data Acquisition (SCADA) is the core subsystem of the Smart Grid. A second and key component to the Smart Grid is several secure, highly available wireless networks, including Worldwide Interoperable Microwave Access (WiMAX), Wireless Local Area Network (WLAN), Wide Area Network (WAN), all generations of cellular technologies, and wireless sensor protocols. The comprehensive security solution is a third key component as privacy remains a major obstacle for implementing Smart Grid technology (Metke and Ekl 2010).

The main driving force of implementing a Smart Grid is the change in electric power areas:

- Rising greenhouse gas emissions (CO_2) have the potential to impact the environment and local economies seriously.
- Power outages can wreak havoc and cost billions of dollars in lost productivity and revenue.
- Security threats are constant to the electric infrastructure. The physical and cybersecurity risks from terrorists and hackers continue to grow exponentially.
- Innovative technology holds significant promise as a "game-changer." Innovation is pervasive across the electricity value chain (from smart appliances to advanced energy storage technologies).
- Evolving standards hold the key to the pace of development. Technical interoperability will be vital to ease of use, adoption rates, cybersecurity, and avoiding stranded costs. The National Institute of Standards and Technology (NIST) is developing these standards in conjunction with the GridWise Architecture Council (GWAC).

The following are key applications that will be enabled by the merged electrical/intelligence infrastructure. It is important to note that the intelligence infrastructure will be created through applications like these; that is, a utility is not going to invest in creating the infrastructure for the sake of creating infrastructure. With shared Information and Continuous Optimizing, the road is paved for Intelligent Responses (Yarali and Rahman 2012).

- Demand Response and Dynamic Pricing
- Distributed Generation and Alternate Energy Sources
- Self-Healing Wide-Area Protection and Islanding
- Asset Management and On-Line Equipment Monitoring
- Real-Time Simulation and Contingency Analysis
- Participation in Energy Markets

Figure 13.1 depicts the power grid's diverse focus areas superimposed on the internet, leading to various definitions for the Smart Grid (Rahman 2011). The general objectives are to make the grid reliable, cost-effective, and smarter using the Internet of Things (IoT), high-speed communication technologies, and distributed computing.

As the internet grows in popularity and has become part of our everyday lives and modern advancements in technology across the board, the combination of it all has cleared the way for a new line of IoT technologies to be developed. It is slowly becoming a part of our daily lives. Smart devices such as Amazon Alexa or Google Assistant can be found in many modern residential homes today. These smart devices are just a few of the many smaller specialty devices developed in IoT. Smart devices such as the revolutionary Raspberry Pi

Figure 13.1 Applications of a Smart Grid in different use cases.

can be used in infinite ways, including being implemented for Artificial Intelligence (AI) use on a modern "Smart Grid" for smart cities.

Today's technology allows for remote sensing, remote security, various production uses, etc. This will improve the quality of life residentially, all the way to increased industrial production yields (Sohraby, Minoli, and Znati 2007). With AI technology growing in popularity, both commercially and residentially, more advances can be made for efficiency and convenience.

13.2 Wireless Sensor Networks

Wireless sensors, as we know them, are rapidly advancing as the technology itself expands. Wireless sensors are even embedded in Central Processing Units (Kocakulak and Butun 2017). Often, when smart wireless sensors are linked together, they collectively form a smart Wireless Sensor Network. A Wireless Sensor Network is a set of self-configured wireless sensors linked to a wireless internet connection to monitor physical or environmental conditions such as sound, temperature, vibration, pollutants, pressure, or motion and pass the collected data over the network to be analyzed (Matin and Islam 2012).

The average Wireless Sensor Network is usually quite power-efficient. However, power-efficiency comes with several limitations that go with it. One of the largest limitations is power-related components. Power-efficiency also means reduced system computing power, which leads to a limited speed for system-wide processing/computing. Nonetheless, Wireless Sensor Networks are still rapidly growing in popularity in the commercial field.

The Wireless Sensor devices have also been developed and designed to respond to queries sent from a "control site," so they will perform specific instructions or obtain specific sensing samples (Matin and Islam 2012). This design technique allows the sensing system to remain self-sufficient but still maintains the ability to be controlled and accessed remotely.

Some modern Wireless Sensor Networks are being used in special applications such as civil and military applications to modern healthcare facilities (Sharif, Potdar, and Chang 2009). These sensor systems can even be used to monitor vehicle emissions at vehicle inspection businesses. Wireless Sensor Networks have a vast area of application and are still growing in popularity.

13.3 Power Grid Impact

Artificial Intelligence and Smart Home Systems can positively impact today's power grid, becoming over-worked and pushed to new limits every year. With a growing number of electronic devices in modern homes than ever before and modern electric vehicle (EV) hitting the consumer market yearly, today's aging power grid is becoming extremely overloaded and will be forced to make modern changes. The power grid design that is still in use today was not developed or designed for such modern advancements and power-hungry electronic devices we regularly use today. All this has put a major strain on today's power grid.

Unfortunately, power outages are becoming more common as our aging power grid and systems reach their limits. In 2007, there were about 76 power outages across the United States, and in 2011, there were over 300 power outages, all due to an aging power grid and equipment failures (NPR and Bakke 2016). Renewable resources such as water and wind turbines are slowly being incorporated into our aging power grid as a reliable resource to be used to provide power. However, our aging power grid is not entirely capable of adapting to these renewable resources; thus, a lot of renewable energy is wasted compared to what could be collected and used.

Believe it or not, power companies have not changed their business strategies since the first power plant was erected in 1882 by Thomas Edison (Martin, Wade, and Chediak 2020). Centralized facilities have always been the basic concept for power generation. As one would expect, it is an aging concept. In recent years, power companies have also been under pressure, being under the microscope by larger cities and local governments to develop more efficient and reliable ways to produce clean/green energy to power today's rapidly aging power production methods.

Fortunately, that is where AI comes into play. Smart devices are designed to be extremely power-efficient, balancing processing power with power-efficiency to do various given tasks. Of course, AI is still technically in its infancy, but it can make a huge impact on today's power grid, all starting at home with smart home devices.

Eventually, AI combined with intelligent Internet of Things (IoT) technology will allow for Smart Grids to be deployed on an aging power grid across the globe.

13.4 Benefits of the Smart Grid

As technology develops and advances, our current power grid is expected to slowly develop and transform into a Smart Grid. A Smart Grid is an automated and broadly distributed energy generation, transmission, and distribution network (Chhaya et al. 2016).

- **Economic development**
- **New jobs**. The manufacture, installation, operation, and maintenance of the Smart Grid and its components will create new jobs within the state.
- **Innovation**. Smart Grid innovation will enable the growth of a business while rewarding customers with valuable new products.
- **Lower costs**. Costs rise over time, and energy is no exception, but the Smart Grid should provide less costly energy than otherwise would be possible. As such, it will save customers money, which can be invested or consumed as they choose.
- **Customer satisfaction**
- **Higher customer satisfaction**. The combination of lower costs, improved reliability, and better customer control will raise satisfaction among all types of customers (residential, commercial, industrial, institutional).
- **Improved reliability**. The Smart Grid will reduce and shorten outages and improve the quality of power.
- **Shorter outages**. The incorporation of advanced sensors and phasor measurement units (PMUs), communication networks, and smart systems will allow an unprecedented

degree of system visibility and situational awareness of the electric power system. The smart Grid will result in shorter outages through its "islanding" and "self-healing" features.

- **Customer energy/cost savings**. As pricing becomes more transparent and is aligned with the underlying economics of generation and distribution, customers' decisions to save money will benefit society as well.
- **Highest security**. Security will be incorporated into the Smart Grid design and require the implementation of practices and procedures by individual stakeholders. In this way, physical and cybersecurity risks can be managed to the highest standards possible.
- **Timely renewables**. The Smart Grid is the enabler of more renewable energy. Its development will allow for the timely incorporation of these sustainable sources of power in a user-friendly, cost-effective manner.

When AI is combined with today's power grid, a new infrastructure is born, known as a Smart Grid. A Smart Grid is integrated with AI and can use a series of specialized, network-connected sensors to identify and pinpoint the exact location when power outages occur. With the proper equipment in place, electricity can be temporarily re-routed to restore power. In contrast, electrical equipment is repaired or replaced (Sulikowski 2019). The efficient use of AI allows for power to be restored faster after a blackout and helps to ensure efficient electricity usage and transmission across the grid.

As the IoT technology grows in popularity and becomes more developed, additional sensors, automation systems, controllers, and actuators will be implemented into a modern Smart Grid, making it a modern reality (Sulikowski 2019). AI technology can use that very series of sensors to find the slightest evidence of a potential malfunction, such as electrical wires in poor condition located anywhere on the Smart Grid. AI technology on an aging power grid allows for problems to be detected before they cause electrical problems.

With AI technology and a specialized series of interconnected sensors, a modern centralized network can be used to create a modern Smart Grid. This system can automatically collect grid performance and physical condition data to be analyzed and monitored for any deteriorating conditions, allowing for problems to be repaired or fixed before potential blackouts occur.

13.5 Internet of Things

How, exactly, do Smart Grids collect all this data obtained from network-connected sensors? Smart Grids take advantage of a mesh system of IoT devices and their connected sensors that gather and transmit data both to and from the sensors (Sulikowski 2019). With a network of sensors placed throughout the Smart Grid, large-scale blackouts can be prevented.

Firstly, we will look at a little of the background of the IoT technology. The IoT smart devices are advancing to a point where they can all collectively form a large network of smart devices that can be managed securely. These devices can be integrated into almost any area of our daily lives, including Smart Grids. When in place, these devices can drastically change our way of life for the better, making us more productive overall as a result.

The IoT technology, in general, could be looked at in a variety of different layers (Mo 2019). The first initial layer would start with internet-connected smart IoT devices found in today's modern residential homes, like the Amazon Echo device or Google's Nest.

The middle layer would be where the full-duplex communications pipelines lay. This is where a reliable internet connection would be needed to support smart home devices alongside every other smart device found in modern homes today, such as smartphones, smart TVs, and even laptops. This middle layer would also serve as a connection to cloud servers where smart home devices retrieve their information from and understand and execute verbal commands on the spot.

The final layer is a very high-level layer where IoT smart home devices are powered using a high-level AI by the manufacturer's cloud servers, business-grade intelligence, and even a company algorithm. Thus, a smart home device can properly function based on residential level verbal commands that could be prompted at any given time.

It is important to note that the IoT broad concept is not directly controlled under one company, just like the world-wide-web (Mo 2019). However, independent companies can purchase these smart IoT devices and load their own operating systems on these smart devices, based on their intended use. The IoT smart devices should generally be considered to be a large and productive extension of the world-wide-web as we know it. These devices are very beneficial in many different areas when properly used, especially in a production or industrial environment. These devices eliminate human error out of the equation almost entirely in a commercial environment, especially when it comes to Smart Grids.

The IoT devices are almost guaranteed to explode in popularity because of their compact computing power and efficiency; all are packed into their small size (Mo 2019). They are also rather inexpensive, which is a big benefit to commercial industries. Take these small and efficient IoT devices and pair them with today's aging power grid. A new Smart Grid is born, revolutionizing the way power is transferred everywhere across today's grid.

With the IoT, smart home devices are becoming popular. This revolution introduces various new and additional smart sensors found in modern homes. This concept is intended to provide a whole new level of comfort and control of modern devices and accommodations today in residential homes. Smart home devices simply report to a cloud-based server for communication reasons. When AI is implemented into a smart home device, it is also likely that power grid demands will be reduced, which will lead to a massive impact on the energy sector, especially when the Smart Grid is combined with smart home devices throughout a modern residential home. This could potentially lead to a massive energy conservation.

13.6 Internet of Things on the Smart Grid

With the IoT smart devices in place, there will also be significantly reduced costs to the power grid, which should lower the average consumer's electricity bill and give the end consumer more control over their electricity consumption.

As previously mentioned, human error is eliminated when a modern Smart Grid is deployed. With modern Smart Grids in place, fewer blackouts occur with reduced downtime for repairs or replacements to the power grid itself, because the Smart Grid will be capable of temporarily re-routing electricity itself. With a Smart Grid being capable of monitoring its own system's health, human error is eliminated since power companies will not have to wait until something breaks or is damaged before repair or replacement, saving the company time, money, and resources.

When the Smart Grid is paired with smart home devices, it enables instantaneous feedback from numerous smart network sensors connected to a main smart home device powered by a Smart Grid. The Smart Grid can easily streamline the power delivery process to each home located on the Smart Grid, enabling massive energy conservation across the city.

13.6.1 Smart Grid Security

As Smart Grids are deployed, the cybersecurity side of things is often "kicked under the rug" and forgotten. With Smart Grids being deployed on a city-wide scale where Smart Grids will be linked to hundreds of thousands of homes, security truly needs to be right at the top with the implementation of Smart Grids. Unfortunately, cybersecurity for Smart Grids is likely to be complicated by numerous factors, including the vast complexity of a Smart Grid and the increased demand for power itself to homes and corporate businesses worldwide as in-home electronic devices continue to grow in popularity.

As a side effect, deploying a Smart Grid on a city-wide scale will inevitably introduce a weak entry point for cybercriminals. There have been numerous discussions between the Federal Communications Commission and government legislation about implementing security protocols and guidelines regarding the security of IoT smart devices. However, nothing has been agreed upon and mandated as of now. This means there are no real security policies in place by default for the IoT smart devices, leaving the window wide open for cyber attackers.

13.7 Smart Grid and Artificial Intelligence

Artificial Intelligence can be implemented in many ways, both residentially and industrially. Power usage is only predictable for power companies based on past usage computer models, which help estimate future power demand (Nunez 2019). This is where AI comes into play. When it comes to electrical grids, electrical companies must maintain thousands of assets as part of necessary equipment, such as transformers and generators. One blackout can result from almost a billion different scenarios regarding what caused the blackout to begin with. At that point, electric companies must decide what part requires the most attention for repair. This can be expensive and time-consuming, wasting valuable time and resources, ultimately diminishing company profits and funding.

AI can be very beneficial to power companies. They can feed the AI system a set of data with solutions as if the machine were studying previous "exams" before trying new ones (Nunez 2019). This is referred to as supervised AI learning. Companies can also feed the AI system raw system data without any potential solutions, forcing the AI system to find system patterns and seek out the best solution possible.

The AI system is always "learning" and saves past power disruption event data on either local or cloud-based servers. Future disruptions in service can be rapidly analyzed and compared to past events to identify the problem and compile the best solution based on cost and available company resources. This technology gives the power grid operators and technicians more accurate guidance far more reliable than time-consuming guesswork for system repairs and electrical grid equipment malfunctions. This is extremely beneficial after a large-scale natural disaster or storm, allowing power grid operators to make equipment repairs much faster than before.

Another use of AI technology on the Smart Grid uses this technology to speed up daily calculations that go into regional electric system planning (Nunez 2019). This system can help power grid technicians implement the desired schedule for hourly and daily energy production. This prevents too much power from being produced or accidentally coming up short for larger sudden power demands. Saving this data on either a daily or regular basis allows AI software to compile and analyze data regularly. This allows the AI system to find regular patterns that could solve an issue later down the line.

Any lower-end prediction equipment in place is likely to be assisted rather than completely replaced by AI technology (Nunez 2019). This technology pairing strategy simply gives existing equipment a "boost" with previous data from problems and solutions. This introduces a new adaptive-learning method to any lower-end equipment already in place and will process system-wide issues much faster due to this pairing method.

13.8 Smart Grid Programming

The implementation of Smart Grids on such a broad scale will require a minimal amount of low-level programming. This is due to the vast amount of technology added to the existing power grid, such as an integrated series of specialized sensors that are implemented to monitor electrical system conditions. Smart device sensors are installed directly on the power lines themselves and at electrical substations. These sensors directly monitor the physical and electrical conditions of the power transmission system itself. The programming of the smart devices that control the smart sensors can be as simple as setting the AI system to alert power grid operators of equipment failures when they occur. The AI system will also continue to look for abnormalities in the sensor data.

Using previously collected sensor data, the system compares past with current system data to predict any changes present throughout the Smart Grid system (Nunez 2019). This analysis can accurately pinpoint if something new is found on the electrical grid and where it is located, ultimately alerting power grid technicians if something is going on with the power grid that they may not expect.

Finally, suppose a Smart Grid has access to renewable energy resources such as wind turbines. In that case, AI can work with IoT smart devices, which will have direct internet connectivity to compare current and past weather patterns to predict best what wind speeds will be on a day-by-day basis. This method will help predict how much power generation should be expected daily for power grid companies. The AI system can recognize regular weather patterns and make daily production schedule adjustments based on present and historical weather pattern data.

13.9 Conclusion

The Smart Grid is an emerging technology to provide next-generation power grid and is promoted by many governments to address energy independence, global warming, and emergency resilience issues. As the internet grows in popularity and becomes part of our everyday lives along with modern advancements in technology across the board, it has cleared the way for a new line of IoT technologies to be developed. It is slowly becoming a part of our daily lives. Many smaller smart devices such as Amazon Alexa or Google Assistant can be found today in many modern residential homes. Smart devices such as the revolutionary Raspberry Pi can be used in infinite ways, including being implemented for AI use on a modern "Smart Grid" for smart cities.

Today's technology allows for remote sensing, remote security, various production uses, etc. This will improve the quality of life residentially, all the way to increased industrial production yields (Sohraby, Minoli, and Znati 2007). With AI technology growing in popularity, both commercially and residentially, more advances can be made for efficiency and convenience, especially on the modern Smart Grid.

When AI is implemented into a smart home device, it is likely that there will also be reduced power grid demands. This will have a massive impact on the energy sector, especially when the Smart Grid is combined with smart home devices throughout a modern residential home. This could potentially lead to some massive energy conservation measures.

References

Chhaya, L., Sharma, P., Bhagwatikar, G., and Kumar, A. (2016, October 21). *Wireless Sensor Network Based on Smart Grid Communications* (Vaccaro, A. ed.). MDPI. www.mdpi.com/2079-9292/6/1/5/pdf.

INL Critical Infrastructure Protection/Resilience Center (2009). *Study of Security Attributes of Smart Grid Systems – Current Cyber Security Issues*. Department of Energy.

Kocakulak, M., and Butun, I. (2017). IEEE Annual Computing and Communication Workshop and Conference (CCWC). Retrieved from: https://ieeexplore.ieee.org/xpl/conhome/7864800/proceedings.

Martin, C., Wade, W., and Chediak, M. (2020, January 31). America's Power Grid. (L.P. Bloomberg). The Washington Post. https://www.washingtonpost.com/business/energy/americas-power-grid/2020/01/31/4ef061a8-4472-11ea-99c7-1dfd4241a2fe_story.html (accessed 22 June 2021).

Matin, M.A., and Islam, M.M.. (2012). *Overview of Wireless Sensor Network*. doi:https://doi.org/10.5772/49376. https://www.intechopen.com/books/wireless-sensor-networks-technology-and-protocols/overview-of-wireless-sensor-network.

Metke, A.R. and Ekl, R.L. (2010). Security technology for Smart Grid networks. *IEEE Transaction on Smart Grid* 1 (1): 99–107. Retrieved from: https://ieeexplore.ieee.org/stamp/stamp.jsp?arnumber=5460903.

Mo, D. (2019, January 01). Internet of Things (IoT): the driving force behind 5G. Enterprisetechsuccess https://www.enterprisetechsuccess.com/article/

Internet-of-Things-(IoT):-The-Driving-Force-Behind-5G/c1dvY3UrWTBWS3pwY0pqbEpSM HpIUT09 (accessed 22 June 2021).

NPR and Bakke, G. (2016, August 22). Aging and unstable, the nation's electrical grid is "The Weakest Link." (NPR.org, ed.). NPR. https://www.npr.org/2016/08/22/490932307/aging-and-unstable-the-nations-electrical-grid-is-the-weakest-link (accessed 22 June 2021).

Nunez, C. (2019, June 14). Artificial Intelligence can make the U.S. electric grid smarter (The United States Department of Energy's Office of Science). Argonne National Laboratory. https://www.anl.gov/article/artificial-intelligence-can-make-the-us-electric-grid-smarter (accessed 22 June 2021).

Rahman, S. (2011). Smart Grid as a solution provider for integration of distributed generation https://www.ieee-pes.org/images/files/pdf/appeec2011/APPEEC-2011-Rahman.pdf (accessed 22 June 2021).

Sharif, A., Potdar, V., and Chang, E. (2009). *Wireless multimedia sensor technology: A survey*, 2–9. https://doi.org/10.1109/INDIN.2009.5195872.

Sohraby, K., Minoli, D., and Znati, T. (2007). Wireless sensor etworks. In: *Technology, Protocols, and Applications*. Hoboken, New Jersey: Wiley www.wiley.com.

Sulikowski, M. (2019, June 28). Smart grid – AI at the service of the power distribution network. https://naturally.com/blog/smart-grid-ai-in-power-distribution-network (accessed 22 June 2021).

Yarali, A. and Rahman, S. (2012). Smart Grid networks: promises and challenges. *Journal of Communications* 7 (6): 409–416.

14

Artificial Intelligence, 5G, and IoT: Security

14.1   Introduction

The Internet of Things (IoT) has become a major phenomenon in the last few years. The heightened increase in smart devices has enabled service providers and consumers to retain and manage big data daily. The data that is being gathered has become more complex and uncertain. Therefore, most researchers have turned to Artificial Intelligence (AI) to tackle big data problems. Over the years, there have been two main motivations to expand the IoT. The first one is to increase the amount of information shared by databases and objects in the real world. The second one is to enable users to share information and control objects in the real world. These two motivations make IoT more attractive to people. Therefore, IoT has become a good advancement of the conventional internet.

   However, it should be noted that IoT is still at a young stage in terms of technological development, but it can be greatly improved by endowing its functions with much more intelligence. The progress made in AI has been significant over the past few years. All AI technologies required to make IoT intelligent are currently feasible. However, the main issue that needs to be addressed is comprehending and effectively applying AI technologies to current IoT systems.

14.2   Understanding IoT

There are several building blocks for IoT, which operate simultaneously by operating and communicating with each other. These building blocks include application and user interaction, cloud server, network or connectivity, gateway, and physical objects and devices such as sensors and actuators. The main objective for understanding IoT is to increase the existing internet functions and ensure it is more effective. When using IoT, users can share information provided by human beings, which are contained in the database, as well as the information provided by things in the physical world. The IoT has sensors that get information about the state of things. This processor creates orders that regulate things, such as wireless technology for transferring information from sensors to the internet and the internet to the controller. It also has a control unit for executing human orders, thereby

Intelligent Connectivity: AI, IoT, and 5G, First Edition. Abdulrahman Yarali.
© 2022 John Wiley & Sons Ltd. Published 2022 by John Wiley & Sons Ltd.

regulating the state of things. For example, suppose an IoT is designed to regulate temperature. In that case, a standard room temperature will be established in advance, and the actual room temperature will be obtained by the sensor/sensors and transferred through a wireless medium, such as the internet. After the processor receives the actual room temperature, it compares it with the designated value. It establishes an order to regulate the room temperature and ensure it is within the specified range. However, if the interaction between the physical and the environment becomes complex, the embedded processor function becomes complex, making IoT unsatisfactory. The most successful approach that has been used to solve the complex problem is AI.

14.3 Artificial Intelligence

Conventionally, AI means the simulation of logical human thinking using computer technology (Merriam-Webster 2018). AI technologies include perception, cognition, decision-making, strategy-execution, and strategy optimization. The technology of perception is used to acquire the ontological information (OI) about the objects or problem within the environment. In addition, this technology is used to turn ontological information into epistemological information (EI). The latter is the information perceived by the subject regarding the trinity or the form information is perceived by the subject about the trinity of the form (syntactic information), content/meaning (semantic information), and utility/value (pragmatic information) concerning OI (Bughin 2017). Unlike the traditional concept of information proposed by Claude Shannon, EI comprises the trinity of the form, content/meaning, and utility/value and is the basis of learning. This is why EI is also often called comprehensive information.

On the other hand, the essential function of perception is to convert OI to EI. This is the first class of information conversion in AI. The main function of cognition technology is to convert EI, which the subject from OI perceives, into the object's corresponding knowledge. This is the second class of information conversion needed in AI. The only possible approach to convert EI to knowledge must be learning – there is no other way.

Thirdly, in decision-making EI converts to intelligent strategy (IS) based on knowledge support and is directed by problem-solving. The strategy is just the procedural guidance for problem-solving. This is the third class of information conversion in AI. The radical function of decision-making technology is learning to find the optimal solution for a given problem. There are usually several ways of achieving the designated goal from a starting point expressed by EI. A decision should be made through intelligent use, via learning, of the relevant knowledge provided.

In strategy execution, the technology is used to convert the IS into intelligent action (IA) to solve it. In strategy optimization, there are often errors when intelligent action is applied because of various non-ideal factors in all sub-processes. These errors are regarded as new information and are fed back to the input of the model's perception. With this new information, knowledge can be improved via learning, and the strategy can be optimized. Such an optimization process might continue many times until the error is sufficiently small. In sum, all the AI technologies hereto mentioned are learning-based, which is why AI is so powerful.

While trying to simplify AI, it is the scientific branch that assists machines to find solutions to complex problems in a human-like fashion. For instance, it involves borrowing human intelligence characteristics and applying them to algorithms in a computer-friendly way. AI solutions will depend on the flexibility or the requirements needed, ultimately influencing how artificial and intelligent behavior is manifested.

While attempting to achieve a successful AI transformation, similar elements need to be found in excellent digital and analytic transformations. These include concepts of sources of value, data ecosystems, techniques and tools, workflow integration, and open culture and organization. Firstly, in value sources, AI and IoT need to articulate business needs and create business cases. Secondly, data ecosystems involve breaking down data silos, deciding on the degree of aggregation and pre-assessment, and identifying high-value data. When it comes to AI tools, there needs to be the acquisition to plug capability gaps by assuming a "test and learn" approach.

On the other hand, in workflow integration, businesses or companies need to optimize the human/machine interface. Lastly, in open culture and organization, managers using IoT and AI should adopt an open-collaborative culture and establish trust in all the insights. Moreover, reskilling the personnel is necessary for ensuring complementarity.

The contemporary trends of AI research encompass key systems and various application areas. Firstly, the organization should embrace the concept of large-scale machine learning, which involves the creation and learning of algorithms. Nevertheless, it involves scaling the existing algorithms and managing extremely large data sets. Secondly, robotic utilization currently revolves around how robots can be trained to communicate with the world in generalizable and predictable ways. Robotics also deals with how to manipulate objects in interactive environments as well as interacting with people. According to Buchanan (2005), robotic development will depend on commensurate advances, which enhance the reliability and generality of computer vision and other types of machine perception. Moreover, computer vision has been the most important way of machine perception. It has greatly changed AI in that machines can now do some vision commands better than human beings.

In conclusion, AI means the simulation of logical human thinking using computer technology. AI technologies include perception, cognition, decision-making, strategy execution, and strategy optimization. The technology of perception is used to acquire the ontological information about the objects or problem within the environment. Therefore, the combination of AI and IoT will improve smart industries, ranging from health, education, infrastructure, education, transport, public service, and work.

AI goes past straightforward tedious assignments and into how data can be "acquired, put away, controlled, expanded, utilized, and transmitted" (Sloman 2010). This innovation's human-like profundity is rendering it to be appropriate in more than one or two ways. AI is being utilized in healing centers, cars, and industrial facilities. In reality, technology peculiarity, a term that has been coined more as of late, presents the prospect of super insights. In other words, innovation peculiarity implies coming to the point of refinement that dumbfounds human comprehension.

AI has a huge amount of capacity. Since it imitates people's insights and capabilities, they perform the same wide run of capacities a bit like them. With progress in innovation, calculations, and sheer compute control, it is presently advantageous to utilize AI strategies in regular applications within transportation, healthcare, gaming, efficiency, and media (Khatri et al. 2018). Many are recognizable as voice-based associates such as Apple's Siri and Amazon's Alexa that are "focused on brief, task-oriented intelligence, such as playing music or replying to basic topics" (Khatri et al. 2018). This AI shape essentially helps people exclude the exertion that comes with basic errands like checking the climate or making a phone call. It acts as an individual collaborator and companion to those who claim one by replying to vocalized themes. This shape of counterfeit insights has taken off over a long time, with the foremost recent release appearing within the third quarter of 2018 alone, when 19.7 million units of savvy speakers were shipped, in comparison to the 8.3 million transported within the third quarter of 2017.

Another huge advance of this technology in circulation as of late is mechanized cars. These vehicles do not require human interaction to move from one goal to another. A few Tesla cars have an autopilot highlight in which they can "regulate speed, alter paths, and stop without driver assistance" (Matousek 2018). Fake insights like this would modify transportation significantly. In connection with the therapeutic community, numerous instruments have emerged to help perform assignments that in the past people would have done. One case of this technology is hazard appraisal and decision-support devices. These apparatuses utilize scientific equations to use chronicled and factual information, such as national claims databases, medicine sedation databases, and risk-tolerance devices. Usually, an example of an innovation that helps those within the therapeutic field makes choices that are best for their patients.

The rise of innovations concerning surgery performance can supply more solid work than human specialists, increasing the successful rate for surgeries where this innovation is used. In expansion to surgeries and chance appraisals, counterfeit insights can act remedially for patients. For example, automated pets have been utilized to treat elderly patients diagnosed with dementia. They are programmed to memorize how to act unexpectedly with each quiet time through positive and negative inputs from the patients (Etzioni and Etzioni 2018). Understanding input to alter behavior could be a human-like capacity; fake insights have occurred and seem to offer assistance to patients with other diagnoses as they might feel a more comfortable connection without human nearness. In the exterior of the therapeutic world, it is pertinent to look at manufactured insights and protect missions.

Here calculations are utilized to overview the ethereal film of catastrophe zones to recognize rapidly where individuals are likely to be stranded (Etzioni and Etzioni 2018). Utilizing AI here gives casualties the next chance of being found. There are intelligent cameras, facial acknowledgment, and dreams for gadgets that can react to circumstances in order to list advanced illustrations of developing applications. There are numerous applications of counterfeit insights, but there remains much room for advancement. The innovation included in this range has boundless potential.

AI appears to complement the work of people, even though they state there is no denying that in a few businesses, economies, and parts – particularly those that include monotonous assignments – employment will alter or be eliminated. To supply a more particular piece of information, it was evaluated that in the over 29 nations analyzed, the share of employment at the potential hazard of robotization would be 1% by 2020. From a more financial point of view, the joined together States have been losing dominance in AI new companies to China, which plans to become a world pioneer of manufactured insights by

2030. More particularly, the US had 77% of value bargain offers in 2013 compared with the more minuscule 50% in 2017 (Chaturvedi 2018). Although still a strong sum, the Chinese advancement of AI appears to be overtaking US endeavors. The spar over AI may be a future slant that is likely to proceed over its advancement, as the potential of this innovation is boundless.

Innovation companies such as Amazon, Microsoft, and Letter set have all started to contribute new businesses in manufactured insights in an effort to progress computer security. Also, Palo Alto Systems, Fortinet, and Cisco Frameworks are all within the race to develop AI instruments. This can be since counterfeit insights have become a prevalent usage in cybersecurity items, which includes protective layers. In his proficient conclusion, Eric Jang states that he accepts profound intellect to be the number one company to investigate counterfeit insights, taken after by Google, Facebook, Open AI, and Baidu. The planned capabilities of fake insights have been recognized by numerous companies and are still being executed by more. A Story Science study found 84% of undertakings will be utilizing AI by the end of the decade (TATA 2017).

The run of manufactured insights that capacities can perform is exceedingly valuable for companies in all sorts of businesses. The case of mechanization innovation is not as it was being actualized by Tesla but is now also by Uber, Volkswagen, Lyft, and Waymo. Tesla happens to be actualizing an autopilot highlight with 360 visions that can see 250 m away. JPMorgan Chase, the biggest bank within the Joined together States, has executed a few AI-powered services for its clients, counting on the utilization of AI calculations to assist speculators in making superior venture and exchange choices. The capacity of AI to make exact human-like choices depicts the innovation as being exceedingly invaluable for companies to execute. Other companies that utilize AI are Affectiva, Panasonic, and Phillips.

To address the administrative issues encompassing fake insights, the concerns ought to be handled. "With its fast increasing speed, AI makes fear a robot course that will oppress humankind, annihilate it, or cause major financial disruptions" (Etzioni and Etzioni 2018). Even though as created as these machines may be, they have no inner inspiration, so typically not a concern. Other issues such as cyber assaults and work substitution that stem from human want make a requirement for direction. There are numerous concerns when it comes to the utilization of AI. A few of these, particularly concerning the criminal equity framework, are recorded by Delgado: "Does the government's utilization of AI require a warrant to look at your online information? Can AI be utilized to tune in on American citizens' phone calls without a warrant?"

Indeed, bias can be a potential concern for using AI within the criminal equity framework, as Delgado discussed in a case in 2016. A program was utilized to anticipate recidivism of individuals qualified for parole was found to be one-sided against African Americans. One-sided calculations demonstrate AI ought not to be a sole reliance in performing assignments. Elon Musk, the author of Tesla, tweeted, "We ought to be super cautious with AI. Possibly more dangerous than nukes. I'm progressively slanted to think there ought to be a few administrative oversights, possibly at the national and universal level" (Etzioni and Etzioni 2018). Even though Musk's company, Tesla, is working with counterfeit insights, he still recognizes the innovation's obscure capabilities. The direction is required; in any case, and there is an issue concerning taking a cost toll.

AI's direction is likely to regurgitate wrangles between nations with diverse supposi-tions on the worldwide level. In any case, a direction like this could happen, as shown by the recent panic comparable to the Cold War. Controls on a national level, be that as it may, are as of now input in a few nations. "The General Data Protection Regulation (GDPR) being actualized in Europe put extreme confinements on the use of fake insights and machine learning," particularly any robotized choices that "significantly affect" EU citizens. Controls like this ought to be executed all-inclusively to secure person rights and avoid any potential dangers.

AI has numerous worldwide suggestions. Manufactured insights empower individuals to re-examine how we coordinate data, analyze information, and utilize the emergence of bits of knowledge to progress decision-making. Alone, this innovation has the plausibility of altering how individuals think and make choices. It is not as it was, but efficiency is pro-tected when counterfeit insights are permitted to require over-thoughtless assignments such as thoughtless driving. Moreover, it may decrease the fetched people of transporta-tion, as transport and taxi drivers will not be required. In any case, by making straightfor-ward assignments an unimportant career, numerous will be unemployed and incapable of getting work in other careers due to constrained work positions and immaterial founda-tion. Delgado moreover states that advertisements will end up being more brilliant and more implanted into our day-by-day lives. By analyzing the way people associate with advertisements based on their offer, AI can make choices on how to promote in a more profitable and viable way.

As AI becomes dynamically progressed, owing much to advances in computing control, data analysts' instruction, and the openness of machine learning rebellious for making advanced calculations, the Web of Things is getting closer to becoming an essential stream wonder. 5G speaks to the misplaced component to bring this progress to unused levels and to enable the brilliant network vision. The ultra-fast and ultra-low delay given by 5G frame-works, combined with the tremendous entirety of data collected by the Web of Things and the contextualization and decision-making capabilities of machine learning made experi-ences, will engage advanced transformational capabilities in each industry division, con-ceivably changing our society and the way we live and work.

14.4 5G Network

5G is called 5G because it is the fifth generation of wireless technology. The primary era was first generation (1G) when analog cell phones, to begin with, entered the world. Second generation (2G) came along when modern highlights such as content informing and voice-mail were made. Not long after, higher information exchange rates permitted portable web browsing, picture sharing, and GPS area following, called third generation (3G). By the time fourth generation (4G) came along, individuals could do nearly anything on their smartphones. Figure 14.1 shows the evolution path of wireless mobile generations.

5G is one of the speediest, most affluent innovations the world has ever seen and experi-enced. 5G has faster downloads and an extraordinary arrangement of unwavering quality, which contains a theatrical, outstanding effect on how the world lives, works, and plays. The network advantage of 5G makes businesses more effective.

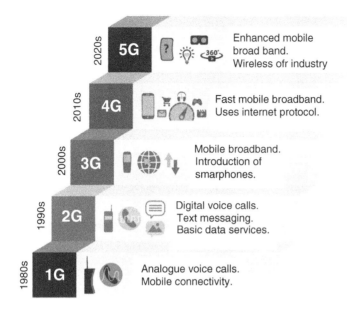

Figure 14.1 Evolution of wireless mobile systems (Katrodiya 2019).

5G systems utilize a framework of cell locales that partition their region into distinctive areas and send encoded information through radio waves. Each cell location has to be associated with an arranged spine, in any case, on the off chance that it is through a wired or remote association. Orthogonal Frequency Division Multiplexing (OFDM) is the sort of coding utilized for 5G. Even though it is comparative to the encoding that Fourth Generation Long-Term Evolution (4G LTE) employs, it is outlined for much less idleness and a much higher adaptability than Long-Term Evolution (LTE).

The objective for 5G is to have higher speeds and distant higher capacity per segment than 4G. The objective is additionally to have much lower idleness than 4G. 5G systems are much more intelligent than the past frameworks. They will boost capacity by four times over current frameworks by leveraging more extensive transfer speeds and will progress radio wave advances.

5G is coming, advertising an enormous boost in transmission capacity that will supply customers with fake insights and more spilling recordings. Even though there are numerous needs to involve the modern arrangement, it is more than likely that the normal buyer will not manage a 5G association. Certain companies, such as Verizon Remote, reported that they would have the primary real mobile 5G benefit within the Joined together States and would be called the 5G Ultra-Wideband. Verizon dispatched its services nationwide in 2021 (Alleven 2021).

The 5G Ultra-Wideband will, as it were, dispatch in select ranges within Chicago and Minneapolis cities. Concurring to Verizon, there will, as it were, be a $10 add-on charge. There will moreover be no additional charges for the primary three months. Even though the 5G comes with awesome highlights, it will be costly.

5G technology will result in awesome changes for customers and endeavors over the country. It will enable companies to form progressions such as being more astute, much better associated cars, progressions in therapeutic innovations, and move forward retail encounters through personalization. 5G will employ radio frequencies that are higher and more directional than the ones utilized by 4G. The directionality of 5G is exceptionally critical since, if towers were to send information everywhere, there would be an awesome sum of squandered control and vitality. It would also debilitate web access.

Since 5G employs shorter wavelengths than 4G, radio wires can be shorter without an interferometer with the wavelengths. As a result of wavelengths being shorter, 5G can back roughly 100 gadgets per meter more than 4G. 5G systems can get the information being requested and self-modulate the control mode, making gadgets more inviting.

5G employs one-of-a-kind radio frequencies that are higher and more directional than those utilized by 4G. The directionality of 5G is exceptionally vital since 4G towers send information everywhere. Since 4G does this, both control and vitality can be squandered and can eventually debilitate the web. The higher the recurrence, the more prominent is its capacity to bolster quick information without interference with other remote signals or to be excessively cluttered.

In expansion to higher frequencies than 4G, 5G will employ shorter wavelengths than 4G. Shorter wavelengths mean that receiving wires can be shorter without an interferometer with the heading of the wavelengths. More information will reach more individuals with less inactivity and disturbance to meet surging information requests. 5G systems can get the information better by being asked to self-modulate the control mode, making gadgets more user-friendly.

Video sharing skyrocketed with the entry of 4G and will heighten overall apps and administrations when 5G arrives. The Contract Manufacturing Organization (CMO) of the cellular supplier AT and T, Moment Katibeh, says that within the not-too-distant future, mirrors may well be supplanted with tall determination screens with cameras that permit individuals to attempt to try on handfuls of combinations of clothing. Moreover, independent cars may utilize live maps for the real-time route, vital to their adequacy. It seems moreover to dispense with a few of the issues that are now experienced with driving cars.

Figure 14.2 shows the requirements and different sets of enabling technologies to meet high throughput, less than a millisecond delay, and higher capacity.

Even though 5G systems come with parts of focal points, there are numerous drawbacks. Greater high-quality applications and user experience demands more transfer speeds than ever experienced recently. 5G systems are introduced to utilize the transmission capacity of amazingly high-frequency millimeter waves that travel for a very short distance. Because of this, they do not travel and penetrate well through buildings. They moreover tend to be ingested by rain and plants and in the long run drive into obstructions and decay.

The unimaginable modern organization brings to the world numerous health concerns. In 2011, the World Health Organization's Worldwide Office for Investigations on Cancer found that cell phones might lead to the creation of brain tumors since they utilize radio frequency radiation, known as RFR. RFR leads to an arrangement of other health issues, such as breaking the DNA strands, the disturbance of the cell digestion system, melatonin, disturbance of the brain glucose digestion system, and the era of stretch proteins.

Microwave radiation is exceptionally destructive to human skin. More than 90% of microwave radiation is ingested by the epidermis and dermis layers, so human skin essentially wipes for it. Moreover, human sweat channels within the skin's upper layer act as

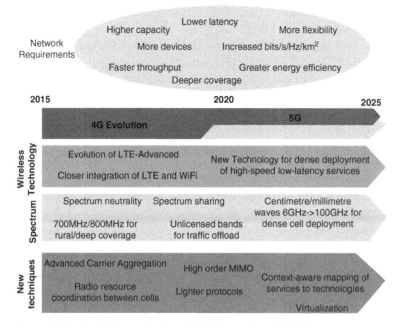

Figure 14.2 Evolution to wireless 5G (El-Hassani et al. 2019).

helical radio wires. Helical radio wires are extraordinary radio wires that particularly react to electromagnetic areas. Since people have millions of sweat channels, our bodies will be exceptionally conductive to microwave radiation.

Rather as radiation hurts people, it moreover could have genuine health dangers for creatures. A Joined Together States Toxicology Program found that male rats exposed to radio frequency radiation create uncommon shapes of tumors within the brain and heart. It moreover demonstrated that rats of both sexes developed DNA harm. Analysts felt that the discoveries of dangers to rats could relate to people. The broad increment in cell phone utilization could lead to a noteworthy effect on people.

In another creature investigation, it was demonstrated that microwave radiation could harm the eyes and a safe framework. Moreover, it appeared that it influences the cell development rate and bacterial resistance. A test conducted at the Kanazawa Therapeutic College found that 60 GHz millimeter-wave receiving wires have a chance of creating warm wounds and rabbit eyes. Warm impacts can also reach underneath the eye's surface. It was also found that introducing versatile phone electromagnetic recurrence caused chickens to develop life retinal cells that separated.

Similarly exasperating, 5G innovation moreover puts the environment's health at risk in numerous diverse ways. Millimeter waves pose a genuine danger to plant health. In 2010, it was found that aspen seedlings exposed to radio frequency radiation displayed indications of rot, which debilitates plants and makes them more susceptible to infections and bugs.

Armenian scientists found that low-intensity millimeter waves caused a push reaction that harms cells in wheat shoots. Even though plant harm is lethal for the planet, it is terrible for people. When plants become sullied, that puts the human nourishment supply at hazard levels, which might inevitably kill people.

In addition to the harming of plants, 5G innovation also poses a risk to the Earth's environment. The usage of 5G will require May satellites that will be conveyed by suborbital rockets. Hydrocarbon rocket motors will impel the suborbital rockets. Propelling as well numerous suborbital rockets will discharge parcels of dark carbon into the air, in the long run contaminating worldwide air conditions and influencing dispersion of ozone and temperature. To form things more harmful still, solid-state rockets produce debilitating substances such as chlorine, which is an ozone-destroying chemical.

5G systems moreover debilitate normal environments. A few reports appear that low-level, non-ionizing microwave radiation have influenced the health of both fowls and bees over the last two decades. It drives winged creatures to leave their nests, conjointly causes crest weakening, motion issues, diminished survivorship, and death. Bee populaces suffer from decreased egg-laying capacities of ruler bees. Some individuals feel that 5G systems are terrible news for all living life forms and the planet that they are living on.

Completely mindful of the issues that 5G brings to the environment, corporations continue to keep their positive states of mind around the jaw-dropping, engaging innovation. The most reasons that business people are proceeding with their thoughts of 5G is the incredible amount of cash that it will bring in. Since companies make 5G seem engaging, business visionaries essentially have mind-control over the customers.

There are numerous ways that communities can come together to ensure themselves against the threats of 5G. Denying utilizing 5G phones, denying purchasing "smart" apparatuses, abstaining from buying shrewd meters, avoiding tall levels of 5G radiations in homes, and restricting introduction to radiation are ways to protect themselves and their families.

5G systems will be based on engineering that will produce an unused mechanical and venture advancements environment. The 5G design will bolster thousands of modern applications within the buyer and trade areas. These shopper and commerce areas incorporate vertical markets such as fabricating, vitality, healthcare, and automobiles.

The 5G design comprises numerous distinctive things that many individuals may know nothing about. The 5G organize layer will utilize level IP concepts so that diverse Radio Access Networks (RANs) or Radio Get-to Systems utilize the same single Nanocore for communication. Many recognizable RANs that are bolstered by 5G engineering are LTE, LTE-advanced, and WiFi.

Like progressive design where ordinary IP addresses are utilized, it has level IP engineering recognized gadgets by utilizing typical names. In this way, the number of organizing components in information is decreased, and costs are incredibly decreased. Inactivity is additionally minimized.

Another component of the 5G design is the aggregator. The aggregator totals all of the RAN traffic and courses them to the portal. 5G portable terminal houses diverse interfacing to supply back all the range in order to get to remote innovations.

Nanocore is additionally a component of the 5G design. It comprises nanotechnology, cloud computing, and all IP designs. In expansion to Nanocore, cloud computing moreover plays a tremendous part within the design of 5G. Cloud computing utilizes the internet and inaccessible central servers to preserve the clients' information and applications. It permits shoppers to utilize applications without any establishment and get to their records from any computer worldwide using the web.

Near the 5G organize engineering layer, there is a 5G convention stack. The convention stack comprises the OWA (Open Wireless Architecture) layer, the organize layer, the open transport layer, and the application layer. All of these layers are exceptionally diverse in numerous ways.

The OWA layer, or the Open Remote Design layer, is a physical layer and data-link layer of the convention stack. The arrange layer is utilized to course information from the source IP gadgets to the goal IP gadgets. It is partitioned into two layers, the upper and the lower arrange layers. Next, there is the open transport layer. The open transport layer combines the usefulness of both transport layers and session layers. Last, there is the application layer. The application layer marks information as per the appropriate organization required. It moreover does encryption and unscrambling of data. The application layer chooses the most excellent remote association for a given service.

The rising of the 5G organize layer is nearly here. By the conclusion of the year, it will be in full impact. Even though companies appear to have it all figured out, there will be parcels of challenges and necessities for the 5G organize layer to be as effective as arranged. Moreover, business visionaries ought to put into thought how hurtful the materials of 5G are. People, creatures, plants, and indeed the environment are influenced by millimeter waves utilized for the working of 5G. Although 5G is preparing to come, there are numerous things to think about. Everything that sounds and looks great is not always good for individuals. Figure 14.3 depicts how small technologies such as Multiple-Input Multiple-Output (MIMO), densification, spectrum aggregation, and farming help to enhance higher capacity and higher throughput.

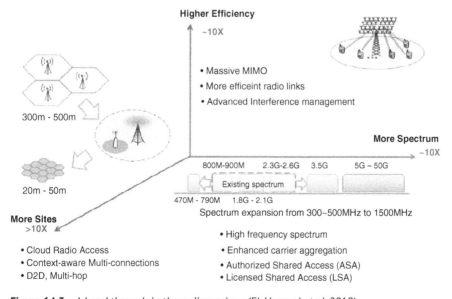

Figure 14.3 A breakthrough in three dimensions (El-Hassani et al. 2019).

14.5   Emerging Partnership of Artificial Intelligence, IoT, 5G, and Cybersecurity

Operations are revolutionized by information technology through smart connected products, which help in device miniaturization and processing power and wireless connectivity. Smart connected products provide greater reliability, expanding opportunities, much high utilization of the product, and its capabilities of transcending traditional products. It involves strategic choices of creating and capturing products, newly generated data, and relationships with conventional business partners. The new technology stack includes identifying and securing the product cloud layers, the external source of information, integration with a business system, interrelated connectivity, and form a product cloud. The product cloud involves smart product applications, rules or analytical engines, and its platform of the application and product data database.

AI works by developing new algorithms and models based on machine learning. Traditionally, AI was about creating human-like systems that can reason and do things like the human brain. AI can be further understood as narrow AI or general AI. Narrow AI, the intelligence that human beings interact with daily, is the intelligence that has been designed to carry out specific functions that surround a particular domain, for example, the translation of one language to another. On the other hand, general AI is hypothetical and does not work in a specific domain. This means that general AI can work in several areas by earning and performing different tasks differently. Both current and previous AI developments have led AI technology to be used diversely in various applications and avenues while simultaneously enhancing the scope of AI and the efficiency, as well as the impact of its different forms. Various applications of AI range from Machine Learning, Deep Learning, Automation, and Autonomy, to Human–Machine Teaming. The implementation of AI through the IoT in different sectors of human life will significantly impact business and job employment.

AI, 5G, and IoT advances are now enhancing each other, making the fifth wave of computing.

There have been some significant developments in Cybersecurity. One of the significant developments in the techniques and tools that are redeveloped is through the support of AI and Machine Learning (ML). With this partnership between AI and Cybersecurity, the current and future application possibilities for Cybersecurity are endless. The detection of threats is one of the significant concerns in Cybersecurity and has emphasized it substantially. Officials, authorities, and organizations have always been keen on developing newer and more advanced ways to detect a potential threat or to be prepared for any advanced threat and attack that can take place. Machine learning has played a vital role in this aspect of Cybersecurity and strengthened the overall relationship. It has provided effective approaches and outcomes in terms of threat detection in Cybersecurity and has been instrumental in detecting threats by analyzing data and identifying threats in the initial stages.

Each year, cyberattacks have been on the rise and are getting worse than their impacts in previous years. The sharp increase of cyberattacks has resulted in more and more security threats and made it complex due to AI's evolution in cyberattacks or the AI of the attackers. As a result, more sophisticated cyberattacks that are more complex than ever are taking place, which is one of the most significant challenges in AI and its implementation and usage in Cybersecurity despite all the promises it has fulfilled and will deliver.

14.5.1 The Current State of IoT Security

The subject that ought to be investigated is the current state of IoT security. The IoT has been developing at a fast rate as vehicles, computer programs, and wearable gadgets have progressed past the fundamental work. According to Ammar, Russello, and Crispo (2018), more than 3.7 billion devices are utilized on day-by-day premises with web associations. As a result, there is a desire for more activity and information on the congested associated web. Considering the development in IoT, it is critical to address the issues related to IoT security. The issues included can incorporate an increment in assaults, subsequently settling the issues to upgrade the IoT security level. The growth within the IoT sensors' entrance and heterogeneous smart gadgets requires a basic requirement for IoT administration arrangements that are dependable in terms of control and setup. Replying to the investigated subject will offer assistance in making organizations mindful of the measures they can take to boost IoT security. Numerous organizations are likely to put fitting measures input to boost the security of their IoT. This section investigates the current state of IoT security to create ways of upgrading the security level.

Ammar, Russello, and Crispo (2018) conducted an investigation that uncovered the fact that organizations need to introduce security frameworks to enhance IoT security. The creators contended that there is a requirement for IoT security due to the expanded utilization of internet-supported gadgets. Concurring to the creators, operations are becoming robotized in numerous organizations to upgrade effectiveness. As a result, web security concerns are expanding as numerous aggressors are focusing on organizational information. The IoT innovations are getting to be assorted due to the expanded network required to convert operations into numerous businesses, like framework, well-being, and funds. IoT security dangers increment as unused gadgets are presented on the web. The IoT security breaches that are now taking place are an indication that there is a requirement for IoT security.

The IoT has driven emotional changes within organizations' operations and the lives of individuals. As a result, numerous organizations are grasping rising innovations. A few firms have discovered that they are powerless due to the expanded number of programmers utilizing advances to hinder operations. Numerous huge firms are receiving IoT frameworks as they offer assistance in improving forms through progressed information analytics. Agreeing with Ammar, Russello, and Crispo (2018), the organizations receiving the IoT frameworks need to be mindful of the possible threats and misfortune that they could have in their systems if they are disturbed by programmers. This source is important to the investigation because it gives the arrangements that can be made to improve IoT security in organizations. It contributes to replying to the question about the theme by clarifying how security frameworks like firewalls can offer assistance in disposing of or minimizing the vulnerabilities of the IoT frameworks. From this source, we learned that the IT office plays a pivotal part in upgrading the IoT security.

Lee and Lee (2015) found that shopper mindfulness is pivotal in upgrading IoT security in organizations. Concurring with the creators, most organizations found that involvement with IoT security breaches can dodge such breaches through expanded buyer mindfulness. This may involve making sure beyond any doubt that the clients of IoT frameworks are mindful of the conceivable aggressors, and subsequently making them take the essential safeguards. One of the IoT security breaches that this source can be connected to is Cisco Talos. The security analysts revealed a botnet connected to Russia. These IoT breaches influenced more than 500000 organizations to get to capacity gadgets and switches in Ukraine, consequently recommending a few political inspirations. The Virtual Private Network (VPN) Channel is the malware that made the takeover conceivable by allowing the programmers to control the tainted gadgets. The control included the chance to turn the tainted gadgets off and in this way taking them offline.

The IoT security breach is driven by the disease of numerous gadgets recommending the need for mindfulness among the buyers on securing the savvy situations. According to Lee and Lee (2015), shopper mindfulness might have made a difference in maintaining a strategic distance from the IoT security breach as the clients may be more cautious. This source is important since it gives a technique that organizations can utilize to minimize their IoT framework vulnerabilities. It may have made a difference in anticipating the IoT security breach by guaranteeing that the clients are mindful of conceivable assailants. Moreover, the source makes a difference in making Cisco Talos develop ways of arranging security that makes it clear that it is, without doubt, a necessary item. We learned from this source that locks in partners within the preparation of upgrading IoT system security are among the finest techniques that can help diminish vulnerabilities.

The study conducted by Nowodzinski, Łukasik, and Puto (2016) uncovered that encryption and verification are vital in improving IoT security. Agreeing with the creators, organizations ought to learn how to apply innovations to boost their arranged framework security. This is often true since programmers are grasping mechanical progressions in assaulting systems. This source seems to have made a difference in avoiding IoT security breaches that included Threat care and IBM, where security analysts distinguished around 17 vulnerabilities from the four keen cities. Rudimentary streams within the security plans, just like the utilization of default passwords, permitted entry to the frameworks, and having systems that were unsecured online was the lion's share of most of the vulnerabilities.

There were concerns after encryption issues and verification blemishes were found within the illustration's server communication frameworks. Concurring to Nowodzinski, Łukasik, and Puto (2016), verification and encryption are among the significant technologies within the avoidance of IoT security breaches. The IoT security breach made clients and merchants of the IoT systems realize the security challenges, particularly within the basic IT foundation. This source is important to the inquiry about points since it gives a few ways organizations can improve IoT security. Concurring to the creators controlling the way to get to the company's organized frameworks is vital in upgrading IoT security. From this source, we learned that the physical way is imperative in improving the security of arranging frameworks.

Addo et al. (2014) ponder whether judgment and confirmation are basic in making strides for IoT security. Confirmation makes a difference in making beyond any doubt that aggressors cannot get to an organization's frameworks. This source can be connected in fathoming the third IoT security breach that included Tesla, the electric car makers. Despite the basic security imperfections in Tesla, it was found that Show S-cars were powerless to key dandy assaults. Key coxcomb assaults are methods utilized within the preparation of taking high-end cars. The KU Leuven College group in Belgium cloned the Show S keys coxcomb and utilized it in the opening. The analysts utilized hardware worth $600 to examine radio and compute signals within the controlling part of learning the vehicle's identifier transmitted by the car.

As a result, the group may trigger the reaction from key parts by mimicking the performance of the cars. The analysts utilize reaction sets to narrow down real keys that may be utilized. As stated by Addo et al. (2014), the IoT breach may be anticipated by implementing tight confirmation frameworks within the electric car. This source is significant since it gives techniques that can be utilized by organizations within the procedure of boosting their IoT security frameworks. From this source, we learned that numerous IoT breaches could be related to destitute confirmation frameworks in organizations, making it simple for aggressors to get to vital frameworks.

Patel and Patel (2016) considered that coordination of human understanding and innovation is vital in upgrading IoT security. Agreeing to the creators, organizations must guarantee that the clients of the frameworks and systems have a legitimate understanding when applying fundamental security measures. This source is pertinent to the inquiry point since it prescribes the measures that organizations can grasp to improve IoT security. For example, fortifying the creators' security culture among the representatives is vital in minimizing vulnerabilities. It is through creating a security culture in an organization that the security of IoT can be moved forward. As a result, this source can help organizations to relieve the dangers of assaults confronting IoT frameworks. This illustrates the need for representatives to be enlightened on methods assailants use as they utilize developing advances.

According to Ammar, Russello, and Crispo (2018), the utilization of security programs can offer assistance within the anticipation of aggressors by denying access to systems and frameworks. This source can help arrange our investigation point because it suggests establishing firewalls and patches to deny unauthorized individuals. For instance, within the IoT security breach, including Cisco Talos, malware played a basic part in permitting the programmers to compromise information security. This included snooping on the activity that passed through influenced switches. This is intended to harm the company's notoriety as clients will question the security measures taken within the company. The circumstance was genuine to a point where the FBI had to intercede. The mediation included empowering the switch's proprietors to reboot the gadgets, utilize a security computer program, and introduce patches. The FBI declared that it was intended to seize the space that was utilized in supporting the botnet. This source might have made a difference in avoiding the IoT security breach as the creators investigated the ways organizations can upgrade IoT security by denying access.

Lee and Lee (2015) contended that mindfulness among the representatives in an organization is pivotal in upgrading IoT security. This source can offer assistance in replying to our investigation theme by presenting measures that should be put in place to boost IoT security frameworks. Nowodzinski, Łukasik, and Puto (2016) contended that confirmation and encryption by organizations are vital in guaranteeing that systems and frameworks are secure. As a result, this source can offer assistance in replying to the investigation point by clarifying how confirmation can be utilized to progress IoT security. As an illustration, within the IoT security breach, Tesla's dependence on a 40-bit figure that was effectively crackable and non-appearance of shared confirmation made key coxcomb innovation of the electric car go astray. The company incurred extra costs that influenced the productivity and image of the company within the industry. Tesla rolled out cryptography that was stronger for the key coxcomb framework utilized by Demonstrate S-cars.

Patel and Patel (2016) contended that innovations need to be coordinated with human understanding. The advances are changing at a fast rate, consequently expanding the plausibility of the need for information essential in understanding the developing security dangers posed by web utilization. This source can help in replying to enquiries about the theme by advising individuals how to find out about dangers that are likely to compromise IoT security.

14.6 Conclusion

In the coming years, AI will meet IoT at the edge of the computing layer. It is believed that many models that are trained in the public cloud could be deployed at the edge. At the top, there is industrial IoT for AI that will perform outlier detection, the main reason analysis, and the precaution maintenance of the equipment. Advanced machine learning models that are developed based on neural networks can be optimized at the edge. They will have the capability to deal with time-series data, unstructured data, and video frames, as well as devices such as sensors, mics, and cameras. IoT will be the most important driver of AI. All the edge devices will have special AI chips equipped with an ASIC (Application Specific Integrated Circuit) and an FPGA (Field-Programmable Gate Array). The following applications will be in operation:

1) Interoperability in neural networks. Selecting a suitable framework is very necessary for developing neural networks. There is a need to select the right tool from different choices, including Tensor Flow, MXNet, PyTorch, Caffe2, and MS Cognitive. Another challenge is that when a model is evaluated in one framework, it is very difficult to place it in another. Low interpretability in the neural network toolkits also affects the adoption of AI. Microsoft and Facebook have made a mutual platform to make an Open Neural Network Exchange that has helped reuse the trained neural network models. In the future, the Open Neural Network Exchange will act as an important technology. It will run as a standard runtime for inferencing.
2) Automated machine learning. Soon the facility of Machine Learning (ML) solutions will be changed to AutoML. This will give more power to business analysts to use ML models that can define complex scenarios. This will help the data scientist to proceed further without considering the typical ML model training. They can focus on business problems with AutoML, which requires less attention to workflow and processes. AutoML suits the cognitive ML platforms and APIs. It offers the best customization without the typical workflow. Unlike the typical APIs, which are considered important as black boxes, the AutoML offers the same flexibility and portability.
3) Automation of DevOps. For analytics, searching, and indexing, there are many different applications and complex infrastructures. There are complex, big data sets taken from

the operating system and application that can be examined and combined to locate patterns. Operations go from reactive to predictive when machine learning models are used. When the power of AI is used in operations, it redefines that infrastructure. The usage of machine learning and AI in IT and DevOps will add intelligence to operations. This is more effective because the analysis can be performed quickly as AIOps will be in the mainstream, allowing public cloud vendors to take advantage when AI is converted to DevOps (Janakiram, MSV 2018).

IoT security has been an issue of concern in numerous organizations as modern advances are rising within the market. Organizations have to be mindful of the security dangers confronting IoT and provide fitting measures for anticipating the assaults. It is critical to understand that the aggressors utilize current advances in assaulting the frameworks and systems. The sources discussed above have significantly contributed to the investigation by examining diverse ways to boost IoT security. Organizations ought to make sure, beyond any doubt, that they execute the security techniques they define, locking in the representative preventative measures. All the organizations' partners have to be aware of the security dangers and measures that ought to be taken. The suggestion of this conclusion is to expand mindfulness concerning the dangers of confronting IoT security in organizations.

References

Addo, I.D., Ahamed, S.I., Yau, S.S., and Buduru, A. (2014). A reference architecture for improving security and privacy in the internet of things applications. In: *IEEE International Conference on Mobile Services*, 108–115. IEEE.

Alleven, M. (2021). Verizon launches 5G Ultra Wideband in 3 more markets. *Fierce Wireless.* https://www.fiercewireless.com/operators/verizon-launches-5g-ultra-wideband-3-more-markets (accessed 22 June 2021).

Ammar, M., Russello, G., and Crispo, B. (2018). Internet of Things: A survey on the security of IoT frameworks. *Journal of Information Security and Applications* 38: 8–27.

Buchanan, B.G. (2005). A (very) brief history of Artificial Intelligence. *Computer Science, AI Magazine* 25th Anninversary Issue: 53–60.

Bughin, J. (2017). Ten big lessons learned from Big Data analytics. *Applied Marketing Analytics* 2 (4): 286–295.

Chaturvedi, A. (2018, July 11). Thirteen major Artificial Intelligence trends to watch for in 2018. https://www.geospatialworld.net/blogs/13-artificial-intelligence-trends-2018/ (accessed 22 June 2021).

El Hassani, S., Haidine, A., and Jebbar, H. (2019). Road to 5G key enabling technologies. *Journal of Communications* 14 (11): 1034–1048. http://www.jocm.us/uploadf ile/2019/0930/20190930023333103.pdf.

Etzioni, A. and Etzioni, O. (2018, September 20). Should Artificial Intelligence be regulated? https://issues.org/perspective-should-artificial-intelligence-be-regulated (accessed 22 June 2021).

Janakiram, MSV (2018, December 9). Five Artificial Intelligence trends to watch out for in 2019. https://www.forbes.com/sites/janakirammsv/2018/12/09/5-artificial-intelligence-trends-to-watch-out-for-in-2019/#64c39a015618 (accessed 22 June 2021).

Katrodiya, R. (2019). A survey of 6th generation. https://www.researchgate.net/publication/338249511_A_Survey_on_6th_generation_1_st_Renil_Katrodya (accessed 22 June 2021).

Khatri, C., Venkatesh, A., Hedayatnia, B. et al. (2018, Fall). Alexa Prize — State of the Art in Conversational AI. *AI Magazine* 39 (3) https://ashwinram.org/2018/09/28/alexa-prize-state-of-the-art-in-conversational-ai/.

Lee, I. and Lee, K. (2015). The internet of things (IoT): applications, investments, and challenges for enterprises. *Business Horizons* 58 (4): 431–440.

Matousek, M. (2018, January 29). The most impressive things Tesla's cars can do in Autopilot. https://www.businessinsider.com/tesla-autopilot-functions-and-technology-2017-12#tesla-cars-made-since-october-2016-come-with-eight-cameras-that-have-a-complete-360-degree-range-of-vision-around-the-car-each-of-the-cameras-can-see-up-to-250-meters-away-2 (accessed 22 June 2021).

Merriam Webster (2018, October 23). Artificial Intelligence. Artificial Intelligence | Definition of Artificial Intelligence by Merriam-Webster (accessed 22 June 2021).

Nowodzinski, P., Łukasik, K., and Puto, A. (2016). Internet of things (IoT) in a retail environment. The new strategy for a firm's development. *European Scientific Journal* 12 (10).

Patel, K.K. and Patel, S.M. (2016). Internet of Things – IOT: Definition, characteristics, architecture, enabling technologies, application & future challenges. *International Journal of Engineering Science and Computing* 6 (5).

Sloman, A. (2010, April 11). What is Artificial Intelligence? http://www.cs.bham.ac.uk/research/projects/cogaff/misc/whatsai.html (accessed 22 June 2021).

TATA CS (2017). Getting smarter by the day: How AI is elevating the performance of global companies. TCS global study: Part 1. https://www.tcs.com/content/dam/tcs/pdf/Industries/global-trend-studies/ai/TCS-GTS-how-AI-elevating-performance-global-companies.pdf (accessed 22 June 2021).

15

Intelligent Connectivity and Agriculture

15.1 Introduction

Based on a Food and Agriculture Organization survey in 2018, the world population is projected to increase from 7.6 billion in 2018 to over 9.6 billion by 2050 (Biradar 2019). For arable areas, the augmentation forecasts are as low as 5%. The current agricultural output does not sufficiently feed the 7.7 billion world population, leaving approximately 821 million people suffering from hunger. This indicates that agricultural production will have to increase by 70% to compensate for the shortage. This poses significant challenges to the agricultural sector as the demand for natural resources, freshwater, and other foods surge to unprecedented levels (Biradar 2019). However, as modern urbanization and technological disruptions define almost every sphere of life, the fusion of Artificial Intelligence (AI), the Internet of Things (IoT), LTE, and fifth generation (5G) technologies are expected to spearhead the fourth industrial revolution. This potentially provides a solution that will shape future cultivation.

The implications of smart and efficient farming techniques on food production patterns will inevitably improve yield and reinforce land sustainability efforts. Many of these intelligent technologies provide alternative forms of collecting and processing farming data for real-time analysis and appropriate action. The rapid adoption of wireless sensor networks has led to low-cost designs of small sensor devices, thanks to the IoT input (TEAM 2019). These sensory automated tools aid accurate decision-making in agriculture in favor of high production. Equally, such innovations are mutually complemented by AI. As such, AI has opened the widely untapped cross-disciplinary potential to create a paradigm shift on how much the world derives from agriculture. With an enhanced mix of biological science and technology, IoT, Big Data analytics, and AI-powered elucidations, farmers can produce more quality food with less effort, time, and complexities. This chapter dissects how fusing AI, 5G wireless, and IoT technologies can transform the existing farming latency for future "smart agricultural" practices. Lastly, it explores the likely impact of this intelligent connectivity in farming using modern innovations.

15.2   The Potential of Wireless Sensors and IoT in Agriculture

Today agricultural activities are quickly changing how or how much farmers can produce, thanks to the IoT, which is a modern system that interrelates several devices to uniquely identify and transfer mass data over networks without human-to-computer or human-to-human interventions (Biradar 2019). Tools with such unique identifiers (UIDs) include mechanical, computing, and digital machines, all mutually working with objects, animals, or people (TEAM 2019). Through IoT gadgets in the healthcare sector, manufacturing, and many other innovative areas, smart farming is emerging as an enabler of increased efficient, intelligent crop management. Such developments could potentially help reduce food shortages across the globe, saving millions from the effects of drought, natural disasters, fires, and other calamities.

For instance, to effectively manage and control pests in agriculture, wireless IoT is now able to relay information seamlessly from farms. These low-resolution sensors analyze and send information from large tracts of land to required destinations about the crop health status or potential pest manifestations. They can capture both high-definition and microscopic images of plants that the naked eye cannot see. The IoT wireless sensors come embedded with nodes linked to a central processing unit (CPU) working with an interface, power, and transceiver units (TEAM 2019). A node is a small, minute centralized computer system. The sensory unit uses Radio Frequency (RF) technologies through which nodes communicate data monitored wirelessly to CPUs about farm humidity, temperatures, pressure, vibrations, crop health status, and much more.

The nodes are predefined with specific tasks. They could be located across several parts of the farm forming networks synchronized in structure to interconnect data collected about microclimatic conditions or any other user preferences. Likewise, these wireless IoT sensors can assemble statistics related to pest behavioral patterns straight from ranches to distant data operating centers (Biradar 2019). IoT device users can monitor such regular data for pest application technique adjustments, including when and how to apply pesticides. Interestingly, they can also capture the amount of sunlight received or released by a plant, commonly referred to as a spectral signature. In most cases, the location of these nodes takes into account farm topography for optimal functionality.

IoT data transmissions empower farmers to take timely action to prevent potential losses, further bolstering efforts to increase food production. Agriculturalists can analyze the facts and identify effective research-based methods, treatments, and technologies to control current and future manifestations based on influencing factors (Biradar 2019). Remarkably, the sensors also provide predictive futuristic preventive mechanisms, allowing farmers to explore appropriate pest treatment methods without remedial ideas. As a result, smart farming is now making it easy for farmers to understand the likely impact of pest control methods well in advance, which avoids wasting resources and time on non-productive or unhealthy crop-maintenance procedures.

Thankfully, these devices are comfortable to use across the world to supplement the often-inadequate conventional pest management practices. As IoT devices continue to evolve and significantly impact agriculture's future, for the better, many farmers will be able to avoid unnecessary low productive disappointments characterized by unprofitable farming seasons (Biradar 2019). These modern technologies seek to replace the time-consuming and tiresome manual approaches to maintaining healthy crops. They are likely to define a smart farming future, helping farmers to make informed decisions about healthy crop maintenance instead of hopefully waiting against the odds for good weather.

15.3 IoT Sensory Technology with Traditional Farming

"Smart agriculture" has immense potential to boost future food production and save millions suffering from food shortages or dying of hunger. Many farmers embracing traditional approaches lack fast, reliable internet connectivity through the IoT. The reason is that, to employ IoT sensory technologies, connectivity is necessary throughout the agronomic environment (TEAM 2019). Specifically, such an installation is essential in greenhouses, storehouses, barns, and many other farm places. The connection should also be uninterruptible and able to withstand adverse weather conditions outdoors, which might not work for farmers living in harsh climatic locations. Figure 15.1 depicts the five stages of a sample case of IoT analytics (EDUCB n.d.).

Nonetheless, technological advancement is underway to solve the design problems associated with these limitations. Until IoT sensory systems manufacture devices that can effectively work anywhere, including regions grappling with an unfavorable climate, adopting the know-how remains a challenge in some areas. Some growers or agrarian communities lack enough resources and time to embrace the IoT sensory technology in farms (TEAM 2019). For instance, employing drones with portable sensors linked through grids and operating stations is often expensive for many farmers. Others do not have the time to regularly monitor such functionalities due to several personal, agro

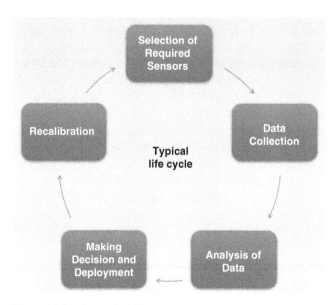

Figure 15.1 The typical life cycle of an IoT analytics-based agricultural use case (EDUCBA).

micro- and macro-environmental limitations. Others lack awareness of such technologies, the potential impact on increasing agricultural productivity and food sustainability, plus much more.

15.3.1 IoT Sensors Available for Specific Agriculture Applications

There are several IoT sensors dedicated to crop growth stages. Such stages include sowing, harvesting, packing, and transportation, among others. These sensors can detect and monitor soil moisture, humidity, solar energy levels, temperature, carbon dioxide, and many other aspects (Biradar 2019). An important factor to consider when selecting a sensor for its suitability to a particular application is to ensure accuracy of the signal report, range coverage, noise fluctuation, resolution and incremental changes, and repeatability performance for a measurement report. Smart vehicle stations are usually installed across the fields with sensors for data collection. Through diverse models from different manufacturers, they can predict how crops can grow in precision farming stages.

For instance, during the early stages of planting and sowing, actuators can provide farmers with invaluable information for the careful nursing of crops (Biradar 2019). These types of sensors scrutinize soil humidity and carbon dioxide levels, including plant health big data analytics. Consequently, farmers can exercise care, ensuring crops grow in a sustainable environment, like greenhouses (TEAM 2019). Actuators come together with the installation capability of intelligent LEDs for plant energy regulation and automation. They support sprinkler systems to activate automated irrigation and cooling mechanisms when temperatures are higher than anticipated levels. Once the crops grow to harvest and storage times, these sensors provide storage heating, including automated packing and transportation capabilities, as farmers reduce waste.

Likewise, digital lumen sensors can nurture crops from the early stages of planting, sowing to maturity before harvesting using an intelligent contiguous heat control. The combination of lighting controls and data collection seamlessly guarantees efficiency in crop growth management for superior farm performance (Biradar 2019). Adopting these types of sensors for smart greenhouses presents up to 10 times average yields compared to conventional agricultural methods. They require less water and minimal use of pesticides due to the healthy, controlled crop environment. Supplementary sensors include those with hydroponic technologies dedicated to smart gardening for urban environments like malls and other skyscraper structures, among other places. The resource-efficient sensors sanction, almost without soil, the growing of crops since they inform farmers of the nutrients that are necessary to provide plants during growth (TEAM 2019). The models have now become the much-sought solutions for twenty-first-century farming challenges in maintaining crops from an early age to maturity, including harvesting and storage.

A brief list is given of the field sensors in agriculture used for monitoring the following parameters:

1) Temperature
2) Humidity
3) Barometric pressure
4) Soil moisture
5) pH level

The modeling software collects data from these sensors and activates the Control Network. This helps farmers to start cultivation with optimal inputs of material. The Control Network has the following responsibilities:

1) Water pressure
2) Irrigation operation
3) Controlling animals
4) Sunlight
5) Pesticide dispersal
6) Heating/cooling

These sensors are also cheap, so many visionary farmers are implementing them.

15.3.2 Challenges Faced While Implementing Sensor Technologies

Though IoT is the future of agriculture, it still has some challenges to face.

Connectivity. Connectivity is a challenge because to work in an IoT system you need to provide connectivity throughout the agricultural environment from storehouses, fields, barn, and greenhouse. It also requires much space and strong connectivity, which should be able to work in certain weather conditions like storms, etc.

Design and durability. As it will be a network of IoT, it must have a proper design with reliability and robustness to work on the farm.

Limited resources and time. Those companies that design IoT for agriculture should design them so that these systems can withstand rapid climate changes and be compatible with limited land and resources.

15.4 IoT Devices and Communication Techniques

There are several IoT and communication devices available in the market to be used in the agriculture field. The following are some of the sensors with their functionality:

- Wireless sensors. These sensors are considered crucial when it comes to collecting crop conditions and other information. Acoustic sensors are used for pest monitoring and detection and classifying seeds into varieties. They are low in price; Field Programmable Gate Arrays (FPGA) sensors are starting to be used to measure real-time plant transpiration, humidity, and irrigation, but they have some limitations, such as size, cost, and greater power consumption. Optical sensors are used to test the soil's ability to reflect light, its moisture, and the presence of minerals and to gain yield information. Mass flow sensors are used.
- IoT-based tractors. Self-driving tractors have been manufactured that avoid revisiting the same area. They can be extremely helpful in the cultivation process, but farmers cannot afford them due to their high prices.
- Harvesting robots. Harvesting the field is a painful process, but thanks to AI and IoT it can now be automated. This saves time because robots work faster than humans, and the field is harvested at the right time and provides flexibility whenever needed.

Communications in agriculture. Communicating the relevant information at the right time is crucial in the agricultural field. Otherwise, it would be difficult to achieve real purpose until better connectivity is provided. There are many communication networks that could be selected based on the requirements of any specific field or availability of the resources. Some of them are mentioned below:

Cellular Communications. Communication modes from second generation (2G) to 5G could be used according to the field's requirements. Connectivity is again a major concern, especially in rural areas, where getting in touch with the satellites for transmission of the data could be the option. Still, its costs are high and would not be suitable for small farms. The need for 5G and wireless is critical for agricultural development. The enhancements and range of effects it will bring will allow for a much smoother transition for farmers worldwide. Wireless protocols like ZigBee will ensure that low-energy cost wireless communication occurs and will allow for adequate techniques to be utilized in wireless sensor networks. There is a wide range of protocols being developed and protocols that have already been developed that will allow sensors to communicate wirelessly without any hassle. In addition, the effectiveness and mobility that wireless will bring for agricultural AI and IoT as an exponential benefit will ensure a haven of great success.

Bluetooth. This is wireless communication and connects small head devices over short distances. Many farms are using this technology due to its low power consumption, user-friendliness, and low-cost benefits.

LoRa. This is a long-ranged type of communication with a low power requirement, considered to perform better in terms of lifespan, and does not require much maintenance. It is better than Bluetooth technology in terms of reliability and effectiveness.

SigFox. This is a French global network operator that provides connectivity to objects that need low power and provides high performance because of its ultra-narrow technology.

ZigBee. ZigBee is suitable for short-range area communications, like the greenhouse environment. Real-time data is transmitted through ZigBee to the end-user.

15.5 IoT and all Crop Stages

- Sowing. By using sensors, farmers can find optimal inputs to the crop. This helps them to save money, time, and energy because they know exactly how many seeds to sow, amount of water to provide, and spray pesticides.
- Harvesting. Robots reduce painful labor work and crops are harvested at the right time within less time.
- Packing. Automated packing would help reduce human effort, time, as well as labor costs. With automated robot packing, all from moving to retrieving of the product is done automatically, and a record of the items is maintained. A track record of the products is maintained as well through various sensors.
- Transportation. Through vehicle tracking systems and connectivity, farmers can be assured of their products' security, and these connected vehicle technologies can monitor tire pressure so that vehicles can carry the exact amounts of loads. They could also make a better choice to select the better route and time for transportation.

15.6   Drone in Farming Applications

Unmanned Aerial Vehicles (UAVs) dedicated to crop surveillance have reinforced the impact of the IoTs and AI in "smart agriculture." They provide superior future solutions, thanks to their spatial resolution, to execute a series of controlled measurements (TEAM 2019). Once activated, they can fly across vast agricultural fields monitoring crop health, including soil properties, while relaying the same information to farm stations. These UAVs seamlessly capture pest manifestations, diseases, irrigation challenges, including plant growth patterns. Technologically, UAVs are designed to tirelessly carry out such repeated tasks since they are smaller versions of computers, things that are dangerous or tedious for humans to do.

Today, UAVs can evaluate crop weed management, plant levels of chlorophyll, moisture content, soil texture, and much more. UAVs routinely spray various pesticides in "smart farms" and have become useful in semi-automated crop scouting. Semi-automated crop scouting is the virtual inspection of farms through image and video UAV relays with in-depth data interpretations to accurately manage their agricultural activities (Biradar 2019). These devices execute vegetation index mapping for real-time agroindustry analysis and significantly save revenue growth costs by optimized crop yields.

Drone technology has a variety of uses in the field of precision farming. Farm management activities involving observation, measurement, and taking action can be now be done based on real-time crop and livestock data. Drones can be used to obtain three-dimensional (3D) maps on soil and help in identifying issues related to soil. This is a great tool in soil and field analysis. The information gathered helps farmers to find effective ways to plant and manage their crops and soil. This results in better utilization of resources like soil and water. Agricultural drones can also aid in planting. This is a new technology that is still developing. These drones can plant vast areas over a short period, thus minimizing the need for an on-the-ground planting operation, which may be costly, time-insensitive, and strenuous.

Crops require constant spraying and fertilization to maintain high yields. Traditionally this was done using methods that were costly, inefficient, and tiresome. However, drones have revolutionized the way it is done today. These drones are usually equipped with reservoirs filled with fertilizers, herbicides, or pesticides and can spray large areas quickly. This method has proved to be cost-effective, efficient, and safer. Spot spraying is also possible using drone technology, and can be accomplished using less time than the traditional way.

Drone technology has become a critical component in large-scale crop and acreage monitoring. It is now easy to manage thousands of acres more effectively. Drones provide real-time footage and time-based animation, which gives a clear image of crop progress. Using drones, one can collect information on overall crop health, crop life cycle, and crop distribution. Therefore, crop mapping and surveying decisions can be made on real-time data rather than guesswork. The final result is the maximized use of land and other resources.

Irrigation can sometimes be cumbersome, especially in the case of large-scale irrigation. However, using drone technology, one can quickly identify regions with irrigation issues and solve them. This information can also aid in better crop layout and avoiding water pooling, which is detrimental to sensitive crops.

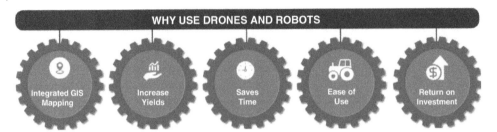

Figure 15.2 The benefits of using a drone in precision agriculture (Chuchra 2016).

Other than crop management, drones are one of the best tools for real-time live-stock monitoring. Drones can be equipped with imaging cameras that enable a farmer to manage and monitor livestock. A farmer with a huge herd can identify any injured or missing animal and observe the process of giving birth from the comfort of his house. Also, drones can be used to spot predators, which is a huge advantage to the farmer. Figure 15.2 shows how drone usage in agriculture for soil and field analysis, planting, crop spraying, crop monitoring, irrigation, and health assessment can benefit farmers.

15.7 Conclusion

The fusion of AI and the IoT inevitably offers immense farming opportunities. As the world population continues to increase, the agriculture sector is under pressure more than ever to boost food production. Thankfully, the technologies behind IoT sensors and AI provide farmers with the ability to collect almost every piece of information about plant or crop health for real-time analytics. Today, wireless IoT sensors installed with nodes in farms analyze crop pest manifestations, surrounding humidity, temperatures, soil properties, and much more for effective crop management. UAVs help farmers fly across vast fields collecting index mapping data, spraying pesticides, and analyzing crop irrigation gaps, plus much more. Such integration has seen these mechanical, digital, and computing devices mutually work together with people.

These technologies predict necessary measures for plant and animal care, enhancing and further increasing food production. However, the lack of awareness of AI and IoT for "smart agriculture" continues to pose challenges for the maximum adoption of these technologies. Other problems include a lack of resources, time, and farmers' commitment to utilize these solutions and solve food-related problems. Though several wireless IoT sensors now exist for greenhouse and crop health monitoring, today's farming methods mainly remain conventional. A lot needs to be done to increase the adoption of AI and IoT technologies for "smart agriculture." However, ambitious futuristic farming goals will involve removing existing limitations to increase food production and boost farmers' revenues. In conclusion, extensive research shows that dedicated IoT sensors will significantly save farming time, resources, and costs. Such efforts will unlock smart farming integration of AI and IoT opportunities for maximum exploitation and help the world achieve sustainable futuristic agribusiness efficiency.

References

Biradar, C., El-Shamaa, K., Singh, R.K., Atassi, L., et al. (2018). Artificial Intelligence (AI) and Internet of Things (IoT) for Inclusive Agro-Ecosystems for Sustainable Development. *Geospatial World Forum*. Hyderabad, India: HICC. https://www.researchgate.net/publication/345807738_Artificial_Intelligence_AI_and_Internet_of_Things_IoT_for_Inclusive_Agro-Ecosystems_for_Sustainable_Development (accessed 22 June 2021).

Chuchra, J. (2016). Drones and robots: Revolutionizing farms of the future. https://www.geospatialworld.net/article/drones-and-robots-future-agriculture/.

EDUCBA (n.d.). IoT in agriculture. https://www.educba.com/iot-in-agriculture/ (accessed 22 June 2021).

TEAM, DIGITEUM (2019). Is IoT the future of agriculture?https://www.digiteum.com/iot-agriculture (accessed November 19, 2019).

16

Applications of Artificial Intelligence, ML, and DL

16.1 Introduction

The basic skills to learn from the data and give output, as a result, are old. Along with the core technologies, real-world Artificial Intelligence (AI) solutions need different tools for managing data, deployed at various scales. The combination of rapidly increasing data and important computing power has given an extension to deep learning and machine learning capabilities. An increase in computing power has given computers the power to deal with big data and run that data on bigger models and complicated algorithms. Machines can analyze a substantial amount of information and then transform the input (what they have read, observed) into an intelligent insight at a high operational scale. AI enables the machine to understand, make interactions, and communicate with humans in a human way (SAS 2019).

Whatever a machine can reason, learn, and comprehend will be useless for humans if they cannot understand the result or intuitively offer new input with a language help. Advancement in machine learning has allowed language abilities to facilitate effective collaboration between machines and humans. It is not possible that machines can chat with humans with the help of text and speech software. They are continuously learning and having an insight through every experience that involves interaction. Machines can now analyze the language nuances such as sarcasm and slang to capture meaning, sentiment, and intent (SAS 2019).

16.2 Building Artificial Intelligence Capabilities

AI algorithms are programmed and designed in such a way that they can make decisions on their own. This is done using real-time data. AI machines are not passive and can only make a predetermined and mechanical response. AI may use different tools such as remote input, sensors or digital data, or combinations to combine information from many resources, evaluate the data, and respond by acting on the derived insight. AI machines are designed and programmed by humans intentionally and conclusions are based on instant analysis.

Intelligent Connectivity: AI, IoT, and 5G, First Edition. Abdulrahman Yarali.
© 2022 John Wiley & Sons Ltd. Published 2022 by John Wiley & Sons Ltd.

The transportation industry is making good use of this technology. Light Detection and Ranging (LIDARS) is a technology-based on AI, and remote sensors are used to take information from a vehicle's surroundings. LIDAR will use the light from the radar to observe different objects around the car and make a rapid decision about the objects present, the distance, and the car's speed if something is about to collapse. The on-board computer uses the information together with the sensor data to analyze dangerous conditions; it will suggest changing lanes in such a case or stopping the vehicle.

There have been many improvements in storage systems, analytic techniques, and processing speeds; they can handle sophistication in decision making and analysis. Financial algorithms based on AI can detect minute differentials in stock valuations and analyze market transactions that may use information.

AI is also used in combination with data analytics and machine learning that results in combination and decision-making. Machine learning will take data and search for underlying trends. If it detects anything related to a practical problem, such knowledge can be used further along with the data analytics to understand the different problems (West 2018).

AI has the adaptability to learn from the information and use it for decision making. AI will shift itself when the circumstances are different, which may involve changes in environmental conditions, road conditions, financial conditions, and military situations. AI integrates the set algorithm changes and makes a different decision based on changed circumstances (West 2018).

16.3   What is Machine Learning?

In 1959, Arthur Samuel used the phrase "Machine Learning." He defined it as "the ability to learn without being explicitly programmed." It is a very basic type to parse data with algorithms, make learning, and make predictions about something. House process can be considered a very good example; websites like Zillow or Redfin make predictions about the price of an old house. At its core, Machine Learning (ML) is about making a line of best fit. As the example given of house price, the model will use a lot of data for predicting the price. With every data point having different dimensions, like the number of bathrooms, bedrooms, parking space, and total size, the system functions from these parameters and moves to the coefficients to all these parameters (Shah 2018).

ML can be termed as an application of AI that offers systems and the ability to learn and improve automatically from the experiences without explicit programming. ML is used to let the machine learn by focusing on developing computer programs with access to data and using the same data for the future. Data is the main source of learning, and learning is highly dependent on the observation of data. The main purpose is to allow machines such as computers to learn without human involvement or help. Computers can do learning automatically and adjust future actions accordingly (Shah 2018). ML is one of the most exciting parts of AI, building and developing an automatic computational strategy to process data in meaningful information. On the other hand, AI comprises computer science areas that make computer programs and machines capable of problem-solving and learning. Figure 16.1 shows different areas of AI and ML functionalities (TM Capital 2017).

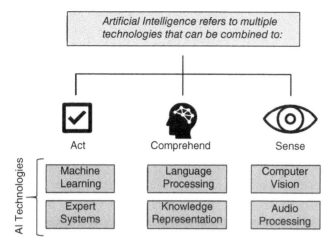

Source: Accenture, "Why is AI The Future of Growth" (2016)

Figure 16.1 Defining AI and ML (TM capital 2017).

16.3.1 Machine Learning Methods

The algorithms of ML can be supervised or unsupervised. In supervised ML algorithms, they can apply past learning in the use of new data to predict future events. If starting from the evaluation of a good training dataset, the learning algorithm outputs an inferred function to make predictions about the output values. The system will be able to offer targets for a new input after training. The learning algorithm may also compare the output with the intended output and find the errors to change the model. On the other hand, in the unsupervised ML algorithms, the information used is not labeled or classified (Expertsystem 2017). In simple words, the output is fed in the system's algorithm, which means in supervised learning, the output is already known to the machine before it is even started. When the output is known, the machine only has to work out the input processes. The algorithm is fed with the help of a training data set that gives instructions to the machine. If the results are different from the algorithm, the training data set will guide the algorithm to the right path. Currently, supervised ML is used in most of the machines used in the world. Both input and output variables are used with the help of an algorithm. Humans will provide the input, output, algorithm, and scenario (Loon 2019).

Unsupervised learning examines how the system infers the functions to explain the hidden structure from unlabeled data. The system usually does not classify the right output; it will examine the data and draw inferences from the datasets to describe the unlabeled data's hidden structures (Expertsystems 2017). The concept of unsupervised ML is not very common and is not used very frequently. It is applicable in very limited sets. Although it is not used in many applications, the methodology of unsupervised ML creates the future of ML. In unsupervised learning, the machine does not have firm data sets and many problems. AI system and ML purpose are blinded when it is in operations. The system has logical operations to pilot it along the way. Lack of input and output algorithms can result in complications in the processes. Unsupervised learning can also find solutions and interprets big data through the binary logic mechanism, which is in all computers; however, there will be no reference data (Loon 2019).

Semi-supervised ML algorithms can be categorized as unsupervised or supervised learning. Both unlabeled and labeled data are used for training; unlabeled data is used in large amounts while labeled data is used in small amounts. The system will improve itself with the help of learning accuracy. Normally, semi-supervised learning is selected when the acquired labeled data needs related resources to learn or train. In other cases, getting unlabeled data does not need more resources. There are reinforcement ML algorithms that make interactions with the environment by making actions and highlighting errors. Error and trial search, along with the reward system, are the dominant characteristics of reinforcement learning. Software and machines can automatically detect the effective behavior in a special context to maximize performance. Simple reward feedback is needed for the agent to learn and determine the best action, called a reinforcement signal (Expertsystems 2017).

ML helps the analysis of large data. It delivers a fast and accurate result to highlight opportunities or potential risks. It also needs more resources for the training purpose.

16.4 Deep Learning

Deep Learning (DL) can be termed as an ML technique. It lets the computers do what humans do in a natural way, i.e. learning through examples. The main technology is based on which driverless class is made to see the stop sign, pedestrian, or any other hurdle. This technology is used in voice control in smartphones, TVs, and other devices as well. In DL, the computer will take inputs or learn from sound, images, or text and perform the action accordingly. The models of DL may perform actions with high accuracy. In some cases, they have exceeded the human level of performance and accuracy. A large data can also be used for the training of the machine along with neural network architectures.

In the modern world, DL is achieving recognition accuracy at a very high level. This is helping consumer electronics meet the customer's expectations, and it is also very important in safety applications. The recent advances have made DL so strong and accurate that it has surpassed the human level in classification of objects. DL has two main reasons for becoming so useful. Firstly, DL needs big labeled data. For instance, the driverless car development needs millions of images and very long video hours to learn. Secondly, DL needs a lot of computing power. There is a need for a strong system of graphical handling units (GPUs), along with strong architecture. This is used along with cloud computing, which reduces the learning or training time for the machine (Mathworks 2019). Figure 16.2 depicts a schematic diagram of the difference between AI, ML, and DL concepts, which revolutionized the world. Companies are investing in these technologies to boost their productivity and solve many complex problems in all industry sectors.

16.4.1 Use Cases

There can be many examples of DL applications that are currently getting known:

- *Aerospace and defense.* DL technology helps in identifying the objects with the help of satellites and knows the location. It also helps to know the safe and unsafe areas for the soldiers.

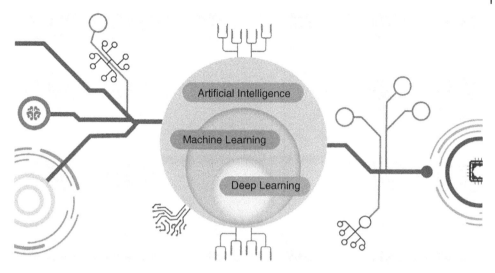

Figure 16.2 The difference between AI, ML, and DL in the digital world (Valencia 2019).

- *Driving cars.* DL is currently used in auto-driven cars, where these cars can detect traffic signals and traffic lights. Similarly, it also helps to detect any other obstacles or pedestrians on the road.
- *Medical.* DL technology is being used in cancer research. The technology helps in detecting cancer cells in the human body. There is also an advanced microscope development that can yield a large amount of high-dimensional data.
- *Industrial automation.* DL is of great use for employees' safety when they are working around heavy machinery; machines can detect workers when they are unsafe, reducing accidents and enhancing workplace safety.
- *Electronics.* DL technology is also used in speech translation and hearing. Home assistance devices that will respond to the human voice and set the preference are normally supported by DL technology.

16.4.2 The Working Mechanism

There are numerous hidden layers in the neural network in DL. The common neural networks may contain around three hidden layers, where the deep and complicated networks may have more than 150 hidden layers. A large set of neural network architectures and labeled data let the machine learn the features (Mathworks 2019).

Convolution neural networks (CNN) are a very common kind of deep neural networks. This network involves many learned features with two-dimensional (2D) layers, a large amount of input data, images, and architecture. There is therefore no need for manual feature extraction in CNNs; there is also no requirement to locate the features used to highlight the images. Convolutional neural networks take features from the images. The most relevant features might not be needed as the network will train using the images. This feature adds a lot of accuracy in DL for the computer machine vision in object classification.

CCNs may detect multiple features of an image with the help of multiple hidden layers. Each hidden layer will add more to the complexity of the learned image features. For example, the first hidden layers can detect edges; the next one will detect more complicated shapes, ultimately detecting the whole object.

16.4.3 Deep Learning Models

There are three common ways to use DL to classify the object:

- Training from scratch
- Transfer learning
- Feature extraction

For a network to be trained in DL, there is a need for many labeled data sets and the network architectural design that will be learning the model's features. This can be very effective for the latest applications. Similarly, it is also very beneficial for applications that have multiple output categories. This approach is not very common due to the longer training period, big data, and learning rate; such networks will take weeks to train (Mathworks 2019).

Transfer learning is a very common approach to DL. This process includes the fine-tuning of a pertained model. Google Net or Alex Net can be a good start, and the new data can be fed containing the unknown classes. After a few changes in the network, the new task can be performed, for example, classifying the only dogs and rabbits among many other objects. This approach needs fewer data processing; therefore, the computation time will be less than our previous approach. The processing would need thousands of images instead of millions, and the computation time will go down from hours to minutes. There is a need for an interface in transfer learning of the pre-existing network. There are good chances of modification and enhancement of the new task. The tools of MATLAB® are specifically developed in transfer learning.

Feature extraction is not a very common approach to DL. This is only to use the feature extractor in DL as all the layers are assigned to learn the special features from the images. These features can be pulled out from the network at any given time during the training process. Such features can be used as a mode of input in the machine. A good example of this can be support vector machines (Mathworks 2019).

16.4.4 Deep Learning and MATLAB®

DL has been made very easy by MATLAB®. Along with the functions and tools to manage big sets of data, there are special toolboxes offered by MATLAB® to work with ML. MATLAB® can help us in DL with a few code lines. There is no expertise required in this. It offers a quick start by creating and visualizing the model, applying the model, and embedding the application or the device. Combining MATLAB® with DL can create DL models with fewer codes and import the pertained models for debugging the initial results as the training parameters are adjusted.

Similarly, MATLAB® can also be used to get expertise in DL. MATLAB® makes learning about the special field. It also helps domain experts in DL. It will enable the user to label the objects in the images, and it can also automate the ground truth labeling for testing within the videos. MATLAB® can combine different domains in one workflow. Programming and thinking can be done in the same environment. It also gives different tools for DL and a long-range of domains fed in DL algorithms, for example, signal processing, data analytics, and computer vision. MATLAB® also helps in integrating the outcomes in the existing applications. It can automate the DL models on embedded machines, clouds, and enterprise systems (Mathworks 2019).

16.5 Machine Learning vs. Deep Learning Comparison

The comparison between ML and DL can be done on the following basis:

- Data dependencies
- Hardware dependencies
- Problem-solving approach
- Feature engineering
- Execution time
- Interpretability

Table 16.1 shows the main differences between DL and ML (Guru99).

16.5.1 Data Dependencies

ML is the development of historical data in computer programs called training data. There are many texts that we have access to, like government, embassies, the United Nations, and Non-Government Organizations (NGOs), that publish a text in hundreds of other languages and most importantly in English. The tools that use ML to translate, such as

Table 16.1 DL and ML differences (Guru99 2019).

	Machine learning	Deep learning
Data dependencies	Excellent performances on a small/medium dataset	Excellent performance on a big dataset
Hardware dependencies	Work on a low-end machine	Requires a powerful machine, preferably with GPU: DL performs a significant amount of matrix multiplication
Feature engineering	Need to understand the features that represent the data	No need to understand the best feature that represents the data
Execution time	From a few minutes to hours	Up to weeks. The Neural Network needs to compute a significant number of weights
Interpretability	Some algorithms are easy to interpret (logistic, decision tree), some are almost impossible (SVM, XGBoost)	Difficult to impossible

Google, translate to this kind of translated library as its training data. For instance, the German–English translation training uses a version of English and German of various documents. When we require translating the specific text from German to English, it can happen successfully by choosing the right pair of German and English languages.

The DL concept is not new to us as it has been working for a few years. However, people are now paying more attention to the DL concept, as we saw in ML. We will now discuss the definition of DL and further break it down with an example (Levine 2018).

The major difference between DL and data dependencies is its performance as it increases with its scale. DL algorithms will not perform well when the data is in a small form. That is why DL requires a huge amount of data to understand it perfectly. On the other side, the concept of ML algorithms with their old rules prevails in this scenario (Dörner 2018).

16.5.2 Hardware Dependencies

The DL algorithms will need high-end machines, in contrast to traditional ML algorithms, which can work on low types of machines. The reason behind the DL algorithm with high-end machines is that this machine includes GPUs, which are an important part of how it works. DL machines do a large number of medium multiplication operations and there are several requirements of hardware in the ML process. If your job is minor and can fit in chronological processing, you do not need to purchase a big system. You can leave the GPUs together. A central processing unit (CPU) could be enough for the processing. If you are working on another ML area, a GPU is not necessary. If the task is too difficult and has adaptable data, a more powerful GPU would be required for you. A high level of a graphics card laptop should work for this. If you are working for a big organization or business, you will require building your DL system. If your task is larger than usual and you have sufficient funds to cover the GPU cost, you should select the GPU to process the data (Marcus 2018).

When a business is trying to gain value through ML, access to the best hardware will support all the main functions at a high level, with a wide range of hardware like CPUs, GPUs, TPUs, and ASICs (application specific integrated circuits). Selecting the correct hardware could be a little confusing. The first thing you should determine is what kind of resource would be required to complete the task. In the future, we will see more powerful gadgets that would not require more power. If you are trying to increase value through ML in your company, you will need to use the best hardware for this task because it produces the best results. Chips are the main parts of your computer because chips are the brain of every computer, and without the chips, the computer cannot process the information for further purposes. Processors check all the instructions that different hardware and software work around them. When we discuss ML, the processor has a major role in executing the sense in a given algorithm. The main strength of the CPU is to execute the difficult operation very efficiently. The best-advanced chip for ML is another major processor, which is called mass-manufactured (Cheng 2018).

16.5.3 Problem-Solving Approach

In the problem-solving approach, we use the usual algorithms to solve problems. It requires breaking the problem into chunks so that every part can be solved separately, which will take less time and will be more efficient. Although DL is a substrate of ML, it has become a popular problem-solving approach because of its sky-high accuracy. The "deep" part of DL comes with more than one layer in its architecture. Several advantages are introduced, as it can classify data more and more accurately, learn better, and even found application in self-driving cars (Nyshadham et al. 2018).

Although the **machine learning** approach of problem-solving might requires less amounts of data than the **deep learning** approach, which is a data-hungry process, it would still produce integrated results. These techniques pass information legitimately to the system and have a decent act, unlike different strategies where the best highlights are chosen to ignore the calculation. Because of this, it may very well be effectively adjusted to various spaces contrary to DL vertical applications.

Deep learning strategies work out how to extricate highlights from the dataset. The best way to build exactness is to enter more information, and the precision accomplished is a lot higher using these strategies, although sometimes the dataset will need to modify, invent, and transform. Different strategies work just with set information. If the information is transformed, it comes up as incomplete and must be prepared once more. Profound learning adjusts to the changes. It examines issues in its shrouded layers that are generally computationally hard to explain. Even though it can be concluded that the dataset is small, ML algorithms/approaches should be preferred for that problem (D. Mesal 2018).

16.6 Feature Engineering

Highlight designing is key to the use of AI and is both troublesome and costly. In simple words, the expression "Deep Learning" is a strategy for factual discovery that removes highlights or traits from crude information. Interestingly, information portrayals are hard-coded, as many AI calculations highlight, requiring further procedures, including choice and extraction.

As compared to ML, DL is an appropriate technique for separating important highlights from crude information. It does not rely on hand-created highlights, like nearby twofold examples, a histogram of slopes, and so forth. In particular, it carries out a progressive element extraction. It learns highlights layer-wise, which implies that in beginning layers it adapts to low-level highlights. As it climbs the chain of command, it becomes familiar with a progressively conceptual portrayal of the information (Wongsuphasawat 2018). However, AI is not a decent strategy for removing important highlights from the information. It depends on available highlights as a contribution to performing well.

16.6.1 Layerwise Features of Deep Learning

Although AI calculations frequently function admirably regardless of whether the dataset is small, profound learning is data hungry. The more information you have, the better it is probably going to perform. It is regularly said that with more information, the number of layers in the system likewise subsequently increases more (Sharma 2018) Figure 16.3 depicts a relationship between the bulk of data availability and performance, with layer-wise features showing data dependency.

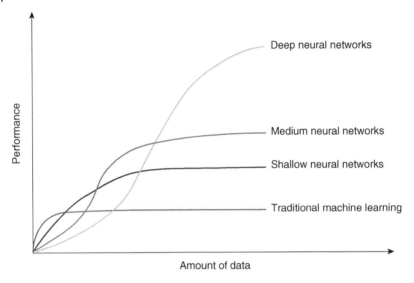

Figure 16.3 The plot of data vs. performance (Tang 2018).

As it tends to be inferred that profound learning systems are information subordinate, they need more than a CPU can offer. You need a GPU for the profound learning system preparation, which has many centers, in contrast with a CPU with extremely insignificant centers. The calculation control relies upon the sum of information and how expansive your system is; therefore, as you increase the measure of information or the number of layers, you increasingly need more calculation control. Then again, a conventional AI calculation can be actualized on a CPU with genuinely tolerable particulars (Sharma 2018).

Finally, it can be concluded that both profound learning and AI will be around for a long time, probably remaining for something like 10 years from now. As enterprises send profound learning and AI calculations to produce more income, their workers will be instructed to gain proficiency with this expertise. Many new businesses are concocting novel profound learning arrangements, which can take care of testing issues (Sharma 2018).

In an industry and scholarly world, much earth-shattering examination occurs each day, and how profound learning is altering the world is awesome. The profound learning models have played out to be significantly superior to contemporary strategies and have accomplished best in class in exhibitions.

16.6.2 Execution Time in DL

DL algorithms usually need time to learn. This is because, in DL algorithms, there are many parameters where learning takes longer than usual. The ResNet learning algorithm takes two weeks to train someone fully while machine training is shorter, from a few seconds to a few hours.

The time for deep training can range from one hour to a few hours. For neural and brain analysis, for example, the machine training can last for several months. If you have a lot of data, learning with essential data takes time. Additionally, when you increase the number of layers in your network, the number of parameters known as the weight will increase, which will lead to slow learning.

Not only learning, but deep nerve networks can take a long time to complete because testing will pass through all the layers in your network. Increasing numbers will happen, which will take a lot of time.

ML algorithms normally work from a few hours to a longer time, depending on the applications and modeling outcome requirements. State-of-the-art DL algorithm ResNet takes about two weeks to train entirely from scratch due to a massive data analysis, whereas ML comparatively takes much less time to train because of less analytical processes. It is turned in reverse on testing process time. At test time, a DL algorithm takes less time to run, whereas, if we compare it with k-nearest neighbors (a type of ML algorithm), the test time increases as the data size increases. However, this does not apply to all ML algorithms, as there are also some small testing times, depending on the applications.

As an example, effective planning and optimized execution of the e-Science workflows in distributed systems such as the Grid need predictions of the workflow execution times. However, predicting the execution times of e-Science workflows in heterogeneous distributed systems is a challenging job due to their complex structure, variations due to input problem sizes, and the heterogeneous and dynamic nature of the shared resources.

16.6.3 Interpretability

Finally, we do not know whether we can interpret it as a computational model for learning or learning rules to adapt its system to a particular environment. DL with its massive data usage is still 10 times better than before in industrial applications.

As an example, we could use DL to provide automatic app ratings. The performance it gives in scoring is perfect and compatible with human performance. However, there are problems as we do not know how it gave the result. You can determine whether nodes found on the deep nervous system are activated, but we do not know which nucleus is assumed to be an example, and these nerves are combined. Therefore, we failed to translate the results.

On the other hand, ML algorithms, such as decision trees, give us clear rules about why they choose what they choose, so it is easy to interpret their wishes. Thus, algorithms such as trees, decision-making, and logistic regression are mainly used in the translation industry.

In ML, the exact rules are given by the algorithm to explain the decision behind a specific option, while the DL's decision seems to be "empowered" to give the user the option of translation in order to make a choice. Thus, the DL algorithm cannot work in medical matters, where the evidence should be properly explained in court.

Many of the methods of criticism concerning ML are about vectors, machine vectors, or support (probably because you can see the probability of the composition of the output). For example, when modeling an electronic health record or data set, a bank loan with an ML technique is easy to understand for many predictive models (Shickel 2018).

One of the best examples of interpretation is the tree of decision, where you follow the logical tests on the wooden nodes until you reach the solution. The machine translation algorithm with a high conversion capability is the nearest neighbor. This is not a parameter learning algorithm, but it still falls under the heading of an ML algorithm (Battaglia 2018).

Many industries use DL models as a standard procedure in their fields because of DL reproducibility and interpretability features. The results obtained by models are not reproducible as a huge number of parameters with these high parameters are involved; uncertainty remains in such a case. Although exact results might not be reproduced, an average needs to be taken.

We do not know what a specific neuron is doing in the exact quantified manner in a DL model. We can understand which nerve cells are active, but we do not know what these nerve cells need to do and what the nervous layer does. For MA algorithms like a decision tree, the tree gives clear rules and the SVM gives a clear demarcation with its hyper-planes, which is much easier to interpret.

16.7   Applications of Machine Learning

AI is all around us. There are many possibilities that we are using many of the technologies based on AI and are not aware of it. The main application of AI is ML. Software and computers and similar devices come into this category. The following are a few examples of ML in our daily use.

16.7.1   Virtual Personal Assistants

Search engines like Google and Alexa are based on ML. We often give voice commands to these search engines and they process our information. This is a very advanced form of ML where a command is given in the form of voice and the machine will process it further. For example, a command is given to Google, "Please set an alarm for 6 a.m. tomorrow." The smartphone will take the command through Google and the alarm will be set. A more advanced form of ML can be searching for flights. A command can be given to Google, "Please search for a possible flight of tomorrow from London to Australia." In such a command, Google will further process the information to other applications or websites and automatically collect data and present it. In ML, the data is collected and can be used for future reference. The machine learns from the data provided to it and sets preferences obtained from previous records. Virtual assistants based on ML help people on many platforms, such as:

- Mobile applications: Google Allo
- Smartphones taking multiple commands: Samsung S8 and Bixby
- Smart speakers: Google Home and Amazon Echo

16.7.2   Predictions While Commuting

Traffic predictions. ML can predict traffic if it is present in a vehicle. Many people use GPS, which is the service that can take our speed and locations to manage traffic. The data can be taken to map the current traffic and alert for upcoming traffic jams; however, all vehi-cles are not equipped with this technology. Therefore, it becomes difficult for the machine to do accurate predictions.

Online transportation networks. Online transportation services are very common today. Companies like Uber are using ML to predict customer demand and apply peak hours by automatically collecting the data from the users and the driver. The machine will collect data from both ends of the journey and set the price of the ride.

16.7.3 Video Surveillance

ML has made video detection very easy. Before ML, a single person monitored multiple cameras, which is quite a boring and difficult job. With the help of ML, machines are pro-grammed to observe the video cameras and detect any unusual behavior, such as a person standing for a very long time, napping on a bench, or any other suspicious activity. The machine will alert the person present on the surveillance cameras, and crime can be pre-vented before it takes place.

16.7.4 Social Media Services

Facebook is a very popular social media platform. We often see "People you may know" where the suggestion is made to add people to our friends list who can be known to us. This process is done through ML, because the machine collects data based on our preferences, locations, likes, interest, and social media accounts. Face recognition is also done through ML. We upload pictures on Facebook and it will automatically suggest us to tag certain people in the picture. This process looks simple, but it is very complicated. There are many patterns behind this technology and Facebook uses different pictures of people in certain poses and then offers to tag them.

16.7.5 Spam Email and Malware Filtering

We often see emails in our spam folders that are from advertisers and other companies. Similarly, suspicious emails are also automatically transferred to our spam folder. All of this is done through ML. Clients use different spam filtering techniques, which need to be regularly updated. Some of the famous spam filtering techniques are C 4.5 Decision Tree Induction and Multi-Layer Perception.

There are more than 325 000 malwares designed every day with almost a similar pattern to the previous ones. ML helps the computer track this malware based on their previous patterns and variations and offer protection.

16.7.6 Online Customer Support

Following the machine learning algorithms, we see many websites that offer online chats for their customers. However, there does not need to be live people behind these chat boxes as some bots do the chatting. In reality, these bots are taking information from the customer and filter it to obtain a suitable answer already fed into the system. Bots will only filter the information and give the best answer from the information they process. With time, these bots are becoming more advanced and can understand the customer queries.

16.7.7 Improved Search Engine Results

Machine learning has made search engine results more refined. Whenever someone searches for something on Google and opens the first two links at the top, and stays on these pages, Google will consider that the search results are accurate. If the user has not opened any link, Google will consider that the search results are not effective. The better search results are then saved for future preferences and referred to other users who search for the same keywords.

16.7.8 Product Recommendations

A person shops something online, and after some days, recommendations for similar products will appear on social media platforms or search results pages. This is all done through machine learning, where the shopping pattern and option is saved and further processed to offer better options to the users. Sometimes, the search engine may also sell these data to third parties or promote their products from the search results without the customer's consent.

16.7.9 Fraud Detection on the Web

Companies like PayPal are using special machine learning algorithms to prevent online fraud detection. Machines specially monitor the transactions in millions, and the verification is done on different levels to check if the transaction is legal or illegal (Daffodil 2017).

16.8 Applications of Deep Learning

DLis a method used to analyze and provide a learning process in Big Data Analytic, which is a fascinating tool with many endless applications in entertainment, manufacturing, healthcare, fraud detection, and many other areas in our lives.

16.8.1 Self-Driving Cars

Google has made a completely self-driven car, and a lot of its technology is based on deep learning, where a large amount of data and algorithms have been used along with sensors to detect motion, hurdles, and other things around the car. The car's movement depends on these sensors, which has been done based on deep learning, which is how a child learns through continuous experience and repetition. These cars are equipped with the same deep learning technology, and is being enhanced day by day.

16.8.2 Healthcare

AI is constantly reshaping healthcare, medicine, and life sciences, whether it is diagnosing skin-cancer, bio-bank data, or personalized medicine. AI innovations are making the

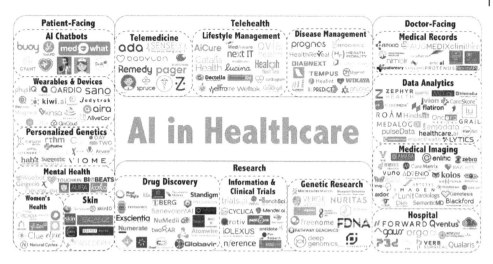

Figure 16.4 The industry landscape of AI and ML healthcare applications.

future with precision medicine and health management in different ways. There has been a lot of improvements in decision support tools, computer-aided detection, and quantitative imaging.

Figure 16.4 shows AI companies with healthcare applications (TM capital 2017). As shown, the healthcare market for AI and ML is highly fragmented. There are three main categories: diversified healthcare corporations increasingly developing AI capabilities, technology giants exploring AI applications in multiple industries, and AI-focused startups.

16.8.3 Voice Assistants and Search

Voice-activated assistants are gaining in popularity. Market giants like Apple and Samsung are continuously working on this technology. Apple's Siri is based on deep learning that can take voice commands and process information further. Google Now is another voice-activated assistant that can be used if a smartphone has Android. The latest version of voice assistant is Microsoft Cortana.

16.8.4 Movies and Sound Effects

Deep learning is used to synthesize a silent video to match a sound. The system is developed with 1000 examples of video with the sound of a stick that is hit on different surfaces and making different sounds. A deep learning model is associated with the video frames and a database of prerecorded sounds is used to select a sound to play that is an accurate match on what is happening in the video. After that, the system is evaluated using a tuning test, and human input is added to allocate which video has genuine or fake sound. The technology of recurrent neural networks and long short-term memory (LSTM) is used.

16.8.5 Auto Translator

Auto translation can now be easily seen even on social media platforms such as Facebook, where people's comments can be translated into another form. Google is also offering this service, which is quite popular. There are many automatic translation machines that people have been using for a long time, which are all based on deep learning, which includes the translation of texts and images.

16.8.6 Auto Text Generation

This can be observed in Gmail's updated version, where the email server gives the suggested words. It is very interesting and saves time and effort where the machine learns a corpus of text from the model text. These models can spell, make sentences, and punctuate. Big recurrent neural networks are also used to learn the link between things in a sequence of the input and make text.

16.8.7 Automatic Handwriting Generation

A part of handwriting is given and new handwriting is generated for a given phrase. The part of handwriting is used as a sequence of coordination used by a pen when handwriting samples are generated. With this corpus help, the link between the pen and letter movement is learned and new samples are generated.

16.8.8 Image Colorization

DL is used in the coloring of black and white images. The objects and their context are used in the image, in the same way that humans can give ideas about colors. There have been past movies that have been converted to color using this technology. A very large set of CNN and supervised layers are used in this technology to recreate the photo.

16.8.9 Earthquake Prediction

Scientists have trained computer machines through deep learning to do viscoelastic computations to predict earthquakes. These computations were intensive in history; however, the application of deep learning has highly boosted the calculation time by an enormous 50 000%. Earthquakes can be disastrous and an early prediction is required, which is where deep learning comes in handy.

16.8.10 Detection of Brain Cancer

It was becoming difficult to detect brain cancer cells due to light in operating rooms. Neural networks have made it very easy with the combination of Raman spectroscopy during the operations, which have detected the brain cancer cell more easily and lowered the rate of residual cancer.

16.8.11 Finance

The Capital Asset Pricing Model (CAPM) is the latest trend in finance. The future market related to accounting and finance can see a breakthrough success due to the latest development in machine learning and its application in finance and accounting. The CAPM is a part of it. A technical trading rule is developed and applied from the spot market price. The daily price of the different stock exchanges from 10 different markets is taken for analysis.

16.8.12 Energy Price

Recently in Spain the neural network has been applied to the energy grid stations in order to analyze energy usage and price fluctuations. The daily data is collected along with the price. The pattern is used to make predictions of consumption and energy availability, which will lead to cost-savings and higher efficiency in the energy sector (Mittal, Bhadoria 2017).

16.9 Future Trends

In the past few years, some dramatic changes have been made in AI. The tools of ML and DL have been greatly improved. These technologies greatly impact the internet and software market and other industries such as automobile, healthcare, manufacturing, and social media (Patidar 2018). This chapter will have given you an overview of machine training and deep learning and its difference. In this section, I share my vision of how deep learning and learning will go forward:

- The first consideration is to provide a growing trend of utilization of science, data, and machine learning in the industry, which will become important for any company that wants to practice machine learning in its business. Also, everyone is expected to know the basic roles and benefits of these technologies for their organizations.
- Surprise drills should occur every day, and should continue in the future. This is because deep learning is the best technique to be discovered with the most up-to-date performance.
- Research is to continue in machine learning together with deep learning. However, unlike in previous years, when research was limited, machine research and deep learning have exploded both in industry and education. With more money invested, it is likely to be an integral part of human development.
- In general, a deep training machine/training will give some up-to-date information. At the same time, the matching archives and codes should be followed every day.
- Both deep machine training and training has grown so much that it will last for at least 10 years. The industry uses in-depth learning and machine learning algorithms to generate more revenue. Staff are trained to learn this skill and contribute to their company. Beginnings come with a new, deep training solution that can address the challenges.
- The industry and the researchers are also doing innovative research every day, and the method of learning deep in the revolutionary world is underestimated. Deep learning

architecture has performed better than modern methods and has accomplished the best performance.

- To survive in the industry or the education sector, these deep learning and learning skills will play significant roles in the coming years.
- In the current situation, you are advised to have a complete theoretical analysis of AI and two techniques of artificial innovation, such as machine training and deep learning. You should also learn about machine training and how to solve the problem and how these two training methods differ from one another.
- Today, machine learning and data science are becoming a necessity and the demand for both types is growing fast. They are especially sought by companies who want to survive and integrate engine training into their business.
- Deep learning is open and has the best technique with the most up-to-date performance. In this way, incorporating deep study in a business will bring great surprises and will continue to do so.
- Recently, researchers have continued to learn about machine training and deep learning. In the past, this was limited to academics, but today research in the ML and TD fields has begun in both industry and education.

References

Battaglia, P.H.-G. (2018). Relational inductive biases, deep learning, and graph networks. *Arxiv*. 170-196.

Cheng, G., Yang, C., Yao, X. et al. (2018). When deep learning meets metric learning: Remote sensing image scene classification via learning discriminative CNNs. In: *IEEE Transactions on Geoscience and Remote Sensing*, 2811–2821. Retrieved from: https://www.semanticscholar.org/paper/When-Deep-Learning-Meets-Metric-Learning%3A-Remote-Cheng-Yang/0f78ad40306f7e6bb4d609fa9463a085cfba6f02.

Daffodil (2017, July 31). Nine applications of machine learning from day-to-day life. https://medium.com/app-affairs/9-applications-of-machine-learning-from-day-to-day-life-112a47a429d0 (accessed 22 June 2021).

Dörner, S.C. (2018). Deep learning-based communication over the air. *IEEE Journal of Selected Topics in Signal Processing* 12 (1): 132–143. https://ieeexplore.ieee.org/document/8214233.

Expertsystem (2017, October 5). What is machine learning? a definition. https://www.expertsystem.com/machine-learning-definition/ (accessed 22 June 2021).

Guru99 (2019). AI vs. deep learning vs. machine learning. Gru99.com. https://www.guru99.com/machine-learning-vs-deep-learning.html (accessed 22 June 2021).

Levine, S.P. (2018). Learning hand-eye coordination for robotic grasping with deep learning and large-scale data collection. *The International Journal of Robotics Research*: 421–436.

Loon, R.V. (2019, February 4). Machine learning explained: understanding supervised, unsupervised, and reinforcement learning. https://bigdata-madesimple.com/machine-learning-explained-understanding-supervised-unsupervised-and-reinforcement-learning/ (accessed 22 June 2021).

Marcus, G. (2018). Deep learning: a critical appraisal. *Arixiv*, 75-80.

Marr, B. (2018, February 14). The key definitions of Artificial Intelligence (AI) that explain its importance. https://www.forbes.com/sites/bernardmarr/2018/02/14/the-key-definitions-of-artificial-intelligence-ai-that-explain-its-importance/#bf566164f5d8 (accessed 22 June 2021).

Mathworks (2019). What is deep learning? | How it works, techniques & applications. https://www.mathworks.com/discovery/deep-learning.html (accessed 22 June 2021).

Mittal, M., Bhadoria, R.S. (2017). Aspect of ESB with Wireless Sensor Network. In Exploring Enterprise Service Bus in the Service-Oriented Architecture Paradigm; IGI-global Publications: Hershey, PA, USA, 2017. https://www.igi-global.com/chapter/aspect-of-esb-with-wireless-sensor-network/178066

Mesal, D. (2018, November 28). Deep learning has become the Go-To method. Analytics India: https://www.analyticsindiamag.com/deep-learning-has-become-the-go-to-method-for-problem-solving/ (accessed 22 June 2021).

Nyshadham, C., Morgan, W.S., Bekker, B., and Hart, G. (2018). Materials prediction using machine learning: Comparing MBTR, MTP, and deep learning. In: *Bulletin of the American Physical Society*. Retrieved from: https://www.semanticscholar.org/paper/Materials-prediction-using-machine-learning%3A-MBTR%2C-Nyshadham-Morgan/a781a3c8b8f9b80f28004ebde6ea3d3882822075.

Patidar, S. (2018). Future of Artificial Intelligence. DZone, AI Zone. Retrieved from: https://dzone.com/articles/future-of-artificial-intelligence-1.

SAS (2019). Artificial Intelligence – What it is and why it matters. https://www.sas.com/en_us/insights/analytics/what-is-artificial-intelligence.html (accessed 22 June 2021).

Shah, D. (2018, April 03). AI, machine learning, & deep learning explained in 5 minutes. Retrieved from: https://becominghuman.ai/ai-machine-learning-deep-learning-explained-in-5-minutes-b88b6ee65846.

Sharma, A. (2018). The difference between machine and deep learning. Datcamp. https://www.datacamp.com/community/tutorials/machine-deep-learning (accessed 22 June 2021).

Shickel, B.T. (2018). A survey of recent advances in deep learning techniques for electronic health record (EHR) analysis. *IEEE Journal of Biomedical and Health Informatics*: 1589–1604.

Tang, A., Tam, R., Cadrin-Chenevert, et al. (2018). Health Policy and Practice / Sante: Politique et Pratique Medicale: Canadian Association of Radiologists on Artificial Intelligence in Radiology, white paper. *Canadian Association of Radiologists Journal* 69: 125–135.

TM capital (2017). The next generation of medicine: Artificial Intelligence and machine learning. https://www.tmcapital.com/wp-content/uploads/2017/11/TMCC20AI20Spotlight20-202017.10.2420vF.PDF.

Valencia, J.P. (2019). Artificial Intelligence, innovation. Retrieved from: https://tangocode.com/2019/07/ai-machine-learning-and-deep-learning/.

West, D.M. (2018, October 18). What is Artificial Intelligence? https://www.brookings.edu/research/what-is-artificial-intelligence/ (accessed 22 June 2021).

Wongsuphasawat, K.S. (2018). Visualizing dataflow graphs of deep learning models in tensorflow. *IEEE Transactions on Visualization and Computer Graphics*: 1–12.

17

Big Data and Artificial Intelligence: Strategies for Leading Business Transformation

17.1 Introduction

The telecommunication industry has become significant over time. It has allowed people around the world to connect, making the sharing of ideas easier. The industry has experienced considerable development and continues to extend into the future, both in hardware and software. The industry plans to make modern advancements in the next five years to change its current operation mode. Some of the major changes that are forecast for the industry include technological advances such as Augmented Reality (AR), fifth generation (5G), Artificial Intelligence (AI), Machine Learning (ML), and cross-industry alliances.

Firstly, telecom's future will see a change in service delivery and an increased competition among the players as telecom companies invest heavily in creating exclusive broadcast content. These companies will look at acquiring such content at a cost or try to own broadcast companies that produce entertainment content. Either way, both approaches will be cost-intensive. Telecom companies will look at diversifying their portfolio as consumers become more demanding and discerning.

Another development that the consumer will enjoy is realizing 5G technology's full powers, which will offer higher-speed connectivity. Telecom companies will use 5G as a revenue growth tool as live streaming and broadcasting become bigger. 5G technology holds the enormous potential of trustworthiness and scalability.

Thirdly, telecom companies will face the HR issue of employee retention vis-a-vis automation. Telecom companies are likely to cut their employee base or go for automation, in which case both options have financial ramifications. Thus, companies have to face either of these options sooner or later.

Fourthly, telecom is propping itself to be ready for AR and virtual reality (VR) advancements in the next few years. AR technology is gaining use in social media and the gaming industry, and more sophisticated applications using AR are likely to come up. Smartphone users will particularly use digital world's changing dynamic stent for social media. The technology will improve efficiency at the workplace, thereby increasing customer satisfaction and experiences. VR technology will help to enhance entertainment and viewer experiences for customers. Consequently, technology development will increase competition among the various telecom service providers, making the customer the winner of this competitive race.

Intelligent Connectivity: AI, IoT, and 5G, First Edition. Abdulrahman Yarali.
© 2022 John Wiley & Sons Ltd. Published 2022 by John Wiley & Sons Ltd.

Fifthly, the telecom industry will continue to face regulatory challenges it currently faces. Various new regulations are likely to come up soon, and these will also have financial implications for the companies. The need to ensure consumer privacy is a key issue that will be of prime concern to the telecoms in the next few years. Therefore, industry players should keep up with the changing trends and adapt accordingly.

The concepts of AI and ML are currently popular. These technologies will continue to advance in the future as back-office operations continue to improve. Speech and voice recognition and customer chatbot technologies are already in use and will continue to advance over the coming years.

The development of in-flight connectivity will act as a game-changer in the airline industry. The development will affect customer service delivery on flights and increase competition among flight companies. However, this technology may be highly susceptible to cyber-attacks and calls for higher security and a content control level.

Lastly, the telecom industry will experience improved customer support through digitization. The industry will develop processes in which a customer's problem will be solved in the shortest time possible. Customer self-service will be crucial, real-time chats will help solve other problems, and only a small fraction of customer problems will be handled through actual voice calls. The aim will be to reduce costs and increase customer satisfaction in the long run.

The telecom industry is experiencing rapid changes due to innovations and the need to satisfy consumers. Telecom companies want to increase consumer satisfaction and thus improve profits. The use of newer technologies will also come at a cost, which the players will have to consider. Adherence to specific standards and security levels will act as a major constraint for the industry. However, if the industry participants can remain proactive, they can adapt to the changing trends easily.

This massive advancement has to lead the foundation of Artificial Intelligence (AI), where machines are used to perform human activities and can be used in place of natural intelligence. AI aims to design robots and machines that can be used instead of humans and animals. They are the set of solution software that have been created to facilitate human beings. AI has created an ecosystem under which all business is operated automatically by adding the instruction to perform the assigned task.

Everyone wants to take advantage of rapid digitalization in the business world in order to remain competitive and always keep themselves ahead. AI has set new milestones to achieve that help decide the future of digital business and aims to add additional value in every industry that helps the business to expand. It is supported by initiatives that include digital production, self-driven cars, risk management, customer engagement, speech recognition, and computer vision (Cearley, Burke, Searle and Walker 2018).

Digital twins help in aiding the business to increase this digitalization incorporation in their business. It is creating more business opportunities to expand globally by taking advantage of this digitalization. These new ways help us adapt to new technology that shows a radical transformation of the business that will lasts for five to ten years. Different platforms that include virtual reality, mixed reality, augmented reality, immersive and natural interactions help to interact with the digital world. However, some security concerns are also present to ensure the safety of data present on clouds.

According to the Gartner survey conducted in 2017, more than 59% of organizations suffer from AI strategies when they integrate them into their business due to lack of a plan and

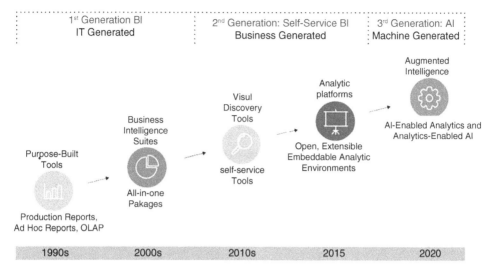

Figure 17.1 The evolution of business intelligence (Eckerson 2018).

knowledge of digital transformation. The market trend on investing in AI strategies has been increasing because they know the digital world's changing dynamics. With the help of AI engineers and data mining scientists, numerous technologies have been designed comprising expert systems, linear regression, decision trees, and neural networks to enable them to slow down so that they can handle a big set of AI (High 2017).

The strategic trends of 2020 revolve around AI. Numerous research projects have been conducted to thoroughly implement the lives of human beings and explore new ways of serving humanity. The widespread AI applications in healthcare, consumer things, flying things, autonomous things, and robot things have revolutionized human lives. A digital twin is the backbone of designing such a system applicable in all industries and enhancing customer experiences. Figure 17.1 shows how AI technology advancements have led us in the right direction by efficiently doing big data analytics.

17.2 Big Data

Big data is an extensive set of data made up of millions of transactions and entries, as well as rules in today's businesses. Due to advancements in technology and recent developments in information technology, there has been a drastic business change. Business is digitalized due to data travel worldwide from one region to another, and increased data usage is easier compared to past years. This data results in big data that is so huge that we need to develop special skills and software to come up with a good outcome (Johnson 2017). There are multiple uses of big data. It depends on us in which direction and in what way we are using it.

Big data is like a huge pile of data that keeps growing at the national and international level due to skyrocketing data consumption by people using this and contributing to this data. On our computer screen, we are doing the work by storing it in the form of different coding.

Hence, these codings combine together in the form of big data (sas.com 2015). The main question is how to use this big data to be useful in decision-making and how we can apply it in different life fields. Unfortunately, this data has not been used in the way it was supposed to be used.

Be that as it may, from 2003 to 2012, the sum stretched around 2.7 ZB (or 2700 Exabytes or 2.7 trillion GB) [sources: Intel and Lund]. As indicated by Berkeley scientists, we are presently delivering approximately five quintillion bytes (or around 4.3 Exabytes) of data every two days [source: Romanov].

The term "big data" is generally used to allude to huge, quickly growing, shifted, and regularly unstructured digitized data arrangements that are hard to keep up utilizing customary databases. It can incorporate all the advanced data gliding around out there in the ether of the internet, the restrictive data of organizations with whom we have worked together, and official government records, among a considerable number of different things. There is additionally the ramifications of the fact that the data is being broken down for some reason.

There are multiple applications of this data that can be utilized in a good way. There is no significant work done on the usage of big data. That is why there is a lack of it. According to recent research, it is evaluated that this data has not been using properly. Only a small portion of it is analyzed and used for constructive patterns.

The term of big data is new in IT. Therefore, not many people know how to use this data to find the trends and analyze them. Big data is the act of gathering data from multiple sources and storing it in one place that can be used in various analyses. Data gathering has been taking place for many generations, but how to use this data, and its purpose, is still ambiguous (Big Data Analytics 2015). Big data gained momentum in 2000 when the industry analyst found its value and wanted to use it for business. According to Doug Laney, this new mainstream data is defined in three ways:

Volume. The volume of big data is huge and comes from multiple sources. The sources where big data is generated are the business exchange, data sensor, online networking sites, and machine-to-machine information (sas.com 2015). Putting all the data in one place is an issue. Therefore, the new advancements in analyzing data facilitate much in this regard. For example, Hadoop is widely used in an analysis of this data.

Velocity. The data that is gathered is compiled at high speed. Its speed is so high that no one can analyze it. For example, radio frequency identification (RFID) labels and sensors are the best examples that show how speedily this data can be managed.

Variety. The data is present in different forms, or we can say that there are multiple channels of information through which this data is generated. This extensive information is present in numeric foam that is extended to an unstructured content. Videos, audios, email, soundtrack, and stock ticker are the budgetary exchange of this data.

Variability. There is variability in data. It means that this data is assorted and conflicting. This data increases due to online networking sites where millions of people transfer their data from one place to another. Hence, we can say that unstructured information is present with this data, which is ambiguous.

Complexity. The data can be very complex, where the common man cannot understand and analyze it. Hence the understanding and implementation of this data are difficult. Therefore, big data software is designed to enable the data to be used in the system. Hence, we can say that big data is so complex that a layman would not be able to use it unless and until software is applied to it. That will tell us how to use it in a different foam based on any specific requirement.

17.2.1 Big Data Need for Organizations

Due to advancements in technology, the ways of doing business have also changed. This means that how the business explores markets is also different. Big data has come to mean a lot to businesses and industries as they came to know about recent trends and preferences of people. Now the data is linked up with one another (sas.com 2015). Just having the concept of big data is not enough for business. Still, they have to learn about the widespread application of data and define how they incorporate this big data in business and maximize benefits.

Big data analysis tools prove to be a great help where different software and analytical tools are used. This software is made up of processing systems and servers, scalable and different technologies. The software that is used for the analysis of big data is Hadoop and NoSQL database. These are specially designed data analysis tools where this large amount of data is analyzed under the real-time window.

There are multiple ways through which this data can be used for the benefit of the business and the benefits are widespread (Belfiore 2016). Some of the advantages of using this data are mentioned below:

- It helps in cost reduction. Hadoop is the latest technology of the big data used to analyze this data and develop reduction methods to reduce cost.
- Hadoop applications on big data are helpful in memory analytics when combined with new sources of data. It helps analyze the available information and makes instant decisions that are safe, reliable, and fruitful.
- Davenport points out that the big data of customer satisfaction can be used in analyzing the needs, want, and demand of customers (Big Data Analytics 2015). This would help companies in developing new and unique products and services according to the need of customers.

The following are tools and technologies used for big data:

- Map Reduce
- Python
- Hadoop
- Pig
- Dryad
- Hadapt
- Scala
- Hive
- NoSQL (Big Data Analytics 2015)

17.2.2 Big Data and Applications

Big data have set a new trend in information technology and other fields of life as well. Now every business is big or large using this big data to achieve excellence in business and remain consistent in the market. Some of the business sectors using big data are given below:

Telecommunication. The telecommunication sector has been booming for the last few years due to the latest trends in mobile phones. Many telecommunication companies have been opened. Also, this communication mode in business highlights the importance of data available through the business sector. According to a recent survey, millions of documents, images, and manuals are passed every minute. Millions of call center agents serve in different regions to solve customer issues (Belfiore 2016). It is also analyzed that $1 is saved on every call. Hence, in this way, millions of dollars are saved every year. Therefore, this sector is the main source of big data used by many businesses to expand their business and maintain direct contact with clients.

Fitness. Big data is not related to customers only for their satisfaction but can also be used for fitness where such apps are designed to make use of calorie data of users and keep records of it to analyze health issues.

Insurance. Insurance companies are using this big data to reduce this claim time from 10 days to 10 minutes. The company is also using this data to save their business from fraud (Belfiore 2016). This big data results in a more customer-centric and profitable company.

Banking. Banks are the ones who are getting the maximum benefit from this data and increase customer engagement and satisfaction. According to a survey, it has been analyzed that it increases customers' participation from 40 to 92%. Customers can sign in to the bank app and pay their bills and allocate their investment wherever they want. There is no need to go to the bank.

Banks and other monetary establishments have approved the use of Artificial Intelligence (AI), which can have a huge effect on business and trade in financial business. Many significant banks worldwide have actualized these developing advancements to use these incredible assets for their compelling tasks. The advances have been fruitful in the value capital market and help associations to upgrade their hierarchical structure. The execution of simulated intelligence in banking helped in installment endeavors and decreased complex procedures through basic chatbot discussions to proceed with the tasks. Some progressive banks likewise have utilized the simulated intelligence innovation in smart menial helpers to improve their client administrations. Simultaneously, some money-related foundations have been utilizing measures to avert extortion and screen potential dangers to clients in trade.

Astronomy. We will take a look at the sky and attempt to discover the appropriate responses concerning the most perplexing subject, which is space science. Until now, science has progressed to a specific dimension, and researchers are taking care of the business of addressing each question identified with the universe. In any case, not every one of the inquiries, as we are probably aware of our impediments, concerning simulated intelligence could assist us with dealing with the restrictions. From an examination distributed in a diary month by month in Notification of the Imperial Galactic Culture, specialists demonstrate that human-made brainpower estimations can make more precise forecasts than people can about the long-haul security of other planets. The innovation could help us understand our whole universe and how it functions. This procedure could give the best tips to humankind to comprehend their very own cause.

Construction. It is correct to state that the development division of construction will gain an advantage by using computer-based intelligence or AI. AI-based applications have been broadly utilized in the development segments. Simulated intelligence could propose the perfect structure and prescribe the best highlights to make our lives progressively secure. The computer-based intelligence will likewise help in hazard relief as it comprehends the intricate language and is adept at fixing any issues. The AI-based application will make the architects progressively gainful and equipped for conveying amazing work in the stipulated period. Moreover, the innovation will be valuable in dissecting the work and the procedure of the development business.

Agriculture. Horticulture is one of the central parts of this technology, and we have been changing the development procedure to yield more from it. There are tremendous ways for human-made intelligence or AI to be used in farming. Yet the execution of innovation is the most unpredictable part in industries like farming. The advancements in human-made intelligence and IoT will be exceptionally valuable in understanding auspicious planting, getting forecasts, utilizing manures, collecting, and the atmosphere. Mechanization of cultivating exercises is conceivable with the usage of the advancements like computer-based intelligence and IoT. Ranchers need to adjust to the new advances to actualize and get the most yield from their fields.

Sports. The execution of human-made reasoning in the games business is a distinct advantage and is unquestionably going to change the game world. The trend-setting innovation will make the games all the more fascinating and help competitors to go past the ability to rehearse and get the best out of them. There has been a colossal interest in simulated intelligence-based applications in the games business as it has noteworthy abilities. The execution of the innovation is positively going to illuminate many real changes in the game world and could bring a genuine challenge to the players and competitors.

Entertainment. Computer-based intelligence or AI has acquired a major change in media outlets. Generally, we can use the media when we need it, where we need it, and how we need it because of the rising innovations. AI is everywhere and is having a major effect on our lives. With regards to amusement, the calculations being utilized by different applications make our lives less difficult. AI has truly changed media outlets and will make it all the more inviting in the days to come.

Education. It is the most imperative and tremendous area that touches each life, paying little heed to age. AI-based arrangements have been helping understudies and instructors at different levels. AI makes our training framework more brilliant and simulated intelligence and synergistic virtual systems are being utilized to make an ideal learning condition for understudies just as educators. Simulated intelligence and developing advances have been making an appropriate mix of learning environments. Twenty-first century homerooms are outfitted with rising innovation answers for conveying the best learning conditions to understudies.

E-Commerce. Web-based business is generally a clamoring portion of the retail business. Real internet business organizations have been utilizing cutting edge innovations like human-made intelligence or AI. The effect of the usage is unmistakably obvious in a web-based business space. Organizations utilize human-made intelligence, AI associates, savvy coordination, and calculations to anticipate and dissect clients' practices. AI-based applications are being actualized to expand the showcasing technique. Mechanization developed as the way to powerful distribution center activities and the innovation has helped numerous organizations to accomplish conveyance productivity. The definitive point is to diminish shipping costs. AI helps organizations to achieve sought-after anticipation, item look positioning, item and arrangements proposals, promotion of situations, extortion locations, interpretations, and substantially more.

Marketing and sales. Advertising should be proficient and constantly dynamic with their leads and prospects and take advantage of every opportunity that presents itself. Recently, SMEs have been additionally receiving some type of AI or AI-based applications in their business. Two advancements – AI and prescient knowledge – have helped business groups to meet their objective and manage the most important and qualified leads. The execution of computer-based intelligence or AI will help organizations to utilize their profitable time and cost effectively in diverse phases of the client lifecycle. The applications could help them lead in both B2B and B2C.

17.3 Machine Learning-Based Medical Systems

The benefits of information technology are not limited to the development of new technologies for the amazement and entertainment of people. The widespread application of information technology in healthcare has facilitated the provision of the best healthcare practices for patients. It has created ease for doctors and healthcare providers as well, where they can deeply diagnose the problem and then treat it. In the past few decades, the recent development in information technology under the healthcare domain helps doctors diagnose those diseases that have been impossible or difficult to treat in the past. Hence, we can say that it has improved the survival rate of patients. The information technology development is not limited only to the development of machines that will provide testing and treatment, but healthcare software, data retrieval, and management helps in providing a huge amount of big data so that by merely clicking on desired options, we can get the desired data. It also helps in maintaining the data of patients for proving better healthcare. The use of AI and the incorporation of the ML-based system has completely altered healthcare services.

AI is used in healthcare, where doctors and medical staff are considered important for providing quality services. "Medical artificial intelligence, data mining, expert's system, ML along with image processing are used extensively for clinical diagnosis that suggests treatments. Several artificial intelligent approaches that are exploited in informatics technology and application help provide better healthcare services" (Bates 2006).

With the power of cognitive computing of big data and AI advancement, AI helps in overcoming communication barriers. After thoroughly searching for different journals in order to find an article related to AI communication, David W. Bates and his co-authors described the use of AI in communicating medical records of a patient in the Harvard Business Review (Bates 2006). In this article, the author described the difficulty in communicating a patient's records from one hospital to another as it requires a lot of time, which is a loss to both the hospital and patient. Sometimes, this data is so critical that timely delivery is important for saving the patient's life. Hence, he states that it is essential to incorporate digital technology in healthcare so that timely delivery of reports through this communication channel can be made easy (Bates 2006).

Furthermore, it helps in enhancing the delivery of better healthcare services. It is analyzed from the article that although the incorporation of information technology in healthcare is expensive for the hospital with time, it helps in saving costs and efforts of the doctors and can be utilized for different purposes. This AI will help maintain the data of a patient in a sequential way and maintains his or her records. When anyone needs this record, it will be easily available rather than physically accessing all the files for many hours to get the required information. Hence, the installation of this ML is a one-time expense that will save other expenses.

AI is useful in healthcare. The findings of Sukel (2017) are interesting and so it is important to incorporate his findings on AI in healthcare and its uses. Sukel has given negative reviews because he believes first that the relationship between the physician or the doctor must be established to provide the best healthcare services without incorporating AI and ML. However, this chapter focuses on how doctors are benefitting from AI, along with medical diagnostic application apps for the diagnosis of diseases by the British National Health Service.

With the inclusion of this technology, doctors can easily diagnose diseases and prescribe the treatment. This also helps in lowering errors as it helps to lessen the ratios of unnecessary deaths. However, the reviews of Sukel on this issue are different. He states that underperforming doctors will easily use these apps to treat patients; however, the chances of error are most likely to occur due to lack of knowledge of doctors in particular who would not be able to ensure whether the app was giving accurate results or not. From the doctors' perspective, however, they state that this AI and ML help them to do their duties with more efficiency and less effort. With AI, the patients' big data can easily be managed as a 10-year-old record can be found within seconds. Restorative human-made consciousness, information mining, a master framework, and AI alongside a picture can be prepared for utilizing a clinical conclusion that proposes what medicines to prescribe. A few counterfeit wise methodologies misused in informatics innovation and application help to give better human services administration.

AI can only be used in monitoring medical records and updating the data of patients. Still, it is surprising that AI can also diagnose those diseases that could not be detected before using this technology. Hence, Temming shares findings in her paper in the *Journal of Math and Technology*, which states that "Computers can diagnose eye problems." In this article, the author elaborates on how AI algorithms can be used to diagnose eye diseases. Under the Food and Drug Administration of the US, those artificial intelligence programs are implemented to help diagnose critical health issues (Temming 2018). The extensive use of IDX–DR (a software for diabetic retinopathy) in healthcare helps to analyze the data of one million eyes and also helps to identify the symptoms of diabetic retinopathy. From this article, it was found that this AI algorithm will help to provide fast treatments to patients.

In his article, Duncan shares very interesting information regarding Chinese scientists' inventions using unique technology. With the help of a computer screen and a mirror, they made AI software with the name ICX, that is iCrabonX; it will analyze the internal position of the body that ranges from the temperature of the body, pulse rate, DNA, and various viral enzymes, and many more things (Duncan 2017). He developed a kind of personalized device that will help monitor the internal situation and helps to detect early signs of disease. This is a kind of personalized medicine that helps in treating disease.

In her research, Hall states that AI is the major step that will bring revolution in medicine. She stated that AI is like a human mind that can take critical decisions by thoroughly analyzing the situation and the consequences and benefits of those decisions (Hall 2016). She states that AI is a complete software that can be used to monitor personalized medicine. It depends on us how we can take maximum benefits from it.

17.4 Artificial Intelligence for Stock Market Predictions

The stock market is where company stock and financial instruments of the capital and money market are traded. The stock market has a great impact on the economy of a company. Stock markets have positive and negative effects on the economy. If the stock market is stable, then the economy is considered strong and hence we can say that the stock market directly relates to the economy. For smooth functioning of this market, it is essential to reinvest in this market. Therefore, from time to time, predictions for investment in the stock market are important.

A stock market prediction is a well-defined term that must be understood first before investing in the stock market. A stock market prediction is an act through which we define the future value of a company's stock or the traded financial instruments. If the prediction of the stock is successful, then it results in significant profits. A stock market prediction is not an easy job as it is a detailed analysis of a stock market hypothesis given as a technical analysis of stock market factors that predict the future stock market (Laszlo Gerencser 2000). Historically, theories of the stock market are considered to be a strong point for stock market prediction. Social media instruments are also revealing strong support for predicting the stock market.

AI in stock trading refers to the use of artificial techniques to predict the stock market. These include AI, like computers, laptops, and software specially designed for prediction. This software has the capacity to think like a person or make decisions. The world around us is now very dependent on artificial things. Therefore, implementation of this AI is a good addition to stock market predictions (Kim 2000).

We create technology and machines, and it is now considered an essential part of humanity. The intention of creating this technology and machines is to serve humanity and make life easy for them. The field of computer science is extended so far that its multiple applications serve us in many different ways.

AI is a branch of computer science. This intelligence function is to perform tasks assigned to them as humans; therefore, they are specially designed like the human brain. There are multiple functions that these machines perform, like audio and visual recognition, decision making, and computation. AI is further divided into subtypes. One is ML (Kuo, Chen and Hwang 2001). Under ML, multiple layers are composed that interpret the input with the output. Amazon, Google, and Yahoo currently use this system to save their users from fraud. Big companies are using it for their benefit through which they can save on labor costs. Figure 17.2 shows a schematic diagram of the AI working process.

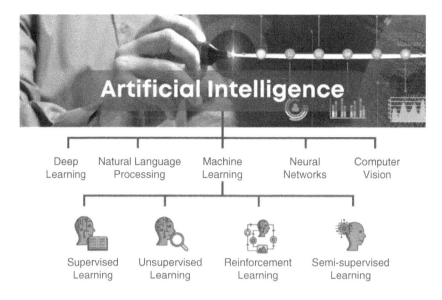

Figure 17.2 Working of the AI system (Kurzweil 2016).

However, the important question is how we can use these systems for our personal use. Early in 1965, Alexey Grigorevich Ivakhnenko revised this Deep Learning (DL) and developed a DL algorithm theory. Under this algorithm, multiple layers all join together and are connected to different layers from each layer data that is received to produce intended results (Boyacioglu and Avci 2010).

17.4.1 Application of Artificial Intelligence by Investors

Investors continuously use this system so that they can secure their investments. Investors use this system to put large data in a summary that gives them a complete picture of the past, present, and future stock market. The advancement in the algorithm or AI accounts for 60 to 70% of the whole stock market. Along with the traditional analysis, these are used by professionals and retailers (Kim 2000). Algorithmic methods are used by traders for their analysis and as a second choice while making decisions. These AI structures analyze the trends in the market. Predictable patterns are present that are derived by machines; machine forecasted decisions are then displayed to investors.

Every algorithm predicts market dynamics. They are based on AI and ML and certain genetic algorithms and neural networks. ML mainly shows the results of market dynamics. Combining an algorithm that develops in ML statistically analyzes the share price and predicts future prices. This AI predicts about approximately 1400 assets and predicts the multidimensional stock's future trajectory (Op 1999).

These AI predictions are so accurate that the return on this investment is 66.66%, beating the S&P 500 by 30%. This system is improving with time and continues beating the S&P 500 throughout the year. From the graphs in Figure 17.3, we can see that AI software predictions are very close to market stock prices.

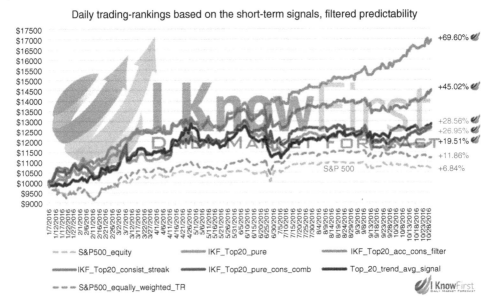

Figure 17.3 AI predictions (Kurzweil 2016).

17.5   Trends in AI and Big Data Technologies Drive Business Innovation

Programming and web advancement organizations nowadays, particularly those in Australia, convey innovation and development to clients wherever they might be situated on the planet. The two most famous innovation advancements are Huge Information and Artificial Intelligence (AI). Specialist organizations utilize these most innovating patterns to keep pace with the extreme challenge and furnish customers with exceedingly powerful and dynamic arrangements.

At the crossing point of shrewd innovation and investigation, organizations are starting to understand the hotly anticipated advantages of computerized reasoning. Following quite a time of guarantees and expectation, this might be when AI increases a significant footing inside Fortune 1000 associations. A mind-boggling 97.2% of administrators report that their associations are putting resources into making or propelling huge information and computer-based intelligence activities. Among the administrators, a rising accord is that huge amounts of information and artificial reasoning activities are becoming intently interlaced, with 76.5% of officials showing that the more noteworthy accessibility of information and expansion is enabling simulated intelligence and intellectual activities inside their undertakings.

Presently, administrators see an immediate connection between AI activities and huge information capacities. Out of the blue, gigantic companies report directly to be accessing significant sources and volumes of information, which could sustain computer-based intelligence calculations to obtain practices and distinguish designs. Not being subject to information subsets to do investigations, these associations join enormous information, processing forces, and computer-based intelligence calculations to deliver a variety of business benefit structures to provide continuous shopper credit endorsements to new item contributions. Associations like Morgan Stanley and American Express have recently freely shared their examples of overcoming adversity.

As expressed by the "Gushing Investigation Market by Verticals – Overall Market Figure and Examination (2015–2020)" report, the continuous examination was anticipated to watch a normal yearly development of 31.3% somewhere in this time range, which appears to be approaching this.

The term big data will unobtrusively leave its universe. Even though it has expansive importance, without other input, it will not continue. Like IT, enormous information is a term that incorporates a great deal in the brains of individuals to truly have a careful significance aside from saying to individuals who realize very little to clarify that "I work in huge information." There is an incredible number of components arranged under enormous information from AI and information gathering, investigation, and information security, none of which truly need anything to do with one another, yet are as yet sorted as "large information." Indeed, you will even find that those who do not connect with huge information are likewise monitoring these zones. The explanations for this are simply the hacks, mechanical technology, driving autos, and hordes of other information-driven advancements. From this, we can assess that the utilization of enormous amounts of information will not be out at any time soon.

Benjamin Franklin appropriately cited that "In this world, nothing can be said to be sure, aside from death and assessments"; however, in 2020, we can include "enormous hacks will affect organizations."

Over the last three years, eight of the best 10 hacks have effectively occurred, with no incident. You may see that information security shows signs of improvement. Yet, the improvement in information security is working practically parallel with the upgraded ability of the individuals who are making further attempts to take it. We can relate that hacks are taking the expanding measure of information. The more information there is, the more attacks there will be. Taking the genuine size of Uber hacks and its cover-up, which are yet to be exposed, an announcement clarified that around 57 million records were separated. The organization needed to pay $100 000 to keep the programmers calm and keep up the market mystery.

This situation is turning into a dread, which is exacerbating things more. As expressed before, the explanation is that more information is gathered. The organizations are compelled to pay more to the programmers to get their information open or prevent it from being uncovered. There has been a huge spike in the sum remunerated by organizations to the programmers as ransomware compared with previous years. In the meantime, some extremely uncommon individuals are captured for hacking. Suppose there is an expansion in the reward given for hacking and a next to no possibility of being obtained; then, in that case, the general population will accept it as an open door and will take a stab at rehearsing this action all the more regularly.

17.5.1 Driving Innovation Through Big Data

In the enormous information world, where developing volumes of data from a greater assortment of sources are made at consistently developing speeds, the unenviable test to those ordering data is to completely value the greater use of the arrangements of information they hold. Genuinely, those creations or order information are not all the time wagered puts in deciding its most stretched out applications.

It may not be amazing that the promoting and deals executives of BMW at the North American Universal Car Expo uncovered a significant number of solicitations to utilize the ordered information of its vehicle; however, these solicitations were normally declined. This may have been incited by security concerns and conceivable unintended results of giving open client information to outsiders, where it could be helpless against undesirable introductions.

While uncertain security is critical for an extensive information investigation, any discount dismissal makes information progressively accessible on the grounds of protection dangers, disregarding the inborn incentive for pioneers. It ought to be recollected that protection issues emerge to such a degree that individual data is included. Businesses must concentrate on the quality and nature of the information caught. An appraisal should be made at the start regarding whether it is carefully essential for information that has an individual quality to it to be ordered.

17.5.2 The Convergence of AI and Big Data

Big data is a term used to describe datasets that are so large and complex that it is now difficult to process using traditional standard statistical and data processing software and applications. Big data has attracted the attention and has become a very important component for many scientific research segments, for instance, in the chemistry, biology, medical, physics, and astronomical divisions. The data sets are larger now than they were before because, at present, more and more data are unstructured, and complex data comes from numerous new sources comprised of social media (Facebook, Twitter), email (Yahoo, Gmail, Hotmail), and others. The businesses that tend to make increasing use of big data are primarily located in well-developed countries. After that, there are billions of mobile phone users, more data in the cloud, and billions of users accessing the internet worldwide. These developed countries have the capacity and technology to provide a larger dataset. The telecommunications network capability to exchange data has grown exponentially from petabytes in the early 1980s. The flow of data over the internet has been way over being Exabytes at present.

For businesses in various industries and even in academic institutions, big data is expanding the cloud infrastructure, platform, and applications to represent the best data and to deliver the data in order to allow subscribers to have better decision-making and action. Big data characteristics make it look attractive and seen as beneficial for use in conjunction with cloud computing within businesses.

Cloud computing technology offers flexibility to businesses in terms of services and efficiency in using resources that can be cost-effective to businesses, especially to startup, smaller, and medium-sized businesses. They can save costs by using the pay-as-you-go models for testing purposes. Primarily, it all comes down to the issue of security; if the subscribers do not understand the models or types of clouds to implement properly, it may hurt their business. When a certain purpose or capability such as security is required, but is not provided within the paid service (IaaS, PaaS, or SaaS), the subscriber must converse with the cloud service provider and reach an agreement on the particulars of the level of service. The subscriber has to be aware that there are limitations for each cloud computing service model to prevent any form of misplaced expectation towards the cloud service providers. The threats and disadvantages of cloud computing must also always be considered. The business confidential and non-confidential data is stored on a system that does not belong to the business.

On the other hand, the application of cloud computing services within large organizations can also be adapted to count the benefits, firstly, within a small business segment to monitor any positive results from the service. Secondly, larger organizations can also invest in more complex developed application projects globally, but the same security concerns also apply to larger organizations. The subscribers have to place some level of trust towards the cloud service provider. Preferably, the cloud service provider must have some form of reputable background and recognition from various well-known institutions for a business to place trust in it.

Cloud computing is growing and continues to grow at present as big data increases at an accelerated rate per year. Big data and cloud computing are interrelated as each one intensifies the other's capabilities. Regarding businesses, the availability of the data stored is massive. Hence cloud computing came into play to take advantage of this pool of resources. Figure 17.4 depicts the role of big data and AI in the business world (Verma 2018).

The union of human-made intelligence and huge information rises as the absolute most vital advancement molding the eventual fate of how organizations drive business esteem structure their information just as examination capacities. The accessibility of more noteworthy sources and volumes of information gives abilities access to simulated intelligence and AI, which stayed lethargic for quite a long time in light of the absence of accessible information, constrained example sizes, and failure to examine huge information sums in milliseconds. Computerized abilities moved information from cluster to ongoing, constantly accessible online access.

While a great deal of simulated intelligence advances has been around for a considerable length of time, it is solitary since they can exploit adequate size for important outcomes and

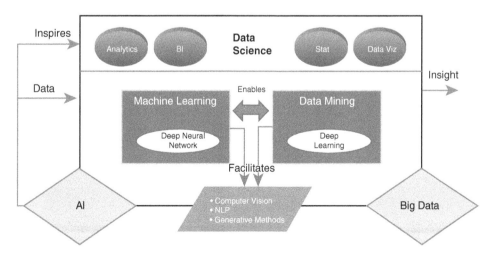

Figure 17.4 Transformation of business data with AI-powered business intelligence systems (Verma 2018).

learning. The capacity of getting to enormous information volumes with prepared access and deftness is prompting a quick advancement in the utilization of AI and computer-based intelligence applications. Enormous amounts of information allow a situation that supports the revelation of information using emphasis. Accordingly, organizations could test more, move rapidly, and adapt quicker.

17.5.3 How AI and Big Data Will Combine to Create Business Innovation

Large-scale data analysis. A simulated intelligence framework can be utilized to peruse huge amounts of information at lightning speed. Think about the unlimited outcomes produced by a solitary Google look with a significant inquiry instead of putting in several worker hours at a library. Computer-based intelligence enables organizations to rapidly discover the open doors in their business forms and proceed onward to distinguishing arrangements quickly. Google's hunt item could be the most exceptional human-made reasoning framework on the planet right now. Ordering whatever number of information focuses on you would be prudent and utilizing them to recognize the correct substance on the web would fulfill your pursuit expectation. Google's whole plan of action relies upon helping you discover data rapidly and precisely. Figure 17.5 depicts the relationship between AI solutions with big data, algorithms, and hardware.

Improved basic leadership. One thing each business will concur upon is that great data is reasonable. Firms lose a large number of dollars each equitable by neglecting to follow up on data. As a general rule, this stems from the data not being promptly accessible. Since AI is insider savvy, such data will be promptly accessible to officials to settle on a quicker choice. In a perfect world, basic leadership is completely improved – for instance, when you shop at Amazon, and they propose that "individuals like you" purchased "things like this," this kind of suggestion depends on AI investigations of comparable shopping practices and what those individuals purchased. Customers are given a

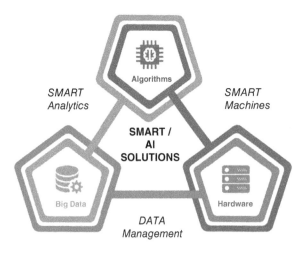

Figure 17.5 Artificial Intelligence solutions as the interplay of three central components (Foster & Company n.d.).

superior web-based business experience, the business sells more items, and the entire event is done naturally, utilizing computer-based intelligence.

Improvement in product development. By distinguishing market patterns and implicit client needs from the advanced communication logs they create, collaborating with organizations is, maybe, the most critical part of enormous information. For instance, Netflix broadly tracks the demonstrations its clients watch, which they observe repeatedly, the amount they are "marathon watched," and the majority of that data that they utilize in order to decide the following project they are going to make. For instance, Cards' place has grown absolutely on the investigation of this kind of information log.

17.5.4 AI and Big Data for Technological Innovation

The most important factors for increasing AI are the limit and the driving force, the data, and the algorithms. The execution and the limit of the processors have been completely extended. Today, there is a huge amount of data about the atmosphere, online networks, and medicines, and machines can eventually use that data. In the meantime, data storage costs for executives and improved data storage have led to the faster investigation of a large amount of data. There are two types of AI: subtle AI and general AI. Incoming AI can solve a problem, such as detecting malignant growth through artificial vision, classifying home and business registers, and responding to customers' direct questions. For all purposes, all current AI is regulated. General AI is confronted with several problems, for example, driving, dialects, and cooking. No general intelligence has yet been created, but AI experts differ in the speed with which they become a reality (Tekoäly 2018).

17.5.5 Disruptive Innovation

Innovation requests comparable aptitudes to deal with existing conditions and new apparatus and a new taskforce. The inundation of increasingly logical inclusion expects to change how tasks are completed. Likewise, a tremendous change accordingly requests a period longer than anticipated to make a move. Subsequently, it is a disturbance in the prior ordinary everyday practice. How far and to what degree it is in support can be contended.

17.6 Advancements and New Entries

As we watch non-stop progressions in huge information, at the comparative size, we can likewise watch an ever-increasing number of undertakings entering the market instead of an extension to embrace innovations when they enter. Enormous information is not new to any business, simply that its examination and administration is pivotal and requires consolation. In any case, taking off dimensions of the piece in this field paints the canvas as requested. Advantages of enormous information are ceaselessly welcoming more organizations under the umbrella, expanding the network of huge information in the end. Here, the major mechanical change is a developing, technically knowledgeable market hungry for the investigation to deal with the new innovations.

17.6.1 Recruitment of a Skilled Taskforce

Adequate necessities emerging with enormous information examination bring mechanical progressions and make a colossal vacuum in the taskforce proper for the ability required to deal with it. There are plenty of employments looking for a substitution and many others looking for new participants. As it is a human intercession, a gifted information examiner is significant despite the fact that the innovation is changing and bringing new changes. Jobs and obligations of newcomers are in this way settled based on how huge information should be overseen. Abilities become the main factor here, first of the examiner and after that of the venture. Such high prerequisites place an inbuilt channel and, consequently, the best of the parcel is delegated with such duty. This therefore raises the challenge levels in this manner, making more space for advancement.

17.6.2 Reliable Performance

The market has made another territory and has influenced individuals to acknowledge enormous information examination and its developments attributable to its unwavering quality and consistent usefulness. The energetic execution that puts the required outcomes investigated by the administration of information by talented experts helps in business insight and increases the client trust in the meantime. As and when a firm extends the measure of information, the execution considers pay. It would have been a Titanic assignment to sort out such enormous information on the off-chance that it would not become a huge information investigation. Awed by the productivity and execution, an abundant number of endeavors settled on a huge information investigation, making an influx of impact-driven mechanical headways.

Concluding the uses of big data in a nutshell, it is pertinent to mention that big data has completely altered the way of doing business. Hence the widespread application of big data helps many business people remain successful in the market and take advantage of others who do not take advantage of it. Therefore, many businesses nowadays, whether they are providing and public, are taking advantage of it. This big data has also made the job easy for marketers. Now they provide ample information for a new business startup.

Based on the research findings, it is pertinent to mention that AI and ML are a blessing for healthcare to provide the best healthcare services to a patient. It helps in providing quality services and ensures patient safety as well. It helps in performing the duties of doctors and lessens the burden for doctors as well. Hence, they will be able to treat the patients better. The hospitals must incorporate this technology for the best healthcare services that every patient needs from the analysis of these articles.

By summarizing the results of finding the role of AI in the stock market, it is observed that neural networks in AI consider both quantitative and qualitative factors while making predictions. In a traditional prediction, only qualitative factors are analyzed, but, under AI, it becomes convenient for investors to predict an outcome by keeping in view all the factors. In buying and selling performance, their prediction proves to be more accurate.

17.7   AI and Production

Production of goods through manufacturing is the cornerstone of the economic development of different countries. Efforts towards continuously innovating in the sector have always ensured that the manufacturing sector takes advantage of new and emerging technologies to make the systems better and more effective in producing goods as desired by the consumers. The roots of industrial manufacturing go back to the industrial revolution. At the beginning of the twentieth century, mass production became entrenched. Using machine tools became a field where the company with the best-optimized tool would have an advantage over the competitors (Nguyen and Chan 2006). Since the introduction of machine tools in mass production, newer technologies have been integrated into the processes, including numerical control systems, flexible manufacturing, and computer integrated manufacturing. The advances have ensured scientific systemization of the processes while giving proper dissemination of information for advanced analysis and control. Operation research over the years has focused on the improvement of the systems with an increased emphasis on enhancing manufacturing for economic growth. In the recent past, manufacturing has embraced AI and ML tools to exhibit human intelligence and behavior characteristics. The deployment of artificial intelligence in production will help the manufacturing processes make independent decisions on complex algorithms associated with human intelligence.

More than at any other time, the manufacturing industry is experiencing an increase in data-driven processes that consist of various formats informing on the quality, semantics, and formats of the processes. Sensor data in the production lines, machine tool parameters, environmental data, and processes data inform the production decisions across different manufacturing processes. Different names have been floated to explain how the manufacturing processes are data-driven, including smart manufacturing, smart factory, industry 4.0, and intelligent manufacturing. The increase of large amounts of data in the production processes, like in other spheres in modern life, is largely regarded as big data (Kersting and Meyer 2018). The availability of such big data offers the potential to increase production quantities while maintaining quality and ensuring sustainable production. Even as information can help the production processes, there is also a likelihood that it can pose a challenge to the processes by distracting from the main role or offer wrong conclusions concerning the appropriateness of desired actions. For the manufacturing industry to benefit from the increased availability of data, quality improvement initiatives, cost estimation, and process optimization have to be refined to allow for a more consistent application of the inputs while getting the desired output. A better understanding of the consumer requirement, for example, would be integrated into the decision-making processes and refined in a way that ensures that the end product reflects consumer choices while maintaining the quality of the end product. High dimensionality, complexity, and integration of all the dynamics involved would emerge from data-driven processes.

The developments emerging from mathematics and computer-driven processes have allowed the industry to benefit from easy-to-use and at times freely available software tools that offer great potential of transforming the manufacturing processes sustainably. Emerging from the most exciting development is the concept of ML that has included data mining, knowledge discovery that has, in turn, informed AI (Bratko 1993). The field of ML is wide and diverse, incorporating different theories, methods, and algorithms. For many practitioners in the manufacturing industry, the diversity represented by ML presents a barrier to adopting the systems, hindering the wide deployment that would benefit the systems. In exploring the diversity represented by AI systems, work will proceed towards expounding on:

- The essence of the appropriateness and applicability of machine ML in industrial processes from the manufacturing perspective.
- The introduction of different terminology used in diverse fields covered in AI.
- Presenting an overview concerning different areas of ML and, where applicable, propose the right structuring mechanisms.
- Providing a high level of understanding concerning the benefits and drawbacks of adopting certain methods in the production processes.
- The necessity of different processes in improving manufacturing through AI.

17.7.1   Methodology

AI encompasses a diverse field of application leading to situations where its definitions are largely intertwined. However, AI is projected as the dynamic learning system that allows for better decision making and applications across a wide range of industrial processes. Manufacturing equally is a broad field encompassing the production of commodities ranging from automobiles, agricultural equipment, electronics, and the textile sector. Here the focus is not on any specific industry but on the incorporation of the "brain-related" algorithm to help in the production processes. Therefore, the literature reviewed has included a wide range of intelligent systems in the manufacturing processes that embraces system robotics, natural language processing, ML, computer vision, smart factory, neural networks, and automation based on varying inputs.

17.8   AI and ML Operations Research

While traditional operation research focused on optimizing the processes, AI in manufacturing has leaned on offering satisfaction and generating solutions acceptable to decision-makers across a different range of manufacturing processes. AI in manufacturing has come a long way since adopting ML tools in the 1950s. Although AI, ML, and operations research interrelate, they represent different aspects of using the processes to improve the product.

ML has emerged from the neural networks fashioned to learn from the human brain concerning different production processes. In the brain, nerve cell interaction helps store information that informs in the making of low-level decisions, including the determination of the rate of breathing, body temperature, heartbeat, satiety, and wakefulness (Wiegerinck 2003). Advances in technology have focused on implementing decision-making processes that would imitate the human brain in the production processes, allowing for changes in the outputs when there is a variance in the inputs.

AI is broader than ML and includes aspects regarded as complex in the ML processes. In AI, the systems are optimized to learn inputs like natural languages, such as speech and text, and, in turn, are expected to interpret while offering solutions like human recognition from spoken words. This would allow for granting access to different systems based on recognition of speech patterns and associating the spoken words to an individual (Bishop 2016). In AI, the systems would be optimized to deconstruct speech patterns to recognize emotions, humor, irony, and aspects like laughter and expletives. AI integrates structured data processing and unstructured data processing to develop the desired solutions as expected by the users. Using AI would allow the system to recognize patterns within structured or unstructured data, resulting in instances where the system can match aspects like unstructured data from random images and videos.

Operation research, on the other hand, is optimized towards improving operations in real-world scenarios. Operation research analysts use mathematical modeling to solve problems that may arise out of the production processes. Real-world scenarios are simulated beforehand, and programmers develop the right modeling to solve issues that would realistically happen. The analysis of large problems requires simulations that help model the right output based on the input in place.

17.8.1 Smart Maintenance

Maintenance of the production lines in an industrial setting is an important element representing a major expense to the plants involved. Unplanned maintenance of equipment in production lines has been estimated to cost industries billions of dollars every year as equipment breaks down, leading to the restructuring of the production processes and a halt to the production while awaiting maintenance. Incorporating artificial intelligence into the production processes by using predictive maintenance algorithms eases the processes as it allows those in decision-making positions to make predictions and schedule for maintenance. When the technology is in place running along with the different machines in the production processes, there is a drastic reduction in the downtimes since the embedded neural networks continually provide information concerning the remaining useful life of the different parts. When maintenance cannot be avoided, a shutdown would be needed; the exercise is optimized to allow for minimal disruption in the production processes. If a plant or parts of production are to be serviced in a week, for example, the production preceding the maintenance period would be increased to cater for the period that the machines would not be running. Equally, planning allows for mobilizing the right technicians to undertake the task, resulting in a minimal time when the machines would be decommissioned.

17.8.2 Intelligent Manufacturing

Smart manufacturing or intelligent manufacturing encompasses a broad concept in manufacturing where advanced information informs product transactions and optimal production. The life cycle of the whole production process is integrated to allow for the variation of the processes based on input data and information. Different sensors in the production process inform aspects like product quality and make subsequent decisions based on the need to correct or enhance the processes. Intelligent manufacturing, therefore, would imply the combined intelligence of processes, people, and machines aimed at impacting the economics of the production process. The purpose of intelligent manufacturing is to optimize the manufacturing resources to improve the product and reduce the wastage of critical resources (Edwards, Holt, and Robinson 2002). Consumers demand quality at all times. Through smart manufacturing, the production processes would use available data to vary the production lines and allow for consumer specific modeling of the desired quality and expectations.

Manufacturers in the automotive industry, construction, agriculture, and heavy truck industries rely on intelligence manufacturing systems to optimize the systems and allow data to inform the processes. Through intelligent manufacturing, integration of a product's life cycle is made possible, allowing the people in charge to make decisions that affect the final product.

17.8.3 IoT-Enabled Manufacturing

Manufacturing processes have been taken a notch higher above smart manufacturing by incorporating sensors that allow the process to benefit from human-like intervention through smart manufacturing objects (SMOs). The SMOs help sense the inputs, communicate with each other, and vary the processes based on the desired outcome. Carrying out the manufacturing logic requires constant tinkering with the processes to ensure that the end product conforms to the production process's expectations. With the incorporation of the IoT (see Figure 17.6), decisions can be made on the spot through the constant monitoring of sensors, allowing human to human, human to machine, and machine to machine communications that play a part in determining how the resources would be shared. The application of IoT in manufacturing allows for close monitoring of the processes. The system can intervene and change through data sharing and analysis consistent with the cutting-edge technology that seeks to acquire and share data to inform subsequent systems. Equally, IoT enabled manufacturing processes to have the real-time data collection capacity that allows for sharing the information concerning tasks, workers, material, and percentages of the

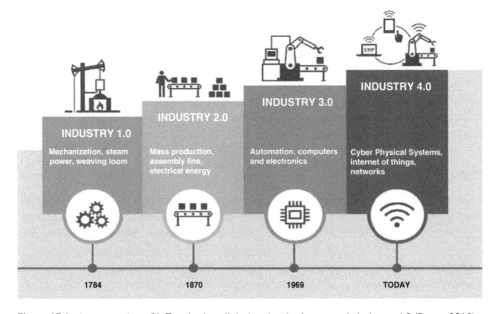

Figure 17.6 Incorporation of IoT and other digital technologies towards industry 4.0 (Dyson 2018).

tasks, thus enabling the floor managers to deploy and redeploy workers based on the areas where they are needed the most. Using radio frequency identification and wireless communications, the systems closely update different ends of the process allowing for decisions to be made on the spot. The materials' physical movement can be followed across the system, allowing for traceability and determination of different parameters across warehouses and production floors. Integrating the warehouse floor with the production would allow for a variation in the units produced based on the numbers moving towards the market.

The internet has impacted the production processes in real-time using embedded chips and RFID technology in real-time production management. The RFID helps the Loncin Motorcycle Company, for example, to collect real-time data on raw materials and work-in-progress in a way that informs trackability and traceability across the production lines. Rather than buy the raw materials in bulk and wait for them to be used effectively in the production process, companies use a combination of IoT and just-in-time inventory processes, allowing for a minimal investment in dead stocks in terms of raw materials.

17.8.4 Cloud Manufacturing

Under the support of cloud computing, cloud manufacturing refers to a model that uses advanced computing systems to virtualize the production processes transforming manufacturing into a service that can be shared and used across different platforms. Cloud manufacturing encompasses extended lifecycles of products in all the steps, including design, simulation, and maintenance, creating a parallel network system that uses intelligence to drive the processes. Thriving in today's society and global market requires optimizing the bulk of the production processes as competitors can have a competitive edge if they were to put in more efficient place systems. In a cut-throat competitive industry like the ones meeting global demands, adopting the wrong approach may be the difference between emerging the winner in reducing costs or the company bogged down by bulky processes. Therefore, companies are opting to use the available data in the systems to drive the processes and make optimal production decisions. In the era of big data, AI is proving a hit for the manufacturers who have become producers of volumes of data concerning the processes and the different metrics outlined by the embedded chips in the production floor.

Moving the production processes away from the mechanical processing of the different parameters to a place where data plays a big role in decision-making has been the focus of industries in an era of Big Data and Cloud Computing. The market for AI has continued to grow, with manufacturers realizing the benefits of encompassing Big Data into making critical decisions. For example, smart manufacturers allow the wealth of information contained in Big Data to inform the processes concerning the health of the equipment used. With AI, predictive maintenance would be assured since the systems use various sensors to predict imminent maintenance schedules for running machines. An AI-driven predictive type of maintenance can play a critical role in reducing maintenance costs across the manufacturing sector.

AI has gained some wide deployment in yield enhancement by decreasing the scrap rate previously abundant in the production processes from defective outcomes (Reed 1996). Using more optimized production systems, yield losses are significantly reduced or completely avoided through better simulation mechanisms in the production design. Using AI in the production process allows the system to identify the causes of errors and rectify them in real-time, cutting the prospect of realizing mistakes after producing a batch line of products. The scrap rates and high testing costs to check on conformity are avoided when optimized production processes are used. It has been estimated that the savings emanating from the use of AI in aiding yield enhancement have resulted in up to 30% of savings, making AI an indispensable component in the process.

Working with AI breaks new grounds for quality testing procedures that would optimize the production process. Advancements in ML, such as the facial recognition software, allow for better learning on fault detection on products triggering the system to reject commodities or products that do not conform to the specified range of measurements (Spacek, Kubat, and Flotzinger 1994). Rather than mass produce and reject already finished products, AI enhances the system to continually test the products for conformity and make the necessary adjustments or reject products at every step in the process. The prospect of identifying errors through testing has been cited as capable of increasing productivity by 50%. Equally, the detection rates of defective products through AI have improved the detection rates of products that would be deemed defective by 90%, showing the technology's essence in improving the product life cycle (Leo Kumar 2017).

On supply chain management, the manufacturers have optimized complex supply chains with diverse components and specialty tools that need to constantly keep communicating with each other and come up with the right way of ensuring coordination. When AI is present in a supply chain, the system's prospect of shutting down due to the breakdowns or small mistakes in the processes is reduced since the technology can predict the complex interactions involved before they happen and automate the requests for parts, tools, and repairs. The proactive approach adopted reduces the forecasting errors by a factor of almost 50% and, at the same time, optimize the stock replenishments.

AI is important in the research and design realm. It helps in the virtualization in the design process, allowing the designers to visualize the best materials to use and identifying designs prone to failure. Through constraints and goals during the design process, there is a greater likelihood that products that may be prone to failure would be identified and corrective measures adopted through AI instead of the use of human-driven design processes. The application of ML and the wide availability of big data to inform the design process would come a long way to improve the designs and offer them a chance to simulate the final product before they are rolled out to the consumers. Therefore, AI becomes a critical component in the production cycle, offering the designers the chance to simulate processes and analyze outputs before products are rolled out in the shopping stores.

17.8.5 Suitability of ML with AI

Applications of ML techniques have been gaining ground over the last few years due to the abundance of data on different platforms and changing the outcome when applied. The increased usability of ML tools has equally created situations where computers are allowed to solve problems without active involvement on the part of human beings. As outlined by Samuel (1959), ML would involve scenarios where machines would develop the ability to solve problems that arise out of their work areas even as they may not be explicitly pro-grammed to do so. Presently, ML is applicable in the manufacturing processes through con-trol, optimization, and troubleshooting.

Production of goods and materials through the factory floor involves many repetitive actions used to garner desired results. Factory floors have been a common feature for the last part of the twentieth century and continue to become integral in the production cycle. There is a vast amount of data concerning the different processes that can be harnessed by introducing AI in driving the processes (Spelda 2018). ML has been proven to be useful in analyzing the trends through the technologies and using the data to identify future trends. The future demands for raw materials or the power to drive the machines would be noted by ML, allowing for the optimization of the processes to result in lesser power production. In essence, the systems would note the historical power consumption patterns allowing for better visualization of future demands and possible fluctuations that would affect the pro-duction process (Vora and Iyer 2018). Using such a system would enable companies to make more precise predictions and analyze different parameters that would affect produc-tion processes.

The rise of autonomous vehicles is a culmination of advances in technology that allow the machine to learn from human interactions and actions, easing the processes, espe-cially where the deployment involves many repetitive tasks. Autonomous vehicles on the production floor would represent robotic processes that would allow for working in areas where human input would be at risk (Witman 2017). Automating the processes through autonomous vehicles represents a wide range of possibilities on the deployment of tech-nology to solve human-related issues (Koinoda, Kera, and Kubo 1984). Autonomous vehi-cles have been manufactured out of factory environments and deployed to real-life experiences, allowing for better optimizing the resources. Self-driving transport systems represent advances in technology that have allowed machines to learn human ways and perform as desired. Incorporating different techniques within the autonomous vehicle units represents the possibilities of allowing machines to learn from human beings and make critical decisions.

17.9 Collaboration Between Machines and Humans

For AI systems to learn and adopt human ways, a great amount of emphasis has been put in place to allow close collaboration between humans and machines in their operation areas. Workers constantly interact with robotic instructions at different levels during the production processes, allowing for the machines to refine and make them less dependent on human input to perform their designated roles. The human–robot collaboration contin-ues to grow with advances in AI and the determination that they provide imminent cost-savings expected when industries embrace technology. The development of robotic and intelligent manufacturing systems is largely reliant on technological advances, breaking new grounds with every innovation (Ostrosi and Fougères 2018). Real-time environmental data, coupled with the analytical capacity of production processes, allow AI to become deeply embedded in the processes to ensure that the automated systems' decisions are rel-evant and desired in production.

17.10   Generative Designs

AI has changed the way that designers come up with acceptable designs of various products. With the availability of AI, newer ways have emerged in designing. Designers and designers use algorithms regarded as generative design software that uses the input and proposed designs (Li et al. 2013). Designers would input information regarding different parameters like material types, budget limitations, time constraints, and production methods in the software to explore possible configurations used in the coming product. Once the software proposes different options, the designers would then work hand in hand with the decision-makers concerned in selecting the right option to represent the ideal choices desired. With the availability of generative design software, designers are handed a template that would then be refined to meet the design team's expectations and offer the output desired. The design process refines the design through the software while testing different parameters until the final design offers the output originally envisaged. There are no assumptions taken at face value in designing with a great amount of time resource devoted to offering a sensible product that would meet the designer team's demands.

17.11   Adapting to a Changing Market

Industry 4.0 has relied on AI to drive the processes but is not confined to improving the design floor methods. Manufacturing encompasses more than the turning of raw materials into viable products. Optimizations using AI can equally happen at the supply chain or the logistic levels. Using AI in manufacturing encompasses all aspects of the processes and benefits the system by anticipating market changes and demands while varying the production processes to meet the expectation. There is a wealth of information concerning the consumer needs that big data would provide to the production processes. For example, in the beverage market, tastes keep changing, and consumer sentiments drive the process in ways that the products reflect the end-users' requirements. When the fad in the market, for example, is on turning green, the research and development teams analyze the available data to develop viable products that would meet consumer expectations. Without AI that would combine the designing and the demand aspects into one, so designing a product from the ground up would take a considerable time to perfect.

17.11.1   Conclusion

As outlined in this chapter, AI is profoundly important in informing the production process and making sure that significant changes can be attempted during the product development phases. With big data becoming critical in informing the processes about the desired changes, AI from the embedded chips in the production process allow for the variation of the inputs, thereby leading to real-time intervention necessary to produce products that would meet consumer demands without fail. There have been significant changes brought about by industry 4.0 that have allowed significant benefits emerging from the processes. In essence, AI will continue informing the correct interventions to make to optimize the production process.

References

AMFG (2018). Seven ways Artificial Intelligence is positively impacting manufacturing. https://amfg.ai/2018/08/10/artificial-intelligence-manufacturing-impact/. (accessed 22 June 2021).

Bates, D.W. (2006). *Digital Age*, vol. 148 (16):, –63. Harvard Medical School.

Belfiore, M. (2016, July 28). How ten industries are using big data to win big. bm.com: https://www.ibm.com/blogs/watson/2016/07/10-industries-using-big-data-win-big/ (accessed 22 June 2021).

Big Data Analytics (2015, 12 January). Big data analytics. sas.com: https://www.sas.com/en_us/insights/analytics/big-data-analytics.html (accessed 22 June 2021).

Bishop, C. (2016). *Pattern Recognition and Machine Learning*. New York, USA: Springer-Verlag.

Boyacioglu, M.A. and Avci, D. (2010). An adaptive network-based duzzy inference system (ANFIS) for predicting stock market return: The case of the Istanbul Stock Exchange. *Expert Systems with Applications* 37 (12): 7908–7912.

Bratko, I. (1993). Machine learning in artificial intelligence. *Artificial Intelligence in Engineering* 8 (3): 159–164. https://doi.org/10.1016/0954-1810(93)90002-w.

Cearley, D.W., Burke, B., Searle, S., and Walker, M. (2018). *Top 10 Strategic Technology Trends for 2018*, 1–34. Retrieved from: https://www.gartner.com/en/doc/3811368-top-10-strategic-technology-trends-for-2018. (282) Gartner Top 10 Strategic Technology Trends 2018 - YouTube.

Duncan, D.E. (2017). Constant monitoring + AI = Rx for personal health. *Mit Technology Review*, Retrieved from: https://medium.com/mit-technology-review/constant-monitoring-ai-rx-for-personal-health-4cef06517287 (accessed 22 June 2021).

Dyson (2018). Mind the gap – Industry 4.0 and the future of manufacturing, IBTimes. https://www.ibtimes.co.uk/mind-gap-industry-4-0-future-manufacturing-1665243 (accessed 22 June 2021).

Eckerson (2018). The Impact of AI on Analytics: Machine-Generated Intelligence, Eckerson Group. https://www.eckerson.com/articles/the-impact-of-ai-on-analytics-machine-generated-intelligence (accessed 22 June 2021).

Edwards, D., Holt, G., and Robinson, B. (2002). An artificial intelligence approach for improving plant operator maintenance proficiency. *Journal of Quality in Maintenance Engineering* 8 (3): 239–252. https://doi.org/10.1108/13552510210439810.

Foster and Company (n.d.) Artificial Intelligence and Machine Learning (ML). https://www.fostec.com/en/competences/digitalisation-strategy/artificial-intelligence-ai-machine-learning-ml/ (accessed 22 June 2021).

Gerencsér, L., Torma, B., and Orlovits, Z. (2009). Fundamental modelling of financial markets. *ERCIM News*: 52. Retrieved from: https://ercim-news.ercim.eu/en78/special/fundamental-modelling-of-financial-markets and https://www.researchgate.net/publication/220571865_Fundamental_Modelling_of_Financial_Markets.

Hall, J. (2016). The next major advance in medicine will is the use of AI. PC Magazine. https://www.extremetech.com/extreme/228830-the-next-major-advance-in-medicine-will-be-the-use-of-ai (accessed 22 June 2021).

High, P. (2017, April 10). Gartner: Top 10 strategic technology trends for 2018. https://www.gartner.com/en/newsroom/press-releases/2017-10-04-gartner-identifies-the-top-10-strategic-technology-trends-for-2018 (accessed 22 June 2021).

Johnson, B. (2017, January 1). What is "big data"? howstuffworks.com: https://computer.howstuffworks.com/internet/basics/what-is-big-data-.htm (accessed 22 June 2021).

Kersting, K. and Meyer, U. (2018). From big data to big Artificial Intelligence? *KI – Künstliche Intelligenz* 32 (1): 3–8. https://doi.org/10.1007/s13218-017-0523-7.

Kim, K.-J. (2000). Genetic algorithms approach to feature discretization in artificial neural networks for the prediction of a stock price index. *Expert Systems with Applications* 19: 125–132.

Koinoda, N., Kera, K., and Kubo, T. (1984). An autonomous, decentralized control system for factory automation. *Computer* 17 (12): 73–83. https://doi.org/10.1109/mc.1984.1659029.

Kuo, R.J., Chen, C.H., and Hwang, Y.C. (2001). An intelligent stock trading decision support system through integration of genetic algorithm based fuzzy neural network and artificial neural network. *Fuzzy Sets and Systems* 118 (1): 21–45.

Kurzweil, R. (2016). *Deep learning stock prediction: Artificial Intelligence expanding applications*. I Know First-Daily Market Forecast.

Leo Kumar, S. (2017). State of the art-intense review on Artificial Intelligence systems application in process planning and manufacturing. *Engineering Applications of Artificial Intelligence* 65: 294–329. https://doi.org/10.1016/j.engappai.2017.08.005.

Li, Z., Shi, Z., Zhao, W. et al. (2013). Learning semantic concepts from an image database with a hybrid generative/discriminative approach. *Engineering Applications of Artificial Intelligence* 26 (9): 2143–2152. https://doi.org/10.1016/j.engappai.2013.07.004.

Nguyen, H. and Chan, C. (2006). Applications of Artificial Intelligence for optimization of compressor scheduling. *Engineering Applications of Artificial Intelligence* 19 (2): 113–126. https://doi.org/10.1016/j.engappai.2005.06.008.

Op, B.N. (1999). Time-series properties of an artificial stock market. *Journal of Economic Dynamics and Control*: 1487–1516.

Ostrosi, E. and Fougères, A. (2018). Intelligent virtual manufacturing cell formation in cloud-based design and manufacturing. *Engineering Applications of Artificial Intelligence* 76: 80–95. https://doi.org/10.1016/j.engappai.2018.08.012.

Reed, N. (1996). Robust strategies for diagnosing manufacturing defects. *Applied Artificial Intelligence* 10 (5): 387–406. https://doi.org/10.1080/088395196118470.

Samuel, A. (1959). Some studies in machine learning using the game of checkers. *IBM Journal of Research and Development* 3 (3): 210–229. https://doi.org/10.1147/rd.33.0210.

Sas.com. (2015). Big Data. sas.com: https://www.sas.com/en_us/insights/big-data/what-is-big-data.html (accessed 22 June 2021).

Spacek, L., Kubat, M., and Flotzinger, D. (1994). Face recognition through learned boundary characteristics. *Applied Artificial Intelligence* 8 (1): 149–164. https://doi.org/10.1080/08839519408945436.

Spelda, P. (2018). Machine learning, inductive reasoning, and reliability of generalizations. *AI & Society*. https://doi.org/10.1007/s00146-018-0860-6.

Sukel, K. (2017). Artificial Intelligence will soon be a standard part of your medical care – if it isn't already. Can you trust it?

Tekoäly 2018. Tekoälyn historia. http://xn--tekoly-eua.info/tekoaly_historia/ (accessed April 6, 2018).

Temming, M. (2018). *Computers Can Diagnose Eye Problems*, 1–2. Society for Science & the Public.

Verma, A. 2018. How are Big Data and AI Changing the Business World? Whizlabs Blog.

Vora, D. and Iyer, K. (2018). Evaluating the effectiveness of Machine Learning algorithms in predictive modelling. *International Journal of Engineering and Technology* 7 (3.4): 197. https://doi.org/10.14419/ijet.v7i3.4.16773.

Wiegerinck, W. (2003). Clinical applications of artificial neural networks. *Artificial Intelligence in Medicine* 27 (2): 223–226. https://doi.org/10.1016/s0933-3657(02)00081-7.

Witman, S. (2017). Detecting gas leaks with autonomous underwater vehicles. *Eos* https://doi.org/10.1029/2017eo080597.

Index

Intelligent Connectivity: AI, IoT, and 5G, First Edition. Abdulrahman Yarali.
© 2022 John Wiley & Sons Ltd. Published 2022 by John Wiley & Sons Ltd.